CRIMINAL L
STATUTES

Selected and annotated by
MICHAEL HIRST, LLB(Manc), LLM(Wales),
Lecturer in Law, University College of Wales,
Aberystwyth

WATERLOW PUBLISHERS

First edition 1990
Introduction and notes
© Michael Hirst 1990

Waterlow Publishers
50 Fetter lane
London EC4A 1AA

A division of Pergamon Professional & Financial Services PLC

ISBN 0 08 033106 8

British Library Cataloguing in Publication Data
Criminal law statutes
   1. England. Criminal law — (Waterlow criminal law guides)
   I. Hirst, Michael 1954—
   344.205

Origination by BPCC Whitefriars Ltd, Tunbridge Wells, and printed and bound in Great Britain by BPCC Wheatons Ltd, Exeter.

Contents

Table of statutes excerpted   vii
Table of cases   ix
Preface   xx

Treason Act 1351 (25 Ed III c 2)   1
Treason Act 1795 (36 Geo III c 7) s 1   3
Vagrancy Act 1824 (5 Geo IV c 83) s 4   4
Treason Act 1842 (5 & 6 Vict c 51) ss 2, 3   6
Accessories and Abettors Act 1861 (24 & 25 Vict c 94) s 8   8
Malicious Damage Act 1861 (24 & 25 Vict c 97) ss 35, 36, 47, 48   11
Forgery Act 1861 (24 & 25 Vict c 98) ss 34, 36, 37   13
Offences against the Person Act 1861 (24 & 25 Vict c 100) ss 4, 5, 9, 10,
    16, 18, 20–5, 27–35, 38, 44, 45, 47, 57–60, 64, 68, 78   15
Territorial Waters Jurisdiction Act 1878 (41 & 42 Vict c 73) Preamble,
    ss 2, 3, 5–7   36
Explosive Substances Act 1883 (46 & 47 Vict c 3) ss 2–5, 7, 9   39
Trial of Lunatics Act 1883 (46 & 47 Vict c 38) s 2   43
Public Bodies Corrupt Practices Act 1889 (52 & 53 Vict c 69) ss 1–4, 7 44
Merchant Shipping Act 1894 (57 & 58 Vict c 60) ss 686–7   47
Prevention of Corruption Act 1906 (6 Ed VII c 34) ss 1, 2   49
Perjury Act 1911 (1 & 2 Geo V c 6) ss 1, 1A, 2–8, 15, 18   51
Official Secrets Act 1911 (1 & 2 Geo V c 28) ss 1, 3, 6–8, 10, 12   58
Prevention of Corruption Act 1916 (6 & 7 Geo V c 64) ss 2, 4   63
Official Secrets Act 1920 (10 & 11 Geo V c 75) ss 1, 3, 6–8   64
Criminal Justice Act 1925 (15 & 16 Geo V c 86) s 47   69
Infant Life (Preservation) Act 1929 (19 & 20 Geo V c 34) ss 1, 2   70
Children and Young Persons Act 1933 (23 Geo V c 12) ss 1, 3, 50   72
Infanticide Act 1938 (1 & 2 Geo VI c 36) s 1   75
British Nationality Act 1948 (11 & 12 Geo VI c 56) s 3(1)   77
Prevention of Crime Act 1953 (1 & 2 Eliz II c 14) s 1   78
Children and Young Persons (Harmful Publications) Act 1955 (3 & 4 Eliz
    II c 28) ss 1, 2, 4, 5   80
Sexual Offences Act 1956 (4 & 5 Eliz II c 69) ss 1–7, 9–17, 19–36, 44–7,
    Sch 2   82
Homicide Act 1957 (5 & 6 Eliz II c 11) ss 1–4   111
Restriction of Offensive Weapons Act 1959 (7 & 8 Eliz II c 37) s 1   116
Street Offences Act 1959 (7 & 8 Eliz II c 57) s 1   117
Obscene Publications Act 1959 (7 & 8 Eliz II c 66) ss 1, 2, 4   119
Indecency with Children Act 1960 (8 & 9 Eliz II c 33) s 1   123
Suicide Act 1961 (9 & 10 Eliz II c 60) ss 1, 2   124
Police Act 1964 (c 48) s 51   126
Obsence Publications Act 1964 (c 74) ss 1–3   128
Criminal Law Act 1967 (c 58) ss 1, 3–5   130
Sexual Offences Act 1967 (c 60) ss 1–8, 11   135
Criminal Justice Act 1967 (c 80) s 8   140
Abortion Act 1967 (c 87) ss 1–7   142
Firearms Act 1968 (c 27) ss 1–5, 16–25, 57, 58, 60, Schs 1, 6   148
Theft Act 1968 (c 60) ss 1–25, 30, 34, 36, Sch 1 para 2   168
Criminal Damage Act 1971 (c 48) ss 1–5, 10   198

Sexual Offences (Amendment) Act 1976 (c 82) ss 1, 7 205
Criminal Law Act 1977 (c 45) ss 1–10, 12, 13, 51, 54 208
Suppression of Terrorism Act 1978 (c 26) ss 4, 8, Sch 1 224
Theft Act 1978 (c 31) ss 1–5 230
Protection of Children Act 1978 (c 37) ss 1, 3, 6, 7 235
Magistrates' Courts Act 1980 (c 43) ss 44, 45 238
Forgery and Counterfeiting Act 1981 (c 45) ss 1–6, 8–10, 13–22, 25, 27, 28, 33 240
Criminal Attempts Act 1981 (c 47) ss 1–4, 6–9 256
Civil Aviation Act 1982 (c 16) s 92 264
Taking of Hostages Act 1982 (c 28) ss 1, 2, 6 266
Firearms Act 1982 (c 31) ss 1, 2 267
Aviation Security Act 1982 (c 36) ss 1–6, 8, 38, 41 269
Child Abduction Act 1984 (c 37) ss 1–5, Sch 279
Companies Act 1985 (c 6) s 458 285
Sexual Offences Act 1985 (c 44) ss 1, 2, 4 287
Public Order Act 1986 (c 64) ss 1–9, 17–19, 23, 26–9, 38 289
Crossbows Act 1987 (c 32) ss 1–3, 5, 6 303
Criminal Justice Act 1987 (c 38) s 12 305
Malicious Communications Act 1988 (c 27) s 1 306
Criminal Justice Act 1988 (c 33) ss 39, 134, 135(a), 139, 141, 160 308
Road Traffic Act 1988 (c 52) s 1 314
Prevention of Terrorism (Temporary Provisions) Act 1989 (c 4) ss 2, 3, 8–13, 17–20, 27 316
Official Secrets Act 1989 (c 6) ss 1–10, 12–16 327

Index 341

Table of Statutes Excerpted

Abortion Act 1967	142
Accessories and Abettors Act 1861	8
Aviation Security Act 1982	269
British Nationality Act 1948	77
Child Abduction Act 1984	279
Children and Young Persons Act 1933	72
Children and Young Persons (Harmful Publications) Act 1955	80
Civil Aviation Act 1982	264
Companies Act 1985	285
Criminal Attempts Act 1981	256
Criminal Damage Act 1971	198
Criminal Justice Act 1925	69
Criminal Justice Act 1967	140
Criminal Justice Act 1987	305
Criminal Justice Act 1988	308
Criminal Law Act 1967	130
Criminal Law Act 1977	208
Crossbows Act 1987	303
Explosive Substances Act 1883	32
Firearms Act 1968	148
Firearms Act 1982	267
Firearms Amendment Act 1988—see Firearms Act 1968	
Forgery Act 1861	13
Forgery and Counterfeiting Act 1981	240
Homicide Act 1957	111
Indecency with Children Act 1960	123
Infant Life (Preservation) Act 1929	70
Infanticide Act 1938	75
Magistrates' Courts Act 1980	238
Malicious Communications Act 1988	306
Malicious Damage Act 1861	11
Merchant Shipping Act 1894	47
Obscene Publications Act 1959	119
Obscene Publications Act 1964	128
Offences against the Person Act 1861	15
Official Secrets Act 1911	58
Official Secrets Act 1920	64
Official Secrets Act 1989	327
Perjury Act 1911	51
Police Act 1964	126
Prevention of Corruption Act 1906	49
Prevention of Corruption Act 1916	63
Prevention of Crime Act 1953	78
Prevention of Terrorism (Temporary Provisions) Act 1989	316
Protection of Children Act 1978	235

Public Bodies Corrupt Practices Act 1889   44
Public Order Act 1986   289

Restriction of Offensive Weapons Act 1959   116
Road Traffic Act 1988   314

Sexual Offences Act 1956   82
Sexual Offences Act 1967   135
Sexual Offences Act 1985   287
Sexual Offences (Amendment) Act 1976   205
Street Offences Act 1959   117
Suicide Act 1961   124
Suppression of Terrorism Act 1978   224

Taking of Hostages Act 1982   226
Territorial Waters Jurisdiction Act 1878   36
Theft Act 1968   168
Theft Act 1978   230
Treason Act 1351   1
Treason Act 1795   3
Treason Act 1842   6
Trial of Lunatics Act 1883   43

Vagrancy Act 1824   4

Table of Cases

Prosecutions brought by the Crown are listed under the name of the defendant.

Abbott v Smith [1965] 2 QB 662	100
Abernethie v. A M & N Kleinman Ltd [1969] 2 All ER 790	150
Adams v Metropolitan Police Commissioner [1980] RTR 289	314
Adesanya, The Times 16/17.7.74	30
Albert v Lavin [1982] AC 546	126
Alexander (1912) 107 LT 240	92
Allen (1872) LR 1 CCR 367	31
Allen [1985] AC 1029	233
Anderson [1972] 1 QB 304	119
Anderson [1986] AC 27	209
Anderson and Morris [1966] 2 QB 110	9
Anderton v Ryan [1985] AC 560	257
Andrews [1981] Crim LR 106	231
Andrews-Weatherfoil Ltd [1972] 1 All ER 65	44
Ansell [1975] QB 215	99
Appleyard [1985] Crim LR 723	204
Atkin v DPP [1989] Crim LR 581	292
Atkinson [1985] Crim LR 314	113
Att Gen v Able [1984] 1 All ER 277	124
Att Gen for N Ireland's Reference (No 1 of 1975) [1977] AC 105	131
Att Gen's Reference (No 1 of 1974) [1974] QB 744	194
Att Gen's Reference (No 1 of 1975) [1975] 2 All ER 684	8, 9
Att Gen's References (Nos 1 and 2 of 1979) [1980] QB 180	177, 257
Att Gen's Reference (No 4 of 1979) [1981] 1 All ER 1193; (1980) 71 Cr App R 341	191, 193
Att Gen's Reference (No 1 of 1980) [1981] 1 WLR 34	187
Att Gen's Reference (No 3 of 1980) [1980] 3 All ER 273	149
Att Gen's Reference (No 6 of 1980) [1981] QB 715	30
Att Gen's Reference (No 1 of 1982) [1983] 2 All ER 721	305
Att Gen's Reference (No 1 of 1983) [1984] Crim LR 570	174
Audley (Lord) (1631) Hut 115	206
Ayres [1984] AC 447	213, 305
Bagley [1980] Crim LR 503	257
Bailey (1978) 66 Cr App R 31n	113
Bailey [1983] 2 All ER 503	43
Baker [1895] 1 QB 795	52
Baker [1961] 2 QB 550	155
Banks (1873) 12 Cox CC 393	15
Banks [1916] 2 KB 621	85
Barnet LBC v Eastern Electricity Board [1973] 2 All ER 319	198
Barr [1978] Crim LR 244	180
Baxter [1972] 1 QB 1	258
Bayley [1980] Crim LR 503	175
Beal v Kelley [1951] 2 All ER 763	90
Bean (1842) 4 St Tr (NS) 1382	6
Becerra and White (1975) 62 Cr App R 212	9
Beck [1985] 1 All ER 571	189

Beckford v R [1987] 3 All ER 425; [1987] 3 WLR 611   19, 131, 203
Behrendt v Berridge [1976] 3 All ER 285   100, 118
Belfon [1976] 3 All ER 46   199
Benstead (1982) 75 Cr App R 276   189
Bentham [1973] QB 357   153
Bently [1923] 1 KB 403   89
Berriman (1854) 6 Cox CC 388   34
Berry [1984] 3 All ER 1008   42
Bettaney [1985] Crim LR 104   58
Betts v Stevens [1910] 1 KB 1   127
Bevan (1987) 84 Cr App R 143   186
Bingham [1973] 2 All ER 89   67
Bland [1988] Crim LR 41   9
Bloxham [1983] 1 AC 109   171, 191
Board of Trade v Owen [1975] AC 602   15
Bogacki [1973] QB 832   181
Boggeln v Williams [1978] 2 All ER 1061   169, 182
Bolton (H L) (Engineering) Co Ltd v T J Graham & Sons Ltd [1957]
   1 QB 159   187
Bonner [1970] 1 WLR 838   173
Bouch [1982] 3 All ER 918   39, 42
Boulden (1957) 41 Cr App R 105   73
Bourne [1939] 1 KB 687   71, 142, 143, 146
Bow (1976) 64 Cr App R 54   181
Boyce 1 Mood CC 29   23
Boyle (1986) 84 Cr App R 270   257
Brangwynne v Evans [1962] 1 WLR 267   261
Bratty v Att Gen for N Ireland [1963] AC 386   43
Breckenridge [1984] Crim LR 174   206
Breeze [1973] 2 All ER 1141   50, 150
Bridge v Campbell [1947] WN 223   118
Briggs (1856) Dears & B 98   31
Brindley [1871] 2 QB 300   132
Brooks (1982) 76 Cr App R 66   233
Broome v Walter [1989] Crim LR 725   162
Brown (1870) LR 1 CCC 244   34
Brown (1889) 24 QBD 357   88
Brown [1970] 1 QB 105   191
Brown [1985] Crim LR 212   177
Brutus v Cozens [1973] AC 854   292
Bryan v Mott (1976) 62 Cr App R 71   78
Burdon (1927) 20 Cr App R 60   28
Bundy [1977] 2 All ER 382   195
Burfitt v A & E Kille [1939] 2 KB 743   162
Burke [1987] Crim LR 336   114
Burns v Currell [1963] 2 All ER 297   314
Burt v Burt (1860) 2 Sw & Tr 88   31
Byrne [1960] 2 QB 396   112, 113

C v S [1981] 1 All ER 1230   70
Cafferata v Wilson [1936] 3 All ER 149   162
Calder and Boyars Ltd [1969] 1 QB 151   119, 122
Caldwell [1982] AC 341   19, 30, 185, 199, 206
Calhaem [1985] 2 All ER 266   9, 82, 94
Callow v Tillstone (1900) 83 LT 411   238
Calvert v Mayes [1954] 1 QB 342   99
Cameron v HM Advocate 1971 SC 50   37
Campbell (1984) 80 Cr App R 47   240, 247

Camplin (1845) 1 Den 89   205
Carruthers (1844) 1 Cox CC 138   18
Cascoe [1970] 2 All ER 833   114
Casement [1917] 1 KB 98   1
Cash [1985] QB 801   191
Cato [1976] 1 All ER 269   21
Chan Man-Sin v R [1988] 1 All ER 1   172, 184
Chan Wing-Siu v R [1984] 3 All ER 877   9
Chandler v DPP [1964] AC 763   58, 65
Chapman [1959] 1 QB 100   82
Chappell v DPP (1989) 89 Cr App R 82   293
Charles [1977] AC 177   185, 230
Chief Constable of Avon and Somerset v Shimmen [1986] Crim LR
  800   199
Christian (1913) 23 Cox CC 541   94
Churchill v Walton [1967] 2 AC 224   209
Clarence (1888) 22 QBD 23   20, 29, 206
Clarke [1976] 2 All ER 696   99
Clarkson [1971] 3 All ER 344   8
Clayton [1962] 3 All ER 500   120
Clear [1968] 1 QB 670   190
Clegg (1868) 19 LT 47   52
Closs (1857) D & B 460   245
Clotworthy [1981] Crim LR 501   182
Coffin v Smith (1980) 71 Cr App R 221   126
Cogan [1976] QB 217   206
Collins [1973] QB 100   156, 177
Collister (1955) 39 Cr App R 199   190
Coney (1882) 8 QBD 534   9
Cooke [1971] Crim LR 44   28
Cooke [1986] AC 909   213, 305
Cooper v Shield [1921] 2 QB 334   99
Cooper (Gerald) Chemicals Ltd, re [1978] Ch 262   285
Copus v DPP [1989] Crim LR 577   79
Conegate v Customs & Excise [1987] QB 254   120
Corcoran v Anderton (1980) 71 Cr App R 104   176
Corcoran v Whent [1977] Crim LR 52   173
Court (1912) 7 Cr App R 127   69
Court [1988] 2 WLR 1071   90
Courtie [1984] AC 463   88, 89, 137
Cousins [1982] 2 All ER 115; [1982] QB 526   18, 130
Cox (1982) 75 Cr App R 291   285
Cox v. Army Council [1962] 1 All ER 880   314
Cox v White [1976] RTR 248   214
Cramp (1880) 5 QBD 307   21
Crook v Edmondson [1966] 1 All ER 833   288
Crossman [1986] Crim LR 406   315
Crowden (1911) 6 Cr App R 190   27
Cugullere [1961] 2 All ER 343; [1961] 1 WLR 858   78, 303
Cumberworth [1989] Crim LR 591   48
Cunningham [1957] 2 All ER 412   19, 23, 30, 184
Curr [1986] Crim LR 470   239

D [1984] AC 778   280, 282
Dale v Smith [1967] 2 All ER 1133   100, 288
Darroch, The Times 11.5.90   288
Davies [1975] QB 691   114
Davidge v Bunnett [1984] Crim LR 296   174

Dawson [1976] Crim LR 692   176
Dayle [1973] 3 All ER 1151   79
Debreli [1964] Crim LR 53   154
De Munck [1918] 1 KB 635   94
Denham (1983) 77 Cr App R 210   193
Dent [1955] 2 QB 510   83
Denton [1982] 1 All ER 65   203
Diamond (1920) 84 JP 211   15
Dix (1981) 74 Cr App R 306   113
Dobson v General Accident Assurance Co [1990] Crim LR 271   170
Dodd (1977) 66 Cr App R 87   100
Dodge [1972] 1 QB 416   186
Donnelly [1984] 1 WLR 1017   241, 242, 246
Donovan [1934] 2 KB 498   30, 89
Donovan v Gavin [1965] 2 QB 648   101
Douce [1972] Crim LR 105   245
Doughty [1986] Crim LR 623   114
Downes (1983) 77 Cr App R 260   175
DPP v AB & C Chewing Gum Ltd [1968] 1 QB 159   122
DPP v Camplin [1978] AC 705   114
DPP v Doot [1973] AC 807   15, 209
DPP v Holly [1977] 1 All ER 316   63
DPP v Holmes, The Times 7.4.88   151
DPP v Jordan [1976] 3 All ER 775   122
DPP v Khan (1989) 139 NLJ 1455   29
DPP v Majewski [1977] AC 443   141, 203, 206, 294
DPP v Morgan [1976] AC 182   32, 205, 206
DPP v Newbury [1977] AC 500   26, 111
DPP v Nock [1978] AC 979   209
DPP v Ray [1974] AC 370   184
DPP v Smith [1961] AC 290   140
DPP v Stonehouse [1978] AC 55   15, 257, 258
DPP v Whyte [1972] 3 All ER 12   119
DPP for N Ireland v Lynch [1975] AC 653   69
DPP for N Ireland v Maxwell [1978] 3 All ER 1140   9
Du Cross v Lambourne [1907] 1 KB 40   238
Dudley and Stephens (1884) 14 QBD 273   48
Duffy [1949] 1 All ER 932   114
Dunbar [1958] 1 QB 1   103
Dunnington [1984] 1 All ER 676   257
Durkim [1973] QB 786   180
Duru [1973] 3 All ER 715   175
Dyson (1823) Russ & Ry 523   115

Easom [1971] 2 QB 351   175
Eden (1971) 55 Cr App R 193   186
Eddy v Niman (1981) 73 Cr App R 237   170
Edgington v Fitzmaurice (1885) 29 Ch D 459   83
Edwards v Ddin [1976] 3 All ER 705   173
Edwards v R [1975] 1 All ER 152   115
Eldershaw (1828) 3 C & P 316   84, 205
El Hakkaoui [1975] 2 All ER 146   154
Ellames (1974) 60 Cr App R 7   195
Elliott v C (a minor) [1983] 2 All ER 1005   199
Evans v Ewels [1972] 2 All ER 22   5
Evans v Hughes [1972] 3 All ER 412   78

Fagan v Metropolitan Police Commissioner [1969] 1 QB 439   30

Fairclough v Whipp [1951] 2 All ER 834   90, 123
Falkingham (1870) LR 1 CCC 222   23
Faulkner v Talbot [1981] 3 All ER 468   91
Faulkes (1903) 19 TLR 250   31
Feely [1973] 1 QB 530   169
Ferguson v Weaving [1951] 1 KB 814   8, 9
Field v Chapman, The Times 9.10.53   100
Field v Metropolitan Police Receiver [1907] 2 KB 853   289
Firth [1990] Crim LR 326   185, 233
Fisher v Bell [1961] 1 QB 394   116
Flack v Baldry [1988] Crim LR 610   153
Fleming [1989] Crim LR 658   290
Fletcher (1859) Bell CC 63   205
Ford [1978] 1 All ER 1129   100
Ford v Falcone [1971] 2 All ER 1138   5
Fordham [1970] 1 QB 77   157
Francis [1982] Crim LR 363   178
Frankland v R [1988] Crim LR 117   140, 141
Freeman [1970] 2 All ER 413   153, 162
Frickey [1956] Crim LR 421   54
Fritschy [1985] Crim LR 745   170, 184
Frost (1964) 48 Cr App R 284   191

Garcia [1988] Crim LR 115   240
George [1956] Crim LR 52   90
Georgiades [1989] Crim LR 574   154
Ghosh [1982] 1 QB 1053   169, 182, 184, 186, 189, 192, 230
Gilks [1972] 3 All ER 280   174
Gillard, The Times 7.4.88   21, 84
Gillick v W Norfolk and Wisbech Area Health Authority [1986]
   AC 112   86
Gittens [1984] QB 698   113
Gold [1987] QB 1116 CA; [1988] 2 All ER 186 HL   247
Golechha (1990) 90 Cr App R 241   187
Goodfellow [1986] Crim LR 469   111
Gorman v Standen [1963] 3 All ER 627   100
Gould [1968] 1 All ER 849; [1968] 2 QB 65   31, 32
Grace v DPP [1989] Crim LR 365   161
Graham-Kerr (1989) 88 Cr App R 302   236
Grantham [1984] QB 675   285
Green (1863) 3 F & F 274   93
Green v Moore [1982] QB 1044   127
Greenstein [1976] 1 All ER 1   169
Grey [1982] Crim LR 176   100
Griffiths [1966] 1 QB 589   209
Griffiths (1974) 60 Cr App R 14   192
Griffiths v Freeman [1970] 1 All ER 1117   191
Grimshaw [1984] Crim LR 108   19
Gullefer [1987] Crim LR 195   257

Hadfield (1870) LR 1 CCR 253   11
Halai [1983] Crim LR 624   230
Hale (1978) 68 Cr App R 415   176
Hall [1973] 1 QB 126   174
Hall, The Times 15.7.87   86
Hall v Cotton [1986] 3 All ER 332   149
Hamilton (1849) 8 St Tr (NS) 1130   6
Hancock [1986] AC 455   111

Handley (1855) 1 F & F 648   92
Hardie [1984] 3 All ER 848   199
Hardy (1871) LR 1 CCR 278   11
Harris [1966] 1 QB 184   242
Harrison v Hill 1932 SC(J) 13   314
Harvey (1981) 72 Cr App R 139   190
Haughton v Smith [1975] AC 476   192, 194, 256, 257
Hayles [1969] 1 All ER 34   73
Hennington [1971] 3 All ER 133   314
Herrah (1877) 13 Cox CC 547   21
Hewitt (1866) 4 F & F 1101   34
Hibbert (1869) LR 1 CCR 184   92, 93
Higgins (1801) 2 East 5   239
Hill [1964] 1 QB 273   89
Hillman (1863) 9 Cox CC 386   33
Hinchcliffe v Sheldon [1955] 3 All ER 406   127
Hircock (1978) 68 Cr App R 278   174, 184
Hobday v Nicol [1944] 1 All ER 303   222
Holt [1981] Crim LR 499   232
Hornby [1966] 2 All ER 487   89
Horton v Mead [1913] 1 KB 154   100, 118, 287
Houston v Buchanan [1940] 2 All ER 179   25, 26, 73, 201, 281, 323
Howe and Bannister (1987) 85 Cr App R 32   8, 9, 113
Howell [1982] QB 416   291
Howells [1977] QB 614   149
Humphrys [1977] Crim LR 225   178
Hunt [1950] 2 All ER 291   89
Hunt [1987] 1 All ER 1   93, 303
Hussein [1981] 2 All ER 287   149

Ibrams (1982) 74 Cr App R 154   114
ICR Haulage Ltd [1944] KB 551   203

Jackson [1983] Crim LR 617   231, 232
Jaggard v Dickinson [1980] 3 All ER 716   203
James & Son v Smee [1955] 1 QB 78   12, 201, 236
JJC (a minor) v Eisenhower [1983] Crim LR 567   18
JM (a minor) v Runeckles (1984) 79 Cr App R 255   74
Johnson [1964] 2 QB 404   82, 94
Johnson v Youden [1950] 1 All ER 300   9
Jones [1973] Crim LR 621   92, 281
Jones [1981] Crim LR 119   30
Jones and Smith [1976] 3 All ER 154   177
Jordan (1956) 40 Cr App R 152   314
Joyce v DPP [1946] AC 347   1

Kaitamaki v R [1985] AC 147   206
Kell [1985] Crim LR 239   169
Kelly [1982] AC 665   47
Kelly v Purvis [1983] 1 All ER 525   95–6, 100
Kelt (1977) 65 Cr App R 74   155
Kemp [1957] 1 QB 399   43
Kenlin v Gardiner [1967] 2 QB 510   126
Keyn (1876) 2 Ex D 63   36
Khan, The Times 3.2.90   257
Kimber [1983] 3 All ER 316   90
King [1964] 1 QB 285   32
King [1965] 1 All ER 1053   324

King [1979] Crim LR 122 — 185
Kingerlee [1986] Crim LR 735 — 198
Knox v Anderton (1983) 76 Cr App R 156 — 79
Knuller v DPP [1972] 2 All ER 898 — 119, 136, 213
Kohn (1864) 4 F & F 68 — 209
Kohn (1979) 69 Cr App R 395 — 172
Kong Cheuk Kwan v R (1985) 82 Cr App R 18 — 315
Korie [1966] 1 All FR 50 — 100
Kylsant (Lord) [1932] 1 KB 442 — 184, 187

Lack (1986) 84 Cr App R 342 — 246
Lambie [1982] AC 449 — 185
Lang (1975) 62 Cr App R 50 — 205
Lang v Hindhaugh [1986] RTR 271 — 314
Lawrence [1982] AC 510 — 315
Lawrence (Alan) [1972] AC 626 — 170
Lawrence (Rodney Brian) (1971) 57 Cr App R 64 — 175, 190
Laws (1928) 21 Cr App R 45 — 85, 90
Leathley [1979] Crim LR 314 — 177
Leung Ping Fat v R (1973) 3 HKLJ 342 — 115
Lewis (1857) Dears & Bell 182 — 17
Lewis v Cox [1985] QB 509 — 127
Lewis v Erol [1906] AC 299 — 25
Lewis v Lethbridge [1987] Crim LR 59 — 174
Lincoln [1980] Crim LR 575 — 192
Liverpool JJ ex p Molyneux [1972] 2 All ER 471 — 47
Lloyd [1985] QB 829 — 175
Lockwood [1986] Crim LR 244 — 285
London and Globe Finance Corporation Ltd, re [1903] 1 Ch 728 — 184
Low v Blease [1975] Crim LR 513 — 172, 182

McCormack [1969] 3 All ER 371 — 86, 90
Macdonagh [1974] RTR 372 — 314
McDonnell [1966] 1 QB 233 — 209
McEachran v Hurst [1978] RTR 462 — 314
McGowan v Longmuir 1931 SC 10 — 5
McHugh (1988) 88 Cr App R 385 — 170
McInnes [1971] 3 All ER 295 — 114, 130
McKenzie [1971] 1 All ER 729 — 13
McKeon v Ellis [1987] RTR 26 — 314
McKnight v Davis [1974] RTR 4 — 181
McLeod v Buchanan [1940] 2 All ER 179 — 12, 54
M'Naughten (1843) 10 C & Fin 200 — 112
McPherson [1973] Crim LR 191 — 170
McShane (1977) 66 Cr App R 97 — 124
Macer [1989] Crim LR 659 — 246
Mahroof [1989] Crim LR 72 — 290
Mainwaring (1981) 74 Cr App R 99 — 174
Makins v Elson [1977] 1 All ER 572 — 25
Malcherek [1981] 2 All ER 422 — 314
Mallett [1978] 3 All ER 10 — 50, 53, 187, 217
Mancini [1942] AC 1 — 114
Mandla v Dowell Lee [1983] 2 AC 548 — 296
Mankletow (1853) Dears CC 159 — 92
Mansfield [1975] Crim LR 101 — 195
Marchant (1984) 80 Cr App R 361 — 181
Marcus [1981] 2 All ER 833 — 21, 22, 84

Marlow (1964) 49 Cr App R 49   32, 33
Martin (1881) 8 QBD 54   19, 29
Masterton v Holden [1986] 1 WLR 1017   292
Matheson [1958] 1 WLR 474   113
May (1867) 10 Cox CC 489   34
Mayling [1963] 2 QB 717   213
Mearns, The Times 4.5.90   308
Meech [1974] QB 549   174
Millar (Robert) Contractors Ltd [1970] 2 QB 54; [1970] 1 All ER 577
                                                       9, 41, 82, 94, 314
Miller (1854) 6 Cox CC 353   191
Miller [1954] 2 All ER 529; [1954] 2 QB 282   29, 30, 206
Mills [1963] 1 QB 522   33
Millward [1985] QB 519   52
Mohamad v Knott [1968] 2 All ER 563   85
Mohan [1976] 1 QB 1   259
Mohan v R [1967] 2 AC 187   9
Moloney [1985] AC 905   76, 111, 140, 141, 199
Monaghan [1979] Crim LR 673   186
Monger [1973] Crim LR 301   18
Moon [1910] 1 KB 818   98
More [1987] 1 WLR 1578   246
Morgan [1972] 1 QB 436   132
Morgan v DPP [1970] 3 All ER 1053   50
Morphitis v Salmon [1990] Crim LR 48   198
Morris (1867) LR 1 CCR 90   29
Morris (1963) 47 Cr App R 202   99
Morris [1966] 1 QB 148   242
Morris (1984) 79 Cr App R 104   179
Morris (David) [1984] AC 320   168, 170
Morris-Lowe [1985] 1 All ER 400   94, 98
Most (1981) 7 QBD 244   15, 239
Moussa Membar [1983] Crim LR 618   270
Mowatt [1967] 3 All ER 47   18, 19, 21
Munks [1964] 1 QB 304   25
Murray [1984] RTR 203   315

Nanayakkara [1987] 1 WLR 265   189
Neal v Gribble [1978] RTR 409   181
Nedrick [1986] 1 WLR 1025   111, 141, 199
Newell (1980) 71 Cr App R 311   114
Newell [1989] Crim LR 906   114
Newton [1958] Crim LR 469   71, 142
Newton (1983) 77 Cr App R 13   88, 137
Norton [1977] Crim LR 478   154

O'Brien v Anderton [1979] RTR 388   314
O'Grady [1987] QB 995   131, 203
Ohlson v Hylton [1975] 2 All ER 490   79
O'Leary (1986) 82 Cr App R 341   178
O'Moran [1975] QB 864   317
Olugboja [1982] QB 320   190, 205
Orum [1988] Crim LR 848   294
Ostler v Elliott [1980] Crim LR 584   127
Owen [1988] 1 WLR 134   235
Oxford v Moss [1979] Crim LR 119   172

Palmer v R [1971] AC 814; [1971] 1 All ER 1077   30, 131

Papadimitropoulos v R (1958) 98 CLR 247   205
Park, The Times 14.12.87   191
Parke (1922) 17 Cr App R 22   32
Parker (1895) 59 JP 793   27
Parker (1985) 83 Cr App R 69   44
Parker v British Railways Board [1982] QB 1004   173
Parkes [1973] Crim LR 358   190
Parkin v Norman [1983] QB 92   292
Parrott (1913) 8 Cr App R 186   59
Pearce [1966] 3 All ER 618   27
Pearce [1973] Crim LR 321   181
Peart [1970] 2 QB 672   181
Pembliton (1894) LR CCR 119   199
Pethick [1980] Crim LR 242   192
Philippou [1989] Crim LR 559   170, 285
Pierre [1963] Crim LR 513   303
Pigg [1982] 2 All ER 591   257
Pilgram v Rice-Smith [1977] 1 WLR 671   171
Pitchley (1973) 57 Cr App R 30   191
Pitham (1976) 65 Cr App R 45   171, 191
Plastow [1988] Crim LR 604   291
Preece [1977] 1 QB 370   88, 89
Prince (1875) LR 2 CCR 154   84, 85, 92
Purly (1933) 149 LT 432   34

R (Stephen Malcolm) (1984) 79 Cr App R 334   199
Rainbird [1989] Crim LR 505   19
Ralphs (1918) 9 Cr App R 86   98
Ram (1893) 17 Cox CC 609   84, 205
Read v Donovan [1947] KB 326   161
Reader (1977) 66 Cr App R 33   192
Reakes [1974] Crim LR 615   136
Reed [1982] Crim LR 819   209
Rice v Connolly [1966] 2 QB 414   127
Richards [1974] QB 776   8, 113
Rider [1954] 1 All ER 5   85
Rider (1986) 83 Cr App R 210   52
Roberts (1971) 56 Cr App R 95   29
Roberts [1986] Crim LR 188   206
Robinson [1915] 2 KB 342   257
Robinson [1977] Crim LR 173   169, 175
Rolfe (1952) 36 Cr App R 4   90
Royal College of Nursing v DHSS [1981] 1 All ER 545   143
Russell [1901] AC 466   31, 32
Russell (1984) 81 Cr App R 315   78
Russell and Russell [1987] Crim LR 494   9

Sage v Eicholz [1919] 2 KB 171   50
Sagoo [1975] QB 885   31
Salisbury [1976] VR 452   19
Sambasivam v Public Prosecutor [1950] AC 458   29
Sanders [1982] Crim LR 615   191
Sangha [1988] 1 WLR 519   199
Sarjeant 12.9.81 (unreported)   6, 7
Sarwan Singh [1962] 3 All ER 612   31
Satnam Singh (1985) 78 Cr App R 149   206
Saunders (1879) 14 Cox CC 180   24
Scott v Metropolitan Police Commissioner [1975] AC 319   213, 305

Scott v Shepherd (1773) 96 ER 526   29
Secretary of State for Trade v Markus [1976] AC 35   17
Seers [1985] Crim LR 315   112
Selby v DPP [1872] AC 515   248
Senior [1899] 1 QB 283   7, 25, 52, 60, 73, 75
Seymour [1983] 2 AC 493   206, 315
Shacter [1960] 2 QB 252   188
Shama [1990] Crim LR 411   187
Shannon [1980] 71 Cr App R 192   131
Shaw v DPP [1962] AC 220   99, 119, 121, 213
Shephard [1919] 2 KB 125   15
Sheppard [1980] 3 All ER 899; [1981] AC 394   27, 28, 70, 73, 76, 144
Sherriff [1969] Crim LR 260   126
Shivpuri [1987] AC 1   257
Sibartio [1983] Crim LR 470   232
Simpson [1983] 3 All ER 789   79
Singh [1989] Crim LR 724   161
Singleton v Ellison [1985] 1 QB 601   100
Siracusa [1989] Crim LR 712   209
Siviour v Napolitano [1931] 1 KB 636   101
Skipp [1975] Crim LR 114   170
Skirving [1985] QB 819   119
Slack [1989] Crim LR 903   9
Smith (1858) D & B 566   245
Smith [1959] 2 QB 35   314
Smith [1960] 2 QB 423   44
Smith, re (1858) 3 H & N 227   8
Smith v Koumourou [1979] Crim LR 116   185
Smith (David George) [1985] Crim LR 42   30
Smith (David Raymond) [1974] 1 All ER 632   202, 203
Smith (John) [1974] 1 All ER 376   143
Sockett (1980) 72 JP 428   32
Spanner [1973] Crim LR 704   78
Speck [1977] 2 All ER 859   123
Spratt, The Times 14.5.90   30
Steele (1976) 65 Cr App R 22   206
Steer [1988] AC 111   199
Stokes [1982] Crim LR 695   181
Stonehouse v Mason [1921] 2 KB 818   5
Straker v DPP [1963] 1 QB 926   129
Studer (1915) 11 Cr App R 307   190
Sullivan [1983] 3 All ER 673   43
Sutcliffe, The Times 26.5.82   113
Sykes v DPP [1962] AC 528   324

Tait [1989] Crim LR 834   18
Tan [1983] 2 All ER 12   99, 100
Tandy [1988] Crim LR 308   112, 113
Taylor v DPP [1973] AC 964   291
Taylor v Granville [1978] Crim LR 482   30
Thomas [1957] 2 All ER 181   99
Thorpe [1987] 2 All ER 108   149
Timmins (1860) 8 Cox CC 401   92
Titley (1880) 14 Cox CC 502   33
Tobierre [1986] 1 WLR 125   240, 241
Tolson (1889) 23 QBD 168   32
Tophams Ltd v Sefton [1967] 1 AC 50   201
Topping (1856) 7 Cox CC 103   31

Treacy v DPP [1971] AC 537   15, 190, 240
Turner (No 2) [1971] 2 All ER 441   173
Turner v Shearer [1972] 1 WLR 1387   25
Turner v Sullivan (1862) 6 LT 130   299
Tweedie [1984] 2 All ER 136   50
Tyrell [1894] 1 QB 710   86, 88

Utting [1987] 1 WLR 1375   240, 241

Venna [1976] QB 421   30
Vickers [1957] 2 QB 664   111
Vinagre (1979) 69 Cr App R 104   112

W (a minor) v Dolbey [1983] Crim LR 681   19
Waite [1892] 2 QB 600   84
Waites [1982] Crim LR 369   186
Wakely [1990] Crim LR 119   9
Walker [1962] Crim LR 458   209
Walkington [1979] 2 All ER 71   177
Walters v Lunt [1951] 2 All ER 645   74, 194
Walton v R (1978) 66 Cr App R 25   113
Ward (1987) 85 Cr App R 71   9
Watkins [1976] 1 All ER 578   185
Watson v Herman [1952] 2 All ER 70   162
Waugh, The Times 1.10.76   127
Webb [1964] 1 QB 357   94
Webster (1885) 16 QBD 134   96
Weiz v Monghan [1962] 1 All ER 262   118
Westminster City Council v Croyalgrange Ltd [1986] 2 All ER 353   50
White (1871) LR 1 CCC 311   23
White [1910] 2 KB 124   257
Whitefield [1984] Crim LR 97   9
Whitehouse (1977) 65 Cr App R 33   223
Whiting (1987) 85 Cr App R 78   178
Whittaker v Campbell [1983] 3 WLR 676   181
Whyte [1987] 3 All ER 416   131
Widdowson (1985) 82 Cr App R 314   257
Wilcox v Jeffrey [1951] 1 All ER 464   8-9
Wilkins (1861) Le & Ca 89   21
Williams [1893] 1 QB 320   84, 205
Williams (1898) 62 JP 310   83
Williams [1923] 1 KB 340   83, 205
Williams [1980] Crim LR 589   184
Williams v Boyle [1963] Crim LR 204   118, 287
Williams (Gladstone) (1984) 78 Cr App R 276   18, 126, 131
Williamson v Wright 1924 JC 57   118
Wilmott v Atack [1977] QB 498   127
Wilson (1855) Dears & B 127   33
Wilson [1983] 3 All ER 448   29
Windsor (1865) 10 Cox CC 118   246
Woodman [1974] QB 754   173
Woolven [1983] Crim LR 632   184
Wuyts [1969] 2 QB 476   244

Preface

My first objective in this book has been to provide legal practitioners, police officers, and students with a fully updated selection of statutory provisions dealing with matters of substantive criminal law; and I have sought to enhance the value of this selection by including my own commentaries and annotations to each selected provision. My hope is that readers will be able to refer to it, as to a conventional textbook, when in need of guidance on the content and interpretation of particular statutory provisions, and that on points of detail, such as the interpretation of individual words or phrases, it will often provide them with a more direct and easily accessible answer.

No book of this kind and this size can attempt to include all, or even most, of the criminal legislation presently in force, and I have therefore been obliged to concentrate on mainstream criminal law. Provisions dealing with evidence and procedure, or with road traffic, company, tax, customs or licensing offences, fell outside my original remit, although the inclusion of section 1 of the Road Traffic Act 1988 and section 8 of the Criminal Justice Act 1967 illustrate the difficulties I experienced in drawing rigid distinctions. I would have liked to have included some provisions dealing with the misuse of drugs, but satisfactory treatment of such a vast topic would have made it difficult to keep the book within reasonable bounds, and so these too have been omitted.

The production of this book proved to be a more difficult and more protracted exercise than I had first envisaged, and was not assisted by the acquisition of single parent status shortly after beginning work on it. My thanks to James Lamb and Waterlows for their patience and support as production of the typescript fell behind schedule. During that time, I learnt at last to use a p.c.w., but it still fell to Ann Watkin-Jones and Christine Davies to type out those sections of text that had originally been produced in manuscript. My thanks to them, and my apologies for the state of the manuscripts they had to work from.

I must also thank Rosy Daud and Balvir Sidhu, students at UCW, for their help in assembling and checking the typescript.

Christine Davies provided further assistance at the proof-reading stage, as did my colleague and fiancée Pat Jones. Proof-reading, especially reading aloud, is not ordinarily the most exciting of activities, but it has its moments, as where Pat stumbled upon the barbaric (and quite widespread) penalty of 'imprisonment — in square brackets — for life'. Ugh!

The most important help I received during the writing of this book was that provided by my mother. She typed nothing and did no proof-reading; but to a struggling single parent her help in other areas was invaluable. Without it, I think that I would have fallen much further behind schedule, or given up altogether. This book is accordingly dedicated to her. I have attempted to state the law as of 1 June 1990.

Michael Hirst

UCW, Aberystwyth
11 June 1990

NOTE

References in this work to 'the prescribed sum' or 'statutory maximum' are references to the maximum fine which may be imposed by magistrates under s 32 of the Magistrates Courts Act 1980, as amended (currently £2,000).

Treason Act 1351

(25 EDW III STAT 5 C.2)

Declaration what offences shall be adjudged treason
Item, whereas divers opinions have been before this time in what case treason shall be said, and in what not; the King, at the request of the lords and of the commons, hath made a declaration in the manner as hereafter followeth, that is to say; when a man doth compass or imagine the death of our lord the King, or of our lady his Queen or of their eldest son and heir; or if a man do violate the King's companion, or the King's eldest daughter unmarried, or the wife [of] the King's eldest son and heir; or if a man do levy war against our lord the King in his realm, or be adherent to the King's enemies in his realm, giving to them aid and comfort in the realm, or elsewhere, and thereof be [properly] attainted of open deed by the people of their condition: ... and if a man [slay] the chancellor, treasurer, or the King's justices of the one bench or the other, justices in eyre, or justices of assise, and all other justices assigned to hear and determine, being in their places, doing their offices: and it is to be understood, that in the cases above rehearsed, that ought to be judged treason which extends to our lord the King, and his royal majesty.

NOTES

Treason involves a breach of a duty of allegiance towards the Crown. This duty is owed by all persons (other than enemy forces) who voluntarily enter British territory, ships, or (presumably) aircraft in flight, since they thereby come under the protection of the Crown, and the duty of allegiance is owed in return for this protection. See *Calvin's Case* (1608) 7 Co Rep 1A.

Allegiance is also owed by British Nationals, including British Overseas Citizens and British Dependent Territories Citizens, anywhere in the world. This is in return for the diplomatic and consular protection to which they are entitled. Even an alien may incur a duty of allegiance on this basis, should he be the holder of a British passport: see *Joyce v DPP* [1946] AC 347, in which an Irish–American was thereby found guilty of committing treason in Nazi Germany.

'compass or imagine the death of [the Queen] etc' Liability depends on proof of an 'overt act', such as an assassination attempt or a conspiracy. See also the Treason Act 1795, which makes it treason to compass *etc* the wounding, maiming or imprisonment of the Queen or the heir to the throne.

'or of our lady his Queen' This does not appear to apply to a prince consort.

'levy war' Strictly speaking, this is a wide concept that could be applied to certain acts of IRA terrorism, but treason charges are not in fact used in such cases.

'or be adherent to the [Queen's] enemies' As interpreted in *R v Casement* [1917] 1 KB 98 and *Joyce v DPP*, *supra* this form of treason can be committed where D goes abroad and adheres there to the Queen's enemies. It is doubtful whether this was the original meaning of the Act, which created no other forms of extraterritorial treason, and no procedure for trying it; but this interpretation is now firmly established.

'slay the chancellor, treasurer or ... justices' The office of Treasurer no longer exists. It is not the same as the First Lord of the Treasury (Prime Minister). It is most unlikely that the assassination of the Lord Chancellor or of a judge would attract anything more serious than a charge of murder.

'treason which extends to [the Queen]'. This means high treason, rather than petit treason, (which no longer exists as a distinct offence). Note also the lesser offence created by the Treason Act 1842 (*infra*).

Penalty Treason remains a capital offence, the penalty being prescribed by the Treason Act 1814 s 1 (not printed in this work).

Treason Act 1795

(36 GEO III C 7)

Persons who shall compass, advise, etc, the death, restraint, etc, of his Majesty or his heirs, to be deemed traitors
[1] If any person or persons whatsoever . . . shall, within the realm or without, compass, imagine, invent, devise or intend death or destruction, or any bodily harm tending to death or destruction, maim or wounding, imprisonment or restraint, of the person of . . . our sovereign lord the King, his heirs and successors, . . . and such compassings, imaginations, inventions, devices or intentions, or any of them shall express, utter or declare, by publishing any printing or writing, or by any overt act or deed, being legally convicted thereof upon the oaths of two lawful and credible witnesses upon trial, or otherwise convicted or attainted by due course of law, then every such person and persons so as aforesaid offending shall be deemed, declared and adjudged to be a traitor and traitors, and shall suffer pains of death, . . . as in cases of high treason.

NOTES
This Act extends the concept of treason beyond that prescribed in the principal Act of 1351 (qv). It does so:
 (a) by giving an extraterritorial ambit to the offence of treason by compassing *etc* the death of the Queen or of the heir to the throne;
 (b) by making it treason to compass *etc* maim, wounding, imprisonment or restraint as well as death; and
 (c) by making it treason to commit such offences against heirs other than the eldest son.

Note that an intent to injure (without wounding *etc*) or to alarm is not sufficient, but it may suffice for liability under the Treason Act 1842 (qv), which creates a less serious offence.

'**compass, imagine etc**' See the notes to the 1351 Act.

2–4 [*repealed*]

5–6 [*omitted*]

Vagrancy Act 1824

(5 GEO IV C 83)

Persons committing certain offences shall be deemed rogues and vagabonds and may be imprisoned for three months

4. . . . Every person committing any of the offences herein-before mentioned, after having been convicted as an idle and disorderly person; every person pretending or professing to tell fortunes, or using any subtle craft, means, or device, by palmistry or otherwise, to deceive and impose on any of his Majesty's subjects; every person wandering abroad and lodging in any barn or outhouse, or in any deserted or unoccupied building, or in the open air, or under a tent, or in any cart or waggon, . . . and not giving a good account of himself or herself; every person wilfully, openly, lewdly, and obscenely exposing his person . . ., with intent to insult any female; every person wandering abroad, and endeavouring by the exposure of wounds or deformities to obtain or gather alms; every person going about as a gatherer or collector of alms, or endeavouring to procure charitable contributions of any nature or kind, under any false or fraudulent pretence; . . . every person being found in or upon any dwelling house, warehouse, coach-house, stable, or outhouse, or in any inclosed yard, garden, or area, for any unlawful purpose; . . . ; and every person apprehended as an idle and disorderly person, and violently resisting any constable, or other peace officer so apprehending him or her, and being subsequently convicted of the offence for which he or she shall have been so apprehended; shall be deemed a rogue and vagabond, within the true intent and meaning of this Act; and [subject to section 70 of the Criminal Justice Act 1982,] it shall be lawful for any justice of the peace to commit such offender (being thereof convicted before him by the confession of such offender, or by the evidence on oath of one or more credible witness or witnesses,) to the house of correction . . . for any time not exceeding three calendar months:

NOTES

Many of the offences dealt with by this provision appear antiquated today, but it is still quite widely used, particularly in London, where there are a large number of vagrants and homeless persons. Some of the offences created here have little to do with vagrancy; e.g. the offence of indecent exposure, which is also widely used. Occasional use may also be found for the offence of being found in a dwelling house, inclosed yard *etc.*, where a charge of burglary or attempted burglary might be harder to prove.

This is one of two statutory provisions creating offences of indecent exposure, the other being s 28 of the Town Police Clauses Act 1847 (not included in this book). There is also a common law offence which, unlike the others, is capable of applying to women as well as men; and local byelaws may apply in certain areas.

'**any person ... exposing his person**'   The offence can only be committed by a male, because the 'person' which has to be exposed is the penis: *Evans v Ewels* [1972] 2 All ER 22.

'**wilfully, openly, lewdly and obscenely**'   This requires something more than mere indecency. Nudity on an ordinary public beach might be indecent, but would not be obscene unless there were aggravating factors. See *McGowan v Longmuir* 1931 SC 10, *per* Lord Parker at p. 13.

The offence may be committed on private property: *Ford v Falcone* [1971] 2 All ER 1138.

'**with intent to insult a female**'   This is a specific intent, and must be proved, although the proof may take the form of inferences from the circumstances of the exposure. It is not however necessary to prove that any females saw the exposure, or that they would have felt insulted if they had seen it. Contrast the offence under the 1847 Act, which does not require any such specific intent, but does require that some person (male or female) should be 'annoyed, obstructed or endangered' by the conduct.

'**shall be deemed a rogue and a vagabond**'   A person who has previously been convicted of an offence under this provision may on a subsequent conviction be deemed an 'incorrigible rogue' under s 5, and may then face up to one year's imprisonment on committal to the Crown Court for sentence. This sentence may also be imposed where D 'violently resists' a constable arresting him for a s 4 offence.

'**offences herein-before mentioned**'   These are offences of public begging etc under s 3 of the Act (not printed in this work).

'**professing to tell fortunes**'   No intent to deceive need be proved: *Stonehouse v Mason* [1921] 2 KB 818; but it would seem that the law is not generally enforced.

'**wandering abroad**' **etc**   As to the position of homeless persons who have no access to a proper place of shelter, see s 1 of the Vagrancy Act 1935 (not printed in this work).

'**tent, ... cart or waggon**'   This excludes one belonging to D in or with which he travels (1935 Act s 1).

'**to the house of correction**'   This now means imprisonment.

[*other sections omitted*]

Treason Act 1842

(5 & 6 VICT C 51)

1 [*repealed*]

Punishment for discharging or aiming firearms, or throwing or using any offensive matter or weapon with intent to injure or alarm her Majesty
2. ... If any person shall wilfully discharge or attempt to discharge, or point, aim, or present at or near to the person of the Queen, any gun, pistol, or any other description of fire-arms or of other arms whatsoever, whether the same shall or shall not contain any explosive or destructive material, or shall discharge or cause to be discharged, or attempt to discharge or cause to be discharged, any explosive substance or material near to the person of the Queen, or if any person shall wilfully strike or strike at, or attempt to strike or to strike at, the person of the Queen, with any offensive weapon, or in any other manner whatsoever, or if any person shall wilfully throw or attempt to throw any substance, matter, or thing whatsoever at or upon the person of the Queen, with intent in any of the cases aforesaid to injure the person of the Queen, or with intent in any of the cases aforesaid to break the public peace, or whereby the public peace may be endangered, or with intent in any of the cases aforesaid to alarm her Majesty, or if any person shall, near to the person of the Queen, wilfully produce or have any gun, pistol, or any other description of fire-arms or other arms whatsoever, or any explosive, destructive, or dangerous matter or thing whatsoever, with intent to use the same to injure the person of the Queen, or to alarm her Majesty, every such person so offending shall be guilty of [an offence], and being convicted thereof in due course of law, shall be liable, at the discretion of the court before which the said person shall be so convicted, to be [imprisoned] for the term of seven years, ...

NOTES
A genuine attempt to assassinate the Queen would amount to High Treason under the Acts of 1351 and 1795 (qv), the penalty for which remains death by hanging under the Treaon Act 1814 (see s.3 *infra*).
This provision is concerned with actions which are not intended to do more than injure or alarm her, the law of assault being considered an inadequate sanction for such actions (see *R v Bean* (1842) 4 State Trials (N.S.) 1382). It has been invoked in a number of cases, including *R v Hamilton* (1849) 8 State Trials (N.S.) 1130, and most recently in the unreported case of *R v Sarjeant* (12 Sept 1981) in which a sentence of five years imprisonment was passed on a youth who had fired 'blanks' at the Queen from a replica revolver during the Trooping of the Colour ceremony in June that year.

6

'wilfully'   As to the meaning of this term, see *R v Senior* [1899] 1 QB 283 at pp. 290–291; but in view of the need for a specific intent to injure or alarm, it is really otiose.

'gun, pistol etc.'   Imitation firearms are not expressly mentioned in the Act, but can clearly be used to cause alarm etc; and note *R v Sarjeant, supra*.

'with intent'   This is an ulterior intent; D need not in fact succeed in his purpose.

Act not to alter the punishment of high treason, etc

3. Provided always, . . . that nothing herein contained shall be deemed to alter in any respect the punishment which by law may now be inflicted upon persons guilty of high treason or misprision of treason.

NOTE
See the notes to s 2 *supra*.

Accessories and Abettors Act 1861

(24 & 25 VICT C 94)

1–7 [*repealed*]

As to abettors in [indictable offences]

8. Whosoever shall aid, abet, counsel, or procure the commission of any indictable offence whether the same be an offence at common law or by virtue of any Act passed or to be passed, shall be liable to be tried, indicted, and punished as a principal offender.

NOTES

This provision deals only with indictable offences. Complicity in summary offences is dealt with under s 44(1) of the Magistrates' Courts Act 1980, s 44(2) of which ensures that an accessory to an offence triable 'either way' may himself be tried in either way.

Being primarily declaratory of the common law on the subject, the 1861 Act provides little in the way of definitions, and cannot be understood without reference to the case law.

'aid, abet, counsel or procure' These are alternative forms of participation in an offence perpetrated by another person. Each word has its own distinct meaning: *Att-Gen's Reference (No 1 of 1975)* [1975] 2 All ER 684. Nevertheless, it is not usually essential for either the indictment or the court to distinguish precisely between them. An indictment may properly allege that D 'aided, abetted, counselled and [*sic*] procured' without specifying which of these terms is actually appropriate to describe D's involvement: *Re Smith* (1858) 3 H & N 227; *Ferguson v Weaving* [1951] 1 KB 814.

A clear distinction can however be drawn between 'aiding and abetting' on the one hand, and 'counselling and procuring' on the other. As Lord Goddard CJ said in *Ferguson v Weaving*:

> 'The words "aid and abet" are apt to describe the actions of a person who is present at the time of the commission of an offence and takes some part therein ... whereas the words "counsel and procure" are appropriate to a person who though not present at the commission of the offence is an accessory before the fact.' [*ie* someone who assists, causes or encourages prior to the commission of the offence but without being present himself at the scene].

It was until recently held that an accessory before the fact could not be convicted of a more serious offence than his principal offender, but that an aider and abettor could be (*R v Richards* [1974] QB 776). This distinction no longer exists, and accessories before that fact can now be so convicted in appropriate cases: see *R v Howe & Bannister* (1987) 85 Cr App R 32.

The distinctions between 'aiding' and 'abetting' or between 'counselling' and 'procuring' are most frequently glossed over by the courts; but it appears that to 'aid' means to render practical assistance, whereas to 'abet' means to encourage or instigate. Both concepts require something more than mere passive presence at the scene of the crime: *R v Clarkson* [1971] 3 All ER 344; but *cf Wilcox v Jeffery* [1951] 1

8

All ER 464 and *R v Coney* (1882) 8 QBD 534 concerning abetting by audiences at illegal spectacles or fights. See also *R v Bland* [1988] Crim LR 41.

Likewise, in respect of accessories before the fact, it appears that 'procuring' refers to acts which actually cause, bring about or facilitate the commission of the offence, whereas 'counselling' refers to the provision of encouragement, solicitation or advice: *Att-Gen's Reference (No 1 of 1975) supra; R v Calhaem* [1985] 2 All ER 266. In respect of 'procuring', there need not necessarily be any understanding or agreement between the procurer and the perpetrator. Thus, D may procure E's offence of driving with excess alcohol by surreptitiously 'lacing' E's drinks. The question is primarily one of causation. (*Att-Gen's Reference, supra*). But in respect of 'counselling', causation is not critical. If D suggests to E that E should kill X, and E does kill X, D is guilty of counselling X's murder even if there is no evidence that his advice influenced E's actions: *R v Calhaem, supra*.

Mens Rea of Secondary Parties Aiding, abetting *etc* are originally common law concepts, and they accordingly require *mens rea*, even where the charge is one of complicity in an offence which (as regards the perpetrator) is one of strict liability: *Ferguson v Weaving, supra; Johnson v Youden* [1950] 1 All ER 300.

In contrast, a secondary party may incur liability for a crime requiring a specific intent on the part of the perpetrator without himself having any such specific intent. Thus, in cases involving a joint criminal enterprise (*eg* robbery) each participant will be jointly liable for any further criminal act (*eg* murder) committed by another in the course of that enterprise, unless that further act was both unauthorised and unforseen by him: *Chan Wing-Siu v R* [1984] 3 All ER 877; *R v Ward* (1987) 85 Cr App R 71; *R v Anderson and Morris* [1966] 2 QB 110; *R v Slack* [1989] Crim LR 903. But see also *R v Wakely* [1990] Crim LR 119.

Likewise, if D assists E, or provides him with weapons *etc*, knowing or believing that E intends to commit some criminal offence, but without knowing exactly what offence E has in mind, D may still become guilty of complicity in that offence, as long as it is one which he had contemplated as being a serious possibility: *DPP for N Ireland v Maxwell* [1978] 3 All ER 1140.

'shall be liable to be tried, indicted and punished as a principal offender' The liability of the secondary party on conviction is exactly the same as that of the perpetrator; and although it is preferable that an indictment should indicate the nature of D's alleged involvement in the offence charged, an indictment which does not distinguish between perpetrators and accessories is not defective: *DPP for Northern Ireland v Maxwell* [1978] 3 All ER 1140 *per* Viscount Dilhorne at p 1142. It does not generally matter if the prosecution cannot show which of D and E was the principal and which the secondary party — both may be convicted as principals: *Mohan v R* [1967] 2 AC 187 (*cf R v Russell and Russell* [1987] Crim LR. 494).

In *R v Howe and Bannister* (1987) 85 Cr App R 32 the House of Lords ruled that an aider and abettor to murder is, like the principal, unable to rely on any defence of duress. This is probably true also of an accessory before the fact, although the *ratio decidendi* of the case does not extend that far.

Withdrawal from Criminal Enterprise On the issue of what amounts to an effective withdrawal (*ie* so as to avoid incurring liability) see *R v Becerra and White* (1975) 62 Cr App R 212 and *R v Whitefield* [1984] Crim LR 97.

Jurisdictional Problems The general rule is that if D, outside the jurisdiction, counsels or procures an offence committed by E within the jurisdiction, then both are equally liable to be tried here for the offence: *R v Robert Millar Contractors Ltd* [1970] 2 QB 54.

In the converse situation, jurisdiction will only lie if the offence concerned has an extraterritorial ambit (*eg* hijacking, murder, *etc*), but note special provisions in the Misuse of Drugs Act 1971, s 20.

Assisting Offender after Commission of the Offence The 'accessory after the fact', as he used to be called, may now be guilty of a specific offence under s 4 of the Criminal Law Act 1967, although this applies only in cases where an arrestable offence has been committed.

9 [*repealed*]

10 [*omitted*]

11 [*repealed*]

Malicious Damage Act 1861

(24 & 25 VICT C 97)

Placing wood, etc, on railway, taking up rails, etc, turning points, showing or hiding signals, etc, with intent to obstruct or overthrow any engine, etc
35. Whosoever shall unlawfully and maliciously put, place, cast, or throw upon or across any railway any wood, stone or other matter or thing or shall unlawfully and maliciously take up, remove, or displace any rail, sleeper, or other matter or thing belonging to any railway, or shall unlawfully and maliciously turn, move, or divert any points or other machinery belonging to any railway, or shall unlawfully and maliciously make or show, hide or remove, any signal or light upon or near to any railway, or shall unlawfully and maliciously do or cause to be done any other matter or thing, with intent, in any of the cases aforesaid, to obstruct, upset, overthrow, injure, or destroy any engine, tender, carriage, or truck using such railway, shall be guilty of [an offence] and being convicted thereof shall be liable, at the discretion of the court, to imprisonment for life.

NOTES
As to the differences between this provision and the similarly constructed s 32 of the Offences Against the Person Act 1861, see the notes to that provision.

Obstructing engines or carriages on railways
36. Whosoever, by any unlawful act, or by any wilful omission or neglect, shall obstruct or cause to be obstructed any engine or carriage using any railway, or shall aid or assist therein, shall be guilty of [an offence], and being convicted thereof shall be liable, at the discretion of the court, to be imprisoned for any term not exceeding two years.

NOTES
As with s 35 *supra*, there is a similarly constructed provision in the Offences Against the Person Act 1861—in this case it is s 34 (qv). It is nevertheless possible to envisage cases of obstruction under this provision which would not involve any endangerment under the other Act. An unlawful demonstration or picket preventing locomotives from leaving their depot might, for example, be mounted in complete safety.

'obstruct' See *R v Hadfield* (1870) LR 1 CCR 253 and *R v Hardy* (1871) LR 1 CCR 278.

Exhibiting false signals, etc
47. Whosoever shall unlawfully mask, alter, or remove any light or signal, or unlawfully exhibit any false light or signal, with intent to bring any ship, vessel, or boat into danger, or shall, unlawfully and maliciously

do anything tending to the immediate loss or destruction of any ship, vessel, or boat, and for which no punishment is herein-before provided, shall be guilty of [an offence] and being convicted therof shall be liable, at the discretion of the court, to imprisonment for life.

NOTES
The practice of 'wrecking' ships for the sake of plunder may be a thing of the past, but note that this provision might also apply to commonplace acts of vandalism if these were of a kind that might cause the loss of a vessel. In practice, such acts would be more likely to be charged under s 1(2) of the Criminal Damage Act 1971 (qv).

'maliciously' See the notes to s 20 of the Offences Against the Person Act 1861.

Removing or concealing buoys and other sea marks
48. Whosoever shall unlawfully and maliciously cut away, cast adrift, remove, alter, deface, sink, or destroy, or shall unlawfully and maliciously do any act with intent to cut away, cast adrift, remove, alter, deface, sink, or destroy, or shall in any other manner unlawfully and maliciously injure or conceal any boat, buoy, buoy rope, perch, or mark used or intended for the guidance of seamen, or for the purpose of navigation, shall be guilty of [an offence] and being convicted therof shall be liable, at the discretion of the court, to [imprisonment for life].

NOTE
In practice, actions such as these would probably be charged as criminal damage under the 1971 Act (qv).

[ss. 58 & 72 *omitted as otiose; all other provisions repealed*]

Forgery Act 1861

(24 & 25 VICT C.98)

Acknowledging recognizance, bail, cognovit, etc, in the name of another
34. Whosoever, without lawful authority or excuse (the proof whereof shall lie on the party accused), shall in the name of any other person acknowledge any recognizance or bail, or any cognovit actionem, or judgment or any deed or other instrument, before any court, judge, or other person lawfully authorized in that behalf, shall be guilty of [an offence] and being convicted thereof shall be liable ... to be [imprisoned] for a term not exceeding seven years ...

NOTES
The Forgery and Counterfeiting Act 1981 would appear to be applicable in cases where D has forged P's acknowledgment, authorisation or consent on forms or instruments served on him in connection with legal transactions or proceedings (see ss 1, 8(1)(c), 9(1) & 10(1)(a)–(c) of that Act); but this more specific provision has been left in force.

'recognizance' This must be a valid one. Thus in *R v McKenzie* [1971] 1 All ER 729 Cantley J directed the jury to acquit D of using a false name when entering into a recognizance, because D had been improperly required to enter into that recognizance in the first place.

'cognovit actionem' This is an obsolete instrument, which has long ceased to be used. Its modern equivalent is a court order made by consent. This would be within the scope of this section as a species of 'other instrument'.

Destroying, injuring, forging, or falsifying registers of births, baptisms, marriages, deaths, or burials, or certified copies
36. Whosoever shall unlawfully destroy, deface, or injure, or cause or permit to be destroyed, defaced, or injured, any register of births, baptisms, marriages, deaths, or burials which now is or hereafter shall be by law authorized or required to be kept in England or Ireland, or any part of any such register, or any certified copy of any such register, or any part thereof, ... or shall knowingly and unlawfully insert or cause or permit to be inserted in any such register, or in any certified copy thereof, any false entry of any matter relating to any birth, baptism, marriage, death, or burial, or shall knowingly and unlawfully give any false certificate relating to any birth, baptism, marriage, death, or burial, or shall certify any writing to be a copy or extract from any such register, knowing such writing, or the part of such register whereof such copy or extract shall be so given, to be false in any material particular, ... or shall offer, utter, dispose of, or put off any such register, entry, certified copy, certificate, ... knowing the same to be false, ... or shall offer, utter, dispose of, or put off

13

any copy of any entry in any such register, knowing such entry to be false,
... shall be guilty of [an offence] and being convicted thereof, shall be
liable ... to [imprisonment] for life ...

NOTES

As with s 34 *supra*, this provision appears to overlap with those of the 1981 Act, but
its scope is wider in some respects, since it extends to the unlawful destruction etc of
registers; and where false entries are made it need not be proved that there was any
intent to induce another person to act to his prejudice through accepting them as
genuine. Note that the maximum penalty for offences under this provision or s 37
infra is far higher than that which may be imposed for falsification offences under
s 37 of the Births and Deaths Registration Act 1953.

'cause or permit' As to the meaning of these terms, see *McLeod v Buchanan*
[1940] 2 All ER 179 at p 187; *James & Son Ltd v Smee* [1955] 1 QB 78. 'Cause' is
used in its imperative sense (ie ordering), but a person who supplies a registrar
with false information might nevertheless be guilty of 'causing' the insertion of a
false entry in the register, since in most cases the registrar is effectively obliged to
enter such details as he is given by his informants.

*Making false entries in copies of registers of baptisms, marriages, or burials,
directed to be sent to any registrar, or destroying or concealing copies of registers*

37. Whosoever shall knowingly and wilfully insert or cause or permit to
be inserted in any copy of any register directed or required by law to be
transmitted to any registrar or other officer any false entry of any matter
relating to any baptism, marriage, or burial, ... or shall knowingly and
wilfully sign or verify any copy of any register so directed or required to be
transmitted as aforesaid, which copy shall be false in any part thereof,
knowing the same to be false, or shall unlawfully destroy, deface, or injure,
or shall for any fraudulent purpose take from its place of deposit, or
conceal, any such copy of any register, shall be guilty of [an offence] and
being convicted thereof shall be liable ... to imprisonment for life ...

NOTE

This offence largely corresponds to s 36 *supra*, but deals with the falsification,
destruction etc of *copies* of registers.

[s 55 *omitted; all other sections repealed*]

Offences Against the Person Act 1861

(24 & 25 VICT C 100)

Conspiring or soliciting to commit murder

4. ... whosoever shall solicit, encourage, persuade, or endeavour to persuade, or shall propose to any person, to murder any other person, whether he be a subject of her Majesty or not, and whether he be within the Queen's dominions or not, shall be guilty of [an offence], and being convicted thereof shall be liable ... to [imprisonment for life].

NOTES

This provision (as amended) creates what is in effect a statutory offence of incitement to murder, but it is doubtful whether it extends or modifies the common law concept of incitement in any way.

'solicit, etc.' It was held in *R v Krause* (1902) 18 TLR 238 that, even in respect of 'endeavouring to persuade', communication between the inciter and the person incited is an essential element in the offence. If, for example, there is no evidence that a letter containing the incitement has been received and read by the intended murderer, it can on this view be no more than an attempt to commit the offence. See also *R v Banks* (1873) 12 Cox CC 393. (A charge of attempting to solicit, *etc* is *not* precluded under s 1(4) of the Criminal Attempts Act 1981.) Note however that in *Treacy v DPP* [1971] AC 537 the House of Lords held that a blackmail demand is complete when posted; and it is difficult to see why 'demands' and 'proposals' should be construed differently in that respect.

It is clear that the person solicited need not be influenced by the approach: *R v Diamond* (1920) 84 JP 211; *R v Krause, supra*.

'to any person, to murder any other person' Neither the persons solicited, nor the intended victims, need be named individuals. A generalised incitement directed against a whole class of potential victims (eg Jews) will suffice (*R v Most* (1881) 7 QBD 244), as will solicitation of a pregnant woman to murder her child after its birth (*R v Shephard* [1919] 2 KB 125).

'murder' The general rule in respect of inchoate offences such as incitement or conspiracy is that the incitement, *etc* must take place or be furthered within England and Wales (or on a British ship, *etc*) and that the offence incited must be one which would be justiciable under English law: see *Board of Trade v Owen* [1957] AC 602; *DPP v Stonehouse* [1978] AC 55; *DPP v Doot* [1973] AC 807. There are some statutory exceptions to this rule, but this provision does not appear to be one of them. It contemplates the incitement of murders which may be committed abroad, but it is submitted that such murders must nevertheless be punishable in England (e.g. under s 9 *infra*) before it applies. It does not extend to cases in which the incitement itself takes place outside the jurisdiction.

'whether he be within the Queen's dominions or not' This must also be a reference to the victim. As to victims outside the jurisdiction, see note on *'murder'*, *supra*.

'imprisonment for life' Penalty substituted by s 5(10)(b) of the Criminal Law Act 1977.

Manslaughter

5. Whosoever shall be convicted of manslaughter shall be liable, at the discretion of the court, to [imprisonment] for life.

NOTE
This provision merely lays down the maximum penalty for manslaughter. It does not purport to provide any kind of definition of that offence, nor does it make the offence statutory. Involuntary manslaughter, whether constructive or reckless, remains a common law offence. Voluntary manslaughter, where the defendant was acting under provocation, or in pursuance of a suicide pact, or was suffering from diminished responsibility, is now governed by the Homicide Act 1957.

6–8 [*repealed*]

Murder or manslaughter abroad

9. Where any murder or manslaughter shall be committed on land out of the United Kingdom, whether within the Queen's dominions or without, and whether the person killed were a subject of Her Majesty or not, every offence committed by any subject of Her Majesty in respect of any such case, whether the same shall amount to the offence of murder or of manslaughter, may be dealt with, inquired of, tried, determined, and punished in England or in Ireland;

Provided, that nothing herein contained shall prevent any person from being tried in any place out of England or Ireland for any murder or manslaughter committed out of England or Ireland, in the same manner as such person might have been tried before the passing of this Act.

NOTES
'on land out of the United Kingdom' Offences committed in Scotland or Northern Ireland do not come within this provision. However, the Isle of Man and the Channel Islands do, as they are *not* part of the United Kingdom (Interpretation Act 1978 s 5 and Sch 1).

As to offences committed on British or foreign ships, see the Merchant Shipping Act 1894 s 686. As to offences committed on aircraft, see the Civil Aviation Act 1982 s 92 and the Aviation Security Act 1982, ss 1–3. As to hovercraft, see the Hovercraft (Application of Enactments) Order 1972 (SI 1972 No 971). The shipwrecked cannibals, Dudley and Stephens, were convicted of murder by virtue of what is now the Merchant Shipping Act 1894 s 687. Offences on or near British oil or gas exploration or drilling platforms, even if committed outside the new 12 mile territorial limits, may be covered by the Continental Shelf Act 1964 s 3 and the Mineral Workings (Offshore Installations) Act 1971 s 8.

'committed by any subject of Her Majesty' By virtue of s 3(1) of the British Nationality Act 1948 and s 51 of the British Nationality Act 1981, this provision now applies only to British citizens, British Overseas citizens and British Dependent Territories Citizens.

Provision for the trial of murder and manslaughter where the death or cause of death only happens in England or Ireland

10. Where any person being criminally stricken, poisoned, or otherwise hurt upon the sea, or at any place out of England or Ireland, shall die of such stroke, poisoning, or hurt in England or Ireland, or, being criminally stricken, poisoned, or otherwise hurt in any place in England or Ireland, shall die of such stroke, poisoning, or hurt upon the sea, or at any place out of England or Ireland, every offence committed in respect of any such case, whether the same shall amount to the offence of murder or of manslaughter may be dealt with, inquired of, tried, determined, and punished, in England or Ireland.

NOTES
This provision covers two situations: (1) death within the jurisdiction following a criminally inflicted injury elsewhere; and (2) death elsewhere following a criminally inflicted injury within the jurisdiction.

As to the former situation, s 10 would now appear to be superfluous, because murder and manslaughter are 'result crimes' (the death of the victim being the proscribed result) and, as Lord Diplock explained in *Secretary of State for Trade v Markus* [1976] AC 35 at 61:

'In the case of what is a result crime in English law, the offence is committed in England and justiciable by an English court if any part of the proscribed result takes place in England.'

Moreover, it will be seen that s 10 cannot apply unless the original blow, *etc* was 'criminal' in the sense of being punishable under English law (see *R v Lewis infra*).

In the latter situation, where the original blow is inflicted in England, but death occurs elsewhere (eg in a Scottish hospital), s 10 serves a useful function in ensuring that English courts have jurisdiction where otherwise they might not.

'criminally stricken' In *R v Lewis* (1857) Dears & Bell 182, it was held that a blow struck by an alien aboard a foreign ship on the high seas was *not* criminal under English law and that s 10 did not apply, notwithstanding the victim's subsequent death in Liverpool. Had the blow been struck aboard a British ship, it would have been criminal because it would have been punishable under Admiralty jurisdiction. (See following note.)

'upon the sea' Note that English courts have jurisdiction over offences committed within British territorial waters (Territorial Waters Jurisdiction Act 1878, as amended by the Territorial Sea Act 1987) or on British ships (Merchant Shipping Act 1894, s 686) or by British subjects aboard foreign ships to which they do not belong (*ibid*).

'England or Ireland' 'England' includes Wales, 'Ireland' now means Northern Ireland.

11–15 [*repealed*]

Threats to kill
16. A person who without lawful excuse makes to another a threat, intending that that other would fear it would be carried out, to kill that other or a third person shall be guilty of an offence and liable on conviction on indictment to imprisonment for a term not exceeding ten years.

NOTES
This provision was substituted for the original, narrower, s 16 ('Sending letters threatening to murder') by the Criminal Law Act 1977 s 65 and Sch 12, and clearly extends to all kinds of such threats, whether oral, written or otherwise. Some such threats might also amount to blackmail under s 21 of the Theft Act 1968 (qv).

'without lawful excuse' A person may actually *use* lethal force in self–defence, in defence of another person, or for the purpose of preventing crime, *etc* under s 3 of the Criminal Law Act 1967, and will commit no offence provided the force used is reasonable in the circumstances, or even in the circumstances as he mistakenly believes them to be. (See *R v Williams (Gladstone)* (1984) 78 Cr App R 276 and *Beckford v R* [1987] 3 All ER 425, which show that the mistake need not even be a 'reasonable' one). Clearly, a threat of force cannot be criminal where its actual use would not be; and in *R v Cousins* [1982] 2 All ER 115, the Court of Appeal approved of a suggestion in *Smith and Hogan* that:

> 'A threat to kill may ... be excusable where actual killing would not. To cause fear of death might be reasonable to prevent crime or to arrest an offender whereas actually to kill would be quite unreasonable.'

'threat' As in the case of blackmail demands, threats can be implied as well as openly expressed (see the notes to Theft Act 1968 s 21); but if there is any dispute as to whether a statement contains a threat, this is a question for the jury (*R v Carruthers* (1844) 1 Cox CC 138).

'or a third party' This may be a child yet unborn, but only if the threat is that it will be killed after birth. See *R v Tait* [1989] Crim LR 834.

17 [*omitted*]

Shooting or attempting to shoot, or wounding, with intent to do grievous bodily harm or to resist apprehension

18. Whosoever shall unlawfully and maliciously by any means whatsoever wound or cause any grievous bodily harm to any person with intent to do some grevous bodily harm to any person, or with intent to resist or prevent the lawful apprehension or detainer of any person, shall be guilty of [an offence], and being convicted thereof shall be liable ... to [imprisonment] for life.

NOTES
There are four distinct variants of this offence;
    (1) wounding with intent to do grievous bodily harm;
    (2) causing grievous bodily harm with intent to do so;
    (3) wounding with intent to resist lawful apprehension *etc*;
    (4) causing grievous bodily harm with intent to resist lawful apprehension *etc*.
The offence is distinguishable from the less serious one created by s 20, primarily by the need to prove a specific or ulterior intent. It is triable only on indictment.

'maliciously' Where the indictment alleges an intent to do grievous bodily harm, the requirement of maliciousness 'adds nothing' and can be ignored (see *R v Mowatt* [1967] 3 All ER 47 *per* Lord Diplock LJ at p 50); but where what is alleged is an intent to resist lawful apprehension, *etc*, it is essential that the prosecution proves the injury in question to have been caused maliciously. The meaning of the term is explained in the notes to s 20 *infra*.

'wounds' A wound need not be a serious injury, but it must involve penetration of the skin (dermis and epidermis). This means that ruptured blood vessels or internal injuries are not wounds: *JJC (a minor) v Eisenhower* [1983] Crim LR 567. Serious internal injuries may however constitute grievous bodily harm.

'to any person' Under the doctrine of transferred malice, it would be no defence on a charge of wounding P to show that one intended to cause grievous bodily harm to Q; but see *R v Monger* [1973] Crim LR 301 on the need to word the indictment correctly in such a case.

'or with intent to resist the lawful apprehension ... of any person' 'Any person' must here include the accused himself. An offence under s 18 can be committed in the course of resisting or escaping from an *unlawful* arrest; but in such a case it could be necessary to show an intent to do grievous bodily harm. Even then, the accused might be able to plead self–defence, unless his reaction was clearly excessive on the facts as he believed them to be (see *Beckford v R* [1987] 3 All ER 425).

On lawful and unlawful arrest, see s 28 of the Police and Criminal Evidence Act 1984 (not printed in this work) and the notes to s 51 of the Police Act 1964.

19 [*repealed*]

Inflicting bodily injury, with or without weapon

20. Whosoever shall unlawfully and maliciously wound or inflict any grievous bodily harm upon any other person, either with or without any weapon or instrument shall be guilty of [an offence], and being convicted thereof shall be liable to [a term of imprisonment not exceeding five years].

NOTES
This offence is similar in many respects to the more serious variant created by s 18 *supra* but is distinguishable by the absence of the need to prove a specific or ulterior intent, so that 'maliciousness' becomes the key element in the *mens rea*. A further, more subtle, distinction is that any grievous bodily harm must be 'inflicted', rather than merely 'caused by any means whatsoever' as in s 18.

The offence is triable either way.

'maliciously' What is required is *either* an intent to do the particular kind of harm that in fact was done *or* recklessness as to whether such harm would occur or not (*R v Cunningham* [1957] 2 All ER 412); but 'particular kind of harm' need not mean harm of the same severity as alleged in the charge or indictment: an intent *etc* to inflict any bodily harm is sufficient: *R v Mowatt* [1967] 3 All ER 47. See also *R v Grimshaw* [1984] Crim LR 108. Recklessness meanwhile 'postulates foresight of consequence' (*R v Cunningham, supra*). It does not for these purposes include what is generally known as *Caldwell* recklessness (ie a failure to consider an obvious risk). See *W (a minor) v Dolbey* [1983] Crim LR 681; *R v Rainbird* [1989] Crim LR 505.

'wound or ... grievous bodily harm' See the notes to s 18 *supra*.

'inflicts' It was once argued that the concept of 'inflicting' harm necessarily involves some kind of assault and battery, so that injuries caused by indirect means (eg traps) fell outside the scope of this provision; but in *R v Salisbury* [1976] VR 452 the Supreme Court of Victoria reviewed the authorities and stated (at p 461):

> 'We have come to the conclusion that, although the word "inflicts" ... does not have as wide a meaning as the word "causes" ... [it] does have a wider meaning than it would have if it were construed so that inflicting grievous bodily harm always involved assaulting the victim. In our opinion, grievous bodily harm may be inflicted ... either where the accused has directly and violently inflicted it by assaulting the victim, or where the accused has inflicted it by doing something intentionally which, though it is not itself a direct application of force to the body of the victim, does directly result in force being applied violently ... so that he suffers grievous bodily harm.'

This passage was in turn approved by the House of Lords in *R v Wilson* [1983] 3 All ER 448, their Lordships being 'content to accept that there can be an infliction of grievous bodily harm without an assault.' See also *R v Martin* (1881) 8 QBD 54. The distinction between 'causing' and 'inflicting' was not in issue in *Wilson*, but appears to be consistent with some of the views expressed in *R v Clarence* (1888) 22 QBD 23. In *Clarence*, D infected his wife with venereal disease through an act of consensual intercourse, she being unaware of his infection. This intercourse lacked the 'violence' necessary for infliction, but Clarence clearly 'caused' his wife's infection, and would have been guilty of a s 18 offence had he intended to cause her serious harm.

Attempting to choke, etc., in order to commit or assist in the committing of any indictable offence

21. Whosoever shall, by any means whatsoever, attempt to choke, suffocate, or strangle any other person, or shall by any means calculated to choke, suffocate, or strangle, attempt to render any other person insensible, unconscious, or incapable of resistance, with intent in any of such cases thereby to enable himself or any other person to commit, or with intent in any of such cases thereby to assist any other person in committing, any indictable offence, shall be guilty of [an offence], and being convicted thereof shall be liable to [imprisonment] for life.

NOTES
This provision is little used and covers only attempts to choke *etc* which are performed with the ulterior intent of enabling some other crime to be committed. When this ulterior intent is theft, then the more obvious charge would be assault with intent to rob under s 8 of the Theft Act 1968. Where it is sexual intercourse, however, a charge under this provision might sometimes offer the prosecution advantages over a charge of attempted rape. It might, for example, save the court from having to consider whether the attack was 'more than merely preparatory' to the intended act of rape itself.

'choke' etc The popular term for this was 'garrotting'.

Using chloroform, etc., to commit or assist in the committing of any indictable offence

22. Whosoever shall unlawfully apply or administer to or cause to be taken by, or attempt to apply or administer to or attempt to cause to be administered to or taken by, any person, any chloroform, laudanum, or other stupefying or overpowering drug, matter, or thing, with intent in any of such cases thereby to enable himself or any other person to commit, or with intent in any of such cases thereby to assist any other person in committing, any indictable offence, shall be guilty of [an offence], and being convicted thereof shall be liable . . . to [imprisonment] for life.

NOTES
See the notes to s 21 *supra*, although s 8 of the Theft Act would only be a viable alternative where force is used in administering the drug. S 22 might be considered as an alternative charge to the common law offence of kidnapping or attempted kidnapping in appropriate cases.
   Where the ulterior intent is that of having unlawful intercourse with a female victim, a more specific offence is enacted in s 4 of the Sexual Offences Act 1956.

Maliciously administering poison, etc, so as to endanger life or inflict grievous bodily harm

23. Whosoever shall unlawfully and maliciously administer to or cause to be administered to or taken by any other person any poison or other destructive or noxious thing, so as thereby to endanger the life of such person, or so as thereby to inflict upon such person any grievous bodily harm, shall be guilty of [an offence], and being convicted thereof shall be liable to [imprisonment] for any term not exceeding ten years.

NOTES

This is the more serious of the two provisions in the Act relating to the administering of poisons and other noxious substances. S 24 *infra* creates the less serious offence. It contains a specific intent requirement not found in s 23, but a jury is nevertheless entitled to convict under it where the accused has been charged under s 23 (see s 25 *infra*).

'unlawfully and maliciously ... so as thereby to endanger life' etc. See notes to s 20 *supra*. In this context a person who poisons another will be regarded as having acted maliciously where he has done so intentionally or recklessly (using recklessness in the *Cunningham* sense of deliberate risk taking). If he knows that the substance concerned is noxious or harmful to any extent, that will suffice. He need not intend or appreciate that it may endanger life or cause serious injury: *R v Cato* [1976] 1 All ER 269. In other words, the endangering of life *etc.* is an *actus reus* element (*cf R v Mowatt* [1967] 3 All ER 47 in relation to s 20).

'administer' Squirting CS gas, ammonia *etc* at another person can be described as 'administering' a noxious substance: *R v Gillard, The Times,* 7 April 1988.

'or cause to be administered to or taken by' If D puts poison *etc* in P's drink and P unwittingly drinks it, this will be a straightforward case of 'causing poison to be taken' (*cf R v Marcus* [1981] 2 All ER 833). But 'cause' may also be interpreted here in its imperative sense, so that if D *orders* E to administer poison to P and E does so, D will have 'caused' the administration.

'poison or other destructive or noxious thing' The following kinds of substances may be considered destructive or noxious for the purpose of ss 23 and 24:

(1) those which are intrinsically dangerous even in 'ordinary' dosages (eg heroin, as in *R v Cato*)

(2) excessive dosages of substances which in ordinary dosages might be harmless or even beneficial (eg aspirin, alcohol or sleeping tablets). See *R v Cramp* (1880) 5 QBD 307; *R v Herrah* (1877) 13 Cox CC 547; *R v Wilkins* (1861) Le & Ca 89.

At the same time, substances which are harmless in the dosages or quantities actually involved will not be considered noxious merely because they are capable of causing harm, *etc* in larger dosages: *R v Cato; R v Herrah, supra.*

Maliciously administering poison, etc, with intent to injure, aggrieve, or annoy any other person

24. Whosoever shall unlawfully and maliciously administer to or cause to be administered to or taken by any other person any poison or other destructive or noxious thing, with intent to injure, aggrieve, or annoy such person, shall be guilty of [an offence], and being convicted thereof shall be liable to [imprisonment for not more than five years].

NOTES
See the notes to s 23 *supra*. Paradoxically, this provision requires a specific or ulterior intent, whereas s 23 does not, so that in some cases evidence of self-induced intoxication might be relevant to help establish a defence to the lesser charge when it could not help establish a defence to the more serious one.

'maliciously . . . with intent to injure, aggrieve, or annoy' In this context the requirement of maliciousness is clearly otiose, since it is eclipsed by the need for a specific intent.

Provided that the noxious substance is administered or taken, there is no need for it to succeed in actually causing injury, annoyance *etc*. Indeed, it was held in *R v Hill* [1985] Crim LR 384 that the offence might be committed where D administers sleeping pills to P with intent to injure him by some other means whilst he is incapacitated.

'poison or other destructive or noxious thing' See notes to s 23 *supra*. For the purposes of the present provision, it may be that obnoxious or unwholesome substances (including itching powder, stink bombs, *etc*) would come within the concept of noxious things: see *R v Marcus* [1981] 2 All ER 833.

Person charged with [an offence] under s 23 may be found guilty of [an offence] under s 24
   25. If, upon the trial of any person for [an offence] in the last but one preceding section mentioned, the jury shall not be satisfied that such person is guilty thereof, but shall be satisfied that he is guilty of [an offence] in the last preceding section mentioned, then and in every such case the jury may acquit the accused of [an offence under s 23], and find him guilty of [an offence under s 24], and thereupon he shall be liable to be punished in the same manner as if convicted upon an indictment for [an offence under s 24].

NOTES
See the notes to ss 23 and 24 *supra*. It may be that, as a result of the more flexible approach which has recently been adopted in relation to alternative verdicts under s 6 of the Criminal Law Act 1967, this provision is now otiose; but it would previously have been held that s 6 could not have been used, because s 24 requires an ulterior intent which s 23 does not.

26 [*omitted*]

Exposing children whereby life endangered
   27. Whosoever shall unlawfully abandon or expose any child, being under the age of two years, whereby the life of such child shall be endangered, or the health of such child shall have been or shall be likely to be permanently injured, shall be guilty of [an offence], and being convicted thereof shall be liable to [imprisonment for any term not exceeding five years].

NOTES
This provision has largely been superseded by s 1 of the Children and Young Persons Act 1933 (*qv*) which is in most respects wider-ranging. The latter provision might nevertheless fail to cover certain situations in which this one would apply (eg where a person aged between 10 and 15 deliberately abandons and endangers his

baby brother or sister — the 1933 provision applying only to the wilful behaviour of persons aged 16 or over) and where both do apply, the 1933 Act provides a normal maximum penalty of two years' imprisonment compared with the five year maximum provided here.

'abandon or expose' See *R v White* (1871) LR 1 CCC 311; *R v Falkingham* (1870) LR1 CCC 222.

Mens rea No *mens rea* is specified, but in view of the potential seriousness of this offence, it is submitted that D must at least be proved to have acted recklessly in abandoning or exposing the child. It should not however be necessary to prove any intent to endanger the child's life *etc.*

Causing bodily injury by gunpowder
28. Whosoever shall unlawfully and maliciously, by the explosion of gunpowder or other explosive substance, burn, maim, disfigure, disable, or do any grievous bodily harm to any person, shall be guilty of an offence, and being convicted thereof shall be liable, at the discretion of the court, to imprisonment for life.

NOTES
This provision overlaps to some extent with ss 29 and 30 *infra* and also with s 2 of the Explosive Substances Act 1883 (qv), although there are significant differences in the essential elements of each. Where damage to property occurs, charges of criminal damage might also be considered.

'maliciously' See the notes to s 20 *supra*. In the present context D must at least be reckless (in the *Cunningham* sense) as to the risk of causing some injury, but he need not intend or foresee the serious consequences specified in this provision.

'maim' This involves the loss of some limb or member (eg eye or finger) which might be useful in fighting.

'disfigure' A disfigurement is any injury, *etc*, which detracts from the victim's physical appearance.

'disable' A disablement is a permanent incapacitation or handicap: *R v Boyce* 1 Mood CC 29

'grievous bodily harm' See the notes to s 18 *supra*.

Causing gunpowder to explode, or sending to any person an explosive substance, or throwing corrosive fluid on a person with intent to do grievous bodily harm
29. Whosoever shall unlawfully and maliciously cause any gunpowder or other explosive substance to explode, or send or deliver to or cause to be taken or received by any person any explosive substance or any other dangerous or noxious thing, or put or lay at any place, or cast or throw at or upon or otherwise apply to any person, any corrosive fluid or any destructive or explosive substance, with intent in any of the cases aforesaid to burn, maim, disfigure, or disable any person, or to do some grievous bodily harm to any person, shall, whether any bodily injury be effected or not, be guilty of [an offence], and being convicted thereof shall be liable, at the discretion of the court, to [imprisonment] for life.

NOTES
In certain respects, this provision ranges wider than s 28 since it covers the misuse of non-explosive substances and does not require that any person should actually have been injured. It may even apply in certain cases where explosives have failed to go off as intended. It does however require a specific intent to burn, maim, disfigure or do grievous bodily harm.

'maliciously' In view of the need for a specific intent to maim, *etc*, the maliciousness requirement is clearly otiose here.

'cause' In this context, 'cause' appears to bear its ordinary meaning rather than its 'imperative' one. See the notes to s 23 *supra* and see also *R v Saunders* (1879) 14 Cox CC 180).

'noxious thing' See the notes to s 23 *supra*.

Placing gunpowder near a building, etc, with intent to do bodily injury to any person
   30. Whosoever shall unlawfully and maliciously place or throw in, into, upon, against, or near any building, ship, or vessel any gunpowder or other explosive substance, with intent to do any bodily injury to any person, shall, whether or not any explosion takes place, and whether or not any bodily injury be effected, be guilty of [an offence], and being convicted thereof shall be liable, at the discretion of the court, to [imprisonment] for any term not exceeding fourteen years.

NOTES
Apart from the obvious overlap with ss 28 and 29 *supra*, note also the overlap between this provision and s 3 of the Explosive Substances Act 1883 (qv).

'maliciously' As with s 29 *supra*, the requirement of a specific intent to do bodily harm renders the requirement of maliciousness superfluous in this context.

'explosive substance' No definition of explosive substances is provided in this Act; but they are defined in s 9 of the Explosive Substances Act 1885 as including components and materials for making an explosive substance or causing an explosion. The definition is not expressly applicable to the present Act, but there is no reason to exclude it. It is submitted that D might therefore commit this offence by planting or throwing a device which, unknown to him, is missing some essential component without which it cannot explode.

Setting spring guns, etc, with intent to inflict grievous bodily harm, or allowing the same to remain
   31. Whosoever shall set or place, or cause to be set or placed, any spring gun, man trap, or other engine calculated to destroy human life or inflict grievous bodily harm, with the intent that the same or whereby the same may destroy or inflict grievous bodily harm upon a trespasser or other person coming in contact therewith, shall be guilty of an offence, and being convicted thereof shall be liable to [imprisonment for any term not exceeding five years] and whosoever shall knowingly and wilfully permit any such spring gun, man trap, or other engine which may have been set or placed in any place then being in or afterwards coming into his possession or occupation by some other person to continue so set or placed, shall be deemed to have set and placed such gun, trap, or engine with such

intent as aforesaid: Provided, that nothing in this section contained shall extend to make it illegal to set or place any gun or trap such as may have been or may be usually set or placed with the intent of destroying vermin:

Proviso as to traps for vermin, and spring guns, etc, set at night for protection of dwelling-houses

Provided also, that nothing in this section shall be deemed to make it unlawful to set or place, or cause to be set or placed, or to be continued set or placed, from sunset to sunrise, any spring gun, man trap, or other engine which shall be set or placed, or caused or continued to be set or placed, in a dwelling house, for the protection thereof.

NOTES

This rarely-invoked and obscurely worded provision appears to create a number of distinct offences:

(1) setting spring guns, 'engines' *etc* with intent to kill (destroy) or do grievous bodily harm to trespassers or other persons;

(2) setting or causing the setting of such traps *whereby* such persons may be killed *etc*;

(3) knowingly and wilfully permitting such traps to remain on one's property (which is deemed equivalent to personally setting them with intent to kill *etc*).

The setting *etc* of ordinary vermin traps is not an offence under this provision, nor is it an offence under this provision to set spring guns, *etc*, for the protection of dwelling houses between sunset and sunrise. This does not mean, however, that the setting of such traps is proper or lawful, and it is submitted that it does not preclude a prosecution for wounding or manslaughter should a trespasser or burglar stumble into such a trap.

'cause to be set or placed' 'cause' appears here to be used in its imperative sense — as in offences of causing (ie ordering) the unlawful user of motor vehicles (see *Houston v Buchanan* [1940] 2 All ER 179).

'or other engine' An 'engine' is a mechanical device. In *R v Munks* [1964] 1 QB 304, it was held that the connection of the handle of a French window to the mains electricity supply did not amount to an offence under this provision because no 'engine' was involved!

'calculated' This means 'likely to' rather than 'intended to' (cf *Turner v Shearer* [1972] 1 WLR 1387).

'with intent that ... or whereby' If the trap is set with intent to kill *etc*, the offence is complete without the need for it to claim any victim. Alternatively, if it *does* succeed in killing or causing grievous bodily harm, the offence is also committed without the need for proof of any intent that it should do so. It is less clear whether the offence can be committed merely by setting a trap which is *capable* of doing such harm. The words, 'whereby the same may ...' could bear such a meaning, but the wording is most unclear.

'wilfully' Ie deliberately and intentionally — see *R v Senior* [1899] 1 QB 283.

'shall be deemed to have set' This fiction appears to be designed to preempt any defence to the effect that D merely allowed existing traps (set by his predecessor) to remain in place.

'dwelling house' This may be a house in which people actually live or one which is capable of being used for human habitation: *Lewis v Erol* [1906] AC 299 *per* Lord Atkinson at 304. A mobile home or static caravan may be a dwelling house: see *Makins v Elson* [1977] 1 All ER 572.

Placing wood, etc on railway, taking up rails, turning points, showing or hiding signals, etc, with intent to endanger passengers

32. Whosoever shall unlawfully and maliciously put or throw upon or across any railway any wood, stone, or other matter or thing, or shall unlawfully and maliciously take up, remove, or displace any rail, sleeper, or other matter or thing belonging to any railway, or shall unlawfully and maliciously turn, move or divert any points or other machinery belonging to any railway, or shall unlawfully and maliciously make or show, hide or remove, any signal or light upon or near to any railway, or shall unlawfully and maliciously do or cause to be done any other matter or thing, with intent, in any of the cases aforesaid, to endanger the safety of any person travelling or being upon such railway, shall be guilty of [an offence], and being convicted thereof shall be liable, at the discretion of the court, to [imprisonment] for life.

NOTES
This offence is largely identical to s 35 of the Malicious Damage Act 1861 (still in force despite the repeal of most other sections of that Act). The only difference is that in s 35 the words 'with intent to endanger the safety of any person travelling or being upon such railway' are replaced by words requiring an intent to obstruct, overturn, injure or destroy engines or rolling stock. In practice, commission of one offence will usually involve commission of the other.

'maliciously'   In view of the requirement of a specific intent to endanger safety, the reference to malice would appear to be unnecessary here.

'with intent to'   Since this is only an ulterior intent, the offence may be committed even if nobody is ever endangered.

'do or cause to be done'   'Cause' here appears to bear its imperative meaning: one 'causes' another person to do a certain thing if one orders it to be done. See *Houston v Buchanan* [1940] 2 All ER 179.

Casting stone, etc upon a railway carriage, with intent to endanger the safety of any person therein, or in any part of the same train.

33. Whosoever shall unlawfully and maliciously throw, or cause to fall or strike at, against, into, or upon any engine, tender, carriage, or truck used upon any railway, any wood, stone, or other matter or thing, with intent to injure or endanger the safety of any person being in or upon such engine, tender, carriage, or truck, or in or upon any other engine, tender, carriage, or truck of any train of which such first-mentioned engine, tender, carriage, or truck shall form part, shall be guilty of [an offence], and being convicted thereof shall be liable to [imprisonment] for life.

NOTES
As with s 32 *supra*, this offence requires a specific intent, but as with s 32, no lives need actually be endangered, and the object thrown *etc* need not even hit its target. As with s 32, any death caused by such behaviour will inevitably amount to manslaughter (ie constructive manslaughter), even if there is no *mens rea* for murder. See *DPP v Newbury* [1977] AC 500.

'maliciously'   See notes to s 32 *supra*.

'cause to fall' In this context 'cause' appears to bear its ordinary meaning (ie simple causation) rather than its 'imperative' meaning (as in s 32 *supra*). The reason for the difference is that this provision involves causing an event, whereas s 32 involves causing something to be done by someone else.

Doing or omitting anything so as to endanger passengers by railway

34. Whosoever, by any unlawful act, or by any wilful omission or neglect, shall endanger or cause to be endangered the safety of any person conveyed or being in or upon a railway, or shall aid or assist therein, shall be guilty of [an offence], and being convicted thereof shall be liable, at the discretion of the court, to be imprisoned for any term not exceeding two years.

NOTES

'by an unlawful act' This would cover breaches of road traffic law relating to level crossings or breaches of railway bye-laws *etc*, as well as acts of vandalism *etc*, committed without actual intent to endanger life. (Where such intent can be proved, see ss 32 and 33 *supra*.)

'or by any wilful omission or neglect' This must involve a deliberate failure to perform a duty, realising, or being reckless as to, the possible consequences of that neglect. Cf *R v Sheppard* [1980] 3 All ER 899.

'shall endanger' On the face of it, this expressly requires actual danger to be caused; but in *R v Pearce* [1966] 3 All ER 618, it was held that proof of actual danger was not essential, as long as D's conduct was potentially dangerous. Thus, damage to signalling *etc* would be within the section, even if a 'fail safe' back up system ensures that no danger arises. This interpretation is difficult to square with the words of the provision itself, but *Pearce* is the only extant authority.

Drivers of carriages injuring persons by furious driving

35. Whosoever, having the charge of any carriage or vehicle, shall by wanton or furious driving or racing, or other wilful misconduct, or by wilful neglect, do or cause to be done any bodily harm to any person whatsoever, shall be guilty of [an offence], and being convicted thereof shall be liable, at the discretion of the court, to be imprisoned for any term not exceeding two years.

NOTES

Where injury is caused by the driving of motor vehicles on roads, the drivers concerned will usually be prosecuted under appropriate provisions of the Road Traffic Act 1988. This provision may nevertheless be worth consideration in some such cases; and where the incident in question does not occur on a 'road' (as defined by s 192 of the 1988 Act) or does not involve the driving of a 'motor vehicle' (as defined by s 185(1) of that Act), it may provide the only suitable charge.

'any carriage or vehicle' This includes motor vehicles but also includes cycles (*R v Parker* (1895) 59 JP 793) and horse-drawn vehicles.

'wanton or furious' In *R v Crowden* (1911) 6 Cr App R 190, 'wanton' was described as a 'good old English word' which a jury would understand without the need for assistance. If true in 1911, this is almost certainly untrue now; but it may be translated as meaning 'wild, unrestrained, impetuous or undisciplined'. 'Furious' driving would fit the same description, but might also be characterised by bad temper and possibly excessive speed. Drunkenness may be a relevant factor in either case: *R v Burdon* (1927) 20 Cr App R 60.

'or other wilful misconduct or by wilful neglect' This may involve driving (or parking) a vehicle or cycle at night without adequate lights (*cf R v Cooke* [1971] Crim LR 44) or in some other dangerous fashion. It may involve either an act or omission. As far as 'wilfulness' is concerned, it was held in *R v Cooke* (*supra*) that the conduct must be deliberate but that the consequence might be entirely unforeseen. This may however need to be reconsidered in the light of the decision of the House of Lords in *R v Sheppard* [1981] AC 394.

36–37 [*omitted*]

Assault with intent to commit felony, or on peace officers, etc
38. Whosoever shall assault any person with intent to resist or prevent the lawful apprehension or detainer of himself or of any other person for any offence, shall be guilty of [an offence], and being convicted thereof shall be liable, at the discretion of the court, to be imprisoned for any term not exceeding two years.

NOTES
An assault on an arresting constable, or a person assisting such a constable, is more likely to be prosecuted under s 51 of the Police Act 1964 (qv).

If D causes a wound or grievous bodily harm in attempting to resist arrest, the prosecution may consider charges under s 18 or 20 of the present Act, although the former offence is not triable summarily.

'assault' See s 42 *infra*.

'lawful apprehension' On lawful and unlawful arrests, see s 28 of the Police and Criminal Evidence Act 1984 (not printed in this work) and the notes to s 51 of the Police Act 1964.

39–40 [*omitted*]

41 [*repealed*]

42–43 [*repealed by the Criminal Justice Act 1988 s 151 and Sch 14. As to common assault and battery, see now s 39 of the 1988 Act*]

If the magistrates dismiss the complaint, they shall make out a certificate to that effect
44. If the justices, upon the hearing of any case of assault or battery upon the merits, where the complaint was preferred by or on the behalf of the party aggrieved, shall deem the offence not to be proved, or shall find the assault or battery to have been justified, or so trifling as not to merit any punishment, and shall accordingly dismiss the complaint, they shall forthwith make out a certificate under their hands stating the fact of such dismissal, and shall deliver such certificate to the party against whom the complaint was preferred.

NOTES
'assault or battery'   See notes to s 47 *infra*.

'certificate'   Note that this certificate is not issued where the prosecution is brought by the Crown. (Such a prosecution is possible under s 39 of the Criminal Justice Act 1988.) As to the significance of the certificate, see s 45 *infra*.

Certificate or conviction shall be a bar to any other proceedings
   45. If any person against whom any such complaint as shall have been preferred by or on the behalf of the party aggrieved, shall have obtained such certificate, or, having been convicted, shall have paid the whole amount adjudged to be paid, or shall have suffered the imprisonment awarded, in every such case he shall be released from all further or other proceedings, civil or criminal, for the same cause.

NOTES
'for the same cause'   This does not give the defendant immunity from a charge of murder or manslaughter should the original complainant die, the 'cause' no longer being the same: *R v Morris* (1867) LR 1 CCR 90. As to the evidential significance of a conviction for assault on a later manslaughter charge, see s 74(3) of the Police and Criminal Evidence Act 1984; and of acquittal on the assault charge, see *Sambasivam v Public Prosecutor* [1950] AC 458.

46 [*repealed by Criminal Justice Act 1988 s 151 and Schedule 14*]

Assault occasioning bodily harm, common assault
   47. Whosoever shall be convicted on indictment of any assault occasioning actual bodily harm shall be liable to ... [imprisonment for not more than five years].

NOTES
This section originally provided, in addition, for the trial of common assault (assault and battery) on indictment. That offence is now triable summarily only (Criminal Justice Act 1988 s 39) except when a count for common assault is added to an indictment for more serious offences. See s 40 of that Act.

'assault'   This will usually mean a battery, since a 'pure' assault (ie an act which merely causes the victim to *apprehend* immediate unlawful violence) will rarely be capable of 'occasioning actual bodily harm'. D's assault (without a battery) on P may however come within s 47 if it causes P to injure himself in attempting to escape (*cf R v Roberts* (1971) 56 Cr App R 95, where P leapt from D's car to escape) or if it causes P injury through nervous shock (*cf R v Miller* [1954] 2 All ER 529).
   An assault necessarily involves some actual or threatened force or violence which is not validly consented to by the victim (see *R v Clarence* (1888) 22 QBD 23), and it must probably be direct rather than indirect force or violence. Thus, throwing an object or setting a dog upon the victim would be an assault (assuming that it at least causes him to fear or apprehend being struck or bitten) but leaving the object *etc* as a trap for him to fall over would not be: *Scott v Shepherd* (1773) 96 ER 526, but see *contra DPP v Khan* (1989) 139 NLJ 1455. An assault or battery is thus a narrower concept than an infliction of injury contrary to s 20 of this Act. See *R v Wilson* [1983] 3 All ER 448 which seems to have been overlooked in *Khan* and the notes to s 20 *supra*. It should be noted that *R v Martin* (1881) 8 QBD 54, which is sometimes cited as a case on 'indirect assault', is in fact a s 20 case.

'actual bodily harm' In *R v Miller* (*supra*) this was defined as 'any hurt or injury calculated (ie likely) to interfere with the health or comfort of the [victim]'. See also *R v Jones* [1981] Crim LR 119 (where minor facial abrasions and bruises were held to be at the 'very margin' of what is actual bodily harm), and *Taylor v Granville* [1978] Crim LR 482.

Assault and consent to actual bodily harm A person can generally consent to an act which would otherwise be an assault, but not where the act is intended or calculated (ie likely) to cause actual bodily harm or worse. Thus most fights (other than playful tussles or properly supervised boxing or wrestling competitions) will be unlawful (*Att–General's Ref (No 6 of 1980)* [1981] QB 715), as will mutilations for religious or tribal purposes (*R v Adesanya, The Times*, 16/17 July 1974) or caning, whipping, etc for sexual enjoyment (*R v Donovan* [1934] 2 KB 498).

Assault and lawful force Where actual bodily harm is occasioned by the lawful use of force (eg lawful arrest, self-defence *etc*) there will obviously be no offence under this provision. Note however that if excessive force is used, the force may become unlawful. In calculating what is excessive, the courts recognise that one cannot be expected to weigh to a nicety the exact measure of defensive action: *Palmer v R* [1971] AC 814.

Actual bodily harm may be inflicted by way of lawful chastisement or correction, but here again, excessive severity may lead to liability under s 47 and the courts are less likely to make allowance for miscalculation on the part of the chastiser: cf *R v Smith* [1985] Crim LR 42.

Mens rea The *mens rea* required for an offence under this provision was considered in *R v Venna* [1976] QB 421. Intent or recklessness was held to be required in respect of the assault and battery — recklessness being used in the *Cunningham* sense (ie deliberate risk-taking). It might be argued that, following the subsequent decision of the House of Lords in *R v Caldwell* [1982] AC 341, recklessness in assault should include failing to consider an obvious risk; but this is clearly not what was originally meant in *Venna*, and that argument was rejected by the Court of Appeal in *R v Spratt*, The Times 14 May 1990, where the *Venna* interpretation was reaffirmed.

Venna does not appear to require recklessness or intent as to the actual bodily harm, but only as to the assault occasioning it. D need not therefore foresee that the assault on P might cause injury.

Assault by omission Many crimes can be committed by omission, in cases where there is a duty to act, but arguably assault is different. The word 'assault' is derived from the Latin *assaltare* which means 'to jump at'. Assault by omission is therefore an improbable concept. See *Fagan v Met Police Commissioner* [1969] 1 QB 439.

48–56 [*repealed*]

Bigamy

57. Whosoever, being married, shall marry any other person during the life of the former husband or wife, whether the second marriage shall have taken place in England or Ireland or elsewhere, shall be guilty of [an offence] and being convicted thereof shall be liable . . . to [imprisonment] for any term not exceeding seven years . . . provided that nothing in this section contained shall extend to any second marriage contracted elsewhere than in England and Ireland by any other than a subject of Her Majesty, or to any person marrying a second time whose husband or wife shall have been continually absent from such person for the space of seven years then last past, and shall not have been known by such person to be

living within that time, or shall extend to any person who, at the time of
such second marriage, shall have been divorced from the bond of the first
marriage, or to any person whose former marriage shall have been
declared void by the sentence of any court of competent jurisdiction.

NOTES
The inclusion of bigamy in the Offences against the Person Act is anomalous, in
that the rationale behind the criminalisation of bigamy is that it involves 'an
outrage on public decency' and the 'prostitution of a solemn ceremony' (see *R v
Allen* (1872) LR 1 CCR 367 *per* Cockburn CJ at p 374). It may (but need not)
involve a deception practised on the other party to the bigamous marriage, but
even that is hardly an offence against the person.
      This provision is badly worded and obscure, but, read in conjunction with s 3(1)
of the British Nationality Act 1948 and s 51 of the British Nationality Act 1981, it
makes the act of bigamy punishable under English law in any of three situations:
      (1) where anyone goes through a ceremony of marriage in England or Wales
whilst still validly married to another person;
      (2) where any British or Commonwealth citizen goes through a ceremony of
marriage elsewhere within the United Kingdom whilst still validly married to
another person; or
      (3) where a British citizen, British Dependent Territories' citizen or British
Overseas citizen goes through a ceremony of marriage anywhere in the world
whilst still validly married to another person.
      In none of these three cases does it matter where the first marriage took place,
but in all cases D may escape conviction by reliance on the 'seven years absence'
proviso or on a reasonable mistake of fact (eg that the original spouse is dead).

'whosoever being married'   The validity of the former marriage is of crucial
importance. A foreign marriage which is not recognised under English law will be
ignored. Moreover, a potentially polygamous first marriage will also be ignored,
even if it might for some purposes be recognised under English law: *R v Sarwan
Singh* [1962] 3 All ER 612; *R v Sagoo* [1975] QB 885.

'shall marry any other person'   This in effect means 'go through a marriage
ceremony' since the second marriage will be void. The ceremony must nevertheless
purport to be a regular marriage: *Burt v Burt* (1860) 2 Sw & Tr 88.

'England or Ireland'   'England' includes Wales but 'Ireland' must now be
construed as extending only to Northern Ireland. S 57 appears to give English and
Northern Irish courts jurisdiction over offences of bigamy committed in each
other's territory. They certainly have jurisdiction over bigamy committed in
Scotland by a 'subject of Her Majesty': *R v Topping* (1856) 7 Cox CC 103.

'or elsewhere'   Ie anywhere in the world: *R v Russell* [1901] AC 446.

'subject of Her Majesty'   This in effect means 'Commonwealth citizen', but by
virtue of s 3(1) of the British Nationality Act 1948 (qv), Commonwealth citizens
who are not also British citizens, British Dependent Territories citizens or British
Overseas citizens (under the British Nationality Act 1981) will generally incur no
criminal liability for acts done outside the United Kingdom, unless aliens would
also incur such liability. Thus a Canadian committing bigamy in Scotland is
(theoretically) punishable in England or Wales under s 57, while one committing
bigamy in France is not.

Seven years' absence   This proviso does not depend upon a presumption of
death, nor does it require that D has made any attempt to trace his spouse: *R v
Briggs* (1856) Dears & B 98. He need not even suspect his spouse to be dead as long
as he has not heard she is alive: *R v Gould* [1968] 1 All ER 849 *per* Diplock J at 853.
It was even held in *R v Faulkes* (1903) 19 TLR 250 that the 'absence' of D's spouse,

as a result of his desertion of her, would give him a defence under the proviso; but this must be regarded as of doubtful authority and is not an appellate decision. On the burden of proof in such cases, see *R v Parke* (1922) 17 Cr App R 22.

Divorce Where D has been granted a final decree of divorce prior to his second marriage, the crucial issue is whether that divorce is valid and recognised under English law: *R v Russell* [1901] AC 446.

Marriage declared void This is not necessary in the case of a marriage which was void *ab initio*, but may be crucial in the case of a voidable marriage. As to mistaken belief in the nullity of the first marriage, see *R v King* [1964] 1 QB 285 and the note on mistake, *infra*.

Mistake and mens rea A fundamental mistake of fact will ordinarily constitute a defence to an offence requiring *mens rea*, in that it will prevent D from forming that *mens rea*. In relation to bigamy, however, it seems clear that any such mistake must be a reasonable one in order to afford D a defence; thus, if D believes his first wife is dead at the time of his second marriage, this will only be a defence if held on reasonable grounds: *R v Gould* [1968] 2 QB 65; *R v Tolson* (1889) 23 QBD 168; *R v King* [1964] 1 QB 285; *DPP v Morgan* [1976] AC 182 at p 192.

Attempts to procure abortion

Administering drugs or using instruments to procure abortion

58. Every woman, being with child, who, with intent to procure her own miscarriage, shall unlawfully administer to herself any poison or other noxious thing, or shall unlawfully use any instrument or other means whatsoever with the like intent, and whosoever, with intent to procure the miscarriage of any woman, whether she be or be not with child, shall unlawfully administer to her or cause to be taken by her any poison or other noxious thing, or shall unlawfully use any instrument or other means whatsoever with the like intent, shall be guilty of an offence, and being convicted thereof shall be liable ... to imprisonment for life.

NOTES
This provision must be read subject to the Abortion Act 1967 (qv), which legalises abortion under certain circumstances and conditions. In cases where the foetus concerned is capable of being born alive, the termination of the pregnancy may also amount to an offence of child destruction under the Infant Life (Preservation) Act 1929 (qv). S 2 of that Act enables a jury to convict the accused of either offence, whichever one is actually charged in the indictment.

Real and imagined pregnancy For the purposes of the present provision, one must distinguish between cases in which the woman concerned acts alone and cases in which some other person is involved.

A woman acting alone cannot commit the offence unless she is genuinely pregnant. If she is not she might perhaps be guilty of an attempt by virtue of s 1(2) of the Criminal Attempts Act 1981.

Another person who acts with intent to procure the woman's abortion may be guilty whether or not the woman is in fact pregnant. Moreover, the woman concerned may then be guilty of secondary participation in the offence, even if not in fact pregnant: *R v Sockett* (1980) 72 JP 428.

'with intent to procure ... miscarriage' This is an ulterior intent; not only is actual abortion unnecessary — it is not even necessary that the methods or drugs used should have been capable of inducing abortion: *R v Marlow* (1964) 49 Cr App R 49.

'**unlawfully**' See s 5(2) of the Abortion Act 1967, which provides that anything done with intent to procure miscarriage is unlawful *unless* authorised by s 1 of that Act.

'**administer**' — see notes to ss 23 and 24 *supra*.

'**poison or other noxious thing**' See notes to ss 23 and 24 *supra*. See also *R v Marlow supra*.

'**instrument or other means**' There has been some academic debate as to whether the use of an intra-uterine device (or 'coil') infringes s 58 in that it effectively prevents the implantation of the ovum *after* fertilisation. In practice this is not considered to be a problem. The term 'other means' is capable of covering cases in which D kicks P in the abdomen, or pushes her downstairs, in order to induce miscarriage.

'**or cause to be taken by her**' 'Cause' here implies some element of command or direction (as in cases of 'causing' the unlawful use of motor vehicles under the Road Traffic Act 1988). Thus, an abortionist who gives the woman some tablets *etc* and tells or directs her to swallow them will be within the provision, even if he is not present when she takes them (see *R v Wilson* (1855) Dears & B 127); but someone who merely leaves some tablets in her room at her request would appear to be guilty of an offence under s 59 (*infra*).

Procuring drugs, etc, to cause abortion
  59. Whosoever shall unlawfully supply or procure any poison or other noxious thing, or any instrument or thing whatsoever, knowing that the same is intended to be unlawfully used or employed with intent to procure the miscarriage of any woman, whether she be or be not with child, shall be guilty of [an offence], and being convicted thereof shall be liable ... to [imprisonment for any term not exceeding five years].

NOTES
Persons who procure drugs or instruments which are later used in an attempt to procure an abortion may well be guilty as accessories to an offence under s 58 (Accessories and Abettors Act 1861 s 8). S 59 applies whether or not any use has been made of the things procured.

'**unlawfully**' See notes to s 58 *supra*.

'**supply or procure**' It was held in *R v Mills* [1963] 1 QB 522 that an abortionist does not 'procure' his drugs or instruments merely by 'getting them together or preparing them for use' (*ibid* at 524). What is required is that he should get possession of something he has not got already. Thus if D sells E an instrument, D 'supplies' it and E 'procures' it. Read in conjunction with s 58, it would appear that the things concerned must be supplied to and procured by someone other than the woman herself.

'**knowing that the same is intended to be unlawfully used**' It was held in *R v Hillman* (1863) 9 Cox CC 386 and *R v Titley* (1880) 14 Cox CC 502 that nobody other than the accused need actually intend that the things concerned should be used to procure abortion. This intepretation is impossible to reconcile with the words of the provision itself. One cannot 'know' something if it may not be true.

Concealing the birth of a child

60. If any woman shall be delivered of a child, every person who shall, by any secret disposition of the dead body of the said child, whether such child died before, at, or after its birth, endeavour to conceal the birth thereof, shall be guilty of [an offence], and being convicted thereof shall be liable, at the discretion of the court, to be imprisoned for any term not exceeding two years.

NOTES

'delivered of a child'   The child may have been born dead or alive; but, if born dead, it must at least have 'arrived at the stage of maturity at the time of birth that it might have been a living child': *R v Berriman* (1854) 6 Cox CC 388 (*per* Erle J at 390); *R v Hewitt* (1866) 4 F & F 1101.

'every person'   This clearly includes the mother herself.

'by any secret disposition ... endeavour to conceal the birth'   It would not be enough that the body was secretly disposed of, if the birth was freely admitted to; nor would it apparently be enough if the body was placed anonymously in some place where it would inevitably be discovered, the sole intention being to conceal its parentage. There must apparently be an intent to conceal the birth by concealing the body. The body need not be burned or buried; it might be enough if it is deliberately left in a place which is unfrequented: see *R v Brown* (1870) LR 1 CCC 244 and cases there cited.

'of the dead body'   Abandonment of a living child in an unfrequented place, so as to cause its death may be murder, manslaughter or infanticide, but not an offence under this provision: *R v May* (1867) 10 Cox CC 489. Nor is concealment an alternative verdict on a homicide charge. If it cannot be proved whether the child was alive or dead when abandoned, it may be impossible to convict of either offence.

Other offences   See s 36 of the Births and Deaths Registration Act 1953 and s 4(1) of the Perjury Act 1911. There is also a common law offence of disposing of a corpse with intent to prevent the holding of an inquest. See *R v Purly* (1933) 149 LT 432.

61–63 [*repealed*]

Making or having gunpowder, etc, with intent to commit any felony against this Act

64. Whosoever shall knowingly have in his possession, or make or manufacture, any gunpowder, explosive substance, or any dangerous or noxious thing, or any machine, engine, instrument, or thing, with intent by means thereof to commit, or for the purpose of enabling any other person to commit, any of the [offences] in this Act mentioned, shall be guilty of [an offence], and being convicted thereof shall be liable, at the discretion of the court, to be imprisoned for any term not exceeding two years ...

NOTES

This offence is of far greater scope than its heading suggests: it makes it an offence to possess or make *anything* with intent to commit (or to enable anyone else to commit) any indictable offence under the Act. It serves a comparable purpose to s 25 of the Theft Act 1968, s 3 of the Criminal Damage Act 1971 and s 5 of the Forgery and Counterfeiting Act 1981.

'in his possession' This is probably a wider concept than that of 'having the thing with him', which is used in s 25 of the Theft Act. It doubtless extends to something more than direct physical possession (eg it would suffice if D is arrested in the street and found to have weapons *etc* at home). Since D must *knowingly* possess *with intent* to commit offences, the strict liability problems created by the concept of possession in drugs and firearms legislation will not arise.

Other offences This provision appears not to be widely used; and other charges are brought instead. As to possession or manufacture of explosives, see s 4 of the Explosive Substances Act 1883. As to possession and supply of firearms, see ss 16–25 of the Firearms Act 1968. As to possession of offensive weapons in public places, see s 1 of the Prevention of Crime Act 1953. As to possession by burglars and robbers, see ss 10 and 25 of the Theft Act 1968. In some cases, however, the present provision may still constitute an appropriate charge.

65 [*omitted*]

66–67 [*repealed*]

Offences committed within the jurisdiction of the Admiralty
68. All indictable offences mentioned in this Act which shall be committed within the jurisdiction of the Admiralty of England or Ireland shall be . . . liable to the same punishments, as if they had been committed upon the land in England or Ireland . . .

NOTES
It is doubtful whether this provision remains strictly necessary.

'jurisdiction of the Admiralty' Admiralty jurisdiction extends over the Territorial Sea and the submerged foreshore, and over British ships on the high seas. (This includes foreign waters and harbours.) Foreign merchant shipping is within Admiralty jurisdiction when within the territorial sea but foreign naval vessels have sovereign immunity.

'indictable offences' Admiralty jurisdiction has never extended over summary offences (but see ss 686 and 687 of the Merchant Shipping Act 1894). Under s 46(2) of the Supreme Court Act 1981, jurisdiction for proceedings on indictment for offences within the jurisdiction of the Admiralty is conferred on the Crown Court. Offences triable either way may be tried summarily under s 2(4) of the Magistrates Courts Act 1980.

69–75 [*repealed*]

76 [*omitted*]

77 [*repealed*]

Extent of Act
78. Nothing in this Act contained shall extend to Scotland, except as herein-before otherwise expressly provided.

79 [*repealed*]

Territorial Waters Jurisdiction Act 1878

(41 & 42 VICT C 73)

Preamble

Whereas the rightful jurisdiction of Her Majesty, her heirs and successors, extends and has always extended over the open seas adjacent to the coasts of the United Kingdom and of all other parts of Her Majesty's dominions to such a distance as is necessary for the defence and security of such dominions:

And whereas it is expedient that all offences committed on the open sea within a certain distance of the coasts of the United Kingdom and of all other parts of Her Majesty's dominions, by whomsoever committed, should be dealt with according to law:

NOTE

'extends and has always extended' This statement conflicts with the decision of the majority of the Court in *R v Keyn* (The *Franconia* case) (1876) 2 Ex D 63, a decision that this Act was designed to reverse.

[1. *Short title*]

Amendment of law as to jurisdiction of the Admiral

2. An offence committed by a person, whether he is or is not a subject of Her Majesty, on the open sea within the territorial waters of Her Majesty's dominions, is an offence within the jurisdiction of the Admiral, although it may have been committed on board or by means of a foreign ship, and the person who committed such offence may be arrested, tried, and punished accordingly.

NOTES

'on the open sea within the territorial waters' The original definition of 'territorial waters', formerly contained in s 7 of this Act, has been replaced by that contained in the Territorial Sea Act 1987. This establishes new territorial limits which extend for twelve nautical miles from baselines established by the Territorial Waters Orders in Council 1964 and 1979. Certain waters which lie '*intra fauces terrae*' (harbours, estuaries and other semi-landlocked waters) are deemed to lie within county boundaries, and are therefore within the jurisdiction of the common law. This is significant insofar as it gives local magistrates' courts jurisdiction over purely summary offences. (See following note.)

'offence within the jurisdiction of the Admiral' Jurisdiction over summary offences is not affected by this provision, because the Admiral (whose criminal jurisdiction is now exercised by the Crown Court) never had jurisdiction over such offences (see s 7 *infra*). See however s 685 of the Merchant Shipping Act 1894 (not printed in this work), which deals with offences committed aboard ships lying off the coast.

'ship'; 'foreign ship' see s 7 *infra*.

Restriction on institution of proceedings for punishment of offence
3. Proceedings for the trial and punishment of a person who is not a subject of Her Majesty, and who is charged with any such offence as is declared by this Act to be within the jurisdiction of the Admiral, shall not be instituted in any court of the United Kingdom, except with the consent of one of Her Majesty's Principal Secretaries of State, and on his certificate that the institution of such proceedings is in his opinion expedient, and shall not be instituted in any of the dominions of Her Majesty out of the United Kingdom, except with the leave of the Governor of the part of the dominions in which such proceedings are proposed to be instituted, and on his certificate that it is expedient that such proceedings should be instituted.

NOTES
This provision is excluded by the Petroleum Act 1987 s 13(6).

'not a subject of Her Majesty' This means someone who is not a Commonwealth citizen (see s 51 of the British Nationality Act 1981) or a British subject under Part IV of the 1981 Act. S 3(1) of the British Nationality Act 1948 (qv) is not applicable in this context.

4. [*omitted*]

Saving as to jurisdiction
5. Nothing in this Act contained shall be construed to be in derogation of any rightful jurisdiction of Her Majesty, her heirs or successors, under the law of nations, or to affect or prejudice any jurisdiction conferred by Act of Parliament or now by law existing in relation to foreign ships or in relation to persons on board such ships.

Saving as to piracy
6. This Act shall not prejudice or affect the trial in manner heretofore in use of any act of piracy as defined by the law of nations, or affect or prejudice any law relating thereto; and where any act of piracy as defined by the law of nations is also any such offence as is declared by this Act to be within the jurisdiction of the Admiral, such offence may be tried in pursuance of this Act, or in pursuance of any other Act of Parliament, law, or custom relating thereto.

NOTES
It was held in the Scottish case of *Cameron v HM Advocate* 1971 SC 50 that this provision preserves British jurisdiction over piracy *jure gentium* committed within territorial waters; but the case in question did not in fact involve that offence, which is now defined in the schedule to the Tokyo Convention Act 1967 as involving robbery *etc* on the high seas or at some other place outside the jurisdiction of any state. Whilst the present provision would have been effective in

preserving any jurisdiction over piracy that existed at the time of its enactment (eg under s 8 of the Piracy Act 1698), it is doubtful whether it could properly be regarded as preventing derogation under subsequent enactments.

Interpretation

7. In this Act, unless there is something inconsistent in the context, the following expressions shall respectively have the meanings herein-after assigned to them; (that is to say,)

'The jurisdiction of the Admiral,' as used in this Act, includes the jurisdiction of the Admiralty of England and Ireland, or either of such jurisdictions as used in any Act of Parliament; and for the purpose of arresting any person charged with an offence declared by this Act to be within the jurisdiction of the Admiral, the territorial waters adjacent to the United Kingdom, or any other part of Her Majesty's dominions, shall be deemed to be within the jurisdiction of any judge, magistrate, or officer having power within such United Kingdom, or other part of Her Majesty's dominions, to issue warrants for arresting or to arrest persons charged with offences committed within the jurisdiction of such judge, magistrate, or officer:

'United Kingdom' includes the Isle of Man, the Channel Islands, and other adjacent islands:

'Offence' as used in this Act means an act neglect or default of such a description as would, if committed within the body of a county in England, be punishable on indictment according to the law of England for the time being in force:

'Ship' includes every description of ship, boat, or other floating craft:

'Foreign ship' means any ship which is not a British ship.

NOTES

'jurisdiction of the Admiral'   This is now exercised by the Crown Court.

'ship'   This includes hovercraft: see the Hovercraft (Application of Enactments) order SI 1972/971.

'British ship'   This term is now defined in s 2 of the Merchant Shipping Act 1988. The ships of independent Commonwealth countries are now 'foreign ships' for the purpose of this Act.

Explosive Substances Act 1883

(46 & 47 VICT C 3)

1. [*Short title*]

Causing explosion likely to endanger life or property
2. A person who in the United Kingdom or (being a citizen of the United Kingdom and Colonies) in the Republic of Ireland unlawfully and maliciously causes by any explosive substance an explosion of a nature likely to endanger life or to cause serious injury to property shall, whether any injury to person or property has been actually caused or not, be guilty of an offence and on conviction on indictment shall be liable to imprisonment for life.

NOTES
There is an element of overlap between this offence and those created under ss 28–30 of the Offences Against the Person Act 1861, although there are significant differences in the essential elements of each. Where damage to property occurs, charges under the Criminal Damage Act 1971 must also be considered: see in particular s 1(2) of that Act.

'United Kingdom' This does not include either the Isle of Man or the Channel Islands.

'citizen of the United Kingdom and Colonies' This now means a British citizen, a British overseas citizen, or a British Dependent Territories citizen: British Nationality Act 1981, s 51(3).

'or ... in the Republic of Ireland' This unusual extraterritorial ambit was introduced by the Criminal Jurisdiction Act 1975. For further extensions, see s 4 of the Suppression of Terrorism Act 1978 which, *inter alia*, extends it to all states which are 'convention countries' under that Act.

'maliciously' See the notes to s 20 of the Offences Against the Person Act 1861.

'explosive substance' See s 9(1) *infra*; and see also *R v Bouch* [1982] 3 All ER 918 (pyrotechnic devices are explosive within the meaning of this Act).

'of a nature likely to' Note that the offence might be committed even though no lives or property were in fact endangered, and it is certainly not necessary to prove any *mens rea* beyond maliciousness as to the causing of the explosion itself. D need not, for example, intend or forsee any harm or damage resulting.

Attempt to cause explosion, or for making or keeping explosive with intent to endanger life or property
3. (1) A person who in the United Kingdom or a dependency or (being a citizen of the United Kingdom and Colonies) elsewhere unlawfully and maliciously —
   (a) does any act with intent to cause, or conspires to cause, by an explosive substance an explosion of a nature likely to endanger life,

39

or cause serious injury to property, whether in the United Kingdom
or the Republic of Ireland, or

(b) makes or has in his possession or under his control an explosive
substance with intent by means thereof to endanger life, or cause
serious injury to property, whether in the United Kingdom or the
Republic of Ireland, or to enable any other person so to do,

shall, whether any explosion does or does not take place, and whether any
injury to person or property is actually caused or not, be guilty of an
offence and on conviction on indictment shall be liable to imprisonment
for [life], and the explosive substance shall be forfeited.

(2) In this section 'dependency' means the Channel Islands, the Isle of
Man and any colony, other than a colony for whose external relations a
country other than the United Kingdom is responsible.

NOTES
'United Kingdom'; **'citizen of the United Kingdom and Colonies'**;
'Republic of Ireland'   See the notes to s 2 *supra*. The ambit of this provision has
been extended by the Suppression of Terrorism Act 1978 in the same way as that
of s 2. See further the notes to s 4 of that Act.

'conspires to cause'   Conspiracy under this provision has exactly the same
meaning as it has under ss 1 & 2 of the Criminal Law Act 1977 and is governed by
the same principles. See s 5(6) of that Act.

'explosive substance'   See s 9(1) *infra*.

'of a nature likely to etc'   See the notes to s 2 *supra*.

'in his possession or under his control'   This is a wider concept than that of
'having it with him', (as used eg in s 25 of the Theft Act 1968). It would cover
cases in which D keeps the items hidden somewhere far from his own person, or
entrusts them to someone for safe keeping on the understanding that they will be
returned or delivered at his direction.
  The difficulties most commonly encountered in relation to offences of possession
involve questions of *mens rea*; D may claim ignorance of the nature of the thing
allegedly in his possession, but may in some cases nevertheless incur liability. In the
case of alleged offences under this provision, however, the prosecution must prove
both maliciousness and an ulterior intent to endanger life etc. One could hardly
have such ulterior intent without being aware of the nature of the thing possessed.

Making or possession of explosive under suspicious circumstances
4. (1) Any person who makes or knowingly has in his possession or
under his control any explosive substance, under such circumstances as to
give rise to a reasonable suspicion that he is not making it or does not have
it in his possession or under his control for a lawful object, shall, unless he
can show that he made it or had it in his possession or under his control for
a lawful object, be guilty of [an offence] and, on conviction, shall be liable
to [imprisonment] for a term not exceeding fourteen years ... and the
explosive substance shall be forfeited.

(2) [*repealed*]

NOTES
'in his possession or under his control' See the notes to s 3 *supra.*

'explosive substance' See s 9(1) *infra.*

'under such circumstances ... etc' The prosecution has the burden of proving that D has knowingly made the items or knowingly has the items in his possession or control, and that the circumstances give rise to the reasonable suspicion specified in the section. (Note that this refers to an absence of a positive lawful purpose, rather than the existence of a positive unlawful purpose: a point which may be relevant if D merely makes explosives for fun and without any particular purpose in mind.) It is then up to the defence to prove the existence of a lawful purpose. If they cannot do so (on the balance of probabilities), D may be convicted. See *R v Berry* [1984] 3 All ER 1008. If the items are intended for use abroad, D may be required to prove that this use will be lawful under the relevant foreign law (*ibid*).

Punishment of accessories
5. Any person who within or (being a subject of Her Majesty) without Her Majesty's dominions by the supply of or solicitation for money, the providing of premises, the supply of materials, or in any manner whatsoever, procures, counsels, aids, abets, or is accessory to, the commission of any crime under this Act, shall be guilty of [an offence] and shall be liable to be tried and punished for that crime, as if he had been guilty as a principal.

NOTES
The question here is whether this provision adds anything of substance to the general rules governing the liability of secondary participants in offences (as to which, see the Accessories and Abettors Act 1861). For most purposes, the answer would appear to be 'no', even from a jurisdictional viewpoint. This is because a secondary party to an offence committed within the jurisdiction is regarded as having committed that offence, even if he himself remained a thousand miles outside the jurisdictional limits: see *R v Robert Millar (Contractors) Ltd* [1970] 2 QB 54. It is possible, however, that it may have some use in cases where the principal offence is committed outside the normal jurisdiction (eg in the Republic of Ireland) but is punishable because of the extended ambit given to ss 2 & 3. There can of course be no liability under this provision unless there is an offence under ss 2 or 3; and the jurisdictional ambit of those provisions therefore governs the ambit of this one. See further s 4 of the Suppression of Terrorism Act 1978.

'subject of Her Majesty' Under s 3(1) of the British Nationality Act 1948 and s 51 of the British Nationality Act 1981, this must now be construed as a reference to British citizens, British overseas citizens and British Dependent Territories' citizens.

6. [*omitted*]

No prosecution except by leave of Attorney-General — Procedure and saving
7. [(1) Proceedings for a crime under this Act shall not be instituted except by or with the consent of the Attorney-General.]
    (2), (3) ...
    (4) This Act shall not exempt any person from any indictment or proceeding for a crime or offence which is punishable at common law, or

by any Act of Parliament other than this Act, but no person shall be punished twice for the same criminal Act.

8. [*omitted*]

Definitions
9. (1) In this Act, unless the context otherwise requires—
The expression 'explosive substance' shall be deemed to include any materials for making any explosive substance; also any apparatus, machine, implement, or materials used, or intended to be used, or adapted for causing, or aiding in causing, any explosion in or with any explosive substance; also any part of any such apparatus, machine, or implement.
The expression 'Attorney-General' means Her Majesty's Attorney-General for England or Ireland, as the case may be, and in case of his inability or of a vacancy in the office, Her Majesty's Solicitor-General for England or Ireland, as the case requires.

(2) [*omitted*]

NOTES
'explosive substance' Note that this definition enables prosecutions to be brought in respect of items such as timers, which are not in themselves explosive at all, but which may be used in time bombs *etc.* See for example *R v Berry* [1984] 3 All ER 1008. As to the position in respect of incendiary or pyrotechnical devices, see *R v Bouch* [1982] 3 All ER 918.

Trial of Lunatics Act 1883

(46 & 47 VICT C 38)

1. [*Short Title*]

Special verdict where accused found guilty, but insane at date of act or omission charged, and orders thereupon

2. (1) Where in any indictment or information any act or omission is charged against any person as an offence, and it is given in evidence on the trial of such person for that offence that he was insane, so as not to be responsible, according to law, for his actions at the time when the act was done or omission made, then, if it appears to the jury before whom such person is tried that he did the act or made the omission charged, but was insane as aforesaid at the time when he did or made the same, the jury shall return a special verdict that the accused is not guilty by reason of insanity.

(2)–(4) [*repealed*]

NOTES

As to the definition of insanity, this remains a matter of common law, and is still governed by the M'Naghten Rules (1843) 10 Cl & Fin 200. See also *R v Sullivan* [1983] 3 All ER 673; *R v Kemp* [1957] 1 QB 399; *R v Bailey* [1983] 2 All ER 503; and *Bratty v Att-General for N Ireland* [1963] AC 386.

'indictment or information' It would appear that this provision governs only trials by jury, and that the reference to 'informations' concerns informations brought in the High Court as an alternative to committal proceedings (see White in (1984) 148 JPN at p 422). If this is correct, then the result is that the insane defendant at summary trial must be acquitted without any special verdict; but note that the court may still make an order under s 37 of the Mental Health Act 1983.

'it appears to the jury that ...' The burden of proving insanity is on the defence.

'not guilty by reason of insanity' The original wording of this provision required a verdict of 'guilty but insane'. The present formula was substituted by the Criminal Procedure (Insanity) Act 1964, s 5 of which then requires the court to 'make an order that the accused be admitted to such hospital as may be specified by the Secretary of State'.

Appeals The special verdict may be appealed against by the defendant under s 12 of the Criminal Appeal Act 1968.

Public Bodies Corrupt Practices Act 1889

(52 & 53 VICT C 69)

Corruption in office [*an offence*]

1. (1) Every person who shall by himself or by or in conjunction with any other person, corruptly solicit or receive, or agree to receive, for himself, or for any other person, any gift, loan, fee, reward, or advantage whatever as an inducement to, or reward for, or otherwise on account of any member, officer, or servant of a public body as in this Act defined, doing or forbearing to do anything in respect of any matter or transaction whatsoever, actual or proposed, in which the said public body is concerned, shall be guilty of [an offence].

(2) Every person who shall by himself or by or in conjunction with any other person corruptly give, promise, or offer any gift, loan, fee, reward, or advantage whatsoever to any person, whether for the benefit of that person or of another person, as an inducement to or reward for or otherwise on account of any member, officer, or servant of any public body as in this Act defined, doing or forbearing to do anything in respect of any matter or transaction whatsoever, actual or proposed, in which such public body as aforesaid is concerned, shall be guilty of [an offence].

NOTES

The offences created by this provision have been supplemented by s 1 of the Prevention of Corruption Act 1906 (corrupt transactions with agents) and amended by the Prevention of Corruption Act 1916 (qqv).

'person' This includes a company or other corporation, and also (by virtue of s 7 *infra*) an unincorporated body.

'corruptly' Any improper and unauthorised gift, payment or inducement is likely to be accounted corrupt, provided that D knows it to be improper and unauthorised. It has been held that no dishonest motive is required, so that the offer of a bribe for the purpose of exposing the corruption of the person to whom it was offered is itself 'corrupt': *R v Smith* [1960] 2 QB 423. See also *R v Parker* (1985) 83 Cr App R 69. In some cases, a gift or payment will be presumed to have been made corruptly unless the contrary is proved: see s 2 of the 1916 Act.

The corruption may be one-sided; it need not involve any agreement or understanding between the parties, and the offence is complete if the bribe etc is offered, even if it is then refused. See further *R v Andrews-Weatherfoil Ltd* [1972] 1 All ER 65.

'advantage' See s 7 *infra*

'reward' This includes rewards for past favours, whether or not promised at the time: *R v Andrews-Weatherfoil supra; R v Parker, supra.*

'public body'   The definition provided in s 7 has been widened by s 4(2) of the 1916 Act to include 'local and public authorities of all descriptions'.

'member, officer etc'   As to defective appointments, see s 3 *infra*.

Penalty for offences
2. Any person on conviction for offending as aforesaid shall, at the discretion of the court before which he is convicted,—
   (*a*) be liable—
      (i) on summary conviction, to imprisonment for a term not exceeding 6 months or to a fine not exceeding the statutory maximum, or to both; and
      (ii) on conviction on indictment, to imprisonment for a term not exceeding 7 years or to a fine, or to both; and
   (*b*) in addition be liable to be ordered to pay to such body, and in such manner as the court directs, the amount or value of any gift, loan, fee, or reward received by him or any part thereof; and
   (*c*) be liable to be adjudged incapable of being elected or appointed to any public office for [five years] from the date of his conviction, and to forfeit any such office held by him at the time of his conviction; and
   (*d*) in the event of a second conviction for a like offence he shall, in addition to the foregoing penalties, be liable to be adjudged to be for ever incapable of holding any public office, and to be incapable for [five years] of being registered as an elector, or voting at an election either of members to serve in Parliament or of members of any public body, and the enactments for preventing the voting and registration of persons declared by reason of corrupt practices to be incapable of voting shall apply to a person adjudged in pursuance of this section to be incapable of voting; and
   (*e*) if such person is an officer or servant in the employ of any public body upon such conviction he shall, at the discretion of the court, be liable to forfeit his right and claim to any compensation or pension to which he would otherwise have been entitled.

Savings
3. (1) ...
   (2) A person shall not be exempt from punishment under this Act by reason of the invalidity of the appointment or election of a person to a public office.

Restriction on prosecution
4. (1) A prosecution for an offence under this Act shall not be instituted except by or with the consent of the Attorney-General.
   (2) In this section the expression 'Attorney-General' means the Attorney- or Solicitor-General for England ...

5–6 [*repealed*]

Interpretation

7. In this Act—

The expression 'public body' means any council of a county or council of a city or town, any council of a municipal borough, also any board, commissioners, select vestry, or other body which has power to act under and for the purposes of any Act relating to local government, or the public health, or to poor law or otherwise to administer money raised by rates in pursuance of any public general Act, but does not include any public body as above defined existing elsewhere than in the United Kingdom:

The expression 'public office' means any office or employment of a person as a member, officer, or servant of such public body:

The expression 'person' includes a body of persons, corporate or unincorporate:

The expression 'advantage' includes any office or dignity, and any forbearance to demand any money or money's worth or valuable thing, and includes any aid, vote, consent, or influence, or pretended aid, vote, consent, or influence, and also includes any promise or procurement of or agreement or endeavour to procure, or the holding out of any expectation of any gift, loan, fee, reward, or advantage, as before defined.

NOTE

The definition of 'public body' is widened by s 4(2) of the 1916 Act (qv).

8–10. [*omitted*]

Merchant Shipping Act 1894

(57 & 58 VICT C 60)

Jurisdiction in case of offences on board ship

686. (1) Where any person, being a British subject, is charged with having committed any offence on board any British ship on the high seas or in any foreign port or harbour or on board any foreign ship to which he does not belong, or, not being a British subject, is charged with having committed any offence on board any British ship on the high seas, and that person is found within the jurisdiction of any court in Her Majesty's dominions, which would have had cognizance of the offence if it had been committed on board a British ship within the limits of its ordinary jurisdiction, that court shall have jurisdiction to try the offence as if it had been so committed.

(2) [*omitted*]

NOTES

This provision supplements the common law jurisdiction which the Crown Court has inherited in respect of crimes formerly within the jurisdiction of the Admiralty. It does however create a wider jurisdiction, in that it extends to both summary and indictable offences, and covers offences committed aboard foreign ships or in foreign ports etc where the old Admiralty jurisdiction would not extend.

'British subject' This term includes the nationals of independent Commonwealth states: s 3(1) of the British Nationality Act 1948 (qv) has no effect on the scope of offences under the Merchant Shipping Acts.

'ship' This includes any vessel used in navigation, other than one propelled by oars (s 742).

'British ship' This term is now defined in s 2 of the Merchant Shipping Act 1988, and no longer embraces ships owned by the nationals of independent Commonwealth countries. Ships of the Royal Navy are not within the scope of the Act, but see s 48 of the Naval Discipline Act 1957.

'on the high seas or in any foreign port or harbour' At first sight, it would appear that Commonwealth ports and harbours are outside the scope of this provision, but in *R v Liverpool JJ ex parte Molyneux* [1972] 2 All ER 471 it was held that the expression 'high seas' bears its old Admiralty meaning, rather than that it bears in international law. A theft committed aboard a ship in the port of Nassau in the Bahamas was therefore held to have been committed on the high seas and within the scope of this provision. The reference to 'foreign ports and harbours' was said to apply only to those parts of such ports etc which were not within Admiralty jurisdiction: these would in fact be artificial dock basins and ports lying upriver from the lowest bridges. See also s 742 of the Act (not printed in this work).

'on board any foreign ship to which he does not belong' The meaning of this phrase was considered by the House of Lords in *R v Kelly* [1982] AC 665, and it was held that it extends the scope of ordinary criminal offences, such as criminal damage, to any persons, including passengers, who are not members of the crew of the foreign ship in question. See also *R v Cumberworth* [1989] Crim LR 591.

Offences committed by British seamen at foreign ports to be within Admiralty jurisdiction

687. All offences against property or person committed in or at any place either ashore or afloat out of Her Majesty's dominions by any master, seaman, or apprentice who at the time when the offence is committed is, or within three months previously has been, employed in any British ship shall ... be liable to the same punishments respectively, and be inquired of, heard, tried, determined, and adjudged in the same manner and by the same courts and in the same places as if those offences had been committed within the jurisdiction of the Admiralty of England; and the costs and expenses of the prosecution of any such offence may be directed to be paid as in the case of costs and expenses of prosecutions for offences committed within the jurisdiction of the Admiralty of England.

NOTES

Although the marginal note refers only to crimes committed by British seamen in foreign ports, the actual scope of this offence is clearly much wider. It could, in theory at least, apply to crimes committed by foreign nationals in foreign or Commonwealth countries, far from the sea, several weeks after ceasing to be employed on a British ship. Its predecessor in an earlier Act was used as the basis for jurisdiction in the famous cannibalism case of *R v Dudley and Stephens* (1884) 14 QBD 273.

'Her Majesty's Dominions' These are areas over which British rule extends.

'within the jurisdiction of the Admiralty' This is exercised by the Crown Court and does not extend to purely summary offences. This provision is therefore similarly restricted.

[*Other sections omitted*]

Prevention of Corruption Act 1906

(6 EDW VII C 34)

Punishment of corrupt transactions with agents

1. (1) If any agent corruptly accepts or obtains, or agrees to accept or attempts to obtain, from any person, for himself or for any other person, any gift or consideration as an inducement or reward for doing or forbearing to do, or for having after the passing of this Act done or forborne to do, any act in relation to his principal's affairs or business, or for showing or forbearing to show favour or disfavour to any person in relation to his principal's affairs or business; or

If any person corruptly gives or agrees to give or offers any gift or consideration to any agent as an inducement or reward for doing or forbearing to do, or for having after the passing of this Act done or forborne to do, any act in relation to his principal's affairs or business, or for showing or forbearing to show favour or disfavour to any person in relation to his principal's affairs or business; or

If any person knowingly gives to any agent, or if any agent knowingly uses with intent to deceive his principal, any receipt, account, or other document in respect of which the principal is interested, and which contains any statement which is false or erroneous or defective in any material particular, and which to his knowledge is intended to mislead the principal;

he shall be guilty of an offence and shall be liable:

(a) on summary conviction, to imprisonment for a term not exceeding 6 months or to a fine not exceeding the statutory maximum, or to both; and

(b) on conviction on indictment, to imprisonment for a term not exceeding 7 years or to a fine, or to both.

(2) For the purposes of this Act the expression 'consideration' includes valuable consideration of any kind; the expression 'agent' includes any person employed by or acting for another; and the expression 'principal' includes an employer.

(3) A person serving under the Crown or under any corporation or any ... borough, county, or district council, or any board of guardians, is an agent within the meaning of this Act.

NOTES

This provision complements the Public Bodies Corrupt Practices Act 1889, and is itself supplemented by the Prevention of Corruption Act 1916. It has a somewhat wider application than the 1889 Act, since it applies to corruption in private business as well as to corruption in public bodies. On the other hand, it applies only to corruption involving 'agents', and the corruption of councillors, for example, must be dealt with under the 1889 Act.

'agent' See the definition provided in subss (2) and (3), and see also s 4(2) and (3) of the 1916 Act. The agent need not be acting as an agent of his principal, as long as the act in question is done 'in relation to his principal's affairs': *Morgan v DPP* [1970] 3 All ER 1053.

'corruptly' See the notes to s 1 of the 1889 Act, together with s 2 of the 1916 Act. Note that corruption or attempted corruption is not expressed to be an element in the offence created by the third paragraph of subs (1) (see *Sage v Eicholz* [1919] 2 KB 171); but in *R v Tweedie* [1984] 2 All ER 136 it was held that the offence cannot be committed in respect of an 'internal' document passing only between the agent and his principal. Any other construction would mean that a falsified time sheet could lead to liability under this Act.

'business' This includes a profession: *R v Breeze* [1973] 2 All ER 1141.

'attempts' This must have the same meaning as in s 1 of the Criminal Attempts Act 1981, even if s 3(2) of that Act is not directly applicable.

'knowingly' This must mean knowledge of the falsity *etc* as well as of the giving. Proof of wilful blindness will however suffice. See *Westminster City Council v Croyalgrange Ltd* [1986] 2 All ER 353 at p 359.

'false' See the notes to s 17 of the Theft Act 1968.

'in any material particular' See *R v Mallett* [1978] 3 All ER 10, where this expression was construed in the context of s 17(1)(b) of the Theft Act 1968 as meaning 'false in an important respect; something which mattered'.

'a term not exceeding 7 years' The maximum penalty was originally two years. It was increased to seven years, but only in respect of government contracts, by the Prevention of Corruption Act 1916 s 1. That section was repealed by the Criminal Justice Act 1988 Sch 16 and the present wording inserted by s 47(2) of the same Act.

Prosecution of offences
2. (1) A prosecution for an offence under this Act shall not be instituted without the consent, in England of the Attorney-General or Solicitor-General, and in Ireland of the Attorney-General or Solicitor-General for Ireland.
(2) ...
(3) Every information for any offence under this Act shall be upon oath.
(4), (5) ...
(6) Any person aggrieved by a summary conviction under this Act may appeal to [the Crown Court].

Perjury Act 1911

(1 & 2 GEO V C 6)

Perjury

1. (1) If any person lawfully sworn as a witness or as an interpreter in a judicial proceeding wilfully makes a statement material in that proceeding, which he knows to be false or does not believe to be true, he shall be guilty of perjury, and shall, on conviction thereof on indictment, be liable to imprisonment for a term not exceeding seven years, or to a fine or to both imprisonment and fine.

(2) The expression 'judicial proceeding' includes a proceeding before any court, tribunal, or person having by law power to hear, receive, and examine evidence on oath.

(3) Where a statement made for the purposes of a judicial proceeding is not made before the tribunal itself, but is made on oath before a person authorised by law to administer an oath to the person who makes the statement, and to record or authenticate the statement, it shall, for the purposes of this section, be treated as having been made in a judicial proceeding.

(4) A statement made by a person lawfully sworn in England for the purposes of a judicial proceeding:

    (a) in another part of His Majesty's dominions; or

    (b) in a British tribunal lawfully constituted in any place by sea or land outside His Majesty's dominions; or

    (c) in a tribunal of any foreign state,

shall, for the purposes of this section, be treated as a statement made in a judicial proceeding in England.

(5) Where, for the purposes of a judicial proceeding in England, a person is lawfully sworn under the authority of an Act of Parliament:

    (a) in any other part of His Majesty's dominions; or

    (b) before a British tribunal or a British officer in a foreign country, or within the jurisdiction of the Admiralty of England;

a statement made by such person so sworn as aforesaid (unless the Act of Parliament under which it was made otherwise specifically provides) shall be treated for the purposes of this section as having been made in the judicial proceeding in England for the purposes whereof it was made.

(6) The question whether a statement on which perjury is assigned was material is a question of law to be determined by the court of trial.

NOTES
'lawfully sworn' A witness or interpreter is lawfully sworn for the purpose of this Act if he has taken the oath or made a solemn affirmation. It does not matter if

he has sworn an oath in which he does not believe, as long as he has accepted it without objection. See s 15(1) *infra*.

Where a child of tender years gives unsworn evidence under s 38 of the Children and Young Persons Act 1933, he cannot be guilty of an offence under this Act, but in the case of a child aged ten years or more, s 38 itself provides sanctions for wilfully false evidence. The child must of course be proved to be *doli capax*, and this may be difficult in the case of a child who has been considered incompetent to take the oath.

Where an incompetent witness has been wrongly sworn, a conviction for perjury is not possible. See *R v Clegg* (1868) 19 LT 47.

'as a witness' This includes defendants in criminal cases and the parties to civil actions if they testify or swear affidavits for the purpose of the proceedings. (See the following note.)

'in a judicial proceeding' The effect of subss (2) and (3) is that perjury need not take the form of false evidence in court. A false affidavit sworn in connection with judicial proceedings will suffice. False written evidence tendered in criminal proceedings under s 9 of the Criminal Justice Act 1967 is dealt with under s 89 of that Act (not printed in this work); and where written statements are admitted in place of depositions in committal proceedings, see s 106 of the Magistrates' Courts Act 1980. Both these provisions apply the principles of the Perjury Act, but with a maximum penalty in each case of two years' imprisonment rather than seven.

The Criminal Justice Act 1988 enables a person outside the United Kingdom to give evidence at a trial in England or Wales through a live television link. This evidence is treated for the purpose of this section as given in the proceedings concerned: see s 32(3) of that Act (not printed in this work).

Judicial proceedings with a foreign element The effect of subss (4) and (5) is that a person may be tried in England or Wales for a wilfully false statement sworn within the jurisdiction in connection with foreign judicial proceedings, or for such a statement sworn abroad in connection with proceedings here, subject in the latter case to the restrictions in subs (5) itself.

As to false oral or written statements made otherwise than on oath for the purpose of foreign proceedings, see s 1A *infra*.

As to perjury before the European Court, see s 11(1)(a) of the European Communities Act 1972 (not printed in this work) which applies the Perjury Act and its penalties, even where the witness in question is not a British citizen.

'wilfully' This means deliberately and intentionally (see *R v Senior* [1899] 1 QB 283; *R v Millward* [1985] QB 519 at p 524). In the present context, what matters is that the statement is not the result of an oversight, a slip of the tongue, or a misunderstanding.

'material in the proceeding' Note subs (6). 'Material' means important or significant. The accused need not realise that the statement is material, nor need the truth or falsity of the statement be crucial to the outcome of the case. It will suffice, for example, if D's lies prevent the other party from pursuing a certain line of questioning which might have been relevant to D's own credibility. See *R v Millward* supra; *R v Baker* [1895] 1 QB 795.

'which he knows to be false or does not believe to be true' It is possible to construe this in such a way that D could commit perjury by making a statement which he does not realise is in fact true. See *R v Rider* (1986) 83 Cr App R 210, where the point was left open. Earlier cases have sometimes assumed that the statement must be false, and in any event, a prosecution for perjury is hardly likely unless it is at least suspected that the statement was false. Problems may however arise where D's *mens rea* can be proved, but the falsity of the statement remains open to reasonable doubt.

False unsworn statement under Evidence (Proceedings in Other Jurisdictions) Act 1975

1A. If any person, in giving any testimony (either orally or in writing) otherwise than on oath, where required to do so by an order under section 2 of the Evidence (Proceedings in Other Jurisdictions) Act 1975, makes a statement:

(a) which he knows to be false in a material particular, or

(b) which is false in a material particular and which he does not believe to be true,

he shall be guilty of an offence and shall be liable on conviction on indictment to imprisonment for a term not exceeding two years or a fine or both.

NOTES

This provision, which was added by s 8 and Sch 1 of the Evidence (Proceedings in Other Jurisdictions) Act 1975, extends the law beyond the limits of s 1(4) *supra*, in that it applies to unsworn evidence given under that Act. Note that in this case there is no possibility of liability arising without proof of the falsity of the evidence in question.

'false in a material particular' See *R v Mallett* [1978] 3 All ER 10, where this expression was construed in relation to s 17(1) of the Theft Act 1968 (qv) as meaning, 'false in a material respect, something which mattered'. See also the notes to s 1 *supra*.

False statements on oath made otherwise than in a judicial proceeding

2. If any person:

(1) being required or authorised by law to make any statement on oath for any purpose, and being lawfully sworn (otherwise than in a judicial proceeding) wilfully makes a statement which is material for that purpose and which he knows to be false or does not believe to be true; or

(2) wilfully uses any false affidavit for the purposes of the Bills of Sale Act 1878, as amended by any subsequent enactment,

he shall be guilty of a misdemeanour, and, on conviction thereof on indictment, shall be liable to [imprisonment] for a term not exceeding seven years [or to a fine or to both such imprisonment and fine].

NOTES

This provision does not extend to statutory declarations, as to which see s 5 *infra*. Nor does it extend to affidavits sworn in connection with a judicial proceeding, as to which see s 1(3).

'wilfully'; 'material'; 'knows to be false etc' See the notes to s 1 *supra*.

False statements, etc, with reference to marriage

3. (1) If any person:

(a) for the purpose of procuring a marriage, or a certificate or licence for marriage, knowingly and wilfully makes a false oath, or makes or signs a false declaration, notice or certificate required under any Act of Parliament for the time being in force relating to marriage; or

(b) knowingly and wilfully makes, or knowingly and wilfully causes to be made, for the purpose of being inserted in any register of marriage, a false statement as to any particular required by law to be known and registered relating to any marriage; or

(c) forbids the issue of any certificate or licence for marriage by falsely representing himself to be a person whose consent to the marriage is required by law knowing such representation to be false; or

(d) with respect to a declaration made under section 16(1A) or 27B(2) of the Marriage Act 1949:

   (i) enters a caveat under subsection (2) of the said section 16, or

   (ii) makes a statement mentioned in subsection (4) of the said section 27B,

which he knows to be false in a material particular,

he shall be guilty of an offence, and, on conviction thereof on indictment, shall be liable to imprisonment for a term not exceeding seven years or to a fine or to both imprisonment and fine [and on summary conviction thereof shall be liable to a penalty not exceeding the prescribed sum].

(2) No prosecution for knowingly and wilfully making a false declaration for the purpose of procuring any marriage out of the district in which the parties or one of them dwell shall take place after the expiration of eighteen months from the solemnization of the marriage to which the declaration refers.

NOTES

'for the purpose of procuring' This does not appear to require the successful procuring of the marriage certificate *etc*. The making of the false oath or declaration is sufficient *actus reus*, provided that the ulterior intent can be proved.

'knowingly and wilfully' See the notes to s 1 *supra*.

'or ... causes to be made' This appears to be an example of 'cause' being used in its imperative sense. One causes another person to do a thing by ordering or instructing him so to do: *McLeod v Buchanan* [1940] 2 All ER 179.

'required by law' The making of a false statement etc cannot be an offence under this provision unless the statement is a strict legal requirement: *R v Frickey* [1956] Crim LR 421.

False statements, etc, as to births or deaths

4. (1) If any person:

(a) wilfully makes any false answer to any question put to him by any registrar of births or deaths relating to the particulars required to be registered concerning any birth or death, or, wilfully gives to any such registrar any false information concerning any birth or death or the cause of any death; or

(b) wilfully makes any false certificate or declaration under or for the purposes of any Act relating to the registration of births or deaths, or, knowing any such certificate or declaration to be false, uses the same as true or gives or sends the same as true to any person; or

(c) wilfully makes, gives or uses any false statement or declaration as to a child born alive as having been still-born, or as to the body of a deceased person or a still-born child in any coffin, or falsely pretends that any child born alive was still-born; or

(d) makes any false statement with intent to have the same inserted in any register of births or deaths:

he shall be guilty of [an offence] and shall be liable:

      (i) on conviction thereof on indictment, to imprisonment for a term not exceeding seven years, . . . or to a fine instead of . . . the said punishments; and

      (ii) on summary conviction thereof, to a penalty not exceeding [the prescribed sum].

(2) A prosecution on indictment for an offence against this section shall not be commenced more than three years after the commission of the offence.

NOTES
As to the falsification of birth or death certificates, see s 37 of the Births and Deaths Registration Act 1953 (not printed in this work).

As to the insertion of false entries in the registers and the supplying of false certificates, see s 36 of the Forgery Act 1861.

There is clearly some degree of overlap between these provisions and the present one, but the Forgery Act offence appears to be directed primarily against registrars *etc*, whilst the present provisions appear to be directed against persons who supply false information to the registrars.

'wilfully' See the notes to s 1 *supra*.

'false' As far as subs (1) is concerned, the most likely subject on which false information might be provided is that concerning the paternity of a child. A married woman who puts her husband's name down as the father of her child commits this offence if she knows another man to be the true father, and so does her husband if he is a party to the falsehood. This may cause further problems where a married woman is artificially inseminated with the semen of a donor. S 27 of the Family Law Reform Act 1967 provides that the child of such insemination 'shall be treated as the child of the parties to the marriage, unless it is proved that the husband did not consent to the insemination'; but this does not necessarily mean he can be registered as the father. Note s 27(3) of the 1967 Act, which precludes the inheritance of titles of honour by such children.

'particulars required to be registered' See s 39 of the Births and Deaths Registration Act 1953, and orders made thereunder.

False statutory declarations and other false statements without oath

5. If any person knowingly and wilfully makes (otherwise than on oath) a statement false in a material particular, and the statement is made:

(a) in a statutory declaration; or

(b) in an abstract, account, balance sheet, book, certificate, declaration, entry, estimate, inventory, notice, report, return, or other document which he is authorised or required to make, attest, or verify, by any public general Act of Parliament for the time being in force; or

(c) in any oral declaration or oral answer which he is required to make by, under, or in pursuance of any public general Act of Parliament for the time being in force, he shall be guilty of [an offence] and shall be liable on conviction thereof on indictment to imprisonment . . . for any term not exceeding two years, or to a fine or to both such imprisonment and fine.

NOTES
'wilfully'   See the notes to s 1 *supra*.

'false in a material particular'   See the notes to s 1A *supra*.

'statutory declaration'   See s 15(2) *infra*, and see also s 36(6) of the Administration of Estates Act 1925 (false statements by personal representatives).

False declarations, etc, to obtain registration, etc, for carrying on a vocation
6. If any person:
  (a) procures or attempts to procure himself to be registered on any register or roll kept under or in pursuance of any public general Act of Parliament for the time being in force of persons qualified by law to practise any vocation or calling; or
  (b) procures or attempts to procure a certificate of the registration of any person on any such register or roll as aforesaid,
by wilfully making or producing or causing to be made or produced either verbally or in writing, any declaration, certificate, or representation which he knows to be false or fraudulent, he shall be guilty of an offence and shall be liable on conviction thereof on indictment to imprisonment for any term not exceeding twelve months, or to a fine, or to both such imprisonment and fine.

NOTES
'procures or attempts to procure'   To have 'procured' means to have succeeded in obtaining. A charge of attempting to procure would be subject to the Criminal Attempts Act 1981: see s 3 of that Act.

'wilfully'   See the notes to s 1 *supra*.

Aiders, abettors, suborners, etc
7. (1) Every person who aids, abets, counsels, procures, or suborns another person to commit an offence against this Act shall be liable to be proceeded against, indicted, tried and punished as if he were a principal offender.

(2) Every person who incites . . . another person to commit an offence against this Act shall be guilty of an offence, and, on conviction thereof on indictment, shall be liable to imprisonment, or to a fine, or to both such imprisonment and fine.

NOTES
This provision appears to be largely superfluous. Subs (1) adds nothing of substance to the general law of complicity. ('Suborning' is merely another term for 'procuring'.) Subs (2) likewise adds nothing to the common law rules governing incitement.

Venue
8. Where an offence against this Act or any offence punishable as perjury or as subornation of perjury under any other Act of Parliament is committed in any place either on sea or land outside the United Kingdom, the offender may be proceeded against, indicted, tried, and punished ... in England ...

NOTES
This provision, although headed 'venue', was probably intended to create extra-territorial liability, in the same manner as s 686(1) of the Merchant Shipping Act 1894 (qv). It is difficult to see what other function it could meaningfully fill. But it does not by any means make all offences under this Act into full-blooded extra-territorial ones. Offences under s 1, for example, must necessarily involve statements material to English judicial proceedings, except where subs (4) applies; and the s 6 offence of making a false declaration to obtain registration as (eg) a medical practitioner can only be committed where an Act of Parliament requires or authorises the keeping of such a register. Despite the present provision, therefore, no offence could be committed under s 6 by a person fraudulently seeking registration as a doctor in some other country.

9–11 [*repealed*]

12–14 [*omitted*]

Interpretation, etc
15. (1) For the purposes of this Act, the forms and ceremonies used in administering an oath are immaterial, if the court or person before whom the oath is taken has power to administer an oath for the purpose of verifying the statement in question, and if the oath has been administered in a form and with ceremonies which the person taking the oath has accepted without objection, or has declared to be binding on him.
(2) In this Act:
The expression 'oath' ... includes 'affirmation' and 'declaration,' and the expression 'swear' ... includes 'affirm' and 'declare'; and
The expression 'statutory declaration' means a declaration made by virtue of the Statutory Declarations Act 1835, or of any Act, Order in Council, rule or regulation applying or extending the provisions thereof; and [. . .]

16. [*omitted*]

17. [*repealed*]

Extent
18. This Act shall not extend to Scotland or Ireland.

19. [*short title*]

Official Secrets Act 1911

(1 & 2 GEO V C 28)

Penalties for spying

1. (1) If any person for any purpose prejudicial to the safety or interests of the State—

(a) approaches [inspects, passes over] or is in the neighbourhood of, or enters any prohibited place within the meaning of this Act; or

(b) makes any sketch, plan, model, or note which is calculated to be or might be or is intended to be directly or indirectly useful to an enemy; or

(c) obtains, [collects, records, or publishes], or communicates to any other person [any secret official code word or pass word, or] any sketch, plan, model, article, or note, or other document or information which is calculated to be or might be or is intended to be directly or indirectly useful to an enemy;

he shall be guilty of [an offence].

(2) On a prosecution under this section, it shall not be necessary to show that the accused person was guilty of any particular act tending to show a purpose prejudicial to the safety or interests of the State, and, notwithstanding that no such act is proved against him, he may be convicted if, from the circumstances of the case, or his conduct, or his known character as proved, it appears that his purpose was a purpose prejudicial to the safety or interests of the State; and if any sketch, plan, model, article, note, document, or information relating to or used in any prohibited place within the meaning of this Act, or anything in such a place [or any secret official code word or pass word], is made, obtained, [collected, recorded, published], or communicated by any person other than a person acting under lawful authority, it shall be deemed to have been made, obtained, [collected, recorded, published] or communicated for a purpose prejudicial to the safety or interests of the State unless the contrary is proved.

NOTES

'spying'; 'purpose prejudicial to the safety etc of the State'   Despite the marginal note, this provision is not exclusively concerned with spying: sabotage *etc* is also covered. See *Chandler v DPP* [1964] AC 763. As to the question of what may be prejudicial to the interests of the State, the views of a spy or saboteur on this issue are irrelevant (*ibid*). See also *R v Bettaney* [1985] Crim LR 104.

'approaches ... or is in the neighbourhood of'   The Act does not define the term 'neighbourhood', which therefore remains a somewhat vague concept. It seems clear that mere preparatory acts, which might not otherwise have amounted even to attempts to commit acts of espionage or sabotage, are made into substantive offences unders subs (1)(a). See further s 7 of the Official Secrets Act 1920.

'prohibited place'   See s 3 *infra*.

'**model**'; '**sketch**'; '**document**'; '**obtains**'; '**communicates**'   See s 12 *infra.*

'**enemy**'   This may include a potential enemy: *R v Parrott* (1913) 8 Cr App R 186.

Penalty   Offences under this section may be punished by up to 14 years imprisonment: see s 8(1) of the 1920 Act (as amended).

Further disclosures   S 5(6) of the Official Secrets Act 1989 creates as further offence of disclosing information etc originally obtained by spying contrary to this section.

2. [*repealed*] (See Official Secrets Act 1989)

Definition of prohibited place
3. For the purposes of this Act, the expression 'prohibited place' means—

[(a) any work of defence, arsenal, naval or air force establishment or station, factory, dockyard, mine, minefield, camp, ship, or aircraft belonging to or occupied by or on behalf of His Majesty, or any telegraph, telephone, wireless or signal station, or office so belonging or occupied, and any place belonging to or occupied by or on behalf of His Majesty and used for the purpose of building, repairing, making, or storing any munitions of war, or any sketches, plans, models, or documents relating thereto, or for the purpose of getting any metals, oil, or minerals of use in time of war];

(b) any place not belonging to His Majesty where any [munitions of war], or any [sketches, models, plans] or documents relating thereto, are being made, repaired, [gotten] or stored under contract with, or with any person on behalf of, His Majesty, or otherwise on behalf of His Majesty; and

(c) any place belonging to [or used for the purposes of] His Majesty which is for the time being declared [by order of a Secretary of State] to be a prohibited place for the purposes of this section on the ground that information with respect thereto, or damage thereto, would be useful to an enemy; and

(d) any railway, road, way, or channel, or other means of communication by land or water (including any works or structures being part thereof or connected therewith), or any place used for gas, water, or electricity works or other works for purposes of a public character, or any place where any [munitions of war], or any [sketches, models, plans] or documents relating thereto, are being made, repaired, or stored otherwise than on behalf of His Majesty, which is for the time being declared [by order of a Secretary of State] to be a prohibited place for the purposes of this section, on the ground that information with respect thereto, or the destruction or obstruction thereof, or interference therewith, would be useful to an enemy.

NOTES
'**ship or aircraft**'   Hovercraft are included by virtue of the Hovercraft (Application of Enactments) Order 1972.

Prohibited places under para (c) See generally *Archbold*, § 21–182, and the Official Secrets (Prohibited Places) Orders (SI 1955/1497 and SI 1975/182). See also Telecommunications Act 1984, s 109(1) and sch 4.

4–5 [*repealed*]

Power of arrest

6. Any person who is found committing an offence under this Act ... or who is reasonably suspected of having committed, or having attempted to commit, or being about to commit, such an offence, may be apprehended or detained ...

NOTES

All offences under this Act are in fact arrestable offences under s 24(1) or (2) of the Police and Criminal Evidence Act 1984, but the power to arrest for offences which are about to be committed is narrower under the 1984 Act, in that it is only exercisable by constables (subs (7)). The present provision does not differentiate between the powers of the police and those of other citizens.

'offence under this Act' See s 12 *infra*.

Penalty for harbouring spies

7. If any person knowingly harbours any person whom he knows, or has reasonable grounds for supposing, to be a person who is about to commit or who has committed an offence under this Act, or knowingly permits to meet or assemble in any premises in his occupation or under his control any such persons, or if any person having harboured any such person, or permitted to meet or assemble in any premises in his occupation or under his control any such persons [wilfully omits or refuses] to disclose to a superintendent of police any information which it is in his power to give in relation to any such person he shall be guilty of an offence ...

NOTES

'wilfully omits or refuses to disclose' 'Wilfully' in this context means 'deliberately' (*cf R v Senior* [1899] 1 QB 283). The omission must presumably follow an express request for information by the superintendent in question (*cf* s 6 of the Official Secrets Act 1920), although the Act does not make this entirely clear.

'superintendent of police' See s 12 *infra*.

Penalty See s 8 of the 1920 Act.

Restriction on prosecution

8. A prosecution for an offence under this Act shall not be instituted except by or with the consent of the Attorney-General.

9. [*omitted*]

Extent of Act and place of trial of offence
10. (1) This Act shall apply to all acts which are offences under this Act when committed in any part of His Majesty's dominions, or when committed by British officers or subjects elsewhere.

(2) An offence under this Act, if alleged to have been committed out of the United Kingdom, may be inquired of, heard, and determined, in any competent British court in the place where the offence was committed, or ... in England ...

(3) An offence under this Act shall not be tried ... by the sheriff court in Scotland, nor by any court out of the United Kingdom which has not jurisdiction to try crimes which involve the greatest punishment allowed by law.

(4) [*repealed*]

NOTES
It is obviously necessary that this Act should have an extra-territorial ambit, and subs (1) provides this.

'British officers or subjects'   This must be read subject to s 3(1) of the British Nationality Act 1948 (qv) and the British Nationality Act 1981. The reference to British subjects must accordingly be read as a reference to British citizens, British Dependent Territories' citizens or British overseas citizens.

11. [*omitted*]

Interpretation
12. In this Act, unless the context otherwise requires,—
Any reference to a place belonging to His Majesty includes a place belonging to any department of the Government of the United Kingdom or of any British possessions, whether the place is or is not actually vested in His Majesty;

The expression 'Attorney-General' means the Attorney or Solicitor-General for England; and as respects Scotland, means the Lord Advocate; and as respects Ireland, means the Attorney or Solicitor-General for Ireland; and, if the prosecution is instituted in any court out of the United Kingdom, means the person who in that court is Attorney-General, or exercises the like functions as the Attorney-General in England;

Expressions referring to communicating or receiving include any communicating or receiving, whether in whole or in part, and whether the sketch, plan, model, article, note, document, or information itself or the substance, effect, or description thereof only be communicated or received; expressions referring to obtaining or retaining any sketch, plan, model, article, note, or document, include the copying or causing to be copied the whole or any part of any sketch, plan, model, article, note, or document; and expressions referring to the communication of any sketch, plan, model, article, note or document include the transfer or transmission of the sketch, plan, model, article, note or document;

The expression 'document' includes part of a document;

The expression 'model' includes design, pattern, and specimen;

The expression 'sketch' includes any photograph or other mode of representing any place or thing;

[The expression 'munitions of war' includes the whole or any part of any ship, submarine, aircraft, tank or similar engine, arms and ammunition, torpedo, or mine, intended or adapted for use in war, and any other article, material, or device, whether actual or proposed, intended for such use;

The expression 'superintendent of police' includes any police officer of a like or superior rank [and any person upon whom the powers of a superintendent of police are for the purpose of this Act conferred by a Secretary of State];

The expression 'office under His Majesty' includes any office or employment in or under any department of the Government of the United Kingdom, or of any British possession;

The expression 'offence under this Act' includes any act, omission, or other thing which is punishable under this Act.

Prevention of Corruption Act 1916

(6 & 7 GEO V C 64)

1. [*repealed*]

Presumption of corruption in certain cases
2. Where in any proceedings against a person for an offence under the Prevention of Corruption Act 1906, or the Public Bodies Corrupt Practices Act 1889, it is proved that any money, gift, or other consideration has been paid or given to or received by a person in the employment of His Majesty or any Government Department or a public body by or from a person, or agent of a person, holding or seeking to obtain a contract from His Majesty or any Government Department or public body, the money, gift, or consideration shall be deemed to have been paid or given and received corruptly as such inducement or reward as is mentioned in such Act unless the contrary is proved.

NOTE
If the defence wish to discharge this burden of proof, they must do so on the balance of probabilities, as is the case with all such reverse burdens. See *R v Carr-Briant* [1943] KB 607.

3. [*repealed*]

Short title and interpretation
4. (1) This Act may be cited as the Prevention of Corruption Act 1916, and the Public Bodies Corrupt Practices Act 1889, the Prevention of Corruption Act 1906, and this Act may be cited together as the Prevention of Corruption Acts 1889 to 1916.

(2) In this Act and in the Public Bodies Corrupt Practices Act 1889, the expression 'public body' includes, in addition to the bodies mentioned in the last-mentioned Act, local and public authorities of all descriptions.

(3) A person serving under any such public body is an agent within the meaning of the Prevention of Corruption Act 1906, and the expressions 'agent' and 'consideration' in this Act have the same meaning as in the Prevention of Corruption Act 1906, as amended by this Act.

NOTE
'public body' This means any body having public or statutory duties to perform for the benefit of the public: *DPP v Holly* [1977] 1 All ER 316.

Official Secrets Act 1920

(10 & 11 GEO V C 75)

Unauthorised use of uniforms; falsification of reports, forgery, personation, and false documents

1. (1) If any person for the purpose of gaining admission, or of assisting any other person to gain admission, to a prohibited place, within the meaning of the Official Secrets Act 1911 (hereinafter referred to as 'the principal Act'), or for any other purpose prejudicial to the safety or interests of the State within the meaning of the said Act —

(a) uses or wears, without lawful authority, any naval, military, air-force, police, or other official uniform, or any uniform so nearly resembling the same as to be calculated to deceive, or falsely represents himself to be a person who is or has been entitled to use or wear any such uniform; or

(b) orally, or in writing in any declaration or application, or in any document signed by him or on his behalf, knowingly makes or connives at the making of any false statement or any omission; or

(c) ... tampers with any passport or any naval, military, air-force, police, or official pass, permit, certificate, licence, or other document of a similar character (hereinafter in this section referred to as an official document), ... or has in his possession any ... forged, altered, or irregular official document; or

(d) personates, or falsely represents himself to be a person holding, or in the employment of a person holding office under His Majesty, or to be or not to be a person to whom an official document or secret official code word or pass word has been duly issued or communicated, or with intent to obtain an official document, secret official code word or pass word, whether for himself or any other person, knowingly makes any false statement; or

(e) uses, or has in his possession or under his control, without the authority of the Government Department or the authority concerned, any die, seal, or stamp of or belonging to, or used, made or provided by any Government Department, or by any diplomatic, naval, military, or air force authority appointed by or acting under the authority of His Majesty, or any die, seal or stamp so nearly resembling any such die, seal or stamp as to be calculated to deceive, or counterfeits any such die, seal or stamp, or uses, or has in his possession, or under his control, any such counterfeited die, seal or stamp;

he shall be guilty of [an offence].

(2) If any person —

(a) retains for any purpose prejudicial to the safety or interests of the State any official document, whether or not completed or issued for use, when he has no right to retain it, or when it is contrary to his duty to retain it, or fails to comply with any directions issued by any Government Department or any person authorised by such department with regard to the return or disposal thereof; or

(b) allows any other person to have possession of any official document issued for his use alone, or communicates any secret official code word or pass word so issued, or, without lawful authority or excuse, has in his possession any official document or secret official code word or pass word issued for the use of some person other than himself, or on obtaining possession of any official document by finding or otherwise, neglects or fails to restore it to the person or authority by whom or for whose use it was issued, or to a police constable; or

(c) without lawful authority or excuse, manufactures or sells, or has in his possession for sale any such die, seal or stamp as aforesaid;

he shall be guilty of [an offence].

(3) In the case of any prosecution under this section involving the proof of a purpose prejudicial to the safety or interests of the State, subsection (2) of section one of the principal Act shall apply in like manner as it applies to prosecutions under that section.

NOTES

This Act is to be construed as one with the 1911 Act , and the definitions provided in that Act are accordingly relevant to the interpretation of this.

'prohibited place' See s 3 of the 1911 Act and notes thereto.

'communicates'; 'document'; 'retains'; 'office under His Majesty' See s 12 of the 1911 Act.

'purpose prejudicial to the safety etc of the state' The views of the defendant as to what may be in the interests of the state are irrelevant: see *Chandler v DPP* [1964] AC 763 at 777.

Penalty The maximum penalty for an offence under this provision is two years' imprisonment: see s 8(2) *infra*.

2. [*omitted*]

Interfering with officers of the police or members of His Majesty's forces

3. No person in the vicinity of any prohibited place shall obstruct, knowingly mislead or otherwise interfere with or impede, the chief officer or a superintendent or other officer of police, or any member of His Majesty's forces engaged on guard, sentry, patrol, or other similar duty in relation to the prohibited place, and, if any person acts in contravention of, or fails to comply with, this provision, he shall be guilty of [an offence].

NOTES
'in the vicinity of' This means '*in* or in the vicinity of', so the offence may be committed within the perimeter of a prohibited place. See *Adler v George* [1964] 2 QB 7.

'obstruct' Note that the adverb 'knowingly' comes *after* 'obstruct' and does not apply to it; nor is it preceded by the adverb 'wilfully' (as in s 51 of the Police Act 1964) (qv). It is accordingly probable that the offence of obstruction is one of strict liability. As to what may amount to obstruction, see the notes to s 51 of the Police Act.

Penalty The maximum penalty for an offence under this provision is two years' imprisonment by s 8(2) *infra*.

4–5. [*omitted*]

Duty of giving information as to commission of offences
6. (1) Where a chief officer of police is satisfied that there is reasonable ground for suspecting that an offence under section one of the principal Act has been committed and for believing that any person is able to furnish information as to the offence or suspected offence, he may apply to a Secretary of State for permission to exercise the powers conferred by this subsection and, if such permission is granted, he may authorise a superintendent of police, or any police officer not below the rank of inspector, to require the person believed to be able to furnish information to give any information in his power relating to the offence or suspected offence, and, if so required and on tender of his reasonable expenses, to attend at such reasonable time and place as may be specified by the superintendent or other officer; and if a person required in pursuance of such an authorisation to give information, or to attend as aforesaid, fails to comply with any such requirement or knowingly gives false information, he shall be guilty of [an offence].

(2) Where a chief officer of police has reasonable grounds to believe that the case is one of great emergency and that in the interest of the State immediate action is necessary, he may exercise the powers conferred by the last foregoing subsection without applying for or being granted the permission of a Secretary of State, but if he does so shall forthwith report the circumstances to the Secretary of State.

(3) References in this section to a chief officer of police shall be construed as including references to any other officer of police expressly authorised by a chief officer of police to act on his behalf for the purposes of this section when by reason of illness, absence, or other cause he is unable to do so.

NOTES
See also s 7 of the 1911 Act. Both provisions are unusual in that it is not generally an offence to fail or refuse to answer police questions.

'fails to comply ... or knowingly gives' Note the lack of any adverb preceding the word 'fails'. This suggests that even an inadvertent failure to keep an appointment would be punishable under this provision.

'chief officer or police'   See s 11(3) *infra*.

Penalty   The maximum penalty for an offence under this provision is two years' imprisonment. See s 8(2) *infra*.

Attempts, incitements, etc
   7. Any person who attempts to commit any offence under the principal Act or this Act, or solicits or incites or endeavours to persuade another person to commit an offence, or aids or abets and does any act preparatory to the commission of an offence under the principal Act or this Act, shall be guilty of a felony or a misdemeanour or a summary offence according as the offence in question is a felony, a misdemeanour or a summary offence, and on conviction shall be liable to the same punishment, and to be proceeded against in the same manner, as if he had committed the offence.

NOTES
For the most part, this merely restates the general law governing attempts, incitement or complicity; but it also does more, in that it criminalises preparatory actions that would not come within the scope of the Criminal Attempts Act 1981. This means that it may be an offence merely to purchase materials or to travel to the part of the country where some prohibited place is located. *Mens rea* must be proved, but it suffices that D contemplated the possibility of the offence being committed. See *R v Bingham* [1973] 2 All ER 89.

'felony'; 'misdemeanour'   See the notes to s 8 *infra*.

Provisions as to trial and punishment of offences
   8. (1) Any person who is guilty of a felony under the principal Act or this Act shall be liable to penal servitude for a term of not less than three years and not exceeding fourteen years.
   (2) Any person who is guilty of a misdemeanour under the principal Act or this Act shall be liable on conviction on indictment to imprisonment with or without hard labour, for a term not exceeding two years, or, on conviction under the Summary Jurisdiction Acts, to imprisonment, with or without hard labour, for a term not exceeding three months or to a fine not exceeding [the prescribed sum], or both such imprisonment and fine:
   Provided that no misdemeanour under the principal Act or this Act shall be dealt with summarily except with the consent of the Attorney General.
   (3) For the purposes of the trial of a person for an offence under the principal Act or this Act, the offence shall be deemed to have been committed either at the place in which the same actually was committed, or at any place in the United Kingdom in which the offender may be found.
   (4) In addition and without prejudice to any powers which a court may possess to order the exclusion of the public from any proceedings if, in the course of proceedings before a court against any person for an offence under the principal Act or this Act or the proceedings on appeal, or in the course of the trial of a person for felony or misdemeanour under the principal Act or this Act, application is made by the prosecution, on the

ground that the publication of any evidence to be given or of any statement to be made in the course of the proceedings would be prejudicial to the national safety, that all or any portion of the public shall be excluded during any part of the hearing, the court may make an order to that effect, but the passing of sentence shall in any case take place in public.

(5) Where the person guilty of an offence under the principal Act or this Act is a company or corporation, every director and officer of the company or corporation shall be guilty of the like offence unless he proves that the act or omission constituting the offence took place without his knowledge or consent.

NOTES

'felony'; **'misdemeanour'** The distinction between felonies and misdemeanours no longer exists in English law; but offences under s 1 of the 1911 Act were felonies and are thus punishable under subs (1), as are attempts or incitement to commit such offences under s 7 *supra*. All other surviving offences were misdemeanours and are therefore punishable under subs (2).

Criminal Justice Act 1925

(15 & 16 GEO V C 86)

Abolition of presumption of coercion of married woman by husband
47. Any presumption of law that an offence committed by a wife in the presence of her husband is committed under the coercion of the husband is hereby abolished, but on a charge against a wife for any offence other than treason or murder it shall be a good defence to prove that the offence was committed in the presence of, and under the coercion of, the husband.

NOTES
The common law presumption abolished by this provision was of somewhat uncertain extent, being apparently inapplicable in respect of a number of offences. Where it could apply, it could always be rebutted by evidence that the wife acted on her own initiative, but it would otherwise be presumed that she acted under her husband's influence.

This provision does more than abolish the presumption of coercion; it clearly places a full legal burden of proof on the defence. It is not therefore sufficient for the defence merely to raise evidence of coercion. Its existence must be established on the balance of probabilities, as is the case with defences such as insanity and diminished responsibility.

The statutory defence is capable of applying to any offences other than murder or treason. Any further restrictions which may have existed at comon law no longer apply.

'wife' The defence cannot be raised in the absence of a valid and subsisting marriage: *R v Kara* [1988] Crim LR 42 (cf *R v Court* (1912) 7 Cr App R 127).

'coercion' The concept of coercion appears to differ from duress in that it does not require the will of the accused to have been overborne by threats of death or serious injury. Moral or mental domination by the husband may suffice. (See *R v Richardson* [1982] Crim LR 507.) There is nevertheless a dearth of appellate authority as to where the exact limits of the defence lie. One thing that is clear is that the defences of coercion and duress are not mutually exclusive. In appropriate cases a wife might put both defences forward at the same time. See *DPP for NI v Lynch* [1975] AC 653 at 713.

Infant Life (Preservation) Act 1929

(19 & 20 GEO V C 34)

Punishment for child destruction

1. (1) Subject as hereinafter in this subsection provided, any person who, with intent to destroy the life of a child capable of being born alive, by any wilful act causes a child to die before it has an existence independent of its mother, shall be guilty of an offence, to wit, of child destruction, and shall be liable on conviction thereof on indictment to imprisonment for life:

Provided that no person shall be found guilty of an offence under this section unless it is proved that the act which caused the death of the child was not done in good faith for the purpose only of preserving the life of the mother.

(2) For the purposes of this Act, evidence that a woman had at any material time been pregnant for a period of twenty-eight weeks or more shall be *prima facie* proof that she was at that time pregnant of a child capable of being born alive.

NOTES

There is clearly some overlap between this offence and the offence of attempting to procure abortion contrary to s 58 of the Offences Against the Person Act 1861, but the following difference should be noted:

(1) S 58 does not require a successful abortion, and in some cases does not even require that the woman should have been genuinely pregnant. In contrast, the present provision requires the actual destruction of a child capable of being born alive.

(2) S 1 of the Abortion Act 1967 may provide a very significant defence to a charge brought under s 58 (or s 59) of the 1861 Act; but s 5(1) of the Abortion Act provides that this defence is inapplicable where the charge is brought under the 1929 Act.

'any person' This presumably includes the mother herself.

'with intent ... by any wilful act' The meaning of 'wilfulness' has caused some interpretational difficulties in other contexts (see *eg R v Sheppard* [1981] AC 394); but since a specific intent is required here, the concept of wilfulness is rendered otiose.

'a child capable of being born alive' The '28 weeks' test in subs (2) does not preclude the prosecution from proving that a child of, say 24 weeks was capable of being born alive. The significance of subs (2) is that from 28 weeks onwards the burden of proof shifts to the defence, who must prove the contrary. It would therefore be dangerous for doctors to assume that the Abortion Act 1967 protects them beyond about 24 weeks, when in practice the foetus sometimes become capable of live birth.

A foetus which is incapable of breathing on its own cannot be considered capable of being born alive: *C v S* [1981] 1 All ER 1230. On the other hand, it is probably not necessary that it should be genuinely viable (*ie* capable of long-term survival).

'before it has an existence independent of its mother'   If the child has such independent existence, for however short a time, its destruction will be homicide (probably murder). On a homicide charge, child destruction is in fact a possible alternative verdict by virtue of s 2(2), but only if the jury are satisfied that it was indeed the latter offence. If there is no proof as to which offence it was, acquittal may be the only option.

The proviso   In *R v Bourne* [1939] 1 KB 687, McNaghten J told the jury that the proviso to subs (1) merely states the common law principle regarding abortion; and that 'preserving the life of the mother' should be interpreted as including the preservation of her health, at least to the extent of preventing her from becoming a mental or physical wreck. See also *R v Newton* [1958] Crim LR 469.

'on indictment'   This offence is not triable summarily.

Prosecution of offences
   2.—(1) [*repealed*]
   (2) Where upon the trial of any person for the murder or manslaughter of any child, or for infanticide, or for an offence under section fifty-eight of the Offences against the Person Act, 1861 (which relates to administering drugs or using instruments to procure abortion), the jury are of opinion that the person charged is not guilty of murder, manslaughter or infanticide, or of an offence under the said section fifty-eight, as the case may be, but that he is shown by the evidence to be guilty of the [offence] of child destruction, the jury may find him guilty of that [offence], and thereupon the person convicted shall be liable to be punished as if he had been convicted upon an indictment for child destruction.
   (3) Where upon the trial of any person for the [offence] of child destruction the jury are of opinion that the person charged is not guilty of that [offence], but that he is shown by the evidence to be guilty of an offence under the said section fifty-eight of the Offences against the Person Act, 1861, the jury may find him guilty of that offence, and thereupon the person convicted shall be liable to be punished as if he had been convicted upon an indictment under that section.
   (4) [*repealed*]
   (5) [*repealed*]

NOTES
As explained in the notes to s 1, the possibility of alternative verdicts does not solve the problem where it is not clear which offence has been committed.
   Note also that verdicts of murder or manslaughter are not permitted on an indictment charging only child destruction.

Children and Young Persons Act 1933

(23 GEO V C 12)

Offences

Cruelty to persons under sixteen

1. (1) If any person who has attained the age of sixteen years and has the custody, charge, or care of any child or young person under that age, wilfully assaults, ill-treats, neglects, abandons, or exposes him, or causes or procures him to be assaulted, ill-treated, neglected, abandoned, or exposed, in a manner likely to cause him unnecessary suffering or injury to health (including injury to or loss of sight, or hearing, or limb, or organ of the body, and any mental derangement), that person shall be guilty of a misdemeanour, and shall be liable —

(a) on conviction on indictment, to a fine . . ., or alternatively, . . . or in addition thereto, to imprisonment for any term not exceeding two years;

(b) on summary conviction, to a fine not exceeding [the prescribed sum] or alternatively, . . . or in addition thereto, to imprisonment for any term not exceeding six months.

(2) For the purposes of this section —

(a) a parent or other person legally liable to maintain a child or young person shall be deemed to have neglected him in a manner likely to cause injury to his health if he has failed to provide adequate food, clothing, medical aid or lodging for him, or if, having been unable otherwise to provide such food, clothing, medical aid or lodging, he has failed to take steps to procure it to be provided under [the enactments applicable in that behalf];

(b) where it is proved that the death of an infant under three years of age was caused by suffocation (not being suffocation caused by disease or the presence of any foreign body in the throat or air passages of the infant) while the infant was in bed with some other person who has attained the age of sixteen years, that other person shall, if he was, when he went to bed, under the influence of drink, be deemed to have neglected the infant in a manner likely to cause injury to its health.

(3) A person may be convicted of an offence under this section —

(a) notwithstanding that actual suffering or injury to health, or the likelihood of actual suffering or injury to health, was obviated by the action of another person;

(b) notwithstanding the death of the child or young person in question.

(4) . . .

(5) If it is proved that a person convicted under this section was directly or indirectly interested in any sum of money accruing or payable in the event of the death of the child or young person, and had knowledge that that sum of money was accruing or becoming payable, then —

(a) in the case of a conviction on indictment, ... the court shall have the power, in lieu of awarding any other penalty under this section, to sentence the person convicted to penal servitude for any term not exceeding five years; and

(b) in the case of a summary conviction, the court in determining the sentence to be awarded shall take into consideration the fact that the person was so interested and had such knowledge.

(6) For the purposes of the last foregoing subsection: —

(a) a person shall be deemed to be directly or indirectly interested in a sum of money if he has any share in or any benefit from the payment of that money, notwithstanding that he may not be a person to whom it is legally payable; and

(b) a copy of a policy of insurance, certified to be a true copy by an officer or agent of the insurance company granting the policy, shall be evidence that the child or young person therein stated to be insured has in fact been so insured, and that the person in whose favour the policy has been granted is the person to whom the money thereby insured is legally payable.

(7) Nothing in this section shall be construed as affecting the right of any parent, teacher, or other person having the lawful control or charge of a child or young person to administer punishment to him.

NOTES

The various offences of assault, neglect *etc* created by this provision overlap to some extent, and so evidence of neglect may be admissible on a charge of ill-treatment. See *R v Hayles* [1969] 1 All ER 34.

'wilfully' As to the meaning of this term in this context, see *R v Senior* [1899] 1 QB 283 and in particular *R v Sheppard* [1981] AC 394.

'assaults' See the notes to s 47 of the Offences Against the Person Act 1861, but note that subs (7) of this section preserves the common law right of a parent *etc* to administer reasonable punishment.

'neglects' Neglect may be the result of indifference, inadequacy, malice or in some cases religious conviction. If it is 'wilful' (in the *Sheppard* sense) — and this requires awareness of the risk of suffering, or indifference towards it — it will be no defence for D to claim that he acted from religious conviction: see *R v Senior, supra*.

'abandons' See *R v Boulden* (1957) 41 Cr App R 105.

'causes or procures him to be assaulted ...' 'Cause' here bears its imperative meaning. If D orders or directs E to assault P, and E complies, D will have 'caused' the offence. See *Houston v Buchanan* [1940] 2 All ER 179. As to the meaning of 'procure', see the notes to the Accessories and Abettors Act 1861.

Subs (2)(b) Where this applies, D is 'deemed' to have committed the *actus reus* of the offence of neglect, but it does not expressly provide that D should be 'deemed' to have done so 'wilfully'.

Subs (7) Note that this merely preserves any rights to administer punishment that are recognised independently of this Act: it does not itself create any such right, and public sector schoolteachers no longer have any right to administer corporal punishment. The 'reasonableness' of any particular parental or school chastisement must be a question of fact, and it cannot be assumed that old cases on this issue match modern notions of what is reasonable.

2. [*repealed*]

Allowing persons under sixteen to be in brothels
3. (1) If any person having the custody, charge or care of a child or young person who has attained the age of four years and is under the age of sixteen years, allows that child or young person to reside in or to frequent a brothel, he shall be liable on summary conviction to a fine not exceeding level 2 on the standard scale, or alternatively ... or in addition thereto, to imprisonment for any term not exceeding six months.

(2) [*repealed*]

NOTE
'brothel' See the notes to s 33 of the Sexual Offences Act 1956.

Juvenile offenders

Age of criminal responsibility
50. It shall be conclusively presumed that no child under the age of [ten] years can be guilty of any offence.

NOTES
Children not given complete immunity under this provision (ie those aged over 10 but not yet 14) can be convicted of criminal offences, but only on proof that they were aware their actions were 'seriously' wrong: *J. M. (a minor) v Runeckles* (1984) 79 Cr App R 255.

Where a child is not criminally responsible by virtue of this provision, the consequences extend beyond the immunity of the child himself. A person cannot be convicted of conspiring with such a child, nor with handling goods 'stolen' by him. If an adult conceals or disposes of goods wrongfully taken by a child, the correct charge may be theft, not handling. See *Walters v Lunt* [1951] 2 All ER 645.

See further s 2 of the Criminal Law Act 1977 and notes thereto.

[*other sections omitted*]

Infanticide Act 1938

(1 & 2 GEO VI C 36)

Offence of infanticide

1. (1) Where a woman by any wilful act or omission causes the death of her child being a child under the age of twelve months, but at the time of the act or omission the balance of her mind was disturbed by reason of her not having fully recovered from the effect of giving birth to the child or by reason of the effect of lactation consequent upon the birth of the child, then, notwithstanding that the circumstances were such that but for this Act the offence would have amounted to murder, she shall be guilty of an offence to wit of infanticide, and may for such offence be dealt with and punished as if she had been guilty of the offence of manslaughter of the child.

(2) Where upon the trial of a woman for the murder of her child, being a child under the age of twelve months, the jury are of opinion that she by any wilful act or omission caused its death, but that at the time of the act or omission the balance of her mind was disturbed by reason of her not having fully recovered from the effect of giving birth to the child or by reason of the effect of lactation consequent upon the birth of the child, then the jury may, notwithstanding that the circumstances were such that but for the provisions of this Act they might have returned a verdict of murder, return in lieu thereof a verdict of infanticide.

(3) Nothing in this Act shall affect the power of the jury upon an indictment for the murder of a child to return a verdict of manslaughter, or a verdict of [not guilty by reason of insanity].

NOTES

The concept of infanticide was introduced by the Infanticide Act 1922. The present Act extended the scope of the concept, which the original Act confined to the killing of 'newly-born' children.

On a charge of murder, it is doubtful whether a defence of infanticide (under subs (2)) offers an accused any advantages over a defence of diminished responsibility under the Homicide Act 1957. Indeed, the Butler Committee considered the concept of infanticide to have been rendered otiose, and recommended its abolition (Cmnd 6244, paras 19, 23–4). Subs (1) does however permit infanticide to be charged as an offence in its own right as a defence on a charge of murder, and it is possible (albeit doubtful) that subs (2) would be construed as requiring the prosecution to disprove a defence of infanticide, whereas the burden of proving diminished responsibility rests on the defence.

Note that a mother may still be guilty of murdering her infant if the terms of the provision are not satisfied.

'by any wilful act or omission' Wilful conduct must at least be deliberate or intentional (*R v Senior* [1889] 1 QB 283) and in this context the *mens rea* must extend not just to the conduct itself but to its consequences (cf *R v Sheppard* [1981] AC 394). The Act appears to be concerned primarily with conduct which would have been murder at common law — and at common law that means there must be an intent to kill or an intent to cause grievous bodily harm: *R v Moloney* [1985] AC 905.

'Child under the age of twelve months' This must presumably be a reference to the age of the child at the time of the act or omission in question (rather than its age at the time of its death).

'her mind was disturbed by ... giving birth to the child' If the mother's mental disturbance results from any other cause, then the killing cannot amount to infanticide. Likewise if the mother kills an older child whilst disturbed by a more recent birth. On a charge of infanticide, however, an alternative verdict of manslaughter would be possible under s 6(3) of the Criminal Law Act 1967. This would have to be involuntary (constructive) manslaughter; but where the charge is murder, defences of diminished responsibility and infanticide could both be advanced (subs (3)).

'or the effect of lactation' Whilst post-natal depression is a well-recognised condition, it is now considered doubtful whether lactation has any significant effect. This reference to it reflects medical views prevalent when the legislation was enacted.

'notwithstanding that ... the offence would have amounted to murder' If intent to kill or cause grievous bodily harm cannot be proved, the offence might still amount to infanticide, but whether the charge be infanticide or murder, a manslaughter verdict might be possible under s 6(3) of the Criminal Law Act 1967.

as if she had been guilty of ... manslaughter.' As to the maximum penalty for manslaughter, see s 5 of the Offences Against the Person Act 1861. A hospital order or a probation order is normal in cases of infanticide.

Subs (3) Either verdict must be possible, even when the charge is infanticide; and see also s 2(2) of the Infant Life (Preservation) Act 1929, which provides a further alternative verdict of child destruction if this offence has been proved.

British Nationality Act 1948

(11 & 12 GEO VI C 56)

3. A British subject or citizen of the Republic of Ireland who is not a citizen of the United Kingdom and Colonies shall not be guilty of an offence against the laws of any part of the United Kingdom ... by reason of anything done or omitted in any Commonwealth country or in the Republic of Ireland or in any foreign country unless:

(a) the act or omission would be an offence if he were an alien; and
(b) in the case of an act or omission in a Commonwealth country or in the Republic of Ireland it would be an offence if that country ... were a foreign country.

Provided that nothing in this subsection shall apply to the contravention of any provision in the Merchant Shipping Acts 1894 to 1948.

NOTES
This provision is one of the few surviving from the Act, which for most other purposes has been supplanted by the British Nationality Act 1981. Many of the terms it uses must now be translated into their 1981 Act equivalents.

'British subject' The modern term for this is 'Commonwealth citizen', and the purpose of this section was to prevent the citizens of independent Commonwealth countries from being subject to extra-territorial UK criminal jurisdiction under such provisions as ss 9 or 57 of the Offences Against the Person Act 1861 (qqv)

'citizens of the United Kingdom and colonies' Persons who held this status prior to the introduction of the 1981 Act became British citizens, British overseas citizens or British Dependent Territories' citizens. These are the categories to whom this provision must now be taken to refer: see s 51 of the 1981 Act.

'Commonwealth citizens in other parts of the United Kingdom' This provision does not abate the potential liability of Commonwealth citizens in the UK (see for example the notes to s 57 of the Offences Against the Person Act 1861).

'offences on ships or aircraft' This provision does not abate the potential liability of Commonwealth citizens on ships or aircraft outside the territories of foreign or Commonwealth countries. In particular, it does not prevent them from incurring liability under ss 686 or 687 of the Merchant Shipping Act 1894 (qqv).

'extra-territorial liability of aliens or Commonwealth citizens' There are various extra-territorial offences for which aliens (and thus Commonwealth citizens) may incur liability under English criminal law. These include piracy *jure gentium*, hijacking, war crimes and, in certain circumstances, offences covered by s 4 of the Suppression of Terrorism Act 1978. Note also that a person in a foreign country may do an act which leads to the commission of a crime within England or Wales.

Prevention of Crime Act 1953

(1 & 2 ELIZ II C 14)

Prohibition of the carrying of offensive weapons without lawful authority or reasonable excuse

1. (1) Any person who without lawful authority or reasonable excuse, the proof whereof shall lie on him, has with him in any public place any offensive weapon shall be guilty of an offence, and shall be liable —

(a) on summary conviction, to imprisonment for a term not exceeding [six months] or a fine not exceeding [the prescribed sum] or both;

(b) on conviction on indictment, to imprisonment for a term not exceeding two years or a fine . . . or both.

(2) Where any person is convicted of an offence under subsection (1) of this section the court may make an order for the forfeiture or disposal of any weapon in respect of which the offence was committed.

(3) . . .

(4) In this section 'public place' includes any highway and any other premises or place to which at the material time the public have or are permitted to have access, whether on payment or otherwise; and 'offensive weapon' means any article made or adapted for use for causing injury to the person, or intended by the person having it with him for such use by him [or by some other person].

NOTES

'without lawful authority or reasonable excuse' Few persons have lawful authority to carry weapons which are offensive in the sense required by subs (4), the police and armed forces being the only obvious exceptions. See *Bryan v Mott* (1976) 62 Cr App R 71 at 73.

Reasonable excuse is a wider concept. It has been held that the routine carrying of weapons for the purpose of self-defence could not generally be regarded as reasonable; but it might be different where D is responding to a threat of immediate danger, and has armed himself in case he is attacked before he can obtain police protection: *Evans v Hughes* [1972] 3 All ER 412; *R v Spanner* [1973] Crim LR 704.

'the proof whereof shall lie on him' This is proof on the balance of probabilities. Note that D. only has to prove authority or excuse if the prosecution can first prove the basic elements of the offence, (eg that D. has a weapon and that it is offensive within the meaning of the Act).

'has with him' As with offences of 'possession', some mental element is required. D does not commit any offence if a weapon is 'planted' or concealed on him without his knowledge: *R v Cugullere* [1961] 2 All ER 343. See also *R v Russell* (1984) 81 Cr App R 315.

D may carry the weapon on his person or in his car *etc*; but it appears that the offence is not committed where D merely grabs a nearby object for immediate use as a weapon: *R v Dayle* [1973] 3 All ER 1151; *Ohlson v Hylton* [1975] 2 All ER 490. The essence of the offence is carrying a weapon before the need to use it arises.

'in any public place' See subs (4). The landings and stairways of buildings containing private flats may be public places, assuming that the public have free access to them (*Knox v Anderton* (1983) 76 Cr App R 156) but it would be different if security staff controlled such access.

'any offensive weapon' See subs (4). The courts will take judicial notice of the fact that some weapons (such as flick knives) are inherently offensive: *R v Simpson* [1983] 3 All ER 789. Where the weapon in question is neither made for, nor adapted for causing injury, but is allegedly carried for that purpose, then the prosecution will have to prove this purpose. In other cases, proof of possession will suffice, and it will then be for D to establish a reasonable excuse under subs (1).

See further *Copus v DPP* [1989] Crim LR 577.

Other legislation The carrying of articles with sharp blades or points is further covered by s 139 of the Criminal Justice Act 1988 (qv). For firearms, see ss 16-20 of the Firearms Act 1968. Trespassers who carry offensive weapons may be dealt with under s 8 of the Criminal Law Act 1977, and burglars under s 10 of the Theft Act 1968 (qqv).

Children and Young Persons (Harmful Publications) Act 1955

(3 & 4 ELIZ II C 28)

Works to which this Act applies
1. This Act applies to any book, magazine or other like work which is of a kind likely to fall into the hands of children or young persons and consists wholly or mainly of stories told in pictures (with or without the addition of written matter), being stories portraying —

(a) the commission of crimes; or

(b) acts of violence or cruelty; or

(c) incidents of a repulsive or horrible nature;

in such a way that the work as a whole would tend to corrupt a child or young person into whose hands it might fall.

NOTES
This Act appears to cover ground which is now also covered by the Obscene Publications Act 1959 (qv), although the latter has a much wider scope.

It is aimed primarily at certain kinds of violent and/or bizarre 'comics' or 'horror comics', many of which were once imported from the United States and which were aimed at young readers; but since many other kinds of publication are also 'likely' on occasions to fall into the hands of children (even if not intended for them), it may have a wider application than this.

'book, magazine or other like work' It may be argued that a video cassette is a 'like work', and thus within the scope of the Act, but the prosecution could avoid any need to argue the point by using the Obscenity Acts instead. It is doubtful whether this Act covers any items that the Obscenity Acts do not.

'tend to corrupt a child or young person' These are persons under the age of 17 (Children and Young Persons Act 1933 s 107). See the notes on 'tend to deprave or corrupt' in s 1 of the Obscenity Act 1959.

Penalty for printing, publishing, selling, &c, works to which this Act applies
2. (1) A person who prints, publishes, sells or lets on hire a work to which this Act applies, or has any such work in his possession for the purpose of selling it or letting it on hire, shall be guilty of an offence and liable, on summary conviction, to imprisonment for a term not exceeding four months or to a fine not exceeding [level 3 on the standard scale] or to both:

Provided that, in any proceedings taken under this subsection against a person in respect of selling or letting on hire a work or of having it in his possession for the purpose of selling it or letting it on hire, it shall be a defence for him to prove that he had not examined the contents of the work and had no reasonable cause to suspect that it was one to which this Act applies.

(2) A prosecution for an offence under this section shall not, in England or Wales, be instituted except by, or with the consent of, the Attorney General.

NOTES

'publishes' etc   The wide definition of 'publishing' in s 1 of the Obscene Publications Act 1959 (as amended) does not apply here, and this means for example that the mere lending of an article (as opposed to its letting for hire) is not within the scope of this provision.

'or has in his possession'   For the meaning of 'possession', see the notes to s 1 of the Firearms Act 1968; but note that, since possession is not an offence under this Act without proof of purpose, there can be no question of liability where D is unaware that he is in possession of the article in question. On the other hand, the offence is still one of strict liability to the extent that D may be convicted without proof that he was aware of the nature of that article. The defence provided by the proviso to subs (1) is not available to persons charged with printing or publishing offences.

3. [*omitted*]

Prohibition of importation of works to which this Act applies and articles for printing them

4. The importation of —

(a) any work to which this Act applies; and

(b) any plate prepared for the purpose of printing copies of any such work and any photographic film prepared for that purpose;

is hereby prohibited.

NOTES

This provision does not in itself create any offences, but brings the articles in question within the scope of relevant offences under the Customs and Excise Management Act 1979. See ss 49-50 of that Act (not printed in this work).

'photographic film'; 'plate'   See s 5(2) *infra*.

Short title, interpretation, extent, commencement and duration

5. (1) This Act may be cited as the Children and Young Persons (Harmful Publications) Act 1955.

(2) In this Act the expressions 'child' and 'young person' have the meanings assigned to them respectively by section one hundred and seven of the Children and Young Persons Act 1933 or, in Scotland, by section one hundred and ten of the Children and Young Persons (Scotland) Act 1937, the expression 'plate' (except where it occurs in the expression 'photographic plate') includes block, mould, matrix and stencil and the expression 'photographic film' includes photographic plate.

(3–4) [*omitted*]

Sexual Offences Act 1956

(4 & 5 ELIZ II C 69)

Intercourse by force, intimidation, etc

Rape
1. (1) It is [an offence for a man to rape a woman.]
(2) A man who induces a married woman to have sexual intercourse with him by impersonating her husband commits rape.

NOTES
This provision makes rape a statutory offence, but provides very little definitional guidance as to what that offence involves. A basic definition of rape is now contained in s 1 of the Sexual Offences (Amendment) Act 1976 (qv).

Penalty   The maximum penalty for rape or attempted rape is life imprisonment. See Sch 2 *infra*.

Procurement of woman by threats
2. (1) It is an offence for a person to procure a woman, by threats or intimidation, to have unlawful sexual intercourse in any part of the world.
(2) A person shall not be convicted of an offence under this section on the evidence of one witness only, unless the witness is corroborated in some material particular by evidence implicating the accused.

NOTES
'procure by threats or intimidation'   As with all offences of 'procuring', the offence is not committed until the specified object is achieved. Thus, if no unlawful sexual intercourse takes place, there can at most be liability for attempting to procure: *R v Johnson* [1964] 2 QB 404.
To 'procure' is to bring about or facilitate; there must therefore be some causal connection between the threats or intimidation and the unlawful intercourse (*cf R v Calhaem* [1988] 2 All ER 266).

'unlawful sexual intercourse'   Unlawful sexual intercourse need not be criminal; and, if it takes place abroad, then as far as English law is concerned it seldom will be. Any intercourse is unlawful except vaginal intercourse between husband and wife: *R v Chapman* [1959] 1 QB 100.
As to the meaning of 'sexual intercourse', see s 44 *infra*. Note that it includes unnatural intercourse (buggery).

'in any part of the world'   It would seem that it is the intercourse itself which may take place in any part of the world. If the woman herself is procured from abroad, but intercourse takes place within the jurisdiction, there may still be liability because the offence is then completed here (*cf R v Robert Millar (Contractors) Ltd* [1970] 2 QB 54), but if both procuring and intercourse take place abroad, there can be no liability unless the offender is a British seaman or subject to service discipline *etc*.

Intercourse with the procurer himself This is not excluded from the scope of the provisions (*R v Williams* (1898) 62 JP 310) but if intercourse takes place under intimidation *etc* and within the jurisdiction, a better charge would probably be rape. See notes to the Sexual Offences (Amendment) Act 1976, *infra*.

The corroboration requirement The strict corroboration requirement in this provision (also found in ss 3, 4, 22 and 23) goes further than the normal rule that a court or jury should be warned of the danger of convicting on the uncorroborated evidence of a complainant in an alleged sexual offence.

For a full discussion of the subject, see Andrews & Hirst, *Criminal Evidence*, Ch. 9.

Mode of trial and penalties See Sch 2 *infra*.

Procurement of woman by false pretences

3. (1) It is an offence for a person to procure a woman, by false pretences or false representations, to have unlawful sexual intercourse in any part of the world.

(2) A person shall not be convicted of an offence under this section on the evidence of one witness only, unless the witness is corroborated in some material particular by evidence implicating the accused.

NOTES
See generally the notes to s 2 *supra*. This offence differs only in that it requires procurement by false pretences or representations rather than by threats or intimidation.

'false pretences or false representations' These would include deceptions as to the very nature of the sexual act, in which case there may also be liability for rape (if committed within the jurisdiction). See *R v Williams* [1923] 1 KB 340. This provision would also appear to cover cases in which women are lured abroad for an ostensibly innocent purpose and then subjected to unlawful intercourse.

It has been held that a statement as to future conduct cannot constitute a false pretence (*R v Dent* [1955] 2 QB 510); but it may possibly constitute a false representation as to the *present* intentions of the person making it. *Cf Edgington v Fitzmaurice* (1885) 29 Ch D 459.

Penalties, etc See Sch 2 *infra*.

Administering drugs to obtain or facilitate intercourse

4. (1) It is an offence for a person to apply or administer to, or cause to be taken by, a woman any drug, matter or thing with intent to stupefy or overpower her so as thereby to enable any man to have unlawful sexual intercourse with her.

(2) A person shall not be convicted of an offence under this section on the evidence of one witness only, unless the witness is corroborated in some material particular by evidence implicating the accused.

NOTES
This is not a 'procuring' offence, and is complete once the drugs, *etc.* have been administered. It is not necessary that the woman should successfully be stupified or overpowered, or that sexual intercourse should be attempted. It does however require a specific intent to facilitate intercourse by such means.

'apply or administer to or cause to be taken by' As in cases of administering noxious substances, contrary to ss 23 or 24 of the Offences Against the

Person Act 1861, substances may be 'administered' in all kinds of ways. Spraying or squirting gas, ammonia *etc* is included: *R v Gillard, The Times,* 7 April 1988. If D encourages P to drink excessive quantities of alcohol, this might possibly be interpreted as 'causing' her to take it, but this would be questionable, because P would be exercising some choice. Secretly lacing P's drinks with strong spirits or drugs would however be a clear case of 'causing to be taken' — see *R v Marcus* [1981] 2 All ER 833.

'drug, matter or thing'   These terms appear to embrace all kinds of incapacitating devices — including ropes and coshes as well as drugs.

'with intent ... to enable any man'   'Man' includes boy (see s 46 *infra*). A boy of under 14 is deemed incapable of sexual intercourse (*R v Waite* [1892] 2 QB 600) but this need not prevent the accused from having the specified intent. One can intend something even if it turns out to be unachievable.

Unlawful sexual intercourse   See s 44 *infra* and the notes to s 2 *supra*.

Administering drugs, etc and rape   If a woman is successfully stupefied or overpowered, and natural intercourse then takes place, there may then be liability for rape (as perpetrator or as a secondary party) since the woman will not have consented. See further the notes to s 1 of the Sexual Offences (Amendment) Act 1976. (If it is unnatural intercourse, the offence will be buggery contrary to s 12 of the present Act).

Corroboration   See notes to s 2 *supra*.

Mode of trial and penalty   See Sch 2 *infra*.

Intercourse with girls under sixteen

Intercourse with girl under thirteen
   5. It is an offence for a man to have unlawful sexual intercourse with a girl under the age of thirteen.

NOTES
An offence under this provision may also amount to rape if the child in question does not consent and the man knows or is reckless as to this fact. In particular a very young girl may not have sufficient understanding to give genuine consent.
   On rape, see s 1 of the Sexual Offences (Amendment) Act 1976.

'man'   A boy aged under 14 years is deemed to be incapable of sexual intercourse (*R v Waite* [1892] 2 QB 600) but may be guilty of indecent assault (*R v Williams* [1893] 1 QB 320) or of secondary participation in an act of unlawful intercourse (*R v Eldershaw* (1828) 3 C & P 316), as may a woman (*R v Ram* (1893) 17 Cox CC 609).

'unlawful sexual intercourse'   See s 44 *infra* and the notes to s 2 *supra*.

'with a girl under the age of 13'   A mistake as to the age of the girl, even if reasonable, will afford no defence. In this respect the offence is one of strict liability (*cf R v Prince* (1875) LR 2 CCR 154).

Liability of girl   See notes to s 6 *infra*.

Mode of trial and penalty   The maximum penalty is life imprisonment. See further Sch 2 *infra*.

Intercourse with girl between thirteen and sixteen
6. (1) It is an offence, subject to the exceptions mentioned in this section, for a man to have unlawful sexual intercourse with a girl under the age of sixteen.

(2) Where a marriage is invalid under section two of the Marriage Act, 1949 (the wife being a girl under the age of sixteen), the invalidity does not make the husband guilty of an offence under this section because he has sexual intercourse with her, if he believes her to be his wife and has reasonable cause for the belief.

(3) A man is not guilty of an offence under this section because he has unlawful sexual intercourse with a girl under the age of sixteen, if he is under the age of twenty-four and has not previously been charged with a like offence, and he believes her to be of the age of sixteen or over and has reasonable cause for the belief.

In this subsection, 'a like offence' means an offence under this section or an attempt to commit one.

NOTES
This offence could originally be committed only in respect of girls between the ages of 13 and 16. As a result of amendment by s 10(1) and Sch 2 of the Criminal Law Act 1967, it will now be no defence on a charge under s 6 to show that the girl was in fact under 13 and that the accused was therefore guilty of the more serious offence under s 5.

'man' See notes to s 5 *supra*.

'unlawful sexual intercourse' See s 44 *infra* and the notes to s 2 *supra*. A foreigner who contracts a valid marriage in his own country with a girl aged 15 would not offend against this section if he has intercourse with her during their honeymoon in England, because the intercourse would be 'lawful' (*cf Mohamad v Knott* [1968] 2 All ER 563).

'with a girl under the age of 16' The general rule is that a mistake as to the girl's age, even if reasonable, will afford no defence. In this respect the offence is one of strict liability, using the principle derived from *R v Prince* (1875) LR 2 CCR 154. The general rule is, however, subject to the 'young man's defence' provided by subs (3).

The 'invalid marriage' exception (subs (2)) Being an exception to the generality of subs (1), the burden of proving this lies with the defence: s 47 *infra*. Cases falling within this subsection will be very rare. (Note that the Age of Marriage Act 1929 was repealed by the Affiliation Proceedings Act 1957 and the original reference to it has accordingly been omitted.)

The young man's defence (subs (3)) Here again, s 47 places the burden of proving the defence on the accused. It has been held that the defence is not available to a man who fails to direct his mind as to the girl's age — even if there would then have been reasonable grounds for him to conclude that she was over 16: *R v Banks* [1916] 2 KB 621. On the other hand, it has been held (at first instance) that a person is not 'charged with a like offence' for these purposes until he appears before a court with jurisdiction to try him. Thus, the fact that he has previously been 'charged' by the police (or even committed for trial) would not prevent him from claiming the defence in respect of an incident taking place before the trial for that first offence: *R v Rider* [1954] 1 All ER 5.

The defence provided by subs (3) does not prevent the man being charged or convicted of an offence of indecent assault under s 24 *infra*: *R v Laws* (1928) 21 Cr

App R 45; *R v McCormack* [1969] 3 All ER 371. Moreover, s 6(3) of the Criminal Law Act 1967 allows a jury to convict under s 14 where the charge is one of unlawful intercourse under s 6: *R v McCormack, supra.*

Liability of girl or of doctors prescribing contraceptives   An underaged girl cannot aid, abet *etc* a sexual offence against herself: *R v Tyrell* [1894] 1 QB 710, although she may be guilty of an indecent assault on her lover if he too is under 16. A doctor providing contraceptive advice or treatment to such a girl does not necessarily counsel or procure an offence under this provision, nor does he necessarily commit an offence under s 28 *infra*; but this depends on the facts:

> 'Clearly a doctor who gives a girl contraceptive advice or treatment, not because in his clinical judgment the treatment is medically indicated for the maintenance or restoration of her health, but with the intention of facilitating her having unlawful sexual intercourse, may well be guilty of a criminal offence.' (*Gillick v West Norfolk AHA* [1986] AC 112 *per* Lord Scarman at 190).

Mode of trial and penalty   See Sch 2 *infra.*

Intercourse with defective

7. (1) It is an offence, subject to the exception mentioned in this section, for a man to have unlawful sexual intercourse with a woman who is a defective.

(2) A man is not guilty of an offence under this section because he has unlawful sexual intercourse with a woman if he does not know and has no reason to suspect her to be a defective.

NOTES
'man'   See notes to s 5 *supra.*

'unlawful sexual intercourse'   See s 44 *infra* and notes to s 2 *supra.*

'subject to the exception'   Under s 47 *infra* the burden of proving the exception lies with the defence. Failing this, it remains an offence of strict liability.

'with a woman'   Or a girl (see s 46 *infra.*)

'who is a defective'   *Ie* suffering from a state of arrested or incomplete development of mind, which includes severe impairment of intelligence and social functioning: s 45 *infra* (as substituted by s 127(1)(b) of the Mental Health Act 1959, now the Mental Health (Amendment) Act 1982, Sch 3). See *R v Hall, The Times,* 15 July 1987.

Mode of trial and penalty   See Sch 2 *infra.*

8. [*repealed*]

Procurement of defective

9. (1) It is an offence, subject to the exception mentioned in this section, for a person to procure a woman who is a defective to have unlawful sexual intercourse in any part of the world.

(2) A person is not guilty of an offence under this section because he procures a defective to have unlawful sexual intercourse, if he does not know and has no reason to suspect her to be a defective.

NOTES

'procure' See notes to s 2 *supra*.

'a woman who is a defective' See notes to s 7 *supra*.

'subject to the exception' See notes to s 7 *supra*.

'unlawful sexual intercourse' See s 44 *infra* and notes to s 2 *supra*.

'in any part of the world' See notes to s 2 *supra*.

Corroboration In contrast to the other 'procurement' offences in this Act, no mandatory corroboration requirement is stipulated here.

Mode of trial and penalty See Sch 2 *infra*.

Incest

Incest by a man
10. (1) It is an offence for a man to have sexual intercourse with a woman whom he knows to be his grand-daughter, daughter, sister or mother.

(2) In the foregoing subsection "sister" includes half-sister, and for the purposes of that subsection any expression importing a relationship between two people shall be taken to apply notwithstanding that the relationship is not traced through lawful wedlock.

NOTES

This provision is mirrored (as regards incest by women) in s 11 *infra*.

'man' See notes to s 5 *supra*.

'sexual intercourse' See s 44 *infra*. Note that intercourse includes unnatural intercourse, but not other sexual behaviour. Thus consensual 'petting' or oral-genital contact between persons over the age of 16 will not generally involve any criminal offence. Where one or both parties are under 16, liability may arise under ss 14 or 15 *infra*).

'with a woman' or girl (see s 46 *infra*).

'grand-daughter, sister or mother' This includes half-sisters and illegitimate daughters *etc* (subs (2)), but note that adopted children or adoptive parents *etc* are not included; nor does the adoption of a child prevent the law of incest applying to subsequent sexual relationships with members of his original family: Adoption Act 1976, s 73 and Sch 4.

Intercourse with cousins, aunts, nieces or grandmothers(!) cannot be incest.

Incest by a woman
11.—(1) It is an offence for a woman of the age of sixteen or over to permit a man whom she knows to be her grandfather, father, brother or son to have sexual intercourse with her by her consent.

(2) In the foregoing subsection "brother" includes half-brother, and for the purposes of that subsection any expression importing a relationship between two people shall be taken to apply notwithstanding that the relationship is not traced through lawful wedlock.

NOTES
See generally the notes to s 10 *supra*. A girl under 16 cannot be guilty either of perpetrating or of aiding and abetting any offence of unlawful intercourse involving herself (*R v Tyrell* [1894] 1 QB 710), but she may be guilty of indecently assaulting her lover if he is under 16.

Unnatural offences

Buggery
12. (1) It is an offence for a person to commit buggery with another person or with an animal.

(2) [*repealed*]

(3) [*repealed*]

NOTES
Buggery is not defined in the Act, but it bears its common law meaning of unnatural sexual intercourse, *viz* anal intercourse (whether homosexual or hetero-sexual) or intercourse (vaginal or anal) with an animal. Except where s 1 of the Sexual Offences Act 1967 applies, consent is not a defence, and in the absence of a defence such as duress, infancy or coercion, the consenting passive (or patient) party is guilty as well as the active (or agent).

Like natural intercourse, the unnatural form is 'complete' upon penetration and no ejaculation is required (s 44 *infra*).

'animal' In this context birds (such as fowls or turkeys) are 'animals' (*R v Brown* (1889) 24 QBD 357).

De-criminalisation of certain homosexual acts Under certain circum-stances covered by the Sexual Offences Act 1967 (*qv*), homosexual buggery may not amount to an offence (although it remains 'unlawful').

Penalties The maximum penalty for buggery with a woman or boy under 16 or an animal is life imprisonment (Sch 2, as amended). In practice, however, the courts view Parliament's failure to decriminalise consensual heterosexual buggery between adults as an anomaly. It is considered important that a man should not be subjected to serious penalties for buggery with an adult woman unless it has been proved that there was no consent (*R v Newton* (1983) 77 Cr Apr R 13).

For homosexual acts, the penalties are set out in s 3 of the 1967 Act. In view of these different penalties, the House of Lords concluded in *R v Courtie* [1984] AC 463 that s 12 now contains several distinct offences.

The 1967 Act imposes further restrictions on prosecutions for homosexual buggery or gross indecency: see s 7 (time limits on institution of proceedings) and s 8 (consent of DPP required).

Indecency between men
13. It is an offence for a man to commit an act of gross indecency with another man, whether in public or private, or to be a party to the commission by a man of an act of gross indecency with another man, or to procure the commission by a man of an act of gross indecency with another man.

NOTES
This provision effectively restates s 11 of the Criminal Law Amendment Act 1885, and cases decided under the earlier provision remain valid (*R v Preece* [1977] 1 QB 370 at 375). In certain circumstances (as with buggery), acts of gross indecency

committed in private have ceased to be criminal by virtue of the Sexual Offences Act 1967.

'gross indecency' There is a dearth of authority as to the exact meaning of this term. It must to some extent be a question of fact for a jury to decide. In practice, cases brought under s 13 generally involve acts of mutual or collective masturbation or oral sex, often with an exhibitionist element.

'with another man' Although it is not necessary for one man to touch or attempt to touch the other, it is necessary for at least two men to be 'acting in concert' and 'making an exhibition of themselves': *R v Hunt* [1950] 2 All ER 291; *R v Hornby* [1966] 2 All ER 487; *R v Preece* [1977] QB 370. Insofar as it suggests otherwise, *R v Hill* [1964] 1 QB 273 is incorrect. One man acting alone in front of others may possibly be guilty of indecent exposure or of attempting to procure the others to commit similar acts of gross indecency: *R v Preece (supra)*. At the same time, the evidence may be such that only one man can be convicted (*ibid.*)

'or to be a party to' *Ie* aid, abet, counsel, *etc.* Such liability for secondary participation would in any case appear to arise under the Accessories and Abettors Act 1861 or the Magistrates' Court Act 1980.

'or to procure' As to the meaning of procuring, see notes to s 2 *supra*. See also *R v Bently* [1923] 1 KB 403 (where D was convicted of unsuccessfully inciting E to procure boys for D's own purposes) and s 4 of the 1967 Act.

De-criminalisation of certain homosexual acts and restrictions on prosecutions See notes to s 12 *supra*.

Penalties The usual maximum penalty is two years' imprisonment, but it may be five years where s 3(2) of the 1967 Act applies. See *R v Courtie* [1984] AC 463.

Assaults

Indecent assault on a woman

14. (1) It is an offence, subject to the exception mentioned in subsection (3) of this section, for a person to make an indecent assault on a woman.

(2) A girl under the age of sixteen cannot in law give any consent which would prevent an act being an assault for the purposes of this section.

(3) Where a marriage is invalid under section two of the Marriage Act, 1949, (the wife being a girl under the age of sixteen), the invalidity does not make the husband guilty of any offence under this section by reason of her incapacity to consent while under that age, if he believes her to be his wife and has reasonable cause for the belief.

(4) A woman who is a defective cannot in law give any consent which would prevent an act being an assault for the purposes of this section, but a person is only to be treated as guilty of an indecent assault on a defective by reason of that incapacity to consent, if that person knew or had reason to suspect her to be a defective.

NOTES
An offence under this provision may be committed by a person of either sex. It may involve some kind of sexual attack, or it may involve some kind of consensual sexual activity in circumstances where the girl's or woman's consent is deemed to be invalid. The inability of a girl under 16 or a defective to give valid consent is dealt with in subss (2) and (4), but the consent of a normal adult woman will also be invalid if the assault in question is calculated to cause her actual bodily harm or worse: *R v Donovan* [1934] 2 KB 498.

'assault' This term has the same meaning as in common assault *etc*. In other words, it may mean either a battery or an act which causes the woman to apprehend an imminent battery: *R v Rolfe* (1952) 36 Cr App R 4; *Beal v Kelley* [1951] 2 All ER 763. Valid consent negatives any assault.

Indecency without assault does not fall within this provision (*Fairclough v Whipp* [1951] 2 All ER 834) but, if directed at children under 14 years old, it may involve an offence under the Indecency with Children Act 1960 (*qv*); and 'flashing' (lewd and obscene exposure of the penis) may, if done with intent to insult a woman, constitute an offence under s 4 of the Vagrancy Act 1824 (*qv*).

'indecent' As the House of Lords has recently emphasised in *R v Court* [1988] 2 WLR 1071, it is the element of indecency which distinguishes this potentially serious offence from the relatively minor offence of common assault.

As far as the *actus reus* is concerned, there must be something 'objectively' indecent about it. If D is sexually excited by touching a woman's foot or removing her shoe, his sexual motive in so doing cannot turn this objectively harmless act into a sexual assault: *R v George* [1956] Crim LR 52. If, however, D's conduct is capable of being construed as indecent, it is still necessary to prove an 'indecent intent'. Recklessness as to indecency will not suffice: *R v Court, supra*. D's intent may, but need not, involve a sexual motive. It will suffice if he intends only to embarrass or humiliate the woman; but evidence of a secret sexual motive may be relevant and admissible to prove that an assault (*eg* a spanking) was indecent (*ibid*).

'on a woman' Or a girl — see s 46 *infra*.

Invalid consent (subss (2) and (4)) These subsections are based on the same principles as ss 6 and 7 *supra*; just as girls or defectives cannot consent to intercourse, so too are they unable to consent to other forms of sexual activity.

Subs (2) is, however, different from s 6 in that there is no equivalent to the 'young man's defence' provided by s 6(3). A man who successfully pleads that defence would have no defence to a charge brought under s 14 (*R v Laws* (1928) 21 Cr App R 45) unless he has remained completely passive throughout the entire sexual act. Moreover, s 6(3) of the Criminal Law Act 1967 allows a jury to convict under s 14 where the indictment alleges only an offence of unlawful intercourse: *R v McCormack* [1969] 3 All ER 371. A mistake as to the girl's age is therefore entirely a matter of strict liability.

In contrast, subs (4) may be *more* favourable to the accused than s 7, in which, by virtue of s 47, he has the burden of proving the defence of 'no knowledge or reason for suspicion'. S 47 does not appear to apply to subs (4); therefore the burden of *disproving* a defence of 'no knowledge or reason for suspicion' will be on the prosecution. As to the meaning of '*defective*' in subs (4), see the notes to s 7.

Mistake as to consent In situations not covered by subss (2) or (4) a mistaken belief in the woman's consent will be a defence, even if the mistake is not a reasonable one: *R v Kimber* [1983] 3 All ER 316.

The 'invalid marriage' exception: (subs (3)) See notes to s 6(2) *supra*.

Penalties The original maximum penalty provided by Sch 2 *infra* was increased by s 3(3) of the Sexual Offences Act 1985 and is now ten years.

Indecent assault on a man

15. (1) It is an offence for a person to make an indecent assault on a man.

(2) A boy under the age of sixteen cannot in law give any consent which would prevent an act being an assault for the purposes of this section.

(3) A man who is a defective cannot in law give any consent which would prevent an act being an assault for the purposes of this section, but

a person is only to be treated as guilty of an indecent assault on a defective by reason of that incapacity to consent, if that person knew or had reason to suspect him to be a defective.

(4) [*repealed*]
(5) [*repealed*]

NOTES
See generally the notes to s 14 *supra*. In most respects this provision merely 'mirrors' s 14.

It is not an offence for a woman or girl to have intercourse with a boy under the age of 16, but, unless the woman adopts a completely passive role in the sexual act, she will almost inevitably be guilty of indecently assaulting him (*Faulkner v Talbot* [1981] 3 All ER 468). A mistake as to the boy's age will be no defence.

Penalties See Sch 2 *infra*.

Assault with intent to commit buggery
16. (1) It is an offence for a person to assault another person with intent to commit buggery.

NOTES
'assault' As to the meaning of assault, see notes to s 47 of the Offences Against the Person Act 1861. In the present context, the only likely cause of difficulty concerns the effect of consent on the part of the alleged victim. Where s 1 of the Sexual Offences Act 1967 would apply so as to prevent an actual act of buggery being an offence, there would equally be no assault for the purposes of this provision. In other cases, however, consent would be invalid for the purpose of the actual buggery (see notes to s 12 *supra*) and it is submitted that the same must probably be true of the assault under this provision.

'buggery' See notes to s 12 *supra*.

'with intent' There is no need for any actual attempt at penetration, *etc*. This is simply a matter of ulterior intent.

Penalty See Sch 2 *infra*.

Abduction

Abduction of woman by force or for the sake of her property
17. (1) It is an offence for a person to take away or detain a woman against her will with the intention that she shall marry or have unlawful sexual intercourse with that or any other person, if she is so taken away or detained either by force or for the sake of her property or expectations of property.

(2) In the foregoing subsection, the reference to a woman's expectations of property relates only to property of a person to whom she is next of kin or one of the next of kin, and 'property' includes any interest in property.

NOTES
With a maximum penalty of 14 years' imprisonment (as against just two years under ss 19–21), this is potentially a very serious offence. Although it appears somewhat archaic, it may well be applicable in a number of modern scenarios, including cases in which women are abducted with a view to rape and cases in

which girls from certain immigrant communities are forcibly taken abroad for the purpose of arranged marriages.

'unlawful sexual intercourse' See s 44 *infra* and the notes to s 2 *supra*.

'woman' Includes 'girl' (see s 46 *infra*).

'by force' This must presumably include a threat of force. Any other interpretation would produce surprising anomalies between cases in which mild force is used and cases in which the mere threat of serious violence ensures the victim's compliance.

Penalty See Sch 2 *infra*.

18. [*repealed*]

Abduction of unmarried girl under eighteen from parent or guardian
19. (1) It is an offence, subject to the exception mentioned in this section, for a person to take an unmarried girl under the age of eighteen out of the possession of her parent or guardian against his will, if she is so taken with the intention that she shall have unlawful sexual intercourse with men or with a particular man.

(2) A person is not guilty of an offence under this section because he takes such a girl out of the possession of her parent or guardian as mentioned above, if he believes her to be of the age of eighteen or over and has reasonable cause for the belief.

(3) In this section 'guardian' means any person having the lawful care or charge of the girl.

NOTES
If it can be proved that the girl in question was taken against her will and by force, then the better charge would appear to be under s 17 *supra*. If no intention to have or to procure unlawful sexual intercourse can be proved, the charge should be under s 20 *infra*.

'subject to the exception mentioned in this section' The burden of proving a defence under subs (2) lies on the accused by virtue of s 47 *infra*. Failing this, a mistake as to the girl's age is a matter of strict liability under the principle established in *R v Prince* (1875) LR 2 CCR 154.

'take out of the possession of her parent or guardian' It is no defence to show that the girl consented to or even suggested the 'taking' (*R v Mankletow* (1853) Dears CC 159); but, if D neither persuades nor assists her in leaving home *etc*, he is not guilty: *R v Alexander* (1912) 107 LT 240. The taking need not be permanent, nor intended to be (*R v Timmins* (1860) 8 Cox CC 401) but it must involve something more than mere 'dating' or going for a walk *etc*: *R v Jones* [1973] Crim LR 621.

If D does not realise that the girl is in her parent's or guardian's 'possession', then he is not guilty (*R v Hibbert* (1869) LR 1 CCR 184) unless perhaps he is accounted reckless as to that fact.

'against his will' *Ie* the parent would not have consented to it had he known: *R v Handley* (1855) 1 F & F 648.

'unlawful sexual intercourse' See s 44 *infra* and the notes to s 2 *supra*.

Penalty See Sch 2 *infra*.

Abduction of unmarried girl under sixteen from parent or guardian

20. (1) It is an offence for a person acting without lawful authority or excuse to take an unmarried girl under the age of sixteen out of the possession of her parent or guardian against his will.

(2) In the foregoing subsection 'guardian' means any person having the lawful care or charge of the girl.

NOTES

There need not in fact be any sexual element or interest in this offence: if there is an intent to have unlawful sexual intercourse a change may be brought under s 19 *supra*. S 20 would however apply where D elopes with P with the object of marrying her.

'acting without lawful authority or excuse'   Although this offence is not triable summarily, the elusive principle stated in s 101 of the Magistrates' Courts Act 1980 is equally valid in trials on indictment: *R v Hunt* [1987] 1 All ER 1. A defence of 'lawful authority' might therefore require the accused to prove the existence of that authority. See generally Andrews & Hirst, *Criminal Evidence*, Ch 3.

'take . . . out of the possession of her parent or guardian'   See notes to s 19 *supra*.

Mens rea   As to the age of the girl, liability is strict: *R v Prince* (1875) LR 2 CCR 154. There is no defence akin to that provided in s 19(2) *supra*. In contrast, *mens rea* is required as to the fact that the girl is in the possession of her parent or guardian: *R v Hibbert* (1869) LR 1 CCR 184; *R v Green* (1863) 3 F & F 274.

Penalty   See Sch 2 *infra*.

Abduction of defective from parent or guardian

21. (1) It is an offence, subject to the exception mentioned in this section, for a person to take a woman who is a defective out of the possession of her parent or guardian against his will, if she is so taken with the intention that she shall have unlawful sexual intercourse with men or with a particular man.

(2) A person is not guilty of an offence under this section because he takes such a woman out of the possession of her parent or guardian as mentioned above, if he does not know and has no reason to suspect her to be a defective.

(3) In this section 'guardian' means any person having the lawful care or charge of the woman.

NOTES

In most respects this provision is similar to s 19 *supra*.

'defective'   See s 45 *infra*.

Penalty   See Sch 2 *infra*.

Prostitution, procuration etc

Causing prostitution of women

22. (1) It is an offence for a person:

(a) to procure a woman to become, in any part of the world, a common prostitute; or

(b) to procure a woman to leave the United Kingdom, intending her to become an inmate of or frequent a brothel elsewhere; or

(c) to procure a woman to leave her usual place of abode in the United Kingdom, intending her to become an inmate of or frequent a brothel in any part of the world for the purposes of prostitution.

(2) A person shall not be convicted of an offence under this section on the evidence of one witness only, unless the witness is corroborated in some material particular by evidence implicating the accused.

NOTES

'procure'   As with other offences of 'procuring', these offences are not committed until and unless one of the specified objects is achieved. Thus, in subs (1)(a) the woman must actually become a prostitute; in (b) she must leave the United Kingdom; and in (c) she must leave her usual place of abode. Failing this, there can at most be liability for an attempt: see *R v Johnson* [1964] 2 QB 404.

To 'procure' is to bring about or facilitate. There must therefore be some causal connection between the accused's behaviour and the woman's actions: *R v Christian* (1913) 23 Cox CC 541. (*Cf R v Calhaem* [1985] 2 All ER 266).

'woman'   or girl. See s 46 *infra*.

'to become ... in any part of the world'   No offence is committed under this provision where the woman is *procured* entirely outside the jurisdiction. An offence under subs (1)(a) might however be committed where a woman is procured from overseas and becomes a prostitute in England and Wales, because the procuring is thus completed within the jurisdiction. (*Cf R v Robert Millar (Contractors) Ltd* [1970] 2 QB 54). Nevertheless, this would be an unintended and secondary consequence of the provision, which was clearly designed to prohibit the procuring of women *from* England and Wales.

'to become'   It has been held that no offence is committed under this provision where the woman involved was aleady a prostitute when first procured: *R v Gold* (1907) 71 JP 360.

'to leave the United Kingdom'   The Act does not apply to Scotland or Northern Ireland (see s 54). No offence is therefore committed under this provision where a woman is procured to leave Scotland for a foreign country, or to leave her usual place of abode in Northern Ireland. But, as far as subs (1)(b) is concerned, it will not suffice that the woman concerned leaves England for Scotland or Northern Ireland.

'common prostitute'   A prostitute is a woman or girl 'who offers her body for purposes amounting to common lewdness for payment in return': *R v de Munck* [1918] 1 KB 635. Sexual intercourse itself is not essential. Thus a woman who masturbates clients in a 'massage parlour' is a type of prostitute: *R v Webb* [1964] 1 QB 357. So too is one who whips her clients (*ibid*). A single act of prostitution does not necessarily make the woman a 'common' prostitute. See *R v Morris-Lowe* [1985] 1 All ER 400.

'brothel'   See notes to s 24 *infra*.

'for the purposes of prostitution (subs (1)(c)) See the notes on the meaning of 'common prostitute' *supra.*

The corroboration requirement See notes to s 1 *supra.*

Penalty See Sch 2 *infra.*

Procuration of girl under twenty-one

23. (1) It is an offence for a person to procure a girl under the age of twenty-one to have unlawful sexual intercourse in any part of the world with a third person.

(2) A person shall not be convicted of an offence under this section on the evidence of one witness only, unless the witness is corroborated in some material particular by evidence implicating the accused.

NOTES

'procure' See notes to s 2 *supra.*

'unlawful sexual intercourse' See notes to s 2 *supra.* In contrast to offences under ss 2 or 3, there need be no coercion or deception involved. The girl may be quite willing.

'in any part of the world' See notes to s 2 *supra.*

The corroboration requirement See notes to s 2 *supra.*

Penalty See Sch 2 *infra.*

Detention of woman in brothel or other premises

24. (1) It is an offence for a person to detain a woman against her will on any premises with the intention that she shall have unlawful sexual intercourse with men or with a particular man, or to detain a woman against her will in a brothel.

(2) Where a woman is on any premises for the purpose of having unlawful sexual intercourse or is in a brothel, a person shall be deemed for the purpose of the foregoing subsection to detain her there if, with the intention of compelling or inducing her to remain there, he either withholds from her her clothes or any other property belonging to her or threatens her with legal proceedings in the event of her taking away clothes provided for her by him or on his directions.

(3) A woman shall not be liable to any legal proceedings, whether civil or criminal, for taking away or being found in possession of any clothes she needed to enable her to leave premises on which she was for the purpose of having unlawful sexual intercourse or to leave a brothel.

NOTES

The meaning and effect of this provision is clear and requires little explanation; but note that where a woman or girl is detained in a brothel there is no need for it to be proved that she is detained there for sexual purposes.

'brothel' This not defined anywhere in the Act, but at common law it means a place wherein women offer themselves as participants in physical acts of indecency for the sexual gratification of men. The women need not be prostitutes and sexual intercourse need not take place, but more than one woman must be involved: *Kelly* *v Purvis* [1983] 1 All ER 525. The wider definition provided by s 6 of the Sexual Offences Act 1967 (which includes places used for homosexual prostitution) is not applicable here.

'woman' Or a girl: see s 46 *infra*.

'unlawful sexual intercourse' See s 44 *infra* and the notes to s 2 *supra*.

Penalty See Sch 2 *infra*.

Permitting girl under thirteen to use premises for intercourse
25. It is an offence for a person who is the owner or occupier of any premises, or who has, or acts or assists in, the management or control of any premises, to induce or knowingly suffer a girl under the age of thirteen to resort to or be on those premises for the purpose of having unlawful sexual intercourse with men or with a particular man.

NOTES
This provision complements s 5 *supra*.

'premises' These may be the girl's own home and the offenders may be the girl's own parents if they knowingly allow her to have sexual intercourse there with her boyfriend(s) or 'clients'. See *R v Webster* (1885) 16 QBD 134.

'unlawful sexual intercourse' See s 44 *infra* and the notes to s 2 *supra*, but note that the offence may be committed even if no such intercourse actually takes place.

Penalty See Sch 2 *infra*.

Permitting girl between thirteen and sixteen to use premises for intercourse
26. It is an offence for a person who is the owner or occupier of any premises, or who has, or acts or assists in, the management or control of any premises, to induce or knowingly suffer a girl ... under the age of sixteen, to resort to or be on those premises for the purpose of having unlawful sexual intercourse with men or with a particular man.

NOTES
This provision is in most respects identical to s 25 *supra* (see notes thereto) but attracts less severe penalties.

'under the age of sixteen' It is no defence to show that the girl was under the age of thirteen. To this extent this provision overlaps with s 25. The overlap was created by s 10(1) and Sch 2 of the Criminal Law Act 1967 to avoid problems for the prosecution in cases where there is some uncertainty as to whether the child was under or over thirteen at the crucial time.

Penalty See Sch 2 *infra*.

Permitting defective to use premises for intercourse
27. (1) It is an offence, subject to the exception mentioned in this section, for a person who is the owner or occupier of any premises, or who has, or acts or assists in, the management or control of any premises, to induce or knowingly suffer a woman who is a defective to resort to or be on those premises for the purpose of having unlawful sexual intercourse with men or with a particular man.

(2) A person is not guilty of an offence under this section because he induces or knowingly suffers a defective to resort to or be on any premises for the purpose mentioned, if he does not know and has no reason to suspect her to be a defective.

NOTES
In most respects this provision is similar to ss 25 and 26 *supra* (see notes to s 25).

As far as the 'exception' under subs (2) is concerned, the burden of proving the defence rests on the accused by reason of s 47 *infra*.

'defective' See s 45 *infra*.

Penalty See Sch 2 *infra*.

Causing or encouraging prostitution of, intercourse with, or indecent assault on, girl under sixteen

28. (1) It is an offence for a person to cause or encourage the prostitution of, or the commission of unlawful sexual intercourse with, or of an indecent assault on, a girl under the age of sixteen for whom he is responsible.

(2) Where a girl has become a prostitute, or has had unlawful sexual intercourse, or has been indecently assaulted, a person shall be deemed for the purposes of this section to have caused or encouraged it, if he knowingly allowed her to consort with, or to enter or continue in the employment of, any prostitute or person of known immoral character.

(3) The persons who are to be treated for the purposes of this section as responsible for a girl are (subject to the next following subsection):

(a) any person who is her parent or legal guardian; and

(b) any person who has actual possession or control of her, or to whose charge she has been committed by her parent or legal guardian or by a person having the custody of her; and

(c) any other person who has the custody, charge or care of her.

(4) In the last foregoing subsection:

(a) 'parent' does not include, in relation to any girl, a person deprived of the custody of her by order of a court of competent jurisdiction but (subject to that), in the case of a girl who is illegitimate, ... means her mother and any person who has been adjudged to be her putative father;

(b) 'legal guardian' means, in relation to any girl, any person who is for the time being her guardian, having been appointed according to law by deed or will or by order of a court of competent jurisdiction.

(5) If, on a charge of an offence against a girl under this section, the girl appears to the court to have been under the age of sixteen at the time of the offence charged, she shall be presumed for the purposes of this section to have been so, unless the contrary is proved.

NOTES
In many cases, persons who cause or encourage the commission of acts of unlawful intercourse or indecent assault on girls under the age of sixteen years will be guilty as accessories to offences under ss 6 or 14 *supra*, but by virtue of subs (2) acts or

omissions which might not amount to counselling or abetting or procuring under s 8 of the Accessories and Abettors Act 1861 may nevertheless be within this provision.

'cause or encourage' Parents *etc* who make no effort to prevent their under-aged daughter spending the night with her boyfriend may be regarded as having caused or encouraged any sexual acts which then take place: see *R v Ralphs* (1918) 9 Cr App R 86; *R v Moon* [1910] 1 KB 818. As for doctors who prescribe contraceptives, see the notes to s 6 *supra*.

'prostitution' See notes to s 22 *supra*.

'unlawful sexual intercourse' See s 44 *infra* and the notes to s 2 *supra*. This may itself constitute an offence under ss 5 or 6 *supra*.

'indecent assault' See s 14 *supra*; in particular s 14(2).

'for whom he is responsible' See subss (3) and (4).

Penalty See Sch 2 *infra*.

Causing or encouraging prostitution of defective
29. (1) It is an offence, subject to the exception mentioned in this section, for a person to cause or encourage the prostitution in any part of the world of a woman who is a defective.

(2) A person is not guilty of an offence under this section because he causes or encourages the prostitution of such a woman, if he does not know and has no reason to suspect her to be a defective.

NOTES
This provision overlaps to some extent with s 22, and carries the same maximum penalty as s 22, which does not stipulate that the woman or girl concened should be either underaged or a defective. If this provision adds anything to s 22, it may be because it does not require that the defective should become a *common* prostitute (see *R v Morris-Lowe* [1985] 1 All ER 400), and it may be that 'encouragement' constitutes a complete offence under this provision even if prostitution itself never occurs in consequence (*ie* as with the common law offence of incitement).

'subject to the exception mentioned in this section' The burden of proving a defence under subs (2) lies on the accused by virtue of s 47 *infra*.

'woman' Or a girl: see s 46 *infra*.

'defective' See s 45 *infra*.

Penalty See Sch 2 *infra*.

Man living on earnings of prostitution
30. (1) It is an offence for a man knowingly to live wholly or in part on the earnings of prostitution.

(2) For the purposes of this section a man who lives with or is habitually in the company of a prostitute, or who exercises control, direction or influence over a prostitute's movements in a way which shows he is aiding, abetting or compelling her prostitution with others, shall be presumed to be knowingly living on the earnings of prostitution, unless he proves the contrary.

NOTES
'man'   Includes a boy (see s 46 *infra*). As to 'sex changes' by surgery, see *R v Tan* [1983] QB 653.

'live ... on the earnings of prostitution'   Clearly, the 'ponce' who enjoys a parasitic dependence on the prostitute's earnings is the chief target of this provision; but its effect is not confined to such men. A man who provides services to prostitutes in return for payment may commit the offence as long as the services (and thus the payment) are manifestly referable to the business of prostitution. Thus, the publishing of a 'directory' of prostitutes, in which the women concerned pay for 'entries', has been held to constitute the offence: *Shaw v DPP* [1962] AC 220. See also *Calvert v Mayes* [1954] 1 QB 342; *R v Ansell* [1975] QB 215; and *R v Thomas* [1957] 2 All ER 181.

Subs (2)   Note that if a man lives with a prostitute, the presumption will arise, without any need for proof of his aiding and abetting her prostitution (and *vice-versa*): *R v Clarke* [1976] 2 All ER 696.

'aiding, abetting etc'   See the notes to s 31 *infra*.

Woman exercising control over prostitute
31. It is an offence for a woman for purposes of gain to exercise control, direction or influence over a prostitute's movements in a way which shows she is aiding, abetting or compelling her prostitution.

NOTES
Prostitution is not itself an offence (although prostitutes who loiter or solicit in public places may commit a summary offence under s 1 of the Street Offences Act 1959) (*qv*). Aiding and abetting prostitution is not therefore an offence either; but it may constitute an element in some other offence such as this one or that created by s 30 *supra*.

'woman'   Or a girl: see s 46 *infra*.

'prostitute'   See the notes to s 22 *supra*.

'aiding, abetting'   See the notes to s 8 of the Accessories and Abettors Act 1861.

Penalty   See Sch 2 *infra*.

Solicitation

Solicitation by men
32. It is an offence for a man persistently to solicit or importune in a public place for immoral purposes.

NOTES
It has been held that this provision does *not* apply to men who solicit adult women for the purpose of having sexual intercourse with them: *Crook v Edmondson* [1966] 2 QB 81. Such men may however be guilty of offences under ss 1 or 2 of the Sexual Offences Act 1985 (*qv*).

'man'   Or boy. See s 46 *infra*.

'public place'   This clearly includes streets (as to which see s 1(4) of the Street Offences Act 1959) but also includes publicly or privately owned land or property to which the public has access, even if that access is improper or subject to an admission fee. See *R v Morris* (1963) 47 Cr App R 202; *Cooper v Shield* [1921] 2 QB 334. In respect of solicitation by women prostitutes under the Street Offences Act

1959, it has been held that it suffices if the prostitute solicits clients who are in public places even if she herself remains on private property whilst doing so. See *Behrendt v Berridge* [1976] 3 All ER 285.

'solicit or importune'   These are different words meaning the same thing: *Field v Chapman, The Times,* 9 October 1953. The offence requires some attempt to pester or attract the attention of the persons solicited. The attempt need not succeed: *Horton v Mead* [1913] 1 KB 154. Ordinary greetings or pleasantries may suffice provided there is proof of their intended purpose: *Dale v Smith* [1967] 2 All ER 1133.

'persistently'   This may involve the repeated importuning of one person or a series of invitations to a number of different persons: *Dale v Smith supra.*

'for immoral purposes'   As already explained, this apparently does not include unlawful sexual intercourse with an adult woman (even if she is a prostitute) but it does include intercourse with under-aged girls (*R v Dodd* (1977) 66 Cr App R 87) and it may include homosexual activity, even if it would not be illegal under the Sexual Offences Act 1967: *R v Grey* [1982] Crim LR 176; *R v Ford* [1978] 1 All ER 1129. In such cases, however, the question whether the 'purpose' is immoral is one of fact for the jury.

Penalty   See Sch 2 *infra.*

Arrest   Under s 41 (not printed in this work) anyone may arrest a person 'found committing' an offence under this section.

Suppression of brothels

Keeping a brothel
   33. It is an offence for a person to keep a brothel, or to manage, or act or assist in the management of, a brothel.

NOTES
'brothel'   This term is not defined in the Act but at common law it means a place resorted to by persons of both sexes for the purpose of prostitution (*Singleton v Ellison* [1985] 1 QB 601 (at p 608)) or a place in which two or more women (whether prostitutes or not) offer themselves as participants in physical acts of indecency for the sexual gratification of men: *Kelly v Purvis* [1983] 1 All ER 525. See also *Abbott v Smith* [1965] 2 QB 662; *R v Korie* [1966] 1 All ER 50. Premises used by a single prostitute cannot be a brothel but may be a disorderly house at common law: *R v Tan* [1983] 2 All ER 12.
   For the purposes of this section (and ss 34 and 35 *infra*) a brothel may additionally constitute a place in which comparable homosexual practices take place: Sexual Offences Act 1967, s 6.

'keep ... or manage ... or assist in the management'   This does not include menial employment within a brothel such as cleaning the stairs or answering the door, nor does the fact that a woman participates in the activities being conducted there make her guilty of assisting in its management. See *Gorman v Stander* [1963] 3 All ER 627; *Abbott v Smith* [1964] 3 All ER 762.

Penalty   See Sch 2 *infra.*

Landlord letting premises for use as brothel

34. It is an offence for the lessor or landlord of any premises or his agent to let the whole or part of the premises with the knowledge that it is to be used, in whole or in part, as a brothel, or, where the whole or part of the premises is used as a brothel, to be wilfully a party to that use continuing.

NOTES

This offence may be committed even where D has let individual rooms to different prostitutes, provided that some at least of the prostitutes operate together — as in *Donovan v Gavin* [1965] 2 QB 648. If all the prostitutes work entirely alone, it is doubtful whether the premises could constitute a 'brothel'. See notes to s 33 *supra*.

Strictly speaking, it would seem that actual use of the premises as a brothel need not be proved. It would suffice if D knows his new tenant *intends* to use the premises for such a purpose.

Penalty See Sch 2 *infra*.

Tenant permitting premises to be used as brothel

35. (1) It is an offence for the tenant or occupier, or person in charge, of any premises knowingly to permit the whole or part of the premises to be used as a brothel.

(2) Where the tenant or occupier of any premises is convicted (whether under this section or, for an offence committed before the commencement of this Act, under section thirteen of the Criminal Law Amendment Act, 1885) of knowingly permitting the whole or part of the premises to be used as a brothel, the First Schedule to this Act shall apply to enlarge the rights of the lessor or landlord with respect to the assignment or determination of the lease or other contract under which the premises are held by the person convicted.

(3) Where the tenant or occupier of any premises is so convicted, or was so convicted under the said section thirteen before the commencement of this Act, and either:

(a) the lessor or landlord, after having the conviction brought to his notice, fails or failed to exercise his statutory rights in relation to the lease or contract under which the premises are or were held by the person convicted; or

(b) the lessor or landlord, after exercising his statutory rights so as to determine that lease or contract, grants or granted a new lease or enters or entered into a new contract of tenancy of the premises to, with or for the benefit of the same person, without having all reasonable provisions to prevent the recurrence of the offence inserted in the new lease or contract;

then, if subsequently an offence under this section is committed in respect of the premises during the subsistence of the lease or contract referred to in paragraph (a) of this subsection or (where paragraph (b) applies) during the subsistence of the new lease or contract, the lessor or landlord shall be deemed to be a party to that offence unless he shows that he took all reasonable steps to prevent the recurrence of the offence.

References in this subsection to the statutory rights of a lessor or landlord refer to his rights under the First Schedule to this Act or under subsection (1) of section five of the Criminal Law Amendment Act 1912 (the provision replaced for England and Wales by that Schedule).

NOTES
'tenant or occupier or person in charge'   This does not include a lessee who sub-lets the whole or part of the premises, *cf Siviour v Napolitano* [1931] 1 KB 636.

'brothel'   See the notes to s 33 *supra*. Where the tenant *etc* allows a single prostitute to operate on the premises no offence is committed under this provision, but there may be liability under s 36 *infra*.

Subs (3)   A landlord who wilfully permits his premises to be used in whole or in part as a brothel may be guilty of an offence under s 34 *supra*; but if he fails to determine a tenancy in accordance with this section and Sch 1 after learning of his tenant's conviction for an offence under subs (1), it will generally be easier for him to be dealt with under this section should his tenant re-offend.

Penalty   See Sch 2 *infra*.

Tenant permitting premises to be used for prostitution
36. It is an offence for the tenant or occupier of any premises knowingly to permit the whole or part of the premises to be used for the purposes of habitual prostitution.

NOTES
'tenant or occupier'   See the notes to s 35 *supra*.

'habitual prostitution'   See the notes to s 22 *supra* insofar as they deal with common (*ie* habitual) prostitutes. Where two or more prostitutes are allowed to operate together, liability may arise under s 35 *supra*.

Penalty   See Sched 2 *infra*.

37–38 [*omitted*]

39–40 [*repealed*]

41–43 [*omitted*]

Meaning of 'sexual intercourse'
44 Where, on the trial of any offence under this Act, it is necessary to prove sexual intercourse (whether natural or unnatural), it shall not be necessary to prove the completion of the intercourse by the emission of seed, but the intercourse shall be deemed complete upon proof of penetration only.

NOTE
Slight penetration suffices: *R v Hughes* (1841) 9 C & P 752.

Meaning of defective
45. In this Act 'defective' means a person suffering from a state of arrested or incomplete development of mind which includes severe impairment of intelligence and social functioning.

Use of words 'man', 'boy', 'woman' and 'girl'
46. The use in any provision of this Act of the word 'man' without the addition of the word 'boy', or vice versa, shall not prevent the provision applying to any person to whom it would have applied if both words had been used, and similarly with the words 'woman' and 'girl'.

Proof of exceptions
47. Where in any of the foregoing sections the description of an offence is expressed to be subject to exceptions mentioned in the section, proof of the exception is to lie on the person relying on it.

NOTE
This requires proof on balance of probabilities: *R v Dunbar* [1958] 1 QB 1

SECOND SCHEDULE
(Section 37)

TABLE OF OFFENCES, WITH MODE OF PROSECUTION, PUNISHMENTS, ETC

PART I

Felonies and attempts at felonies

Offence	Mode of prosecution	Punishment	Provisions as to alternative verdicts etc.
1. (a) Rape (section one)	On indictment	Life	The jury may find the accused guilty— (i) of procurement of a woman by threats (section two); or (ii) of procurement of a woman by false pretences (section three); or (iii) of administering drugs to obtain or facilitate intercourse (section four); …
(b) An attempt to commit this offence.	On indictment	Life	—
2. (a) Intercourse with girl under thirteen (section five).	On indictment	Life	—
(b) An attempt to commit this offence.	On indictment	[Seven years]	—
3. (a) Buggery (section twelve).	On indictment	[If with a boy under the age of sixteen or with a woman or an animal, life; otherwise the relevant punishment prescribed by section 3 of the Sexual Offences Act 1967]	—

(b) An attempt to commit this offence.	On indictment	[If with a boy under the age of sixteen or with a woman or an animal, ten years]
4. Abduction of woman by force or for the sake of her property (section seventeen).	On indictment	Fourteen years
5. ...		
6. Permitting girl under thirteen to use premises for intercourse (section twenty-five).	On indictment	Life

PART II

Offences other than felonies and attempts at felonies

7. (a) Procurement of woman by threats (section two).	On indictment	Two years
(b) An attempt to commit this offence.	On indictment	Two years
8. Procurement of woman by false pretences (section three).	On indictment	Two years
9. Administering drugs to obtain or facilitate intercourse (section four).	On indictment	Two years
10. (a) Intercourse with girl [under sixteen] (section six).	On indictment ...; a prosecution may not be commenced more than twelve months after the offence charged.	Two years
(b) An attempt to commit this offence.	On indictment ...; a prosecution may not be commenced more than twelve months after the offence charged.	Two years

Offence	Mode of prosecution	Punishment	Provisions as to alternative verdicts etc.
11. (a) Intercourse with [defective] (section seven).	On indictment	Two years	—
(b) An attempt to commit this offence.	On indictment	Two years	—
12. ...			
13. (a) Procurement of defective (section nine).	On indictment	Two years	—
(b) An attempt to commit this offence.	On indictment	Two years	—
14. (a) Incest by a man (section ten).	On indictment ...; a prosecution may not be commenced [except by or with the consent] of the Director of Public Prosecutions...	If with a girl under thirteen, and so charged in the indictment, life; otherwise seven years.	The jury may find the accused guilty— (i) of intercourse with a girl under thirteen (section five); or (ii) of intercourse with a girl between thirteen and sixteen (section six);...
(b) An attempt to commit this offence.	On indictment ...; a prosecution may not be commenced [except by or with the consent] of the Director of Public Prosecutions...	[If with a girl under thirteen, and so charged in the indictment, life; otherwise seven years.]	—
15. (a) Incest by a woman (section eleven).	On indictment ...; a prosecution may not be commenced [except by or with the consent] of the Director of Public Prosecutions...	Seven years	—

(b) An attempt to commit this offence.	On indictment . . . ; a prosecution may not be commenced [except by or with the consent] of the Director of Public Prosecutions . . .	Two years
16. (a) Indecency between men (section thirteen).	On indictment	[If by a man of over the age of twenty-one with a man under that age, five years; otherwise two years.]
(b) An attempt to procure the commission by a man of an act of gross indecency with another man.	On indictment	[If the attempt is by a man of or over the age of twenty-one to procure a man under that age to commit an act of gross indecency with another man, five years; otherwise two years.]
17. Indecent assault on a woman (section fourteen).	(i) On indictment [(ii) Summarily (by virtue of section 17(1) of the Magistrates' Courts Act 1980).]	Ten years [As provided by [section 32(1) of that Act] (that is to say, six months or the prescribed sum within the meaning of that section, or both).]
18. Indecent assault on a man (section fifteen).	(i) On indictment [(ii) Summarily (by virtue of section 17(1) of the Magistrates' Courts Act 1980).]	Ten years [As provided by [section 32(1) of that Act] (that is to say, six months or the prescribed sum within the meaning of that section, or both).]
19. Assault with intent to commit buggery (section sixteen).	On indictment	Ten years
20. Abduction of girl under eighteen from parent or guardian (section nineteen).	On indictment	Two years

Offence	Mode of prosecution	Punishment	Provisions as to alternative verdicts etc.
21. Abduction of girl under sixteen from parent or guardian (section twenty).	On indictment	Two years	—
22. Abduction of defective from parent or guardian (section twenty-one).	On indictment	Two years	—
23. (a) Causing prostitution of a woman (section twenty-two).	On indictment	Two years	—
(b) An attempt to commit this offence.	On indictment	Two years	—
24. (a) Procuration of girl under twenty-one (section twenty-three).	On indictment	Two years	—
(b) An attempt to commit this offence.	On indictment	Two years	—
25. Detention of woman in brothel (section twenty-four).	On indictment	Two years	—
26. Permitting girl [under sixteen] to use premises for intercourse (section twenty-six).	On indictment	Two years	—
27. Permitting defective to use premises for intercourse (section twenty-seven).	On indictment	Two years	—
28. Causing or encouraging prostitution, etc, of girl under sixteen (section twenty-eight).	On indictment	Two years	—
29. Causing or encouraging prostitution of defective (section twenty-nine).	On indictment	Two years	—

Section	Offence	Mode of prosecution	Punishment	
30.	Living on earnings of prostitution (section thirty).	(i) On indictment (ii) Summarily	[Seven years] Six months	—
31.	Controlling a prostitute (section thirty-one).	(i) On indictment (ii) Summarily	[Seven years] Six months	—
32.	Solicitation by a man (section thirty-two).	(i) On indictment (ii) Summarily	Two years Six months	—
33.	Keeping a brothel (section thirty-three)	Summarily	For an offence committed after a previous conviction, six months, or [level 4 on the standard scale] or both; otherwise, three months, or [level 3 on the standard scale] or both.	A conviction of an offence punishable under section thirty-four, thirty-five or thirty-six of this Act, or under section thirteen of the Criminal Law Amendment Act 1885 (the section replaced for England and Wales by sections thirty-three to thirty-six of this Act), shall be taken into account as a previous conviction in the same way as a conviction of an offence punishable under section thirty-three of this Act.
34.	Letting premises for use as brothel (section thirty-four)	Summarily	For an offence committed after a previous conviction, six months, or [level 4 on the standard scale] or both; otherwise, three months, or [level 3 on the standard scale] or both.	A conviction of an offence punishable under section thirty-three, thirty-five or thirty-six of this Act, or under section thirteen of the Criminal Law Amendment Act 1885 (the section replaced for England and Wales by sections thirty-three to thirty-six of this Act), shall be taken into account as a previous conviction in the same way as a conviction of an offence punishable under section thirty-four of this Act.

Offence	Mode of prosecution	Punishment	Provisions as to alternative verdicts etc.
35. Tenant permitting premises to be used as brothel (section thirty-five)	Summarily	For an offence committed after a previous conviction, six months, or [level 4 on the standard scale] or both; otherwise, three months, or [level 3 on the standard scale] or both.	A conviction of an offence punishable under section thirty-three, thirty-four or thirty-six of this Act, or under section thirteen of the Criminal Law Amendment Act 1885 (the section replaced for England and Wales by sections thirty-three to thirty-six of this Act), shall be taken into account as a previous conviction in the same way as a conviction of an offence punishable under section thirty-five of this Act.
36. Tenant permitting premises to be used for prostitution (section thirty-six)	Summarily	For an offence committed after a previous conviction, six months, or [level 4 on the standard scale] or both; otherwise, three months, or [level 3 on the standard scale] or both.	A conviction of an offence punishable under section thirty-three, thirty-four or thirty-five of this Act, or under section thirteen of the Criminal Law Amendment Act 1885 (the section replaced for England and Wales by sections thirty-three to thirty-six of this Act), shall be taken into account as a previous conviction in the same way as a conviction of an offence punishable under section thirty-six of this Act.

NOTES

The provisions as to alternative verdicts (column 4) supplement (and do not supplant) the general provisions in s 6(3) and (4) of the Criminal Law Act 1967. Thus a person indicted for rape may be convicted of attempted rape etc.

Homicide Act 1957

(5 &6 ELIZ II C 11)

Part I: Amendments of law of England and Wales as to fact of murder

Abolition of 'constructive malice'

1. (1) Where a person kills another in the course or furtherance of some other offence, the killing shall not amount to murder unless done with the same malice aforethought (express or implied) as is required for a killing to amount to murder when not done in the course or furtherance of another offence.

(2) For the purposes of the foregoing subsection, a killing done in the course or for the purpose of resisting an officer of justice, or of resisting or avoiding or preventing a lawful arrest, or of effecting or assisting an escape or rescue from legal custody, shall be treated as a killing in the course or furtherance of an offence.

NOTES

Under the doctrine of 'constructive malice', which this provision abolished, a person who caused death during the course of carrying out any felony involving violence would necessarily become guilty of murder, however slight the violence actually intended and however unforeseen the fatality. Shortly after the Act came into force, it was nevertheless held in *R v Vickers* [1957] 2 QB 664 to have left unaffected the rule that the deliberate infliction of grievous bodily harm would amount to murder if death ensued; and this was confirmed by the House of Lords in *R v Cunningham* [1982] AC 566.

'malice aforethought (express or implied)'　Under the present law, a person may be guilty of murder if he kills with 'express malice' (intent to kill) or 'implied malice' (intent to do grievous bodily harm). No other mental state or intent will suffice: *R v Moloney* [1985] AC 905; *R v Hancock* [1986] AC 455. Moreover, the mere foresight of the probability of causing death *etc* is not the same thing as an intent to kill: *R v Moloney supra; R v Nedrick* [1986] 1 WLR 1025.

If, however, D does an act (*eg* destroying an airliner in flight) which he realises must inevitably kill, then arguably he intends to kill, even if the killing is a mere side-effect of the principal objective. This is more than just a case of foreseeing a probability.

Where D kills in the course of a deliberate, unlawful and dangerous act (dangerous in the sense of involving an obvious risk of injury), then he may now be guilty of manslaughter: *DPP v Newbury* [1977] AC 500; *R v Goodfellow* [1986] Crim LR 469.

Persons suffering from diminished responsibility

2. (1) Where a person kills or is a party to the killing of another, he shall not be convicted of murder if he was suffering from such abnormality of mind (whether arising from a condition of arrested or retarded development of mind or any inherent causes or induced by disease or injury) as substantially impaired his mental responsibility for his acts and omissions in doing or being a party to the killing.

(2) On a charge of murder, it shall be for the defence to prove that the person charged is by virtue of this section not liable to be convicted of murder.

(3) A person who but for this section would be liable, whether as principal or as accessory, to be convicted of murder shall be liable instead to be convicted of manslaughter.

(4) The fact that one party to a killing is by virtue of this section not liable to be convicted of murder shall not affect the question whether the killing amounted to murder in the case of any other party to it.

NOTES

Prior to the enactment of this provision, English law recognised no defences based on mental abnormality other than that of insanity under the *M'Naughten Rules* (1843) 10 C & Fin 200 and that of infanticide under the Infanticide Act 1938. Insanity necessarily involves a complete lack of responsibility for one's actions: it is difficult to prove and unpopular as a defence owing to the fact that if 'successful' it leads to indefinite detention in a secure mental hospital (Trial of Lunatics Act 1883 s 2(2)).

The concept of diminished responsibility was borrowed from Scots Law and involves the notion of partial excuse: *ie* the person who deliberately kills whilst suffering from diminished responsibility is considered blameworthy enough to merit conviction for manslaughter, but not for murder. A manslaughter conviction leaves the judge with a wide range of sentencing options, in contrast to the mandatory sentence of life imprisonment for murder.

'he shall not be convicted of murder' Like provocation (s 3 *infra*), diminished responsibility is available only as a defence to murder, and not, for example, to attempted murder or any lesser offence.

'abnormality of mind' In *R v Byrne* [1960] 2 QB 396 Lord Parker CJ said:

'Abnormality of mind ... means a state of mind so different from that of ordinary human beings that the reasonable man would term it abnormal. It appears to us to be wide enough to cover the mind's activities in all its aspects, not only the perception of physical acts and matters and the ability to form a rational judgment whether an act is right or wrong, but also the ability to exercise will-power to control physical acts in accordance with that rational judgment.'

On the other hand, it need not involve anything akin to insanity in the popular sense of the term; it may involve something such as depression: *R v Seers* [1985] Crim LR 315. In practice, the defence has sometimes been used successfully where the court has been sympathetic to the plight of an accused who has killed in tragic circumstances and when under severe emotional strain, but this would strictly speaking appear to be improper; the Court of Appeal has held that the defence should succeed only if supported by clear evidence of mental imbalance or abnormality: *R v Vinagre* (1979) 69 Cr App R 104.

In extreme cases, alcoholism (but not intoxication) may bring about abnormality of mind: see *R v Tandy* [1988] Crim LR 308.

'(whether arising from ...)' The words in parentheses in subs (1) effectively cover all kinds of mental handicap, disorder, injury or illness, including reactive depression (*R v Seers, supra*) and alcohol-induced damage; but they exclude conditions attributable to external factors such as intoxication. A person who kills whilst both mentally disordered and drunk can only succeed with a plea of diminished responsibility if he can prove on balance of probability that he would have killed even if he had been sober: *R v Gittens* [1984] QB 698; *R v Atkinson* [1985] Crim LR 314. Medical evidence will in practice be needed to show the cause of D's condition: *R v Byrne, supra; R v Dix* (1981) 74 Cr App R 306. As to the position of alcoholics who cannot resist drinking, see *R v Tandy, supra.*

'as substantially impaired his mental responsibility'

> 'This is a question of degree, and essentially one for the jury. Medical evidence is of course relevant, but the question involves a decision ... whether such impairment can properly be called substantial, a matter on which juries may quite legitimately differ from doctors' (*per* Lord Parker CJ in *R v Byrne, supra*).

The English courts have followed the Scottish approach to the defence, which involves the jury assessing, by means of a subjective value judgment, whether the accused's mental abnormality is such as to merit something less than conviction for murder. Juries can, and sometimes do, convict of murder despite undisputed evidence of mental disorder, as in *R v Sutcliffe* (*The Times*, 26 May 1982). See also *Walton v R* (1978) 66 Cr App R 25.

In some cases, however, medical evidence of substantially impaired responsibility will be so clear that a verdict of murder would be perverse and unsupportable on appeal: *R v Matheson* [1958] 1 WLR 474; *R v Bailey* (1978) 66 Cr App R 31*n*.

'On a charge of murder' The prosecution will not initiate a charge of manslaughter by reason of diminished responsibility: it will charge murder, and it will then be for the defence to raise the issue. The prosecution may however allege diminished responsibility where the defence is one of insanity (or may raise insanity where the defence is one of diminished responsibility): Criminal Procedure (Insanity) Act 1964 s 6.

'it shall be for the defence to prove' The defence must prove that it is more likely than not that the accused was suffering from diminished responsibility. The normal burden of proof is reversed.

Subs (4) At common law, the general rule used to be that a mere accessory before the fact could not be convicted of a greater offence than the principal offender (see *R v Richards* [1974] QB 776). Subs (4) clearly excluded that rule, so that D might be guilty of murder through counselling or procuring E, even if E had a defence of diminished responsibility. The common law rule has in any event been abrogated following the decision of the House of Lords in *R v Howe and Bannister* (1987) 85 Cr App R 32, so subs (4) may now be otiose.

Provocation

3. Where on a charge of murder there is evidence on which the jury can find that the person charged was provoked (whether by things done or by things said or by both together) to lose his self-control, the question whether the provocation was enough to make a reasonable man do as he did shall be left to be determined by the jury; and in determining that question the jury shall take into account everything both done and said according to the effect which, in their opinion, it would have on a reasonable man.

NOTES
Whereas ss 2 and 4 of the Act introduced defences previously unknown to English law, this section merely restates, with some modifications, a defence long recognised at common law. Pre-Act cases on provocation must be approached with circumspection because the Act gives juries a greater say than did the common law on the question of what constitutes a 'reasonable man's' response to provocative

words or deeds; and judges accordingly have less power to reject provocation defences by withholding them from the jury's consideration.

'Where on a charge of murder' As with diminished responsibility under s 2 (*supra*), provocation is a defence only to murder. It would not appear to be available even as a defence to attempted murder (but see P. English in [1973] Crim LR 727) and 'manslaughter by reason of provocation' is not itself a valid charge; the charge must be murder, and the issue or provocation can then be raised by way of defence to that charge.

'there is evidence on which the jury can find' As a general rule, it is up to the defence to raise the issue of provocation if they wish to rely on it; and the defence bears an evidential burden in that respect. In other words, the prosecution cannot be expected to disprove provocation unless and until there is some evidence before the court which suggests it. In some cases, however, the prosecution case will itself throw up evidence of possible provocation and the jury will then need to be directed on that issue even if the accused's defence is one of self-defence or of complete denial: *R v Mancini* [1942] AC 1; *R v Cascoe* [1970] 2 All ER 833; *R v McInnes* [1971] 3 All ER 295; *R v Newell* [1989] Crim LR 906.

'that the person charged was provoked ... to lose his self-control' However extreme the provocation offered, a killer is not entitled to a defence under s 3 unless that provocation actually caused him to lose his self-control. This clearly excludes cases where D uses P's provocative behaviour as a mere excuse to kill him; but it also excludes any other cases where the killing is a premeditated act, however 'understandable' that act and however badly P may have treated D in the past: *R v Ibrams* (1982) 74 Cr App R 154; *R v Duffy* [1949] 1 All ER 932. In *Duffy*, Devlin J said:

> 'The conscious formulation of a desire for revenge means that a person has had time to think, to reflect, and that would negative a sudden temporary loss of self control which is the essence of provocation.'

'by things done or by things said or by both together' At common law, words alone could never amount to sufficient provocation, and a trivial attack could never be sufficient provocation for a killing carried out with a lethal weapon (*R v Mancini, supra*). S 3 clearly changes the law to the extent that words alone, or trivial violence, *may* amount to provocation, at least to the extent that the issue will have to be left to the jury.

The things said or done need not originate from the victim himself: a husband may be provoked by his wife into killing the wife's lover—although it may be difficult to persuade a jury that a 'reasonable man' could react to the provocation in that way. See *R v Davies* [1975] QB 691.

The 'reasonable man' The concept of the reasonable man committing a deliberate unlawful homicide is bizarre. Although the Act appears to contemplate situations in which reasonable men *would* kill, the real question must in practice be whether it would to some extent be understandable for a basically reasonable person of the accused's sex, age and physical characteristics to lose his self-control and kill in the face of the provocation involved: *DPP v Camplin* [1978] AC 705. The jury should not take acccount of any tendency to loss of temper, excitability or pugnaciousness on the part of the accused (*ibid*). It may perhaps be proper to take account of his background, beliefs and experience, since, like physical characteristics, these may be very relevant in assessing the degree of provocation: see *R v Burke* [1987] Crim LR 336; but the reasonable man is never an alcoholic, or intoxicated, or suffering from depression: *R v Newell* (1980) 71 Cr App R 331.

'The question ... shall be left to be determined by the jury' The judge should generally leave to the jury any issue of provocation, however weak or tenuous he considers it to be: *R v Doughty* [1986] Crim LR 623. Even self-induced provocation is included (*eg* where D claims to have been 'provoked' by P's violent reaction to D's own blackmailing of him, as in *Edwards v R* [1975] 1 All ER 152); but in *Leung Ping-Fat v R* (1973) 3 HKLJ 342 it was held (in Hong Kong) that a robber who kills a person for resisting him can have no right to put a provocation defence to the jury. This ruling can perhaps be justified on the basis that there was no evidence on which a jury could have found provocation.

Suicide pacts

4. (1) It shall be manslaughter, and shall not be murder, for a person acting in pursuance of a suicide pact between him and another to kill the other or be a party to the other ... being killed by a third person.

(2) Where it is shown that a person charged with the murder of another killed the other or was a party to his ... being killed, it shall be for the defence to prove that the person charged was acting in pursuance of a suicide pact between him and the other.

(3) For the purposes of this section "suicide pact" means a common agreement between two or more persons having for its object the death of all of them, whether or not each is to take his own life, but nothing done by a person who enters into a suicide pact shall be treated as done by him in pursuance of the pact unless it is done while he has the settled intention of dying in pursuance of the pact.

NOTES

Prior to the enactment of this provision, it had not been unknown for the unwilling survivor of a partially successful suicide pact to be hanged for the murder of the one who died. The survivor will now at worst be guilty of manslaughter, assuming that he can prove (on balance of probabilities) the existence of a pact in which he himself genuinely intended to die (see subs (3)). If he cannot prove this, as required by subs (2), he may be guilty of murder, but only if he in fact killed (or helped another to kill) the one(s) who died.

Where D merely helps P to take his own life, then D's liability will be for complicity in suicide contrary to s 2 of the Suicide Act 1961 (qv), whether or not he acted in pursuance of a joint suicide pact. (At common law, complicity in suicide was punishable as murder: *R v Dyson* (1823) Russ & Ry 523.)

5–16. [*repealed*]

17. [*omitted*]

Restriction of Offensive Weapons Act 1959

(7 & 8 ELIZ II C 37)

Penalties for offences in connection with dangerous weapons

1. (1) Any person who manufactures, sells or hires or offers for sale or hire [or exposes or has in his possession for the purpose of sale or hire], or lends or gives to any other person—

(a) any knife which has a blade which opens automatically by hand pressure applied to a button, spring or other device in or attached to the handle of the knife, sometimes known as a "flick knife" or "flick gun"; or

(b) any knife which has a blade which is released from the handle or sheath thereof by the force of gravity or the application of centrifugal force and which, when released, is locked in place by means of a button, spring, lever, or other device, sometimes known as a "gravity knife",

shall be guilty of an offence and shall be liable on summary conviction to imprisonment for a term not exceeding six months or to a fine not exceeding [level 4 on the standard scale] or to both such imprisonment and fine.

(2) The importation of any such knife as is described in the foregoing subsection is hereby prohibited.

NOTES

This provision is now supplemented by s 141 of the Criminal Justice Act 1988 (qv), which enables the Home Secretary to make orders restricting the manufacture etc, of other weapons, subject to the approval of Parliament.

'person' This may be a corporation, and the fact that the offence appears to be one of strict liability means that a corporation could incur such liability without it being necessary for the prosecution to prove that its directors *etc*, knew of or authorised the prohibited action.

'has in his possession' See the notes to s 1 of the Firearms act 1968.

'or exposes etc' These words were added by the Restriction of Offensive Weapons Act 1961, following the decision in *Fisher v Bell* [1961] 1 QB 394 that the display of goods in a shop window is not an offer to sell, but only an invitation to treat.

Subs (2) This subsection creates no offence in its own right; the relevant offences are now those contained in s 50 of the Customs and Excise Management Act 1979 (not printed in this work).

Street Offences Act 1959

(7 & 8 ELIZ II C 57)

Loitering or soliciting for purposes of prostitution
1. (1) It shall be an offence for a common prostitute to loiter or solicit in a street or public place for the purpose of prostitution.

(2) A person guilty of an offence under this section shall be liable on summary conviction to a fine of an amount not exceeding level 2 on the standard scale, as defined in [section 75 of the Criminal Justice Act 1982, or, for an offence committed after a previous conviction, to a fine of an amount not exceeding level 3 on that scale].

(3) A constable may arrest without warrant anyone he finds in a street or public place and suspects, with reasonable cause, to be committing an offence under this section.

(4) For the purposes of this section "street" includes any bridge, road, lane, footway, subway, square, court, alley or passage, whether a thoroughfare or not, which is for the time being open to the public; and the doorways and entrances of premises abutting on a street (as hereinbefore defined), and any ground adjoining and open to a street, shall be treated as forming part of the street.

(5) The following enactments shall cease to have effect, that is to say—

(*a*) paragraph 11 of section fifty-four of the Metropolitan Police Act 1839; and

(*b*) the paragraph beginning "Every common prostitute" in section twenty-eight of the Town Police Clauses Act 1847 and any later Act in so far as it incorporates that paragraph; and

(*c*) paragraph 11 of section thirty-five of the City of London Police Act 1839 and the paragraph beginning "Every common prostitute" in section one hundred and two of the Manchester Police Regulation Act 1844;

but for the purposes of subsection (2) of this section a conviction of the offence mentioned in any of those paragraphs shall be taken into account as a previous conviction in the same way as a conviction of an offence under this section.

NOTES
Prostitution is not in itself an offence, but this is one of a number of provisions which criminalise various activities connected with prostitution. See also ss 22–36 of the Sexual Offences Act 1956.

'common prostitute', **'prostitution'** See the notes to s 22 of the Sexual Offences Act 1956 *supra*.

'loiter' It has been held in other contexts that loitering 'connotes the idea of lingering', and that it is not enough for D merely to pass slowly on a single occasion

(*Williamson v Wright* 1924 JC 57). It has also been held that D can loiter whilst in a vehicle (*Bridge v Campbell* [1947] WN 223), but it is submitted that an appellate court should not lightly interfere with a decision that certain conduct does or does not amount to loitering.

'solicit' It has been held that this must involve something more than the placing of advertisements: the prostitute must solicit in person (*Weiz v Monaghan* [1962] 1 All ER 262). One can however solicit customers without succeeding in obtaining their custom or even their attention (*Horton v Mead* [1913] 1 KB 154), and without necessarily uttering a word (*ibid*).

'in a street' See subs (4). The prostitute need not be in the street if she solicits persons who are there: *Behrendt v Berridge* [1976] 3 All ER 285.

'public place' It has been held in other contexts that a place is a 'public' one if the public in fact have access thereto, even if it is privately owned (*Williams v Boyle* [1963] Crim LR 204); cf subs. (4) *supra*.

Obscene Publications Act 1959

(7 & 8 ELIZ. II C 66)

Test of obscenity
1. (1) For the purposes of this Act an article shall be deemed to be obscene if its effect or (where the article comprises two or more distinct items) the effect of any one of its items is, if taken as a whole, such as to tend to deprave and corrupt persons who are likely, having regard to all relevant circumstances, to read, see or hear the matter contained or embodied in it.

(2) In this Act "article" means any description of article containing or embodying matter to be read or looked at or both, any sound record, and any film or other record of a picture or pictures.

(3) For the purposes of this Act a person publishes an article who—

(*a*) distributes, circulates, sells, lets on hire, gives, or lends it, or who offers it for sale or for letting on hire; or

(*b*) in the case of an article containing or embodying matter to be looked at or a record, shows, plays or projects it:

Provided that paragraph (*b*) of this subsection shall not apply to anything done in the course of television or sound broadcasting.

NOTES
'tend to deprave and corrupt' An article may tend to deprave and corrupt without being 'obscene' in the popular sense of the word. An obvious example would be a publication encouraging the misuse of dangerous and addictive drugs (See *R v Skirving* [1985] QB 819) or one which encourages illegal violence. Conversely, an article which is obscene in the popular sense may be so revolting that readers would be shocked rather than corrupted by it. Such an article would not be obscene in the legal sense: *R v Calder and Boyars Ltd* [1969] 1 QB 151; *R v Anderson* [1972] 1 QB 304.

The intent of the author or publisher is irrelevant to the question of whether an article is obscene. As Ashworth J said in *Shaw v DPP* [1962] AC 220 at 227, 'Obscenity depends on the article and not on the author.'

The question of what amounts to corruption and depravity nevertheless remains vague and subjective in a number of respects, particularly where sexual morality is involved. See further *DDP v Whyte* [1972] 3 All ER 12; *Knuller v DPP* [1972] 2 All ER 898.

'persons who are likely ...' If the article is unlikely to corrupt anyone other than 'a minute lunatic fringe' of those to whom it is likely to be exposed, then it is not obscene (*R v Calder and Boyars Ltd, supra*); but an article may be obscene even though the majority of its users would be unaffected; *DPP v Whyte* supra. As to the evidential problems which may arise in this context, see Andrews & Hirst, *Criminal Evidence*, Ch 21.

'article' The definition in subs (2) should be read in conjunction with s 2(1) of the Obscene Publications Act 1964 (*qv*) which ensures that photographic negatives *etc*, are within the scope of the Acts.

119

As to the status of inflatable sex dolls, see *Conegate Ltd v Customs and Excise Commissioners* [1987] QB 254.

'publishes' Publication was originally an essential element of the offence created by s 2 of this Act, but s 1 of the 1964 Act has amended it so at to deal with the possession etc, of articles intended for publication for gain. It had previously been held that D would commit no offence by displaying an obscene article in his shop, because this would only be an invitation to treat, rather than an offer for sale (*R v Clayton* [1962] 3 All ER 500).

'for gain' See s 1(5) of the 1964 Act.

Prohibition of publication of obscene matter
2. (1) Subject as hereinafter provided any person who, whether for gain or not, publishes an obscene article [or who has an obscene article for publication for gain (whether gain to himself or gain to another) shall be liable—
   (*a*) on summary conviction to a fine not exceeding [the prescribed sum] or to imprisonment for a term not exceeding six months;
   (*b*) on conviction on indictment to a fine or to imprisonment for a term not exceeding three years or both.
(2) [*repealed*]
(3) A prosecution ... for an offence against this section shall not be commenced more than two years after the commission of the offence.
(3A) Proceedings for an offence under this section shall not be instituted except by or with the consent of the Director of Public Prosecutions in any case where the article in question is a moving picture film of a width of not less than sixteen millimetres and the relevant publication or the only other publication which followed or could reasonably have been expected to follow from the relevant publication took place or (as the case may be) was to take place in the course of a film exhibition; and in this subsection "the relevant publication" means—
   (*a*) in the case of any proceedings under this section for publishing an obscene article, the publication in respect of which the defendant would be charged if the proceedings were brought; and
   (*b*) in the case of any proceedings under this section for having an obscene article for publication for gain, the publication which, if the proceedings were brought, the defendant would be alleged to have had in contemplation.
(4) A person publishing an article shall not be proceeded against for an offence at common law consisting of the publication of any matter contained or embodied in the article where it is of the essence of the offence that the matter is obscene.
(4A) Without prejudice to subsection (4) above, a person shall not be proceeded against for an offence at common law—
   (*a*) in respect of a film exhibition or anything said or done in the course of a film exhibition where it is of the essence of the common law offence that the exhibition or, as the case may be, what was said or done was obscene, indecent, offensive, disgusting or injurious to morality; or

(*b*) in respect of an agreement to give a film exhibition or to cause anything to be said or done in the course of such an exhibition where the common law offence consists of conspiring to corrupt public morals or to do any act contrary to public morals or decency.

(5) A person shall not be convicted of an offence against this section if he proves that he had not examined the article in respect of which he is charged and had no reasonable cause to suspect that it was such that his publication of it would make him liable to be convicted of an offence against this section.

(6) In any proceedings against a person under this section the question whether an article is obscene shall be determined without regard to any publication by another person unless it could reasonably have been expected that the publication by the other person would follow from publication by the person charged.

(7) In this section "film exhibition" has the same meaning as in the Cinemas Act 1985.

NOTES

'publishes'; 'obscene article' See the notes to s 1 *supra*.

'has ... for publication for gain' See s 1(2) of the 1964 Act; and note that where D is prosecuted for having an obscene article for publication, s 1(3) of that Act applies in place of subss (5) and (6) of this section.

Mens rea and defences It can be inferred from subs (5) that the offence is, in part at least, one of strict liability. If D is familiar with the contents of the article, he cannot come within the subs (5) defence, and it must follow that he could be convicted even if he did not know or foresee that the article might deprave or corrupt. See *Shaw v DPP* [1962] AC 220 at 227. Liability under this section is subject to the important defence of 'public good' under s 4 *infra*.

Common law offences Subs (4) does not itself prevent D from being charged with *conspiracy* to corrupt public morals or outrage public decency through publication of an obscene article (*Shaw v DPP supra*); but it is submitted that s 5(3) of the Criminal Law Act 1977 (*qv*) would now preclude such a charge wherever the proposed publication would amount to an offence under this Act if carried out by a single person otherwise than in accordance with an agreement.

3. [*omitted*]

Defence of public good
4. (1) [Subject to subsection (1A) of this section] a person shall not be convicted of an offence against section two of this Act, and an order for forfeiture shall not be made under the foregoing section, if it is proved that publication of the article in question is justified as being for the public good on the grounds that it is in the interests of science, literature, art or learning, or of other objects of general concern.

[(1A) Subsection (1) of this section shall not apply where the article in question is a moving picture film or soundtrack, but—

(*a*) a person shall not be convicted of an offence against section 2 of this Act in relation to any such film or soundtrack, and (*b*) an order for forfeiture of any such film or soundtrack shall not be made under section 3 of this Act

if it is proved that publication of the film or soundtrack is justified as being for the public good on the ground that it is in the interest of drama, opera, ballet or any other art, or of literature or learning.]

(2) It is hereby declared that the opinion of experts as to the literary, artistic, scientific or other merits of an article may be admitted in any proceedings under this Act either to establish or to negative the said ground.

[(3) In this section "moving picture soundtrack" means any sound record designed for playing with a moving picture film, whether incorporated with the film or not.]

NOTES

This provision clearly places a legal burden of proof on the defence, but this burden only arises if the prosecution can prove that the article in question does tend to deprave and corrupt. The court may ultimately have to balance the literary or artistic merits of the article against its tendency to deprave etc. See *R v Calder and Boyars Ltd* [1969] 1 QB 151; *DPP v Jordan* [1976] 3 All ER 775.

'or other objects of general concern' These must be of the same order as those specifically mentioned; the sexually therapeutic qualities of pornography cannot be relevant in this sense: *DPP v Jordan, supra.*

'the opinion of experts' Expert evidence is not necessarily precluded on the more fundamental issue of the article's tendency to deprave or corrupt, but it will only be admissible on that issue in special cases: see *DPP v A & BC Chewing Gum Ltd* [1968] 1 QB 159.

Indecency with Children Act 1960

(8 & 9 ELIZ II C 33)

Indecent conduct towards young child

1. (1) Any person who commits an act of gross indecency with or towards a child under the age of fourteen, or who incites a child under that age to such an act with him or another, shall be liable on conviction on indictment to imprisonment for a term not exceeding two years, or on summary conviction to imprisonment for a term not exceeding six months, to a fine not exceeding [the prescribed sum] or to both.

NOTES
This offence was created in order to remedy the unsatisfactory state of the law which had been revealed by the case of *Fairclough v Whipp* [1951] 2 All ER 834. In that case, D had exposed his penis to a nine year old girl and invited her to touch it. He was held not to be guilty of indecent assault, because there was no evidence to suggest that he had touched her or threatened to do so. That case remains good law in relation to indecent assault, but provided that the 'victim' is a child of under fourteen years of age, it will now be possible to use this provision instead. In addition, s 54 of the Criminal Law Act (*qv*) may apply in cases where a man incites a girl under the age of sixteen to have incestuous intercourse with him.

'any person'   This may be a male of female, and need not be an adult.

'act of gross indecency'   As in the homosexual offence created by s 13 of the Sexual Offences Act 1956, the concept of gross indecency is not defined in the legislation, nor is it fully defined in the case law; but indecent exposure, without any aggravating features, cannot be sufficient. Exposure of the erect penis might be considered grossly indecent; if directed towards a girl it might also amount to an offence under s 4 of the Vagrancy Act 1824 (*qv*). Open masturbation in the presence of others would clearly amount to gross indecency: see the cases cited in the notes to s 13 of the 1956 Act.

'with or towards a child'   It is not enough that D behaves in a grossly indecent way. If he does not do so with a child (eg by allowing the child to stroke or touch him) he must do so towards it. Thus D would not commit the offence by carelessly allowing a child to watch him masturbating, but he would do so if he deliberately made an exhibition of his behaviour in front of that child.

'or who incites a child under that age to such an act with him'   An offence of incitement may be committed without any evidence that the person incited took any notice of it. Incitement may be express or implied (as where D does nothing to stop a child from touching him in a grossly indecent way). See *R v Speck* [1977] 2 All ER 859.

'or another'   D may commit the offence by inciting P to behave in a grossly indecent way with Q. It would not matter for that purpose whether Q was also a child under fourteen.

2–3. [*omitted*]

123

Suicide Act 1961

(9 & 10 ELIZ II C 60)

Suicide to cease to be a crime
1. The rule of law whereby it is a crime for a person to commit suicide is hereby abrogated.

NOTES
Suicide was a felony at common law and resulted *inter alia* in forfeiture of the offender's goods and chattels to the Crown, although a suicide verdict could be avoided by a finding that the deceased killed himself whilst the balance of his mind was disturbed.

Because suicide was a felony, an attempted suicide was a punishable offence, and, under the transferred malice doctrine, if the attempt resulted in the accidental death of another person, that would be murder (there being the requisite unlawful intent to kill).

With the abolition of the basic common law rule, none of these further consequences continue to apply.

As to the position of accessories, see s 2 *infra*.

Criminal liability for complicity in another's suicide
2. (1) A person who aids, abets, counsels or procures the suicide of another, or an attempt by another to commit suicide, shall be liable on conviction on indictment to imprisonment for a term not exceeding fourteen years.

(2) If on the trial of an indictment for murder or manslaughter it is proved that the accused aided, abetted, counselled or procured the suicide of the person in question, the jury may find him guilty of that offence.

NOTES
Complicity in the suicide of another person was formerly punishable as murder, as was killing another person in the course of a suicide pact. The latter is now manslaughter under s 4 of the Homicide Act 1957, provided that the killer genuinely intended to die himself. If not, it will generally be murder.

In contrast, liability for the offence created under this present provision does not depend on whether the offender was involved in any such pact.

'aids, abets, counsels or procures' See the notes to s 8 of the Accessories and Abettors Act 1861. See also *Att Gen v Able* [1984] 1 All ER 277 in respect of the liability of persons who publish or distribute literature dealing with methods of 'self-deliverance' for the terminally ill.

'or an attempt to commit suicide' The full offence under this provision is committed if the person to whom the encouragement or assistance is given either commits suicide or attempts to do so. If no such attempt is made, the person who advised or encouraged suicide may nevertheless be guilty of attempting to aid or abet it: *R v McShane* (1977) 66 Cr App R 97. This principle would appear to remain valid despite s 4(1) of the Criminal Attempts Act 1981, which provides that it is not an offence to attempt to aid or abet the commission of an offence. Suicide is not itself an offence: aiding an abetting it is however an offence in its own right, and can therefore be attempted.

Alternative verdicts (subs (2)). The provisions in subs (2) do not appear to provide any solution to the problem that may arise where it cannot be proved whether the reluctant survivor of a joint suicide pact killed the others or merely aided or abetted their own suicides. It would seem that a court might be obliged in such a case to acquit the survivor entirely.

Police Act 1964

(C 48)

Assaults on constables

51. (1) Any person who assaults a constable in the execution of his duty, or a person assisting a constable in the execution of his duty, shall be guilty of an offence and liable [on summary conviction to imprisonment for a term not exceeding six months or to a fine not exceeding level 5 on the standard scale or to both.]

(2) [*omitted.*]

(3) Any person who resists or wilfully obstructs a constable in the execution of his duty, or a person assisting a constable in the execution of his duty, shall be guilty of an offence and liable on summary conviction to imprisonment for a term not exceeding one month or to a fine not exceeding level 3 on the standard scale or to both.

NOTES

This provision creates a purely summary offence; but see also ss 18 and 38 of the Offences Against the Person Act 1861, which create indictable offences.

'constable' This means anyone holding the office of constable, regardless of rank, and includes special constables. It also includes prison officers: Prison Act 1952 s 8.

'in the execution of his duty' No offence can be committed under this section unless the police officer in question is acting lawfully at the time. Unlawful action cannot be consistent with his duty, even if the only element of unlawfulness is a failure to comply with the prescribed procedures when making an arrest. The officer need not however be doing anything which he has an absolute duty to do. See *Coffin v Smith* (1980) 71 Cr App R 221. Note that an off-duty police officer may put himself on duty if he encounters an emergency or a breach of the peace, and note also that the offence is one of strict liability to the extent that a lack of awareness that the victim is a police officer *etc* is not in itself a defence: *Albert v Lavin* [1982] AC 546. See further the note on 'assault' *infra*.

'assaults' As to what constitutes an assault, see the notes to s 47 of the Offences Against the Person Act 1861. Although the present offence is one of strict liability in respect of the victim's identity (*Albert v Lavin, supra*), this does not mean that D will be guilty of it if he mistakenly defends himself against policemen whom he believes to be muggers, kidnappers etc. In such circumstances, the mistake would prevent D having the *mens rea* for assault. See *Kenlin v Gardiner* [1967] 2 QB 510. The court in that case assumed that such a mistake would have to be 'reasonable'; but subsequent cases on mistaken defence (including *R v Gladstone Williams* (1984) 78 Cr App R 276) indicate that even an unreasonable mistake could suffice.

'resists' This may involve escaping from lawful arrest etc (*R v Sherriff* [1969] Crim LR 260) but most cases of resistance probably involve assault or obstruction or both. D probably need not realise that the person he is resisting is a police officer. The element of 'wilfulness' required in respect of obstruction offences is not a requisite ingredient of resistance offences.

'wilfully obstructs' D cannot commit this offence if he is trying to help the police, even if he in fact makes their job more difficult (*Wilmott v Atack* [1977] QB 498); but if he deliberately sets out to prevent them achieving their purpose he may be guilty, even if he acts from the best of motives (eg where he tries to prevent them arresting a person he thinks is innocent). See *Lewis v Cox* [1985] QB 509. D cannot be regarded as acting 'wilfully' if he does not realise that he is obstructing police officers at all: *Ostler v Elliott* [1980] Crim LR 584. Obstruction may be physical (as in *Lewis v Cox supra*) or it may take the form of tip-offs to suspects, thereby enabling them to avoid detection or arrest: *Green v Moore* [1982] QB 1044; *Betts v Stevens* [1910] 1 KB 1; *Hinchcliffe v Sheldon* [1955] 3 All ER 406.

A failure to give positive assistance to a police officer cannot ordinarily be an offence under this section (*Rice v Connolly* [1966] 2 QB 414); but note that there is a common law offence of refusing to aid a constable who is attempting to prevent or to quell a breach of the peace and who calls for assistance: *R v Waugh, The Times* 1 October 1976. Note also ss 4 and 5 of the Criminal Law Act 1967.

Obscene Publications Act 1964

(C 74)

Obscene articles intended for publication for gain

1. (1) [*repealed*]

(2) For the purpose of any proceedings for an offence against the said section 2 a person shall be deemed to have an article for publication for gain if with a view to such publication he has the article in his ownership, possession or control.

(3) In proceedings brought against a person under the said section 2 for having an obscene article for publication for gain the following provisions shall apply in place of subsections (5) and (6) of that section, that is to say,—

(a) he shall not be convicted of that offence if he proves that he had not examined the article and had no reasonable cause to suspect that it was such that his having it would make him liable to be convicted of an offence against that section; and

(b) the question whether the article is obscene shall be determined by reference to such publication for gain of the article as in the circumstances it may reasonably be inferred he had in contemplation and to any further publication.

(4) [*omitted*]

(5) References in section 3 of the Obscene Publications Act 1959 and this section to publication for gain shall apply to any publication with a view to gain, whether the gain is to accrue by way of consideration for the publication or in any other way.

NOTES

The purpose and effect of this provision is explained in the notes to ss 1 and 2 of the Obscene Publications Act 1959.

'ownership, possession or control' See the notes to s 15 of the Theft Act 1968 *infra*.

Negatives, etc for production of obscene articles

2. (1) The Obscene Publications Act 1959 (as amended by this Act) shall apply in relation to anything which is intended to be used, either alone or as one of a set, for the reproduction or manufacture therefrom of articles containing or embodying matter to be read, looked at or listened to, as if it were an article containing or embodying that matter so far as that matter is to be derived from it or from the set.

(2) For the purposes of the Obscene Publications Act 1959 (as so amended) an article shall be deemed to be had or kept for publication if it

128

is had or kept for the reproduction or manufacture therefrom of articles for publication; and the question whether an article so had or kept is obscene shall—

(a) for purposes of section 2 of the Act be determined in accordance with section 1(3)(b) above as if any reference there to publication of the article were a reference to publication of articles reproduced or manufactured from it; and

(b) for purposes of section 3 of the Act be determined on the assumption that articles reproduced or manufactured from it would be published in any manner likely having regard to the circumstances in which it was found, but in no other manner.

NOTE

Again see the notes to s 1 of the 1959 Act; and see also *Straker v DPP* [1963] 1 QB 926, which precipitated the enactment of this provision.

The tortuous wording disguises the simple principle that negatives, plates *etc* have been brought within the scope of the 1959 Act, even though they may not themselves be intended for sale, hire, distribution or circulation.

3. [*omitted*]

Criminal Law Act 1967

(C 58)

Part I: Felony and misdemeanour

Abolition of distinction between felony and misdemeanour

1. (1) All distinctions between felony and misdemeanour are hereby abolished.

(2) Subject to the provisions of this Act, on all matters on which a distinction has previously been made between felony and misdemeanour, including mode of trial, the law and practice in relation to all offences cognisable under the law of England and Wales (including piracy) shall be the law and practice applicable at the commencement of this Act in relation to misdemeanour.

NOTE

A number of older statutes have not been amended and continue to refer to felonies and misdemeanours; but since this distinction no longer exists, the texts used in this book have been edited so as to refer only to 'offences'.

2. [*repealed*] (see notes to s 4 *infra*).

Use of force in making arrest, etc.

3. (1) A person may use such force as is reasonable in the circumstances in the prevention of crime, or in effecting or assisting in the lawful arrest of offenders or suspected offenders or of persons unlawfully at large.

(2) Subsection (1) above shall replace the rules of the common law on the question when force used for a purpose mentioned in the subsection is justified by that purpose.

NOTES

This provision serves a two-fold purpose. It provides a defence to civil actions which might otherwise be maintained by persons on whom the reasonable force has been used, and it also provides a defence against criminal prosecutions. In both respects it overlaps to some extent with the common law principle of private defence (ie self-defence or the defence of other persons) but the overlap is by no means total. If D kills P's dog in order to save himself from being savaged by it, this is self-defence, but the dog is not being prevented from committing any crime. Conversely, the policeman who uses reasonable force to arrest an escaping offender is protected by this provision even though his actions have nothing to do with self-defence. Where the overlap does exist, D may plead either defence or both together (*R v Cousins* [1982] QB 526), but it is doubtful whether either would offer any significant advantages over the other. It is no longer necessary, for example, for a person to have retreated as far as possible before using force in self-defence; *R v McInnes* [1971] 3 All ER 295.

'such force as is reasonable in the circumstances'   The question whether
D's use of force was reasonable or not is one of fact for the court or jury, and it is
primarily, but not rigidly, objective: *Attorney General for Northern Ireland's Reference
(No 1 of 1975)* [1977] AC 105; *R v Whyte* [1987] 3 All ER 416. The person using
the force is not therefore his own judge of what is reasonable, any more than he is
at common law, but at the same time, the court or jury must recognise that a
person who has to use force in the heat of the moment cannot be expected to
'weigh to a nicety the exact measure of his necessary . . . action': *Palmer v R* [1971]
1 All ER 1077 per Lord Morris at p 1078. See also *R v Shannon* [1980] 71 Cr App R
192.

   If D uses wholly excessive force, even allowing for the pressures of the moment
and any mistake he may have made as to the true circumstances, both the
statutory and the common law defences fail utterly. If, for example, D has
deliberately but needlessly killed his assailant, he will *prima facie* be guilty of
murder. If he is to escape with a manslaughter conviction, it must be on the basis
of provocation (or perhaps diminished responsibility) under the Homicide Act
1957 (*qv*).

Mistake as to circumstances   Where for example D mistakenly believes that P
is attempting to commit an offence, or mistakenly believes that an offender is
armed, and uses a degree of force that would have been lawful under this section
but for his mistake, he will generally be entitled to rely on this mistake as
negativing any intent to use unlawful force, even if his mistake is an unreasonable
one. See generally *R v Williams (Gladstone)* (1984) 78 Cr App R 276; *Beckford v R*
[1987] 3 WLR 611. The position is different where the mistake is induced by
voluntary intoxication; D will then have no defence, even (according to the Court
of Appeal in *R v O'Grady* [1987] QB 995) where he is charged with an offence
requiring a 'specific intent'.

'lawful arrest'   As to what amounts to a lawful arrest, see generally Part III of
the Police and Criminal Evidence Act 1984 (not printed in this work).

Penalties for assisting offenders
   4. (1) Where a person has committed an arrestable offence, any other
person who, knowing or believing him to be guilty of the offence or of
some other arrestable offence, does without lawful authority or reasonable
excuse any act with intent to impede his apprehension or prosecution shall
be guilty of an offence.
   [(1A) In this section and section 5 below "arrestable offence" has the
meaning assigned to it by section 24 of the Police and Criminal Evidence
Act 1984.]
   (2) If on the trial of an indictment for an arrestable offence the jury are
satisfied that the offence charged (or some other offence of which the
accused might on that charge be found guilty) was committed, but find
the accused not guilty of it, they may find him guilty of any offence under
subsection (1) above of which they are satisfied that he is guilty in relation
to the offence charged (or that other offence).
   (3) A person committing an offence under subsection (1) above with
intent to impede another person's apprehension or prosecution shall on
conviction on indictment be liable to imprisonment according to the
gravity of the other person's offence, as follows:—
   (*a*) if that offence is one for which the sentence is fixed by law, he shall
        be liable to imprisonment for not more than ten years;

(*b*) if it is one for which a person (not previously convicted) may be sentenced to imprisonment for a term of fourteen years, he shall be liable to imprisonment for not more than seven years;

(*c*) if it is not one included above but is one for which a person (not previously convicted) may be sentenced to imprisonment for a term of ten years, he shall be liable to imprisonment for not more than five years;

(*d*) in any other case, he shall be liable to imprisonment for not more than three years.

(4) No proceedings shall be instituted for an offence under subsection (1) above except by or with the consent of the Director of Public Prosecutions.

(5) & (7) [*repealed*]; (6) [*omitted*].

NOTES

At common law, a person rendering assistance to one who had committed a felony would become an 'accessory after the fact' and thus guilty of that same felony. The present Act abolished that principle, but in this provision created a specific offence to replace it.

'arrestable offence' The concept of the arrestable offence was created by s 2 of this Act (now repealed), and is now defined in s 24 of the Police and Criminal Evidence Act 1984 as including:

'offences for which the sentence is fixed by law;

offences for which a person of 21 years of age or over (not previously convicted) may be sentenced to imprisonment for a term of five years (or might be so sentenced but for the restrictions imposed by section 33 of the Magistrates' Courts Act 1980);

offences for which a person may be arrested under the customs and excise Acts, as defined in section 1(1) of the Customs and Excise Management Act 1979;

offences under the Official Secrets Act 1911 and 1920 that are not arrestable offences by virtue of the term if imprisonment for which a person may be sentenced in respect of them;

offences under section ... 22 (causing prostitution of women) or 23 (procuration of girl under 21) of the Sexual Offences Act 1956; [and]

offences under section 12(1) (taking motor vehicle or other conveyance without authority etc.) or 25(1) (going equipped for stealing, etc.) of the Theft Act 1968. ...'

Other offences may carry various powers of arrest, but are not 'arrestable offences' within the meaning of this provision.

'knowing or believing him to be guilty' By analogy with the offence of handling stolen goods contrary to s 22 of the Theft Act 1968 (*qv*), this must involve something more than mere suspicion. If D does not have first-hand knowledge that E has committed such a crime, then he must positively believe him to have done so.

'of the offence or some other arrestable offence' This covers the case where D is mistaken as to the exact offence which E has committed (eg he thinks it is robbery when it is really burglary), and it may possibly cover the case where D realises E must have committed some serious offence, but assists him without having any idea what offence it may have been.

'does ... any act with intent to impede' It is the intent, which matters; D's attempt to assist E may lead directly to his arrest etc, but the complete offence may still be committed, See *R v Brindley* [1971] 2 QB 300; *R v Morgan* [1972] 1 QB 436.

An omission would not suffice for liability under this section.

'without lawful authority or reasonable excuse' The classic illustration of assistance with lawful excuse under this provision involves the destruction of a forged cheque etc, by the intended victim of the forgery, perhaps in return for the forger's promise to make good any loss that has been suffered.

Previous conviction or acquittal of the person allegedly assisted   It is not necessary that the person allegedly assisted by D should have been convicted of an arrestable offence, but his conviction will now raise a presumption that he was indeed guilty, and thus simplify the prosecution's task at D's trial (see s 74 of the Police and Criminal Evidence Act 1984). That person's acquittal at a previous trial is not however of any evidential value to the defence at D's trial.

Even where D and E are tried together, it may sometimes happen that D is convicted on the basis of a confession *etc*, that is not admissible against E, who may accordingly be acquited.

Penalties for concealing offences or giving false information

5. (1) Where a person has committed an arrestable offence, any other person who, knowing or believing that the offence or some other arrestable offence has been committed, and that he has information which might be of material assistance in securing the prosecution or conviction of an offender for it, accepts or agrees to accept for not disclosing that information any consideration other than the making good of loss or injury caused by the offence, or the making of reasonable compensation for that loss or injury, shall be liable on conviction on indictment to imprisonment for not more than two years.

(2) Where a person causes any wasteful employment of the police by knowingly making to any person a false report tending to show that an offence has been committed, or to give rise to apprehension for the safety of any persons or property, or tending to show that he has information material to any police inquiry, he shall be liable on summary conviction to imprisonment for not more than six months or to a fine of not more than level 4 on the standard scale or to both.

(3) No proceeding shall be instituted for an offence under this section except by or with the consent of the Director of Public Prosecutions.

(4) [*repealed*]

(5) The compounding of an offence other than treason shall not be an offence otherwise than under this section.

NOTES

At common law, the offence of misprision of treason may be committed by mere failure to report evidence of treason to the proper authorities, and there is a statutory offence of non-disclosure in s 18 of the Prevention of Terrorism (Temporary Provisions) Act 1989 (*qv*). With these exceptions, the non-disclosure of information concerning offences cannot ordinarily be punishable; but under subs (1) of this section, it may be an offence to strike an improper bargain under which a promise of silence or non-disclosure is exchanged for consideration going beyond a reasonable indemnity or compensation for any harm done. Note that it is the *agreement* which constitutes the *actus reus* of this offence; D will remain guilty of any such ofence even if he breaks his agreement and discloses his information to the police. If D demands money *etc* for his silence, he may also be guilty of blackmail contrary to s 21 of the Theft Act 1968 (*qv*), and in that case it will not be necessary to prove the prior commission of an arrestable offence.

Note that D need not bargain with the alleged offender himself: he might for example accept money from the offender's parents.

'arrestable offence'; 'knowing or believing'; prior conviction or acquittal for the arrestable offence   See the notes to s 4 *supra*.

Subs (2)   Note that D need not intend to waste police time; it would suffice if he knowingly makes a false report to E, who then (perhaps to D's horror) calls the police to investigate it. As to bomb hoaxes, see s 51 of the Criminal Law Act 1977.

6. [*omitted*]

7–8. [*repealed*]

9–15. [*omitted*]

Sexual Offences Act 1967

(C 60)

Amendment of law relating to homosexual acts in private

1. (1) Notwithstanding any statutory or common law provision, but subject to the provisions of the next following section, a homosexual act in private shall not be an offence provided that the parties consent thereto and have attained the age of twenty-one years.

(2) An act which would otherwise be treated for the purposes of this Act as being done in private shall not be so treated if done—

(*a*) when more than two persons take part or are present; or

(*b*) in a lavatory to which the public have or are permitted to have access, whether on payment or otherwise.

(3) A man who is suffering from [severe mental handicap] ... cannot in law give any consent which, by virtue of subsection (1) of this section, would prevent a homosexual act from being an offence, but a person shall not be convicted, on account of the incapacity of such a man to consent, of an offence consisting of such an act if he proves that he did not know and had no reason to suspect that man to be suffering from [severe mental handicap].

(3A) In subsection (3) of this section "severe mental handicap" means a state of arrested or incomplete development of mind which includes severe impairment of intelligence and social functioning.

(4) Section 128 of the Mental Health Act 1959 (prohibition on men on the staff of a hospital, or otherwise having responsibility for mental patients, having sexual intercourse with women patients) shall have effect, as if any reference therein to having unlawful sexual intercourse with a woman included a reference to committing buggery or an act of gross indecency with another man.

(5) Subsection (1) of this section shall not prevent an act from being an offence (other than a civil offence) under any provision of the Army Act 1955, the Air Force Act 1955 or the Naval Discipline Act 1957.

(6) It is hereby declared that where in any proceedings it is charged that a homosexual act is an offence the prosecutor shall have the burden of proving that the act was done otherwise than in private or otherwise than with the consent of the parties or that any of the parties had not attained the age of twenty-one years.

(7) For the purposes of this section a man shall be treated as doing a homosexual act if, and only if, he commits buggery with another man or commits an act of gross indecency with another man or is a party to the commission by a man of such an act.

135

NOTES
This provision falls short of 'legalising' homosexual acts. Quite apart from qualifications imposed by subss (2), (3), (4) and (5), and by s 2 *infra,* it is clear that, even where homosexual acts in private are free of criminal penalties, they are still regarded as 'unlawful'; and it may be an offence under s 4(1) *infra* to procure acts of buggery between other men, even if the men concerned are protected by this provision. In *Knuller v DPP* [1973] AC. 435, the House of Lords upheld convictions for conspiring to corrupt public morals, where the defendants had publicly encouraged homosexual acts.

'homosexual act' Under subs (7), the relevant acts are buggery and gross indecency, which may otherwise be punishable under ss 12 or 13 of the Sexual Offences Act 1956 (*qv*).

'in private' Subs (2) provides a partial definition; in other cases privacy is a question of fact for the jury. It would seem that regard must be had, not only to any other persons present, but also to the likelihood of any such persons coming by: see *R v Reakes* [1974] Crim LR 615.

Homosexual acts on merchant ships
  2. (1) It shall continue to be—
  (*a*) an offence under section 12 of the Act of 1956 and at common law for a man to commit buggery with another man in circumstances in which by reason of the provisions of section 1 of this Act it would not be an offence (apart from this section); and
  (*b*) an offence under section 13 of that Act for a man to commit an act of gross indecency with another man, or to be party to the commission by a man of such an act, in such circumstances as aforesaid,
provided that the act charged is done on a United Kingdom merchant ship, wherever it may be, by a man who is a member of the crew of that ship with another man who is a member of the crew of that or any other United Kingdom merchant ship.
  (2) [*repealed*]
  (3) In this section—
  "member of the crew" in relation to a ship, includes the master of the ship and any apprentice to the sea service serving in that ship;
  "United Kingdom merchant ship" means a ship registered in the United Kingdom habitually used or used at the time of the act charged for the purposes of carrying passengers or goods for reward.

NOTE
S 1 is only prevented from applying where *both* parties are merchant seamen on UK registered ships and at least one belongs to the ship on which the act takes place.

Revised punishments for homosexual acts
  3. (1) The maximum punishment which may be imposed on conviction on indictment of a man for buggery with another man of or over the age of sixteen shall, instead of being imprisonment for life as prescribed by paragraph 3 of Schedule 2 to the Act of 1956, be—
  (*a*) imprisonment for a term of ten years except where the other man consented thereto; and

(*b*) in the said excepted case, imprisonment for a term of five years if the accused is of or over the age of twenty-one and the other man is under that age, but otherwise two years;

and the maximum punishment prescribed by that paragraph for an attempt to commit buggery with another man (ten years) shall not apply where that other man is of or over the age of sixteen.

(2) The maximum punishment which may be imposed on conviction on indictment of a man of or over the age of twenty-one of committing an act of gross indecency with another man under that age or of being a party to or procuring or attempting to procure the commission by a man under that age of such an act with another man shall, instead of being imprisonment for a term of two years as prescribed by paragraph 16 of the said Schedule 2, be imprisonment for a term of five years.

(3) References in this section to a person's age, in relation to any offence, are references to his age at the time of the commission of the offence.

(4) [*repealed*]

NOTES

This provision purports to do nothing more than determine the maximum penalties which can be imposed for certain kinds of homosexual offences; but in *R v Courtie* [1984] AC 463, the House of Lords held that it had the effect of creating a number of distinct offences out of each of the basic offence-creating provisions in ss 12 and 13 of the Sexual Offences Act 1956. This means for example that buggery with a consenting male aged 16–20 years is now a distinct offence from buggery with a non-consenting male of the same age and, in the absence of an unequivocal guilty plea (or formal admission), the absence of consent must be an issue for the jury rather than a mere sentencing consideration for the judge.

Note that the maximum penalty for buggery with a woman, girl, or animal, or with a boy under 16 remains life imprisonment under Schedule 2 of the 1956 Act; but where a woman consents to the act, any custodial sentence is recognised to be wholly inappropriate—see *R v Newton* (1983) 77 Cr App R 13.

Procuring others to commit homosexual acts

4. (1) A man who procures another man to commit with a third man an act of buggery which by reason of section 1 of this Act is not an offence shall be liable on conviction on indictment to imprisonment for a term not exceeding two years.

(2) [*repealed*]

(3) It shall not be an offence under section 13 of the Act of 1956 for a man to procure the commission by another man of an act of gross indecency with the first-mentioned man which by reason of section 1 of this Act is not an offence under the said section 13.

NOTES

Procuring an act of buggery which is *not* de-criminalised by s 1 *supra* will be punishable under s 8 of the Accessories and Abettors Act 1861 (*qv*), the procurer being a party to the offence as an accessory before the fact.

Procuring an act of gross indecency between other men is an offence under s 13 of the Sexual Offences Act 1956, and not only where the act itself is punishable under that provision. For this reason it was not necessary for subs (1) of the present

provision to extend to such procuring. It was only necessary for subs (3) to prevent
s 13 applying where D procures another man to commit a non-criminal act with D
himself.

'procures'   See notes to s 2 of the Sexual Offences Act 1956.

Living on earnings of male prostitution
5. (1) A man or woman who knowingly lives wholly or in part on the
earnings of prostitution of another man shall be liable—
  (*a*) on summary conviction to imprisonment for a term not exceeding
       six months; or
  (*b*) on conviction on indictment to imprisonment for a term not
       exceeding seven years.
  (2) [*repealed*]
  (3) Anyone may arrest without a warrant a person found committing
an offence under this section.

NOTES
As to the meaning of 'lives wholly or in part on the earnings of prostitution' see
notes to s 30 of the Sexual Offences Act 1956. Unlike s 30, the offence created by
this provision can be committed by persons of either sex.

Premises resorted to for homosexual practices
6. (1) Premises shall be treated for purposes of sections 33 to 35 of the
Act of 1956 as a brothel if people resort to it for the purpose of lewd
homosexual practices in circumstances in which resort thereto for lewd
heterosexual practices would have led to its being treated as a brothel for
the purposes of those sections.

NOTES
See ss 33–35 of the 1956 Act and notes thereto.

Time limit on prosecutions
7. (1) No proceedings for an offence to which this section applies shall
be commenced after the expiration of twelve months from the date on
which that offence was committed.
  (2) This section applies to—
  (*a*) any offence under section 13 of the Act of 1956 (gross indecency
       between men);
  (*b*) [*repealed*]
  (*c*) any offence of buggery by a man with another man not amounting
       to an assault on that other man and not being an offence by a man
       with a boy under the age of sixteen.

Restriction on prosecutions
8. No proceedings shall be instituted except by or with the consent of
the Director of Public Prosecutions against any man for the offence of
buggery with, or gross indecency with, another man, ... or for aiding,
abetting, counselling, procuring or commanding its commission where

either of those men was at the time of its commission under the age of twenty-one: ...

9. [*repealed*]

10. [*omitted*]

Short title, citation, interpretation, saving and extent

11. (1) This Act may be cited as the Sexual Offences Act 1967 and the Act of 1956 and this Act may be cited as the Sexual Offences Acts 1956 and 1967.

(2) In this Act "the Act of 1956" means the Sexual Offences Act 1956.

(3) Section 46 of the Act of 1956 (interpretation of "man", "boy" and other expression) shall apply for the purposes of the provisions of this Act as it applies for the purposes of the provisions of that Act.

(4) References in this Act to any enactment shall, except in so far as the context otherwise requires, be construed as references to that enactment as amended or applied by or under any subsequent enactment including this Act.

(5) This Act shall not extend to Scotland or Northern Ireland.

Criminal Justice Act 1967

(C 80)

Miscellaneous provisions as to evidence, procedure and trial

Proof of criminal intent

8. A court or jury, in determining whether a person has committed an offence,—

(a) shall not be bound in law to infer that he intended or foresaw a result of his actions by reason only of its being a natural and probable consequence of those actions; but

(b) shall decide whether he did intend or foresee that result by reference to all the evidence, drawing such references from the evidence as appear proper in the circumstances.

NOTES

It is not always possible to draw a clear distinction between matters of criminal law and matters of evidence. This provison was enacted in an attempt to reform the law governing the *mens rea* of offences such as murder, following the widespread criticism which greeted the notorious decision of the House of Lords in *DPP v Smith* [1961] AC 290. That decision was generally interpreted as laying down an 'objective' test for determining whether a person should be found guilty of a crime requiring foresight or intent; if a given consequence was a natural and probable result of his actions, then he would be deemed to have intended it, however plausibly he might deny having done so. If that was indeed what *Smith* decided, then this provision clearly amended the law. Strictly speaking, however, the House of Lords in *Smith* did not decide that the accused should be deemed to have forseen or intended anything. The basis of their decision was that, in a case of murder,

> 'The jury must ... make up their minds whether the accused was unlawfully and voluntarily doing somthing to someone. ... Once, however the jury are satisfied as to that, it matters not what the accused contemplated as the probable result or whether he ever contemplated at all, provided he was in law responsible and accountable for his actions ... the sole question is whether the unlawful and voluntary act was of such a kind that grievous bodily harm was the natural and probable result.'

If it was, then a person who thereby killed would be guilty of murder ([1967] AC 290 at p 327).

Since s 8 determines *how* intent and foresight must be proved, rather than *whether* they need to be proved for any given offence, it follows that it fails to confront the *Smith* principle at all. Subsequent decisions of the House of Lords, culminating in *R v Moloney* [1985] AC 905, nevertheless saw the abandonment of the *Smith* principle in English law; and in *Frankland v R* [1988] Crim LR 117, the Privy Council, in deciding two appeals from the Isle of Man, declined to follow *Smith*, even though s 8 had not been adopted in Manx law at the relevant time. This prompted Professor J. C. Smith to write:

> "*Smith* ... may now surely be regarded as a case which was wrongly decided, and which never truly represented the common law. S 8 ... merely declared what, as we now know, was the law all the time." ([1988] Crim LR 199)

'court' Under s 104(1) of this Act, 'court' does not include courts-martial, but the decision in *Frankland* (*supra*) suggests that this makes no real difference, since s 8 merely restates the common law position.

inferring intent from probability Where D does an act of which the natural and probable consequence is, say, the death of another person, this will usually be cogent evidence that he intended to kill, but even if it can be proved that D was aware of the likely result, it remains nothing more than evidence of intent. It is not the same thing as intent, not is it a substitute for it (*R v Moloney* [1985] AC 905; *R v Nedrick* [1986] 3 All ER 1). It must nevertheless be possible to argue that, if D is aware that his actions must inevitably kill if carried out in accordance with his intentions, then he intends to kill, even if killing is nothing more than a side-effect of the result he intends to achieve. Awareness of inevitability should be regarded as a form of intent (oblique intent) rather than mere evidence of it.

'by reference to all the evidence' This means all the relevant and admissible evidence. Where the offence is one of 'specific intent' this includes evidence of self-induced intoxication (cf *R v Moloney, supra*), but where the alleged offence is one of 'basic intent' evidence of self-induced intoxication cannot be used to support a denial of *mens rea*. See *DPP v Majewski* [1977] AC 443.

Abortion Act 1967

(C 87)

Medical termination of pregnancy

1. (1) Subject to the provisions of this section, a person shall not be guilty of an offence under the law relating to abortion when a pregnancy is terminated by a registered medical practitioner if two registered medical practitioners are of the opinion, formed in good faith—

(*a*) that the continuance of the pregnancy would involve risk to the life of the pregnant woman, or of injury to the physical or mental health of the pregnant woman or any existing children of her family, greater than if the pregnancy were terminated; or

(*b*) that there is a substantial risk that if the child were born it would suffer from such physical or mental abnormalities as to be seriously handicapped.

(2) In determining whether the continuance of a pregnancy would involve such risk of injury to health as is mentioned in paragraph (*a*) of subsection (1) of this section, account may be taken of the pregnant woman's actual or reasonably foreseeable environment.

(3) Except as provided by subsection (4) of this section, any treatment for the termination of pregnancy must be carried out in a hospital vested in the Secretary of State for the purposes of his functions under the National Health Service Act 1977 or the National Health Service (Scotland) Act 1978 or in a place approved for the purposes of this section by the Secretary of State.

(4) Subsection (3) of this section, and so much of subsection (1) as relates to the opinion of two registered medical practitioners, shall not apply to the termination of a pregnancy by a registered medical practitioner in a case where he is of the opinion, formed in good faith, that the termination is immediately necessary to save the life or to prevent grave permanent injury to the physical or mental health of the pregnant woman.

NOTES

The law relating to abortion, as laid down in ss 58 and 59 of the Offences Against the Person Act 1861, is modified, but not supplanted, by the present Act. The 1861 provisions remain the offence-creators; but the somewhat narrow necessity defence recognised by the courts in *R v Bourne* [1939] 1 KB 687 and *R v Newton* [1958] Crim LR 489 is replaced for those purposes by the generally wider defence created by this provision.

The offence of child destruction, created by the Infant Life (Preservation) Act 1929 (*qv*) is *not* affected. Abortions involving infants capable of being born alive will contravene the 1929 Act unless justified under the proviso to s 1 of that Act, as interpreted in *Bourne*.

'the law relating to abortion' See ss 58 and 59 of the Offences Against the Person Act 1861 and s 6 *infra*.

'when a pregnancy is terminated' Ss 58 and 59 of the 1861 Act create offences of acting with intent to procure abortion—whether any abortion takes place or not. It might therefore seem that there could still be a problem with unsuccessful attempts to procure abortion; but the better view is probably that any reasonable treatment intended to procure a lawful abortion is lawful treatment: see *Royal College of Nursing v DHSS* [1981] 1 All ER 545 at 573.

'terminated by a registered medical practitioner' It is sufficient that the practitioner concerned has decided upon and taken overall responsibility for the treatment used. It is not necessary that he should carry out or even directly supervise every stage of the operation. Some such stages may properly be left to nursing staff; and, if so, the nursing staff will have the benefit of the doctor's defence: *Royal College of Nursing v DHSS* (*supra*). As to the meaning of 'registered medical practitioner', see s 56(1) and Sch 6 of the Medical Act 1983.

'opinion formed in good faith' If two medical practitioners form the opinion that abortion is justified by subs (1)(a) or (b), they may have a defence under the Act, whether or not their opinion is a sound or reasonable one. Conversely, the presence of reasonable grounds for forming such an opinion is no defence if it is clear that the opinion was not formed: *R v Smith* [1974] 1 All ER 376 (at p 381). It is difficult to imagine how a genuine opinion could be formed in bad faith; but if D(1) falsely *purports* to have formed a genuine opinion as to the need for abortion and delivers that false opinion to D(2) who relies upon it, D(2) should not be guilty as long as he himself acts in good faith: he would in effect be able to put forward a defence of mistake, so as to negative his *mens rea*. (Likewise, any nursing staff involved).

The grounds for termination Where reliance is placed on subs (1)(b), the doctors must believe there is a *substantial* risk of *serious* handicap, although not necessarily of such a handicap as to make the child, incapable of ever leading a decent life. In contrast, where reliance is placed on subs (1)(a), there is no need for them to believe there is any substantial risk, nor need the perceived risk be one of serious harm (contrast subs (4) *infra*). It is only necessary that the risks should be perceived as greater than if the pregnancy were terminated. Since there is clear statistical evidence that the dangers of childbirth generally outweigh the dangers inherent in medically supervised abortions, it is arguable that this test falls little short of providing abortion on request.

'Secretary of State' *ie* the Secretary of State for Health (or the Secretary of State for Wales in appropriate cases).

Emergency abortions (subs (4)) Subs (4) is intended to cover cases of urgent necessity where compliance with the normal procedures (including the obtaining of second opinions and the use of authorised hospitals) is believed to be impossible. Read in conjunction with s 5(2) *infra*, it might be interpreted as providing the *only* such necessity defence—so that an emergency abortion carried out by a district nurse or medical student in a snowbound country cottage would remain unlawful even if acknowledged to have saved the mother's life. The student *etc* would have a good defence to a charge of child destruction (see *R v Bourne* [1939] 1 KB 687) but no defence to charges under ss 58 or 59 of the 1861 Act. Such an interpretation should be avoided if possible, and to that end it could be argued that the existence of common law defences such as necessity or duress is seldom acknowledged in legislation to which they are applicable.

Notification

2. (1) The Secretary of State in respect of England and Wales, and the Secretary of State in respect of Scotland, shall by statutory instrument make regulations to provide—

(*a*) for requiring any such opinion as is referred to in section 1 of this Act to be certified by the practitioners or practitioner concerned in such form and at such time as may be prescribed by the regulations, and for requiring the preservation and disposal of certificates made for the purposes of the regulations;

(*b*) for requiring any registered medical practitioner who terminates a pregnancy to give notice of the termination and such other information relating to the termination as may be so prescribed;

(*c*) for prohibiting the disclosure, except to such persons or for such purposes as may be so prescribed, of notices given or information furnished pursuant to the regulations.

(2) The information furnished in pursuance of regulations made by virtue of paragraph (*b*) of subsection (1) of this section shall be notified solely to the Chief Medical Officer of the Department of Health or of the Welsh Office, or of the Scottish Home and Health Department.

(3) Any person who wilfully contravenes or wilfully fails to comply with the requirements of regulations under subsection (1) of this section shall be liable on summary conviction to a fine not exceeding level 5 on the standard scale.

(4) Any statutory instrument made by virtue of this section shall be subject to annulment in pursuance of a resolution of either House of Parliament.

NOTES
'Secretary of State' The Secretary of State for Health (or the Secretary of State for Wales in appropriate cases).

'shall ... make regulations' These are the Abortion Regulations 1968 (SI 1968 No 390) as amended by various Abortion (Amendment) Regulations (SI 1969 No 636; SI 1976 No 15; SI 1980 No 1724).

Certification of opinions (subs (1)(a)) See Regulation 4 and the schedule to SI 1976, No 15, which substitutes a new form of Certificate (Certificate A) for that originally contained in Schedule 1 of the principal Regulations.

Notice of the termination (subs (1)(b)) The form of notification originally set out in Sch 2 of the principal Regulations has been replaced by Regulation 2 and the Schedule to SI 1980 No 1724. Notification must be sent within seven days of the termination to the Chief Medical Officer at the DHSS or the Welsh Office as required by Subs (2).

Prohibition on disclosure (subs (1)(c)) Circumstances under which information on abortions may be disclosed are dealt with in Regulations 5 of the principal Regulations, as amended by SI 1969 No 636.

'wilfully contravenes ... or fails to comply' Wilfulness is a troublesome concept (see *R v Sheppard* [1980] AC 394). In this context, it would appear to cover contraventions *etc* which are either deliberate, or the result of a lack of any positive attempt to conform to the Regulations.

Application of Act to visiting forces etc

3. (1) In relation to the termination of a pregnancy in a case where the following conditions are satisfied, that is to say—

(a) the treatment for termination of the pregnancy was carried out in a hospital controlled by the proper authorities of a body to which this section applies; and

(b) the pregnant woman had at the time of the treatment a relevant association with that body; and

(c) the treatment was carried out by a registered medical practitioner or a person who at the time of the treatment was a member of that body appointed as a medical practitioner for that body by the proper authorities of that body,

this Act shall have effect as if any reference in section 1 to a registered medical practitioner and to a hospital vested in the Secretary of State included respectively a reference to such a person as is mentioned in paragraph (c) of this subsection and to a hospital controlled as aforesaid, and as if section 2 were omitted.

(2) The bodies to which this section applies are any force which is a visiting force within the meaning of any of the provisions of Part I of the Visiting Forces Act 1952 and any headquarters within the meaning of the Schedule to the International Headquarters and Defence Organisations Act 1964; and for the purposes of this section—

(a) a women shall be treated as having a relevant association at any time with a body to which this section applies if at that time—

(i) in the case of such a force as aforesaid, she had a relevant association within the meaning of the said Part I with the force; and

(ii) in the case of such a headquarters as aforesaid she was a member of the headquarters or a dependant within the meaning of the Schedule aforesaid of such a member; and

(b) any reference to a member of a body to which this section applies shall be construed—

(i) in the case of such a force as aforesaid, as a reference to a member of or of a civilian component of that force within the meaning of the said Part I; and

(ii) in the case of such a headquarters as aforesaid, as a reference to a member of that headquarters within the meaning of the Schedule aforesaid.

NOTES

The effect of this provision is to prevent s 2 from applying in cases where women associated with visiting forces, *etc* undergo medical terminations of pregnancy in hospitals controlled by those forces (*eg* at a hospital on a US military base). It also enables medical practitioners belonging to such forces *etc* to undertake such operations without being registered in the UK.

'relevant association' S 3 has no application in respect of pregnant women who have no relevant association with the visiting forces *etc*. S 12(2) of the Visiting Forces Act 1952 defines the relevant association as involving *either* membership of the visiting force or of its civilian component, *or* being a dependent of such a member. Such a dependent may not also be a British citizen, British Dependent Territories citizen or British overseas citizen, nor may she be ordinarily resident in the UK. As to the meaning of "membership of its civilian component", see s 10 of that Act. The Schedule to the 1964 Act adopts similar definitions.

Conscientious objection to participation in treatment

4. (1) Subject to subsection (2) of this section, no person shall be under any duty, whether by contract or by any statutory or other legal requirement, to participate in any treatment authorised by this Act to which he has a conscientious objection:

Provided that in any legal proceedings the burden of proof of conscientious objection shall rest on the person claiming to rely on it.

(2) Nothing in subsection (1) of this section shall affect any duty to participate in treatment which is necessary to save the life or to prevent grave permanent injury to the physical or mental health of a pregnant woman.

(3) In any proceedings before a court in Scotland, a statement on oath by any person to the effect that he has a conscientious objection to participating in any treatment authorised by this Act shall be sufficient evidence for the purpose of discharging the burden of proof imposed upon him by subsection (1) of this section.

NOTES

The main purpose of subs (1) would appear to be to protect doctors or nursing staff (especially those working for the NHS) being disciplined or dismissed for refusing to participate in routine abortions on grounds of conscientious objection.

Subs (2) effectively restates the common law position as declared by McNaghten J in *R v Bourne* [1939] 1 KB 687. A doctor who refuses on religious or moral grounds to abort a pregnancy in circumstances where the mother's life is imperilled may be guilty of manslaughter if the mother dies.

Supplementary provisions

5. (1) Nothing in this Act shall affect the provisions of the Infant Life (Preservation) Act 1929 (protecting the life of the viable foetus).

(2) For the purposes of the law relating to abortion, anything done with intent to procure the miscarriage of a woman is unlawfully done unless authorised by section 1 of this Act.

NOTES

See notes to s 1 *supra* (in particular the note on Emergency Abortions).

Interpretation

6. In this Act, the following expressions have meanings hereby assigned to them:—

'the law relating to abortion' means sections 58 and 59 of the Offences against the Person Act 1861, and any rule of law relating to the procurement of abortion;

[*other definition repealed*]

Short title, commencement and extent
7. (1) This Act may be cited as the Abortion Act 1967.

(2) This Act shall come into force on the expiration of the period of six months beginning with the date on which it is passed.

(3) This Act does not extend to Northern Ireland.

NOTES
The Act came into force on 27th April 1968.

Firearms Act 1968

(C 27)

Part I: General restrictions on possession and handling of firearms and ammunition

Requirement of firearm certificate

1. (1) Subject to any exemption under this Act, it is an offence for a person—

(a) to have in his possession, or to purchase or acquire, a firearm to which this section applies without holding a firearm certificate in force at the time, or otherwise than as authorised by such a certificate;

(b) to have in his possession, or to purchase or acquire, any ammunition to which this section applies without holding a firearm certificate in force at the time, or otherwise than as authorised by such a certificate, or in quantities in excess of those so authorised.

(2) It is an offence for a person to fail to comply with a condition subject to which a firearm certificate is held by him.

(3) This section applies to every firearm except—

[(a) a shot gun within the meaning of this Act, that is to say a smooth-bore gun (not being an air gun) which—

(i) has a barrel not less than 24 inches in length and does not have any barrel with a bore exceeding 2 inches in diameter;

(ii) either has no magazine or has a non-detachable magazine incapable of holding more than two cartridges; and

(iii) is not a revolver gun; and,]

(b) an air weapon (that is to say, an air rifle, air gun or air pistol not of a type declared by rules made by the Secretary of State under section 53 of this Act to be specially dangerous).

[(3A) A gun which has been adapted to have such a magazine as is mentioned in subsection (3)(a)(ii) above shall not be regarded as falling within that provision unless the magazine bears a mark approved by the Secretary of State for denoting that fact and that mark has been made, and the adaptation has been certified in writing as having been carried out in a manner approved by him, either by one of the two companies mentioned in section 58(1) of this Act or by such other person as may be approved by him for that purpose.]

(4) This section applies to any ammunition for a firearm, except the following articles, namely:—

(a) cartridges containing five or more shot, none of which exceeds .36 inch in diameter;

(b) ammunition for an air gun, air rifle or air pistol; and

148

(c) blank cartridges not more than one inch in diameter measured immediately in front of the rim or cannelure of the base of the cartridge.

NOTES

'subject to any exemption under this Act' Exemptions to the licence requirement are provided under s 7 (police permits), s 8 (registered firearms dealers and their servants), s 9 (carriers, auctioneers *etc*), s 10 (licenced animal slaughterers), s 11 (sporting, athletics and other approved activities), s 12 (theatrical performances, films *etc*) and s 13 (equipment for ships and aircraft). See also s 54 in relation to Crown servants, s 58 in relation to proof houses *etc*, and the Visiting Forces and International Headquarters (Application of Law) Orders, SI 1965/1536 and SI 1987/928. The Firearms (Amendment) Act 1988, ss 15–19 and Schedule, has now added further exemptions covering clubs, the use of borrowed weapons on private premises, visitors with permits, and certain museums.

'have in his possession' This may, but need not, be physical possession (*Sullivan v Earl of Caithness* (1976) 62 Cr App R 105, *Hall v Cotton* [1986] 3 All ER 332). As with cases involving the possession of drugs, D may be found guilty notwithstanding his possible ignorance of the nature of the thing concerned, and so to that extent the offence is one of strict liability; but D cannot be held to possess something which has been deposited with him without his knowledge or consent. See *R v Hussein* [1981] 2 All ER 287; *R v Howells* [1977] QB 614.

'acquire'; 'firearm'; 'firearms certificate'; 'ammunition' See s 57 *infra*.

'a firearm to which this section applies' See subs (3). As to the position in respect of antiques which are acquired or kept as curiosities or ornaments, see s 58(2) *infra*. As to the position in respect of imitation firearms that are readily convertible into working weapons, see s 1 of the Firearms Act 1982.

'shot gun' The present definition of exempted shotguns was inserted by the Firearms (Amendment) Act 1988. A rifle from which the rifling has been removed may still be a shotgun which is outside the scope of s 1 (*Attorney General's Reference (No 3 of 1980)* [1980] 3 All ER 273); but if it possesses a detachable or multi-shot magazine (as in the above case) it will no longer be so exempt.

'air weapon' This does not include a weapon in which ammunition is propelled by compressed gas rather than air: *R v Thorpe* [1987] 2 All ER 108. The specially dangerous air weapons which require a licence under this section are those which discharge missiles with kinetic energy exceeding 6 ft/lb (in the case of pistols) or 12 ft/lb (other air weapons): SI 1969/47.

Penalties See Sch 6 *infra*.

Requirement of certificate for possession of shot guns

2. (1) Subject to any exemption under this Act, it is an offence for a person to have in his possession, or to purchase or acquire, a shot gun without holding a certificate under this Act authorising him to possess shot guns.

(2) It is an offence for a person to fail to comply with a condition subject to which a shot gun certificate is held by him.

NOTES
'subject to any exemption under this Act'　See the notes to s 1 *supra*. For the purposes of this section, a further exemption exists under s 15 (holders of Northern Ireland shotgun certificates).

'have in his possession'　See the notes to s 1 *supra*.

'Shot gun'　See s 1(3)(a) and notes thereto.

'acquire', 'certificate'　See s 57(4) *infra*.

Penalty　See Sch 6 *infra*.

Business and other transactions with firearms and ammunition
　3. (1) A person commits an offence if, by way of trade or business, he—
　(a) manufactures, sells, transfers, repairs, tests or proves any firearm or ammunition to which section 1 of this Act applies, or a shot gun; or
　(b) exposes for sale or transfer, or has in his possession for sale, transfer, repair, test or proof any such firearm or ammunition, or a shot gun,
without being registered under this Act as a firearms dealer.

　(2) It is an offence for a person to sell or transfer to any other person in the United Kingdom, other than a registered firearms dealer, any firearm or ammunition to which section 1 of this Act applies, or a shot gun, unless that other produces a firearm certificate authorising him to purchase or acquire it or, as the case may be, his shot gun certificate, or shows that he is by virtue of this Act entitled to purchase or acquire it without holding a certificate.

　(3) It is an offence for a person to undertake the repair, test or proof of a firearm or ammunition to which section 1 of this Act applies, or of a shot gun, for any other person in the United Kingdom other than a registered firearms dealer as such, unless that other produces or causes to be produced a firearm certificate authorising him to have possession of the firearm or ammunition or, as the case may be, his shot gun certificate, or shows that he is by virtue of this Act entitled to have possession of it without holding a certificate.

　(4) Subsections (1) to (3) above have effect subject to any exemption under subsequent provisions of this Part of this Act.

　(5) A person commits an offence if, with a view to purchasing or acquiring, or procuring the repair, test or proof of, any firearm or ammunition to which section 1 of this Act applies, or a shot gun, he produces a false certificate or a certificate in which any false entry has been made, or personates a person to whom a certificate has been granted, or makes any false statement.

　(6) It is an offence for a pawnbroker to take in pawn any firearm or ammunition to which section 1 of this Act applies, or a shot gun.

NOTES
'by way of trade or business'　Cf *R v Breeze* [1973] 2 All ER 1141; *Abernethie v A.M. & N. Kleiman Ltd* [1969] 2 All ER 790. In the latter case, Widgery LJ said (at p 794),

'What a man does with his spare time in his home is most unlikely to qualify for the description "business" unless it has some direct commercial involvement in it. . . .'

'firearm . . . to which s 1 of this Act applies'   See also s 1 of the Firearms Act 1982, which brings imitation weapons within the scope of this provision if they are readily convertible into working condition.

'sells'   See *DPP v Holmes, The Times* April 7th 1988, in which it was held that a sale may take place, even though the 'buyer' is acting for the police with a view to entrapping the vendor.

'shot gun'   See s 1(3)(a) *supra* and the notes thereto.

'transfer'; 'acquire'; 'certificate'; 'firearms dealer'; 'ammunition'   See s 57 *infra*.

Penalties   See Sch 6 *infra*.

Conversion of weapons

4. (1) Subject to this section, it is an offence to shorten the barrel of a shot gun to a length less than 24 inches.

(2) It is not an offence under subsection (1) above for a registered firearms dealer to shorten the barrel of a shot gun for the sole purpose of replacing a defective part of the barrel so as to produce a barrel not less than 24 inches in length.

(3) It is an offence for a person other than a registered firearms dealer to convert into a firearm anything which, though having the appearance of being a firearm, is so constructed as to be incapable of discharging any missile through its barrel.

(4) A person who commits an offence under section 1 of this Act by having in his possession, or purchasing or acquiring, a shot gun which has been shortened contrary to subsection (1) above or a firearm which has been converted as mentioned in sub-s (3) above, (whether by a registered firearms dealer or not), without holding a firearm certificate authorising him to have it in his possession, or to purchase or acquire it, shall be treated for the purposes of provisions of this Act relating to the punishment of offences as committing that offence in an aggravated form.

NOTES

S 6 of the Firearms (Amendment) Act 1988 creates a similar offence to that contained in subs (1), but is applicable only in respect of smooth bore weapons which are not exempted shot guns under s 1(3) *supra*. The 'sawn off' shot gun remains a particularly dangerous weapon at short ranges and can be concealed more easily than an ordinary shot gun. Such a weapon is a firearm to which s 1 of this Act applies.

Subs (2)   There is a limited scope to this subsection, since the shortening of a barrel to, say 25 inches cannot in any event be an offence under subs (1), whoever does it, and for whatever reason. It might, however, cover the dealer who shortens a weapon prior to refitting a new part which would restore the total length to 24 inches or more.

Measurement of barrel lengths   See s 57(6)(a) *infra*.

'possession'   See the notes to s 1 *supra.*

'acquire'; **'firearms dealer'**; **'firearm'**; **'registered'**   See s 57 *infra.*

Penalties   See Sch 6 *infra.*

Prohibition of certain weapons and control of arms traffic

Weapons subject to general prohibition

5.—(1) A person commits an offence if, without the authority of the Defence Council, he has in his possession, or purchases or acquires, or manufactures, sells or transfers—

[(*a*) any firearm which is so designed or adapted that two or more missiles can be successively discharged without repeated pressure on the trigger;

(*ab*) any self-loading or pump-action rifle other than one which is chambered for .22 rim-fire cartridges;

(*ac*) any self-loading or pump-action smooth-bore gun which is not chambered for .22 rim-fire cartridges and either has a barrel less than 24 inches in length or (excluding any detachable, folding, retractable or other movable butt-stock) is less than 40 inches in length overall;

(*ad*) any smooth-bore revolver gun other than one which is chambered for 9 mm rim-fire cartridges or loaded at the muzzle end of each chamber;

(*ae*) any rocket launcher, or any mortar, for projecting a stabilised missile, other than a launcher or mortar designed for line-throwing or pyrotechnic purposes or as signalling apparatus;

(*b*) any weapon of whatever description designed or adapted for the discharge of any noxious liquid, gas or other thing; and

(*c*) any cartridge with a bullet designed to explode on or immediately before impact, any ammunition containing or designed or adapted to contain any such noxious thing as is mentioned in paragraph (*b*) above and, if capable of being used with a firearm of any description, any grenade, bomb (or other like missile), or rocket or shell designed to explode as aforesaid].

(2) The weapons and ammunition specified in subsection (1) of this section are referred to in this Act as "prohibited weapons" and "prohibited ammunition" respectively.

(3) An authority given to a person by the Defence Council under this section shall be in writing and be subject to conditions specified therein.

(4) The conditions of the authority shall include such as the Defence Council, having regard to the circumstances of each particular case, think fit to impose for the purpose of securing that the prohibited weapon or ammunition to which the authority relates will not endanger the public safety or the peace.

(5) It is an offence for a person to whom an authority is given under this section to fail to comply with any condition of the authority.

(6) The Defence Council may at any time, if they think fit, revoke an authority given to a person under this section by notice in writing

requiring him to deliver up the authority to such person as may be specified in the notice within twenty-one days from the date of the notice; and it is an offence for him to fail to comply with that requirement.

NOTES
This provision has been heavily amended by s 1 of the Firearms (Amendment) Act 1988, following the Hungerford 'massacre' of 1987, where a gunman armed with semi-automatic weapons went berserk and killed many people. Most of the weapons and ammunition covered by the amended provision are military weapons, some of which (eg those covered by subs (1)(ae)) could only be of interest to military forces or terrorists. Other weapons now covered have in the past been used for sporting purposes or for the purpose of hunting or culling deer *etc.*
The Secretary of State is empowered by s 1(4) of the 1988 Act to make orders by statutory instrument amending the present provision so as to include new types of weapon in the general prohibition.

Measurement of barrel length (subs (1)(ac))   See s 57(6) *infra.*

Subs (1)(b)   This includes an electric 'stunning' device: *Flack v Baldry* [1988] Crim LR 610.

'acquire'; 'transfer'; 'ammunition'; 'firearm' See s 57 *infra.*

Penalties   See Sch 6 *infra.*

6–13 [*omitted*] (See notes to s 1 *supra*)

14 [*repealed*]

15 [*omitted*]

Prevention of crime and perservation of public safety

Possession of firearm with intent to injure
16. It is an offence for a person to have in his possession any firearm or ammunition with intent by means thereof to endanger life ... or to enable another person by means thereof to endanger life ... whether any injury to property has been caused or not.

NOTES
'have in his possession'   See the notes to s 1 *supra.* Possession in a designated 'convention country' outside the United Kingdom is within the scope of this provision, by virtue of the Suppression of Terrorism Act 1978, s 4 (*qv*).

'firearm or ammunition'   See s 57 *infra:* and note that the definition there provided is sufficiently wide as to include component parts, incomplete or unserviceable weapons, and certain accessories. S 1 of the Firearms Act 1982, which deals with imitation firearms that are readily convertible into working order, does not as such apply to offences under this provision, but a convertible replica may still be within the scope of this provision if it contains some genuine working components: see *R v Freeman* [1970] 2 All ER 413.

'with intent by means thereof to endanger life'   This is an ulterior intent, and may only be conditional: *R v Bentham* [1973] QB 357. If the intent can be proved, it is not necessary that any life should actually have been endangered, and if D possesses the weapons within the jurisdiction, it does not matter if he only intended to misuse it abroad: *R v El Hakkaoui* [1975] 2 All ER 146.

The life in question must be that of another: an intent to use the weapon for suicide does not suffice: *R v Norton* [1977] Crim LR 478.

As to possession for the purpose of lawful self-defence, see *R v Georgiades* [1989] Crim LR 574.

Penalty   See Sch 6 *infra*.

Use of firearm to resist arrest

17. (1) It is an offence for a person to make or attempt to make any use whatsoever of a firearm or imitation firearm with intent to resist or prevent the lawful arrest or detention of himself or another person.

(2) If a person, at the time of his committing or being arrested for an offence specified in Schedule 1 to this Act, has in his possession a firearm or imitation firearm, he shall be guilty of an offence under this subsection unless he shows that he had it in his possession for a lawful object.

(3) [*repealed*].

(4) For purposes of this section, the definition of "firearm" in section 57(1) of this Act shall apply without paragraph (*b*) and (*c*) of that subsection, and "imitation firearm" shall be construed accordingly.

(5) [*omitted*].

NOTES

Subss (1) & (2) create quite distinct offences; but in each case the term 'firearm' has a rather more restricted meaning than elsewhere in the Act. Possession of component parts or of accessories for firearms does not come within the terms of the section, owing to the exclusion of s 57(1) (b)–(c) by subs (4). On the other hand, the misuse or possession of an imitation firearm may come within its terms, whether or not the imitation weapon is capable of conversion into working order.

The offence created by subs (1) has an extraterritorial ambit under s 4 of the Suppression of Terrorism Act 1978 (*qv*).

'imitation firearm'   See s 57(4) *infra*. Note that this definition has been held to embrace real weapons which are no longer in working order: *R v Debreli* [1964] Crim LR 53.

'make ... any use whatsoever'   This need not mean use or threatened use as a firearm; it would suffice if the butt of a revolver was used as a cosh.

'or attempt to make'   The reference to attempt seems superfluous, since this is an indictable offence to which the Criminal Attempts Act 1981 in any case applies. Note s 3 of that Act.

'lawful arrest or detention'   The lawfulness of the arrest in question is a crucial element in the offence, and a technical irregularity may make a conviction impossible. Cf s 51 of the Police Act 1964.

'has in his possession'   See the notes to s 1 *supra*.

'at the time of his ... being arrested for an offence specified in schedule 1'   Sch 1 is printed *infra*. It is not necessary for the purpose of a subs (2) offence that D should possess the firearm *etc.* in connection with the offence for which he is arrested; but it has been held that D must actually have been guilty of a sch 1 offence: he cannot be guilty just because he was the victim of a lawful but mistaken arrest. See *R v Baker* [1961] 2 QB 550.

'unless he shows'   This requires proof on balance of probabilities.

Penalties   See Sch 6 *infra*.

Carrying firearm with criminal intent
18. (1) It is an offence for a person to have with him a firearm or imitation firearm with intent to commit an indictable offence, or to resist arrest or prevent the arrest of another, in either case while he has the firearm or imitation firearm with him.

(2) In proceedings for an offence under this section proof that the accused had a firearm or imitation firearm with him and intended to commit an offence, or to resist or prevent arrest, is evidence that he intended to have it with him while doing so.

(3) [*omitted*].

NOTES
'firearm or imitation firearm'   See s 57(1) and (4) *infra*. Note that incomplete and defective weapons are within the scope of this section.

'have with him'   This is a narrower concept than possession (see *R v Kelt* (1977) 65 Cr App R 74). It seems clear that D must know he has the firearm *etc*. since it must be proved that he intended to have it with him when committing the ulterior offence. On the other hand it will not matter if D is mistaken as to whether the thing in question is real or imitation.

Penalty   See Sch 6 *infra*.

Carrying a firearm in a public place
19. A person commits an offence if, without lawful authority or reasonable excuse (the proof whereof lies on him) he has with him in a public place a loaded shot gun or loaded air weapon, or any other firearm (whether loaded or not) together with ammunition suitable for use in that firearm.

NOTES
This provision serves a broadly similar function to s 1 of the Prevention of Crime Act 1953 (*qv*). It is not, however, necessary to prove that the firearm in question is an offensive weapon (*ie* made, adapted or intended for causing injury); and in that respect the present offence will sometimes be easier to prove.

'without lawful authority or reasonable excuse'; 'the proof whereof shall lie on him'   See the notes to s 1 of the 1953 Act; but note that it will often be easier for D to prove lawful authority or reasonable excuse for possession of a loaded shotgun *etc* than for possession of an offensive weapon.

'has with him in a public place'   See the notes to s 1 of the 1953 Act. The definition of 'public place' in s 57(4) of this Act is identical to that in s 1(4) of the 1953 Act.

'air weapon'; 'shot gun'; 'firearm'; 'ammunition'; 'loaded'   See s 57 *infra*.

Penalty   See Sch 6 *infra*.

Trespassing with firearm

20. (1) A person commits an offence if, while he has a firearm with him, he enters or is in any building or part of a building as a trespasser and without reasonable excuse (the proof whereof lies on him).

(2) A person commits an offence if, while he has a firearm with him, he enters or is on any land as a trespasser and without reasonable excuse (the proof whereof lies on him).

(3) In subsection (2) of this section the expression "land" includes land covered with water.

NOTES

Subs (1) creates an offence which is in many respects identical to that of aggravated burglary under s 9(1)(a) and s 10 of the Theft Act 1968 (*qqv*). The only obvious differences are that there is no need for proof of any ulterior intent to steal, rape, *etc* and that D may commit the offence by 'being in' the building as a trespasser, whether he entered as such or not. It was held in *R v Collins* [1973] QB 100 that, to be guilty of burglary, D must at least be recklesss as to the fact that he is trespassing, and it is submitted that a similar rule should apply here.

A less obvious point is that possession of an imitation weapon may lead to liability for aggravated burglary, but not to liability here, even where the weapon is 'convertible' within the meaning of s 1 of the Firearms Act 1982.

The offence created by subs (2) would be committed (*inter alia*) by anyone who goes poaching with a firearm, but D would also commit the offence if he were to take an illicit short cut across his neighbour's land whilst carrying a firearm.

'firearm' See s 57(1) *infra*. Note that the wider meaning under s 1 of the 1982 Act is not applicable here. (See s 2 of that Act.)

Penalties See Sch 6 *infra*.

Possession of firearms by persons previously convicted of crime

21. (1) A person who has been sentenced to custody for life or to preventive detention, or to imprisonment or to corrective training for a term of three years or more or to youth custody or detention in a young offender institution for such a term, or who has been sentenced to be detained for such a term in a young offenders institution in Scotland, shall not at any time have a firearm or ammunition in his possession.

(2) A person who has been sentenced ... to imprisonment for a term of three months or more but less than three years or to youth custody [or detention in a young offender institution for such a term], or who has been sentenced to be detained for such a term in a detention centre or in a young offenders institution in Scotland, shall not at any time before the expiration of the period of five years from the date of his release have a firearm or ammunition in his possession.

(2A) For the purpose of subsection (2) above, "the date of his release", in the case of a person sentenced to imprisonment with an order under section 47(1) of the Criminal Law Act 1977, is the date on which he completes service of so much of the sentence as was by that order required to be served in prison.

(3) A person who—

(*a*) is the holder of a licence issued under section 53 of the Children and Young Persons Act 1933 or section 57 of the Children and Young Persons (Scotland) Act 1937 (which sections provide for the detention of children and young persons convicted of serious crime, but enable them to be discharged on licence by the Secretary of State); or

(*b*) is subject to a recognizance to keep the peace or to be of good behaviour, a condition of whch is that he shall not possess, use or carry a firearm, or is subject to a probation order containing a requirement that he shall not possess, use or carry a firearm; or

(*c*) has, in Scotland, been ordained to find caution a condition of which is that he shall not possess, use or carry a firearm;

shall not, at any time during which he holds the licence or is so subject or has been so ordained, have a firearm or ammunition in his possession.

(3A) Where by section 19 of the Firearms Act (Northern Ireland) 1969, or by any other enactment for the time being in force in Northern Ireland and corresponding to this section, a person is prohibited in Northern Ireland from having a firearm or ammunition in his possession, he shall also be so prohibited in Great Britain at any time when to have it in his possession in Northern Ireland would be a contravention of the said section 19 or corresponding enactment.

(4) It is an offence for a person to contravene any of the foregoing provisions of this section.

(5) It is an offence for a person to sell or transfer a firearm or ammunition to, or to repair, test or prove a firearm or ammunition for, a person whom he knows or has reasonable ground for believing to be prohibited by this section from having a firearm or ammunition in his possession.

(6) A person prohibited under subsection (1), (2), (3) or (3A) of this section from having in his possession a firearm or ammunition may apply to the Crown Court or, in Scotland, in accordance with Act of Sederunt to the sheriff for a removal of the prohibition; and if the application is granted that prohibition shall not then apply to him.

(7) Schedule 3 to this Act shall have effect with respect to the courts with jurisdiction to entertain an application under this section and to the procedure appertaining thereto.

NOTES

'preventive detention'; 'corrective training' These are obsolete forms of sentence in English law, but may still be relevant in the present context if D has served such a sentence in the past.

'imprisonment' This does not include a suspended sentence: *R v Fordham* [1970] 1 QB 77.

'firearm'; 'ammunition' See s 57 *infra*.

'sell' See the notes to s 3 *supra*.

Penalty See Sch 6 *infra*.

Acquisition and possession of firearms by minors

22. (1) It is an offence for a person under the age of seventeen to purchase or hire any firearm or ammunition.

(2) It is an offence for a person under the age of fourteen to have in his possession any firearm or ammunition to which section 1 of this Act or section 15 of the Firearms (Amendment) Act 1988 applies, except in circumstances where under section 11(1), (3) or (4) of this Act he is entitled to have possession of it without holding a firearm certificate.

(3) It is an offence for a person under the age of fifteen to have with him an assembled shot gun except while under the supervision of a person of or over the age of twenty-one, or while the shot gun is so covered with a securely fastened gun cover that it cannot be fired.

(4) Subject to section 23 below, it is an offence for a person under the age of fourteen to have with him an air weapon or ammunition for an air weapon.

(5) Subject to section 23 below, it is an offence for a person under the age of seventeen to have an air weapon with him in a public place, except an air gun or air rifle which is so covered with a securely fastened gun cover that it cannot be fired.

NOTES
'firearm'; 'ammunition'; 'public place' See s 57 *Infra.*

'shot gun'; 'air weapon' See s 1(3) *supra*; and note that some shot guns and air weapons are firearms to which s 1 of the Act applies, and thus within the scope of subs (2) of this section.

'except ... where under s 11' S 11 (not printed in this work) covers the possession of firearms in connection with sporting and other approved activities, including cadet corps and shooting galleries.

'have in his possession' See the notes to s 1 *supra.*

'have with him' See the notes to s 18 *supra.*

Penalties See Sch 6 *infra.*

Exceptions from s 22(4) and (5)

23. (1) It is not an offence under section 22(4) of this Act for a person to have with him an air weapon or ammunition while he is under the supervision of a person of or over the age of twenty-one; but where a person has with him an air weapon on any premises in circumstances where he would be prohibited from having it with him but for this subsection, it is an offence—

(a) for him to use it for firing any missile beyond those premises; or

(b) for the person under whose supervision he is to allow him so to use it.

(2) It is not an offence under section 22(4) or (5) of this Act for a person to have with him an air weapon or ammunition at a time when—

(a) being a member of a rifle club or miniature rifle club for the time being approved by the Secretary of State for the purposes of this section or section 15 of the Firearms (Amendment) Act 1988 he is engaged as such a member in or in connection with target practice; or

(*b*) he is using the weapon or ammunition at a shooting gallery where the only firearms used are either air weapons or miniature rifles not exceeding .23 inch calibre.

NOTES
'premises' See s 57(4) *infra*. Other terms as in s 22 *supra*.

Supplying firearms to minors
24. (1) It is an offence to sell or let on hire any firearm or ammunition to a person under the age of seventeen.

(2) It is an offence—

(*a*) to make a gift of or lend any firearm or ammunition to which section 1 of this Act applies to a person under the age of fourteen; or

(*b*) to part with the possession of any such firearm or ammunition to a person under that age, except in circumstances where that person is entitled under section 11(1), (3) or (4) of this Act to have possession thereof without holding a firearm certificate.

(3) It is an offence to make a gift of a shot gun or ammunition for a shot gun to a person under the age of fifteen.

(4) It is an offence—

(*a*) to make a gift of an air weapon or ammunition for an air weapon to a person under the age of fourteen;, or

(*b*) to part with the possession of an air weapon or ammunition for an air weapon to a person under that age except where by virtue of section 23 of this Act or section 15 of the Firearms (Amendment) Act 1988 the person is not prohibited from having it with him.

(5) In proceedings for an offence under any provision of this section it is a defence to prove that the person charged with the offence believed the other person to be of or over the age mentioned in that provision and had reasonable ground for the belief.

NOTES
See generally the notes to s 22 *supra*.

Penalties See Sch 6 *infra*.

Supplying firearm to person drunk or insane
25. It is an offence for a person to sell or transfer any firearm or ammunition to, or to repair, prove or test any firearm or ammunition for, another person whom he knowns or has reasonable cause for believing to be drunk or of unsound mind.

NOTES
'firearm'; 'ammunition'; 'transfer' See s 57 *infra*.

'knows or has reasonable cause for believing ...' D may commit this offence even if he fails to notice the obvious signs of drunkeness *etc*; but it is submitted that the other person must indeed be drunk or of unsound mind. It should not suffice merely that there was some misleading evidence which might have given D reasonable cause to suspect it.

Penalty See Sch 6 *infra.*

Part IV: Miscellaneous and general

Interpretation

57. (1) In this Act, the expression "firearm" means a lethal barrelled weapon of any description from which any shot, bullet or other missile can be discharged and includes—

(a) any prohibited weapon, whether it is such a lethal weapon as aforesaid or not; and

(b) any component part of such a lethal or prohibited weapon; and

(c) any accessory to any such weapon designed or adapted to diminish the noise or flash caused by firing the weapon;

and so much of section 1 of this Act as excludes any description of firearm from the category of firearms to which that section applies shall be construed as also excluding component parts of, and accessories to, firearms of that description.

(2) In this Act, the expression "ammunition" means ammunition for any firearm and includes grenades, bombs and other like missiles, whether capable of use with a firearm or not, and also includes prohibited ammunition.

(2A) In this Act "self-loading" and "pump-action" in relation to any weapon mean respectively that it is designed or adapted (otherwise than as mentioned in section 5(1)(a)) so that it is automatically re-loaded or that it is so designed or adapted that it is re-loaded by the manual operation of the fore-end or forestock of the weapon.

(2B) In this Act "revolver', in relation to a smooth-bore gun, means a gun containing a series of chambers which revolve when the gun is fired.

(3) For purposes of sections 45, 46, 50, 51(4) and 52 of this Act, the offences under this Act relating specifically to air weapons are those under sections 22(4), 22(5), 23(1) and 24(4).

(4) In this Act—

"acquire" means hire, accept as a gift or borrow and

"acquisition " shall be constructed accordingly;

"air weapon" has the meaning assigned to it by section 1(3)(b) of this Act;

"area" means a police area;

"certificate" (except in a context relating to the registration of firearms dealers) and "certificate under this Act" means a firearm certificate or a shot gun certificate and—

(a) "firearm certificate" means a certificate granted by a chief officer of police under this Act in respect of any firearm or ammunition to which section 1 of this Act applies and includes a certificate granted in Northern Ireland under section 1 of the Firearms Act 1920 or under an enactment of the Parliament of Northern Ireland amending or substituted for that section; and

(b) "shot gun certificate" means a certificate granted by a chief officer of police under this Act and authorising a person to possess shot guns;

"firearms dealer" means a person who, by way of trade or business, manufactures, sells, transfers, repairs, tests or proves firearms or ammunition to which section 1 of this Act applies, or shot guns;

"imitation firearm" means anything which has the appearance of being a firearm (other than such a weapon as is mentioned in section 5(1)(b) of this Act) whether or not it is capable of discharging any shot, bullet or other missile;

"premises" includes any land;

"prescribed" means prescribed by rules made by the Secretary of State under section 53 of this Act;

"prohibited weapon" and "prohibited ammunition" have the meanings assigned to them by section 5(2) of this Act;

"public place" includes any highway and any other premises or place to which at the material time the public have or are permitted to have access, whether on payment or otherwise;

"registered", in relation to a firearms dealer, means registered either—

(a) in Great Britain, under section 33 of this Act, or

(b) in Northern Ireland, under section 8 of the Firearms Act 1920 or any enactment of the Parliament of Northern Ireland amending or substituted for that section,

and references to "the register", "registration" and a "certificate of registration" shall be construed accordingly, except in section 40;

"rifle" includes carbine;

"shot gun" has the meaning assigned to it by section 1(3)(a) of this Act and, in sections 3(1) and 45(2) of this Act and in the definition of "firearms dealer", includes any component part of a shot gun and any accessory to a shot gun designed or adapted to diminish the noise or flash caused by firing the gun;

"slaughtering instrument" means a firearm which is specially designed or adapted for the instantaneous slaughter of animals or for the instantaneous stunning of animals with a view to slaughtering them; and

"transfer" includes let on hire, give, lend and part with possession, and "transferee" and "transferor" shall be construed accordingly.

(5) The definitions in subsections (1) to (3) above apply to the provisions of this Act except where the context otherwise requires.

(6) For purposes of this Act—

(a) the length of the barrel of a firearm shall be measured from the muzzle to the point at which the charge is exploded on firing; and

(b) a shot gun or an air weapon shall be deemed to be loaded if there is ammunition in the chamber or barrel or in any magazine or other device which is in such a position that the ammunition can be fed into the chamber or barrel by the manual or automatic operation of some part of the gun or weapon.

NOTES

'lethal barrelled weapon' No problem arises here in respect of traditional firearms, but in the case of a weapon such as an air pistol it may be necessary for evidence to be adduced in order to show that it is capable of inflicting lethal injury (*Grace v DPP* [1989] Crim LR 365). Lethality if discharged at a particularly vulnerable part of the body at close range suffices to make an air weapon *etc*, a firearm for the purpose of this Act, and note that some air weapons are so powerful that they require a full firearms licence under s 1 *supra*.

See also *Read v Donovan* [1947] KB 326 (signal pistol held to be a lethal barrelled weapon) and *R v Singh* [1989] Crim LR 724 (flare launcher).

'component part' This does not include a removable telescopic sight (*Watson v Herman* [1952] 2 All ER 70); but an imitation weapon which contains genuine component parts will be covered. See *R v Freeman* [1970] 2 All ER 413, following *Cafferata v Wilson* [1936] 3 All ER 149.

Note that subss (1)(b)–(c) are excluded for the purposes of s 17 *supra*.

'accessory' An integral silencer which attaches permanently to the barrel does not require a separate firearms licence from the weapon it fits: *Broome v Walter* [1989] Crim LR 725.

'ammunition' This includes blank cartridges: *Burfitt v A & E Kille* [1939] 2 KB 743.

'imitation firearm' This definition (which could embrace mere toys) is relevant only to ss 17 and 18 of the Act; but see also s 1 of the Firearms Act 1982, which deals with those imitation weapons which are readily convertible into working order, and which has a wider effect.

Particular savings

58. (1) Nothing in this Act shall apply to the proof houses of the Master, Wardens and Society of the Mystery of Gunmakers of the City of London and the guardians of the Birmingham proof house or the rifle range at Small Heath in Birmingham where firearms are sighted and tested, so as to interfere in any way with the operations of those two companies in proving firearms under the provisions of the Gun Barrel Proof Act 1868 or any other Acts for the time being in force, or to any person carrying firearms to or from any such proof house when being taken to such proof house for the purposes of proof or being removed therefrom after proof.

(2) Nothing in this Act relating to firearms shall apply to an antique firearm which is sold, transferred purchased, acquired or possessed as a curiosity or ornament.

(3) The provisions of this Act relating to ammunition shall be in addition to and not in derogation of any enactment relating to the keeping and sale of explosives.

(4) [*repealed*].

(5) Nothing in this Act relieves any person using or carrying a firearm from his obligation to take out a licence to kill game under the enactments requiring such licence.

59. [*omitted*].

Short title, commencement and extent
60. (1) This Act may be cited as the Firearms Act 1968.

(2) This Act shall come into force on 1st August 1968.

(3) This Act shall not extend to Northern Ireland.

SCHEDULES

SCHEDULE 1
(Section 17)

OFFENCES TO WHICH SECTION 17(2) APPLIES

1. Offences under section 1 of the Criminal Damage Act 1971.

2. Offences under any of the following provisions of the Offences Against the Person Act 1861:—

sections 20 to 22 (inflicting bodily injury; garrotting; criminal use of stupefying drugs);

section 30 (laying explosive to building etc.);

section 32 (endangering railway passengers by tampering with track);

section 38 (assault with intent to commit felony or resist arrest);

section 47 (criminal assaults);

2A. Offences under Part I of the Child Abduction Act 1984 (abduction of children).

3. [*repealed*].

4. Theft, burglary, blackmail and any offence under section 12(1) (taking of motor vehicle or other conveyance without owner's consent) of the Theft Act 1968.

5. Offences under section 51(1) of the Police Act 1964 or section 41 of the Police (Scotland) Act 1967 (assaulting constable in execution of his duty).

6. Offences under any of the following provisions of the Sexual Offences Act 1956:—

section 1 (rape);

sections 17, 18 and 20 (abduction of women).

7. [*repealed*].

8. Aiding or abetting the commission of any offence specified in paragraphs 1 to 6 of this Schedule.

9. Attempting to commit any offence so specified, . . .

SCHEDULE 6
(Section 51)

PROSECUTION AND PUNISHMENT OF OFFENCES

PART I

TABLE OF PUNISHMENTS

Section of this Act creating offence	General nature of offence	Mode of prosecution	Punishment
Section 1(1)	Possessing etc firearm or ammunition without firearm certificate.	(a) Summary	6 months or a fine of the prescribed sum; or both.
		(b) On indictment	(i) where the offence is committed in an aggravated form within the meaning of section 4(4) of this Act, 5 years, or a fine; or both, (ii) in any other case, 3 years or a fine; or both.
Section 1(2)	Non-compliance with condition of firearm certificate.	Summary	6 months or a fine of level 5 on the standard scale; or both.
Section 2(1)	Possessing, etc, shot gun without shot gun certificate.	(a) Summary	6 months or the statutory maximum or both.
		(b) On indictment	3 years or a fine or both.
Section 2(2)	Non-compliance with condition of shot gun certificate.	Summary	6 months or a fine of level 5 on the standard scale; or both.
Section 3(1)	Trading in firearms without being registered as firearms dealer.	(a) Summary	6 months or a fine of the prescribed sum; or both.
		(b) On indictment	3 years or a fine; or both.
Section 3(2)	Selling firearm to person without a certificate.	(a) Summary	6 months or a fine of the prescribed sum; or both.
		(b) On indictment	3 years or a fine; or both.
Section 3(3)	Repairing, testing etc firearm for person without a certificate.	(a) Summary	6 months or a fine of the prescribed sum; or both.
		(b) On indictment	3 years or a fine; or both.
Section 3(5)	Falsifying certificate, etc, with view to acquisition of firearm.	(a) Summary	6 months or a fine of the prescribed sum; or both.
		(b) On indictment	3 years or a fine; or both.

Section of this Act creating offence	General nature of offence	Mode of prosecution	Punishment
Section 3(6)	Pawnbroker taking firearm in pawn.	Summary	3 months or a fine of level 3 on the scale; or both.
Section 4(1) (3)	Shortening a shot gun; conversion of firearms.	(a) Summary	6 months or a fine of the prescribed sum; or both.
		(b) On indictment	5 years or a fine; or both.
Section 5(1)	Possessing or distributing prohibited weapons or ammunition.	(a) Summary	6 months or a fine of the prescribed sum; or both.
		(b) On indictment	5 years or a fine; or both.
Section 5(5)	Non-compliance with condition of Defence Council authority.	Summary	6 months or a fine of level 5 on the standard scale; or both.
Section 5(6)	Non-compliance with requirement to surrender authority to possess, etc, prohibited weapon or ammunition.	Summary	A fine of level 3 on the standard scale.
Section 16	Possession of firearm with intent to endanger life or injure property.	On indictment	Life imprisonment or a fine; or ... both.
Section 17(1)	Use of firearms to resist arrest.	On indictment	Life imprisonment or a fine; or ... both.
Section 17(2)	Possessing firearm while committing an offence in Schedule 1 or, in Scotland, an offence specified in Schedule 2.	On indictment	Life imprisonment or a fine; or ... both.
Section 18(1)	Carrying firearms or imitation firearm with intent to commit indictable offence (or, in Scotland, an offence specified in Schedule 2) or to resist arrest.	On indictment	Life imprisonment or a fine; or ... both.
Section 19	Carrying loaded firearm in public place.	(a) Summary	6 months or a fine of the prescribed sum; or both.
		(b) On indictment (but not if the firearm is an air weapon).	5 years or a fine; or both.

Section of this Act creating offence	General nature of offence	Mode of prosecution	Punishment
Section 20(1)	Trespassing with firearm in a building.	(*a*) Summary	6 months or a fine of the prescribed sum; or both.
		(*b*) On indictment (but not if the firearm is an air weapon).	5 years or a fine; or both.
Section 20(2)	Trespassing with firearm on land.	Summary	3 months or a fine of level 4 on the standard scale; or both.
Section 21(4)	Contravention of provisions denying firearms to ex-prisoners and the like.	(*a*) Summary	6 months or a fine of the prescribed sum; or both.
		(*b*) On indictment	3 years or a fine; or both.
Section 21(5)	Supplying firearms to person denied them under section 21.	(*a*) Summary	6 months or a fine of the prescribed sum; or both.
		(*b*) On indictment	3 years or a fine; or both.
Section 22(1)	Person under 17 acquiring firearm.	Summary	6 months or a fine of level 5 on the standard scale; or both.
Section 22(2)	Person under 14 having firearm in his possession without lawful authority.	Summary	6 months or a fine of level 5 on the standard scale; or both.
Section 22(3)	Person under 15 having with him a shot gun without adult supervision.	Summary	A fine of level 3 on the standard scale.
Section 22(4)	Person under 14 having with him an air weapon or ammunition therefor.	Summary	A fine of level 3 on the standard scale.
Section 22(5)	Person under 17 having with him an air weapon in a public place.	Summary	A fine of level 3 on the standard scale.
Section 23(1)	Person under 14 making improper use of air weapon when under supervision; person supervising him permitting such use.	Summary	A fine of level 3 on the standard scale.
Section 24(1)	Selling or letting on hire a firearm to person under 17.	Summary	6 months or a fine of level 5 on the standard scale; or both.

Section of this Act creating offence	General nature of offence	Mode of prosecution	Punishment
Section 24(2)	Supplying firearm or ammunition (being of a kind to which section 1 of this Act applies) to person under 14.	Summary	6 months or a fine of level 5 on the standard scale; or both.
Section 24(3)	Making gift of shot gun to person under 15.	Summary	A fine of level 3 on the standard scale.
Section 24(4)	Supplying air weapon to person under 14.	Summary	A fine of level 3 on the standard scale.
Section 25	Supplying firearm to person drunk or insane.	Summary	3 months or a fine of level 3 on the standard scale; or both.

NOTES

This table shows only the penalties for those offences printed in this work.

Part II of Sch 6 (not printed here) contains supplementary provisions relating to trials and to the confiscation of firearms etc.

Theft Act 1968

(C 60)

Definition of "theft"

Basic definition of theft

1. (1) A person is guilty of theft if he dishonestly appropriates property belonging to another with the intention of permanently depriving the other of it; and "thief" and "steal" shall be construed accordingly.

(2) It is immaterial whether the appropriation is made with a view to gain, or is made for the thief's own benefit.

(3) The five following sections of this Act shall have effect as regards the interpretation and operation of this section (and, except as otherwise provided by this Act, shall apply only for purposes of this section).

NOTES

This provision creates the offence of theft: the basic definition it provides is amplified by ss 2–6, which deal with the five individual elements of 'dishonesty', 'appropriation', *etc*, but which are not themselves offence-creating. Every one of these five elements is a necessary ingredient of theft. If just one is absent, the offence cannot be committed. On the other hand, the House of Lords effectively held in *R. v Morris* [1984] AC 320 that, provided there has been a dishonest appropriation of another person's property and an intent to permanently deprive him of that property, it need not be shown that the appropriation was the intended means of deprivation. This is a surprising interpretation, and results in certain apparently preparatory actions (such as label-switching in self-service shops) being classed as complete offences of theft. See further the notes to s 3 *infra*.

'It is immaterial ...' Coupled with the definition of 'appropriation' in s 3, the effect of subs (2) is that many acts of criminal damage which result in the destruction of another person's property will also amount (in theory at least) to theft. So too may acts which deliberately result in the total loss of such property (as where D throws P's jewellery into the sea).

'except as otherwise provided' SS 4(1) and 5(1) apply generally by virtue of s 34. S 6 applies to s 15 with some adaptations (see s 15(3)); but s 2 does not strictly speaking apply to any offences other than theft and its derivatives (such as robbery, which necessarily involves theft).

Penalty—See s 7 *infra*.

'Dishonestly'

2. (1) A person's appropriation of property belonging to another is not to be regarded as dishonest—
   (a) if he appropriates the property in the belief that he has in law the right to deprive the other of it, on behalf of himself or of a third person; or

(b) if he appropriates the property in the belief that he would have the other's consent if the other knew of the appropriation and the circumstances of it; or

(c) (except where the property came to him as trustee or personal representative) if he appropriates the property in the belief that the person to whom the property belongs cannot be discovered by taking reasonable steps.

(2) A person's appropriation of property belonging to another may be dishonest notwithstanding that he is willing to pay for the property.

NOTES

This does not purport to provide a complete definition of dishonesty in theft (and does not strictly speaking apply at all for the purposes of deception, handling *etc*). It merely specifies three situations which do *not* involve dishonesty and one which *may* possibly do so. Where s 2 does not provide a complete answer, reference must be made to the leading case of *R v Ghosh* [1982] 1 QB 1053, where the Court of Appeal held that a person may be regarded as acting dishonestly if: (1) his behaviour would be so regarded 'according to the ordinary standards of reasonable and honest [sic] people' *and* (2) he realises that it would be so regarded (whether or not he himself thinks his behaviour to be right).

Earlier cases, such as *R v Feely* [1973] 1 QB 530 and *R v Greenstein* [1976] 1 All ER 1 must now be read subject to the more elaborate *Ghosh* definition.

'in the belief that' (subs (1) (a)–(c)) If D had no plausible grounds for holding a belief which he claims to have held, a court or jury is likely to conclude that his claim is false; but as a matter of law the belief need not be reasonable: *R v Kell* [1985] Crim LR 239.

Ignorance of the law and subs (1)(a) Despite the general rule that "ignorance of the law is no excuse" a mistaken belief in the existence of proprietary or other rights under the civil law may found a defence under subs 2(1) (a). See *R v Robinson* [1977] Crim LR 173. Such a belief may still amount to a defence even where s 2 is inapplicable, since it may negative dishonesty under the *Ghosh* principle.

'except where the property came to him as trustee or personal representative' Trustees cannot ordinarily be permitted to profit from their inability to find the proper beneficiaries; but, although they are denied the protection of s 2(1) (c) itself, trustees will only be guilty of theft if their retention of property is dishonest according to the *Ghosh* principle. Note that subs (1) (a) is not excluded, even for trustees.

'reasonable steps' It is not altogether clear whether D's own view is decisive on the question of what would amount to 'reasonable steps'. A belief that the owner cannot be traced is a defence even if unreasonable and mistaken; but it does not necessarily follow that D has a defence merely because he thinks that a visit to the police station or lost property office to report his finding of property would be an 'unreasonable' inconvenience. Arguably this could be seen as a question for the court or jury (*ie* an 'objective' test).

Willingness to pay. Subs (2) does *not* provide that D's willingness to pay for the property he appropriates is irrelevant to the case of his dishonesty. On the contrary, it may be highly relevant under the *Ghosh* principle (*supra*). Subs (2) does, however, ensure that such willingness is not an automatic defence to a charge under s 1; *cf Boggeln v Williams* [1978] 2 All ER 1061, which involved a question of dishonesty under s 13.

'Appropriates'

3. (1) Any assumption by a person of the rights of an owner amounts to an appropriation, and this includes, where he has come by the property (innocently or not) without stealing it, any later assumption of a right to it by keeping or dealing with it as owner.

(2) Where property or a right or interest in property is or purports to be transferred for value to a person acting in good faith, no later assumption by him of rights which he believed himself to be acquiring shall, by reason of any defect in the transferor's title amount to theft of the property.

NOTES

The concept of 'appropriation' was originally adopted so that it would 'easily be understood even without the aid of further definition' (CLRC 8th Report para. 34). It has in fact proved extremely hard to define satisfactorily, and has created a considerable volume of complex case law.

'any assumption ... of the rights of an owner' According to the House of Lords in *R v Morris* [1984] AC 320, appropriation necessarily involves some interference with the property, this interference being (a) unauthorised by the owner and (b) inconsistent with or adverse to that person's rights of ownership. Thus, a person who takes property with the express or implied permission of the owner does not thereby steal, even if he harbours a secret dishonest intent to avoid paying for that property (as in *Eddy v Niman* (1981) 73 Cr App R 237) or to divert it for his own purposes at a later stage (as in *R v Skipp* [1975] Crim LR 114 or *R v Fritschy* [1985] Crim LR 745). A subsequent unauthorised concealment or mis-application of the property will be needed (as in *R v McPherson* [1973] Crim LR 191, where D appropriated goods she had removed from the shelves in a super-market by concealing them in her own shopping bag); and even then it cannot be theft if D has already acquired sole title and possession of the property concerned. See also *R v McHugh* (1988) 88 Cr App R 385.

An earlier decision of the House of Lords in *R v Lawrence* [1972] AC 626 contained powerful *dicta* to the effect that appropriation *can* take place with the consent of the owner. It is possible to argue that in *Lawrence* P merely *allowed* D to help himself to money from P's wallet and did not positively consent to the taking, and that the *dicta* concerning appropriation with the owner's consent were *obiter* and wrong. Such arguments are not altogether convincing, however. It is doubtful whether *Lawrence* retains much authority after *Morris*; but see the Court of Appeal's recent flirtation with the *Lawrence* approach in *R v Philippou* [1989] Crim LR 559 and *Dobson v General Accident* [1990] Crim LR 271.

Although s 3 refers to the 'rights' of the owner, this has been interpreted in such a way that the assumption of any one ownership right suffices. The particular right assumed need not even be the fundamental right to possession of the property. Thus, in *Morris* D was held to have appropriated goods in a self-service store merely by improperly substituting incorrect price labels thereon and placing them in his trolley. More surprisingly, he was held to have stolen the goods at that moment, even though he later took them to the checkout point and paid for them at the price shown on the false labels. (See also notes to s 1 and s 15.)

'where he has come by the property (innocently or not) without stealing it' This covers innocent acquisition (by mistake, by finding, by lawful borrowing *etc*) and unlawful acquisition (by unlawful borrowing or by deception), as well as cases in which D has possession of P's property through his employment.

'any later assumption of a right to it by keeping or dealing with it as owner' Any action taken by a finder, bailee or borrower of goods *etc* which usurps the owner's rights can amount to an appropriation. Whether it also amounts to theft depends of course on whether this appropriation involves a dishonest intent to permanently deprive the owner. Thus, if the borrower of a library book writes has name in it, or if the borrower of a car offers it for sale to another person, these may amount to appropriations; but the scribbler does not steal the book if he intends to return it (a proper charge would be criminal damage) and the person who offers the car for sale does not steal it if the offer is merely a ruse to obtain money from the would-be purchaser. If, on the other hand, D intends P to suffer permanent deprivation of his property, he will commit theft merely by offering it for sale—even if he fails to find a buyer: *cf R v Pitham* (1976) 65 Cr App R 45. Similarly, a shop assistant will commit theft if he offers his employers' goods to his friends at less than the proper price: *Pilgram v Rice-Smith* [1977] 1 WLR 671.

Subs (2) and *bona fide* purchasers A *bona fide* purchaser of goods who only subsequently discovers them to be stolen property, generally acquires no title to them, and may indeed incur tortious liability to the true owner; but he cannot become guilty of theft or of handling stolen goods merely by retaining or disposing of them. See further *R v Bloxham* [1983] 1 AC 109 and s 22 *infra*.

'Property'

4. (1) "Property" includes money and all other property, real or personal, including things in action and other intangible property.

(2) A person cannot steal land, or things forming part of land and severed from it by him or by his directions, except in the following cases, that is to say—

(a) when he is a trustee or personal representative, or is authorised by power of attorney, or as liquidator of a company, or otherwise, to sell or dispose of land belonging to another, and he appropriates the land or anything forming part of it by dealing with it in breach of the confidence reposed in him; or

(b) when he is not in possession of the land and appropriates anything forming part of the land by severing it or causing it to be severed, or after it has been severed; or

(c) when, being in possession of the land under a tenancy, he appropriates the whole or part of any fixture or structure let to be used with the land.

For purposes of this subsection "land" does not include incorporeal hereditaments; "tenancy" means a tenancy for years or any less period and includes an agreement for such a tenancy, but a person who after the end of a tenancy remains in possession as statutory tenant or otherwise is to be treated as having possession under the tenancy, and "let" shall be construed accordingly.

(3) A person who picks mushrooms growing wild on any land, or who picks flowers, fruit or foliage from a plant growing wild on any land, does not (although not in possession of the land) steal what he picks, unless he does it for reward or for sale or other commercial purpose.

For purposes of this subsection "mushroom" includes any fungus, and "plant" includes any shrub or tree.

(4) Wild creatures, tamed or untamed, shall be regarded as property; but a person cannot steal a wild creature not tamed nor ordinarily kept in captivity, or the carcase of any such creature unless either it has been

reduced into possession by or on behalf of another person and possession of it has not since been lost or abandoned, or another person is in course of reducing it into possession.

NOTES

S 4(1) applies generally for the purpose of the Act—(see s 34(1)) and gives 'property' a much wider meaning than it had in relation to the old offence of larceny.

In contrast, the restrictions imposed by subs (2)–(4) apply only in respect of theft itself. They do not, for example, impede prosecution for offences of obtaining land or real property by deception contrary to s 15 of the Act.

'things in action' Ie property (such as a debt) which is intangible but which is enforceable by legal action. Thus it has been held that a person who uses a forged cheque may steal the debt (or credit balance) owed by the bank to its genuine customer: *Chan Man-Sin v R* [1988] 1 All ER 1; and a director who misuses his company's cheques may be regarded as stealing the 'proceeds' from the company's account: *R v Kohn* (1979) 69 Cr App R 395. Note that, although cheques create choses (things) in action, a cheque or cheque book is also a material thing (or chose in possession) which can itself be the subject of a theft charge.

'other intangible property' This may include patents (Patents Act 1977 s 10); but mere infringement of a patent (or of copyright) cannot be theft, because there can be no question of it permanently depriving the holder of his rights. Confidential information is not 'property' at all (*Oxford v Moss* [1979] Crim LR 119) and nor is electricity (*Low v Blease* [1975] Crim LR 513), but see s 13 *infra*.

'things forming part of land' *Ie* structures, fixtures, plants, trees *etc* which are real property as a matter of civil law; but note that under subs (2) (a)–(b) the dishonest severing or removal of any such items (eg roofing materials, gates, shrubs *etc*) may be theft.

'possession under a tenancy' Although tenants can steal their landlords' fixtures and structures (not shrubs or trees) a person who occupies land under a bare licence would appear (surely by mere oversight) to be immune from any of the qualifications which paras (a)–(c) impose on the generality of subs (2), and it is difficult to see how such a person could ever be guilty of stealing the land or anything forming part of it.

'picks' If given its usual meaning, this would not appear to cover the uprooting of complete plants or the severing of substantial branches using axes or saws. A 'wide' interpretation would appear to be called for here.

'reward, sale or other commercial purpose' Picking wild strawberries *etc* to make jam for sale on a market stall *can* be theft, in that it is not exempted under subs (3), but note that it might be very difficult to prove dishonesty in such cases. See notes to s 2 *supra*.

'wild creatures not tamed or ordinarily kept in captivity' 'Ordinarily' refers to the particular creature or creatures involved. Thus a circus lion *is* ordinarily kept in captivity. The taking of wild creatures from another person's land cannot generally be theft but may constitute an offence of poaching, or an offence under the Wildlife and Countryside Act 1981. See the notes to Sch 1 *infra*.

'Belonging to another'

5. (1) Property shall be regarded as belonging to any person having possession or control of it, or having in it any proprietary right or interest (not being an equitable interest arising only from an agreement to transfer or grant an interest).

(2) Where property is subject to a trust, the persons to whom it belongs shall be regarded as including any person having a right to enforce the trust, and an intention to defeat the trust shall be regarded accordingly as an intention to deprive of the property any person having that right.

(3) Where a person receives property from or on account of another, and is under an obligation to the other to retain and deal with that property or its proceeds in a particular way, the property or proceeds shall be regarded (as against him) as belonging to the other.

(4) Where a person gets property by another's mistake, and is under an obligation to make restoration (in whole or in part) of the property or its proceeds or of the value thereof, then to the extent of that obligation the property or proceeds shall be regarded (as against him) as belonging to the person entitled to restoration and an intention not to make restoration shall be regarded accordingly as an intention to deprive that person of the property or proceeds.

(5) Property of a corporation sole shall be regarded as belonging to the corporation notwithstanding a vacancy in the corporation.

NOTES

Subs (1) applies generally for the purpose of the Act: s 34(1) *infra*. Under it, property can belong to a number of different persons at the same time, and in certain circumstances one type of 'owner' can steal it from another: *R v Turner (No 2)* [1971] 2 All ER 441.

'possession or control' If property belongs to nobody (*eg* because it has been abandoned) it cannot be stolen; but property which has been abandoned by X on Y's land or premises *etc* may thereby come into Y's 'possession or control'. This will be the case if Y has manifested some intention to excercise such control (as by attempting to exclude other persons from the land where the property has been abandoned). Y need not necessarily be aware of the particular property in question. See *R v Woodman* [1974] QB 754.

The position is more complicated where Y does not attempt to exclude other persons from the land or premises in question (see *Parker v British Railways Board* [1982] QB 1004), but note that a person finding and keeping property which he believes has been abandoned may well not be considered 'dishonest'—especially if it has never occurred to him that the landowner *etc* might wish to claim the property for himself.

'or any proprietry right or interest' Examples of such rights *etc* include joint ownership (as in *R v Bonner* [1970] 1 WLR 838, where it was held that one partner could be guilty of stealing partnership property), beneficial interests under trusts (which means that trust property may be stolen from a beneficiary by a trustee) and liens. As to trusts, note also subs (2).

Passing of ownership and theft If D tricks P into transfering ownership, possession *and* control to him, and only afterwards makes off with the property, there may be liability for obtaining that property by deception or for making off without payment, but not for theft: *Edwards v Ddin* [1976] 3 All ER 705; *Corcoran v Whent* [1977] Crim LR 52. If, on the other hand, D has only obtained possession, he may subsequently steal the property by appropriating rights of ownership: *cf R v Hircock* (1978) 67 Cr App R 278 and s 3 *supra*.

Subs (2) Any beneficiary of a trust has a right to enforce it, and is thus an 'owner' for the purpose of the Act. The Attorney General can enforce a charitable trust (Charities Act 1960, s 28). Failing beneficiaries, a trust can be enforced by the persons entitled to the residue.

Subs (3) D must be under a *legal* obligation to deal with the particular property or its proceeds in a particular way. It is not enough that D has received payment in return for a contractual obligation to provide goods or services: *R v Hall* [1973] 1 QB 126. See also *Lewis v Lethbridge* [1987] Crim LR 59; but contrast *Davidge v Bunnett* [1984] Crim LR 296. Where material facts are in dispute, the judge should advise the jury that if certain facts are found then the legal obligation did (or did not) exist: *R v Mainwaring* (1981) 74 Cr App R 99. On principle, the obligation ought to be enforceable in the courts, but see *R v Meech* [1974] QB 549.

'Shall be regarded' Note that this is a legal fiction. If the property *does* belong to another, subs (3) need not be involved.

Subs (4) This primarily covers situations in which D is mistakenly overpaid, or paid for work done by another. As with subs (3), it 'deems' such property to belong to the person entitled to restitution, regardless of whether he does in fact have any proprietary interest in it under the general law: *Att-General's Reference (No.1 of 1983)* [1984] Crim LR 570.

'obligation' As with subs (3), this means a legal obligation: *R v Gilks* [1972] 3 All ER 280.

Corporations sole (subs (5)) These are public offices, the corporate rights and duties of which are distinct from those of the individuals who hold those offices at particular times. The classic example is the office of bishop.

'With the intention of permanently depriving the other of it'
6. (1) A person appropriating property belonging to another without meaning the other permanently to lose the thing itself is nevertheless to be regarded as having the intention of permanently depriving the other of it if his intention is to treat the thing as his own to dispose of regardless of the other's rights: and a borrowing or lending of it may amount to so treating it if, but only if, the borrowing or lending is for a period and in circumstances making it equivalent to an outright taking or disposal.

(2) Without prejudice to the generality of subsection (1) above, where a person, having possession or control (lawfully or not) of property belonging to another, parts with the property under a condition as to its return which he may not be able to perform, this (if done for purposes of his own and without the other's authority) amounts to treating the property as his own to dispose of regardless of the the other's rights.

NOTES
This provision also applies, with slight modifications, to offences under s 15 of the Act. It is not by any means a complete definition of the concept of 'intent to permanently deprive'. It merely extends that concept to certain situations which might otherwise fall outside it.

'without meaning the other permanently to lose the thing itself' Where D *does* mean the other to suffer permanent loss, there can of course be no question but that he has the requisite intent.

'if his intent is to treat the thing as his own to dispose of . . .' This would appear to cover cases in which D takes P's property and then offers to sell it back to him as a 'replacement' for what he has lost, or cases in which D takes P's property and holds it to ransom, offering to return it only if the ransom is paid (see *R v Lloyd* [1985] QB 829 at p 836). It might also cover cases in which D takes P's property with intent to keep or sell it only if on subsequent examination it proves sufficiently valuable; but see *R v Easom* [1971] 2 QB 351 and *R v Bayley* [1980] Crim LR 503, which suggest the contrary.

'borrowing or lending in circumstances equivalent to outright taking or disposal' This covers the 'borrowing' of items which are returned only when they have ceased to retain any value (eg season tickets, dry batteries or valuable securities, which are returned only when expired or cancelled). See *R v Duru* [1973] 3 All ER 715; *R v Downes* (1983) 77 Cr App R 260.

Arguably, the unlawful borrowing of a season ticket for the first half of the season (or even the first day) might still come within subs (1) in that what is returned is no longer the same thing as what was taken (*cf Duru, supra*).

Subs (2) This primarily covers cases in which D pawns P's property in the hope that he may be able to redeem it and return it to D. It is not expressly provided that D must *realise* he may not be able to redeem the property but this may be required by implication.

Theft, robbery, burglary, etc.

Theft
7. A person guilty of theft shall on conviction on indictment be liable to imprisonment for a term not exceeding ten years.

NOTES
Theft is triable either way: Magistrates' Courts Act 1980, Schedule 1, para 28.

In relation to the theft or attempted theft of motor vehicles see also Road Traffic Offenders Act 1988 Sch 2 part II (disqualification and endorsements).

Robbery
8. (1) A person is guilty of robbery if he steals, and immediately before or at the time of doing so, and in order to do so, he uses force on any person or puts or seeks to put any person in fear of being then and there subjected to force.

(2) A person guilty of robbery, or of an assault with intent to rob, shall on conviction on indictment be liable to imprisonment for life.

NOTES
This provision covers two offences, assault with intent to rob (subs (2)) being distinct from robbery. Both offences are triable only on indictment.

'if he steals' All the essential elements of theft are equally essential elements of robbery. Thus, if D uses or threatens force to reclaim property to which he (perhaps wrongly) believes himself to be legally entitled, he cannot be guilty of robbery, even if he knows that the use of such force is unlawful: *R v Robinson* [1977] Crim LR 173. In such a case, however, D's knowledge that the threats are improper would make him guilty of blackmail: see *R v Lawrence* (1971) 57 Cr App R 64 and s 21 *infra*.

As with theft, a complete offence of robbery may be committed even though D never succeeds in making off with the property he has appropriated: eg D grabs P's handbag, but is forced to drop it after a struggle (*cf Corcoran v Anderton* (1980) 71 Cr App R 104).

'uses force' A fairly slight degree of force (*eg* nudging P off balance in order to seize her bag) may suffice, but in marginal cases the question whether D's conduct amounted to a use of force *etc* will be for the jury: *R v Dawson* [1976] Crim LR 692.

'or puts' etc Using threats of immediate force either on the victim or on some bystander will suffice in most cases, even if the force threatened is not serious; but a threat to kill a sleeping baby could not be sufficient, because the baby itself would not be made to feel threatened. Such a threat would however be blackmail under s 21.

'immediately before or at the time of doing so' Force or threats used after the stealing is over will not convert theft into robbery, but in practice theft will often be regarded as continuing for some time after the initial appropriation. Thus in *R v Hale* (1978) 68 Cr App R 415, Eveleigh LJ said;

'the act of appropriation does not suddenly cease. It is a continuous act, and it is a matter for the jury to decide whether or not the appropriation has finished.'

An obvious example of this principle is that violence used to effect a 'getaway' from the scene of the theft could create liability for robbery.

'and in order to do so' If D sexually assaults P and later finds P's purse on the floor where she has fallen, D's taking of the purse will be theft but not robbery, because force was not used *in order* to steal.

'assault with intent to rob' 'Assault' has the same meaning as in s 47 of the Offences Against the Person Act 1861). Where assault can be proved, s 8(2) offers the prosecution a viable alternative to a charge of attempted robbery. (See notes to s 1 of the Criminal Attempts Act 1981.)

Burglary

9. (1) A person is guilty of burglary if—
   (a) he enters any building or part of a building as a trespasser and with intent to commit any such offence as is mentioned in subsection (2) below; or
   (b) having entered any building or part of a building as a trespasser he steals or attempts to steal anything in the building or that part of it or inflicts or attempts to inflict on any person therein any grievous bodily harm.

(2) The offences referred to in subsection (1)(a) above are offences of stealing anything in the building or part of a building in question, of inflicting on any person therein any grievous bodily harm or raping any woman therein, and of doing unlawful damage to the building or anything therein.

(3) References in subsections (1) and (2) above to a building shall apply also to an inhabited vehicle or vessel, and shall apply to any such vehicle or vessel at times when the person having a habitation in it is not there as well as at times when he is.

(4) A person guilty of burglary shall on conviction on indictment be liable to imprisonment for a term not exceeding fourteen years.

NOTES
The offences of burglary and aggravated burglary under this provision and s 10 *infra* have replaced a complex range of offences formerly contained in ss 24–28 of the Larceny Act 1916. It is no longer necessary to distinguish between the types of building involved or the time or method of entry.

'enters' Entry may sometimes be effected without stepping bodily into the buildings. Putting a hand through an open or broken window in order to steal may constitute 'entry' for these purposes: *R v Brown* [1985] Crim LR 212. Climbing onto an outside window ledge would not suffice: *R v Collins* [1973] QB 100, but it might amount to an attempt.

'a building' Subject to subs (3), which deems inhabited vehicles or vessels to be buildings, the Act provides no definition of this term. Case law provides some guidance. Thus sheds, coldstores *etc* have been held to be buildings, even though they lack fixed foundations: *B v Leathley* [1979] Crim LR 314. Except in the case of vehicles and vessels, habitation is quite unnecessary, but a tent, even if inhabited, would be difficult to class as a building.

'or part of a building' There are many situations where D will be entitled to enter one part of a building without any question of trespass, but where he would trespass if he entered some other part. The obvious example would be where a hotel guest enters another guest's room, or the manager's office, looking for money *etc* to steal; but burglary might also be committed where a shopper goes behind a counter in a store, with the same intent: *R v Walkington* [1979] 2 All ER 71.

'with intent to commit ...' *(subs (1)(a))* Burglary under subs (1)(a) requires only that this ulterior intent shall exist on entry. No such act or offence as is mentioned in subs. (2) need ever be committed. Conversely, the commission of such an act or offence after entry will not be burglary within subs (1)(a) unless it is proved that the intent existed at the time of entry.
   A 'conditional intent' to steal any suitable items as might be found will suffice: *R v Walkington (supra); Att General's Refs (Nos 1 and 2 of 1979)* [1980] QB 180.

'or ... having entered ... as a trespasser he steals etc' *(subs (1)(b))*. Note that rape and criminal damage are not relevant offences for the purpose of subs (1)(b). A person who enters a shop as a genuine customer and subsequently steals some item 'on impulse' will not be guilty of burglary, because the original entry is not as a trespasser. It may be otherwise, however if the intent to steal was held at the time of entry: see *R v Jones & Smith* [1976] 3 All ER 154.

'or attempts' See generally the Criminal Attempts Act 1981 *(infra)*.

'as a trespasser' Whether D enters as a trespasser involves a question of law, but liability for burglary cannot be incurred unless there is a *mens rea* element as to this; D must either know he is trespassing or be reckless as to that possibility: *R v Collins* [1973] QB 100. Moreover the doctrine of trespass *ab initio* does not apply, so D does not become guilty of burglary merely because of something he does after making a legitimate entry.
   Where D has the owner's permission to enter a building, he may still do so as a trespasser (and burglar) if he enters for some unauthorised and dishonest purpose of his own: *R v Jones and Smith* [1976] 3 All ER 154.

'inhabited vehicle or vessel' (subs (3)) Caravans, motor caravans and house-boats clearly come within the scope of this provision, together with ships on which the crew or passengers live or sleep: but there is still room for doubt as to whether caravans *etc* are 'inhabited' when not in actual use. There is arguably a difference between an inhabited caravan, the owner of which has gone out shopping, and a touring van which has been 'laid up' for the winter. The former is clearly protected by the law of burglary, but the latter is probably not so protected, even if it is fully furnished and ready for immediate use.

Problems of interpretation may also arise in respect of long-distance lorries which provide sleeping cabins for the crew. Can theft from such a lorry be burglary just because the crew are asleep in their cabins at the time? Is such a lorry 'inhabited'? In what respect might the thief be a trespasser?

Alternative verdicts Subs s (1)(a) and (1)(b) create distinct offences; but on a subs (1)(b) indictment, the jury may be entitled to return a verdict of guilty under subs (1)(a): *R v Whiting* (1987) 85 Cr App R 78. An equivalent alternative verdict is not possible in the converse situation where the indictment charges only an offence under subs (1)(a).

Trial Most burglaries are triable either way; but burglary becomes triable exclusively on indictment if it takes the form of committing or entering with intent to commit an offence which is itself exclusively so triable, and burglary in a dwelling is triable subject to the same principle if anyone in the dwelling was subjected either to violence or to the threat of violence.

Aggravated burglary

10. (1) A person is guilty of aggravated burglary if he commits any burglary and at the time has with him any firearm or imitation firearm, any weapon of offence, or any explosive; and for this purpose—

(a) "firearm" includes an airgun or air pistol, and "imitation firearm" means anything which has the appearance of being a firearm, whether capable of being discharged or not; and

(b) "weapon of offence" means any article made or adapted for use for causing injury to or incapacitating a person or intended by the person having it with him for such use; and

(c) "explosive" means any article manufactured for the purpose of producing a practical effect by explosion, or intended by the person having it with him for that purpose.

(2) A person guilty of aggravated burglary shall on conviction on indictment be liable to imprisonment for life.

NOTES

This provision complements s 9 *supra* by providing a higher maximum penalty (equivalent to that for robbery) where burglary is committed in circumstances 'aggravated' by the carrying of weapons or explosives.

'burglary' This may be either kind of burglary as defined in s 9(1)(a) or (b) *supra*.

'and at the time' In the case of burglary under s 9(1)(a) the crucial time is the moment of entry; in the case of burglary under s 9(1)(b) it is the moment of stealing or of inflicting/attempting grievous bodily harm, see *R v Francis* [1982] Crim LR 363. It is argued by Professor Griew (*The Theft Acts 1968 and 1978*, 5th ed) that aggravated burglary cannot in any event be committed by a trespasser who armed himself after entry, but this argument is not only (as he accepts) difficult to reconcile with the words of the statute—it also overlooks the additional culpability and danger involved in such behaviour. See also *R v O'Leary* (1986) 82 Cr App R 341.

'has with him' By analogy with similarly worded provisions in the Prevention of Crime Act 1953 (*qv*), it would appear that a burglar who grabs a weapon during a struggle and uses it to cause or attempt to cause serious injury would not be guilty of aggravated burglary; he must have armed himself with it in anticipation of use. *Cf R v Humphrys* [1977] Crim LR 225.

'imitation firearm' An imitation firearm need not be a quality replica—it may be a plastic toy or a pair of metal pipes designed to give the appearance of a partly concealed shotgun. See *R v Morris* (1984) 79 Cr App R 104.

'weapon of offence' The definition given in subs (1)(b) is wider than that used in the Prevention of Crime Act 1953, in that it includes items such as ropes which might be used to incapacitate rather than injure. Where an item is not offensive *per se* the burglar's intent at the relevant time will be crucial. Thus in a s 9(1)(a) case, the question may be whether D intended to use his jemmy as a weapon at the time of his entering the building.

Removal of articles from places open to the public
  11. (1) Subject to subsections (2) and (3) below, where the public have access to a building in order to view the building or part of it, or a collection or part of a collection housed in it, any person who without lawful authority removes from the building or its grounds the whole or part of any article displayed or kept for display to the public in the building or that part of it or in its grounds shall be guilty of an offence.
  For this purpose "collection" includes a collection got together for a temporary purpose, but references in this section to a collection do not apply to a collection made or exhibited for the purpose of effecting sales or other commercial dealings.
  (2) It is immaterial for purposes of subsection (1) above, that the public's access to a building is limited to a particular period or particular occasion; but where anything removed from a building or its grounds is there otherwise than as forming part of, or being on loan for exhibition with, a collection intended for permanent exhibition to the public, the person removing it does not thereby commit an offence under this section unless he removes it on a day when the public have access to the building as mentioned in subsection (1) above.
  (3) A person does not commit an offence under this section if he believes that he has lawful authority for the removal of the thing in question or that he would have it if the person entitled to give it knew of the removal and the circumstances of it.
  (4) A person guilty of an offence under this section shall, on conviction on indictment, be liable to imprisonment for a term not exceeding five years.

NOTES
Unlawful borrowing does not generally amount to a criminal offence. This provision and s 12 *infra* create exceptions to the general rule. Of the two, s 12 is of much greater practical significance. The present provision was enacted by way of reaction to a handful of incidents in which works of art had been 'borrowed' from museums and galleries where they had been on public display. Where such items are then held to ransom a charge of theft may be possible by virtue of s 6(1) *supra;* or a charge of blackmail may be preferred under s 21 *infra*. In either case, the need for this provision would appear to be marginal.

'where the public have access to a building' See subs (2). It is not necessary that access should be free of charge; but access to the grounds alone would not be sufficient to bring this provision into play, even if items are then taken from display in those grounds. If access to the building *is* allowed for one of the specified reasons, removal of items from display in the grounds would then appear to be covered.

Purpose of the permitted access   Public access must be permitted for one of the purposes specified in subs (1); see *R v Barr* [1978] Crim LR 244, where the display of items in a church for purely devotional purposes was held not to be within the protection of the provision. If the devotional items were also displayed as works of art (as where a famous religious picture is kept over a church altar) the position would perhaps have been different.

Exhibitions for commercial purposes   The problem here is that an art exhibition may have a twin purpose: general public interest *and* the display of items for private buyers. The latter purpose may be dominant, equal or subservient, and not all the items on display may necessarily be for sale. It is not clear how the courts would apply this provision in such cases.

Subs (2)   An item forming part of a permanent exhibition, and having no other use, is within the scope of this provision at all times, even if the exhibition is temporarily closed or the item has been withdrawn for cleaning or restoration: *R v Durkim* [1973] QB 786. The position is different in respect of items which are exhibited from time to time but which have other uses (*eg* the furniture in a stately house which is used by the owners during periods when the public are excluded). Such items are covered only on days when the public has access; but this cover nevertheless extends beyond 'opening hours' on the days concerned.

Subs (3)   As with s 2(1) *supra* (dishonesty in theft cases) an honest, if perhaps unreasonable, belief in lawful authority or the owner's consent will be a good defence to a charge under this provision.

Conviction on indictment   The offence is also triable summarily: Magistrates Courts Act 1980 Sch 1.

Taking motor vehicle or other conveyance without authority

12. (1) Subject to subsections (5) and (6) below, a person shall be guilty of an offence if, without having the consent of the owner or other lawful authority, he takes any conveyance for his own or another's use or, knowing that any conveyance has been taken without such authority, drives it or allows himself to be carried in or on it.

(2) A person guilty of an offence under subsection (1) above shall [be liable on summary conviction to a fine not exceeding level 5 on the standard scale, to imprisonment for a term not exceeding six months, or to both.]

(3) [*repealed*]

(4) If on the trial of an indictment for theft the jury are not satisfied that the accused committed theft, but it is proved that the accused committed an offence under subsection (1) above, the jury may find him guilty of the offence under subsection (1) [and if he is found guilty of it, he shall be liable as he would have been liable under subsection (2) above on summary conviction].

(5) Subsection (1) above shall not apply in relation to pedal cycles; but, subject to subsection (6) below, a person who, without having the consent of the owner or other lawful authority, takes a pedal cycle for his own or another's use, or rides a pedal cycle knowing it to have been taken without such authority, shall on summary conviction be liable to a fine not exceeding [level 3 on the standard scale].

(6) A person does not commit an offence under this section by anything done in the belief that he has lawful authority to do it or that he would have the owner's consent if the owner knew of his doing it and the circumstances of it.

(7) For purposes of this section—

(a) "conveyance" means any conveyance constructed or adapted for the carriage of a person or persons whether by land, water or air, except that it does not include a conveyance constructed or adapted for use only under the control of a person not carried in or on it, and "drive" shall be constructed accordingly; and

(b) "owner", in relation to a conveyance which is the subject of a hiring agreement or hire-purchase agreement, means the person in possession of the conveyance under that agreement.

NOTES

Like s 11 *supra* this provision is designed to penalise unlawful appropriations which do not necessarily constitute theft. In the case of motor vehicles however, the need for some special provision is unquestionable, because of the large number of such vehicles which are taken, used and abandoned in circumstances where an intent to permanently deprive cannot be inferred.

The maximum penalty for the offence was formerly three years imprisonment following trial on indictment. The offence is no longer triable on indictment, so that the maximum penalty has necessarily fallen to six months imprisonment (plus fine and possible disqualification *etc*): Criminal Justice Act 1988 s 37(1).

It is nevertheless deemed to be an arrestable offence under s 24 of the Police and Criminal Evidence Act 1984.

'conveyance' The definition provided by subs (7)(a) clearly covers boats, aircraft and horse-drawn vehicles as well as motor vehicles; but it excludes trailers, barges *etc* even if these are used for the carriage of persons. It has been held that a horse is not a 'conveyance' even if fitted with a saddle *etc* for that purpose (*Neale v Gribble* [1978] RTR 409) and pedal cycles, although conveyances, are separately provided for by subs (5). It is difficult to see why the taking of a pedal cycle should be a lesser offence than the taking of a dinghy which may be both less valuable and less dangerous when misused, but such is the law.

'takes for his own or another's use' The conveyance need not in fact be 'used' as a conveyance, but if not so used it must at least be taken with a view to future use. Thus removal of a boat on a trailer with intent to sail it will suffice (*R v Pearce* [1973] Crim LR 321) but pushing a vehicle around a corner, without riding in it, in order to play a joke on its owner, will not suffice: *R v Stokes* [1982] Crim LR 695; *R v Marchant* (1984) 80 Crim App R 361.

The engine of a motor vehicle or vessel need not be engaged (*R v Bow* (1976) 64 Cr App R 54) but some movement must take place: *R v Bogacki* [1973] QB 832. If the conveyance is moved in a manner which involves D riding in or on it, it need not be shown that his purpose or motive was so to use it. In *Bow*, D's motive in taking and riding in P's vehicle was to prevent it obstructing his getaway, but it was nevertheless held that he was properly convicted.

'without having the consent of the owner or other legal authority' The offence is not committed where D obtains P's consent to use the conveyance even if that consent is obtained by fraud: *R v Peart* [1970] 2 QB 672; *Whittaker v Campbell* [1983] 3 WLR 676. On the other hand, if D has P's consent to use it for one purpose (eg P's business) and D takes it for some other purpose of his own, that may constitute the offence, whether or not the original consent was obtained by fraud: *McKnight v Davis* [1974] RTR 4. Nevertheless

'Not every brief unauthorised diversion from his proper route by an employed driver in the course of his working day will necessarily amount to a taking of the vehicle for his own use. If however he returns to the vehicle after he has parked it for the night and drives it off on an unauthorised errand he is clearly guilty ... Similarly, if in the course of his working day ... he appropriates it to his own use in a manner which repudiates the rights of the true owner, and shows that he has assumed control of the vehicle for his own purposes, he can properly be [convicted]'

(*ibid* per Lord Widgery CJ at p 6).

Consent authority and mens rea See subs (6). As with s 2(1) in relation to theft, the test is clearly subjective: an unreasonable mistake as to consent *etc* will be a good defence, subject to any problems of credibility. There is admittedly a reference in *R v Clotworthy* [1981] Crim LR 501 to D's right to assert his '*reasonable* belief' but the issue of reasonableness was not crucial to the decision in the case, and it is submitted that the reference to it was erroneous.

Driving or allowing oneself to be carried These secondary offences require knowledge of the unlawful taking. If D merely suspects that E has taken a car without consent he will not incur liability by riding in it *etc*. Note that, whereas s 22 (handling stolen goods) requires knowledge or belief, s 12 does not offer 'belief' as an alternative. It might therefore be possible to argue that D cannot be guilty of riding in a conveyance taken by E unless he has first-hand knowledge of the unlawful taking, and that even a positive (and well-founded) belief would not suffice in the absence of such knowledge. It is unlikely, however, that the courts would find such an argument attractive from a policy viewpoint.

Penalties etc See the general note to this provision (*supra*). On disqualification *etc* see Sch 2 part II of the Road Traffic Offenders Act 1988.

Abstracting of electricity

13. A person who dishonestly uses without due authority, or dishonestly causes to be wasted or diverted, any electricity shall on conviction on indictment be liable to imprisonment for a term not exceeding five years.

NOTES
Electricity cannot be 'stolen', nor does entry as a trespasser followed by the abstraction of electricity constitute burglary: *Low v Blease* [1975] Crim LR 513. Nevertheless the use of a non-rechargeable battery might amount to theft of the battery itself, even if the exhausted battery is left for its owner to reclaim: see s 6(1) *supra*.

Use of a telephone does not necessarily involve any measurable abstraction of electricity; but see s 48 of the British Telecom Act 1981.

'dishonestly' The s 2 definition is not strictly applicable, but the s 13 concept of dishonesty is nevertheless unlikely to differ significantly (if at all) from that in theft cases. See *Boggeln v Williams* [1978] 2 All ER 1061, described by Lord Lane CJ in *R v Ghosh* [1982] 2 All ER 689 as a 'borderline' case. In *Ghosh,* Lord Lane said that such cases 'will depend on the view taken by the jury whether the defendant may have believed what he was doing was in accordance with the ordinary man's idea of honesty'.

Extension to thefts from mails outside England and Wales, and robbery etc, on such a theft

14. (1) Where a person—

(a) steals or attempts to steal any mail bag or postal packet in the course of transmission as such between places in different jurisdictions in the British postal area, or any of the contents of such a mail bag or postal packet; or

(b) in stealing or with intent to steal any such mail bag or postal packet or any of its contents, commits any robbery, attempted robbery or assault with intent to rob;

then, notwithstanding that he does so outside England and Wales, he shall be guilty of committing or attempting to commit the offence against this Act, as if he had done so in England or Wales, and he shall accordingly be liable to be prosecuted, tried and punished in England and Wales without proof that the offence was committed there.

(2) In subsection (1) above the reference to different jurisdictions in the British postal area is to be construed as referring to the several jurisdictions of England and Wales, of Scotland, of Northern Ireland, of the Isle of Man and of the Channel Islands.

(3) For purposes of this section "mail bag" includes any article serving the purpose of a mail bag.

NOTES

The general rule is that the Theft Acts extend only to England and Wales, to British ships and to British-registered aircraft in flight outside the UK. Thefts occurring in other parts of the UK are generally no more justiciable under English law than are thefts committed in foreign countries.

Where, however, items are stolen in postal transit between different jurisdictions, it may sometimes be difficult to prove where exactly the theft took place. Where applicable, this provision obviates the need for such proof. Note that it applies even where the stolen items were in transit between two *other* parts of the British Postal Area (*eg* between Scotland and N Ireland).

Obtaining property by deception

15. (1) A person who by any deception dishonestly obtains property belonging to another, with the intention of permanently depriving the other of it, shall on conviction on indictment be liable to imprisonment for a term not exceeding ten years.

(2) For purposes of this section a person is to be treated as obtaining property if he obtains ownership, possession or control of it, and "obtain" includes obtaining for another or enabling another to obtain or to retain.

(3) Section 6 above shall apply for purposes of this section, with the necessary adaptation of the reference to appropriating, as it applies for purposes of section 1.

(4) For purposes of this section "deception" means any deception (whether deliberate or reckless) by words or conduct as to fact or as to law, including a deception as to the present intentions of the person using the deception or any other person.

NOTES

This is the first of a number of 'deception' offences in the Theft Acts 1968 and 1978. (See also ss 16 and 20 of this Act and ss 1 and 2 of the 1978 Act). As such it has certain elements in common with those other offences. It also has certain elements in common with theft itself, and in some cases it may be difficult to tell whether the conduct in question should attract a charge of theft or a charge under this provision. Theft, however, necessarily involves an 'appropriation' which must probably be unauthorised (see s 3 *supra*), whereas a s 15 offence must involve P or his representative being deceived into allowing D or another to obtain the property in question. This might appear to make 'overlap' between the two offences impossible; but note that if D forges P's cheques and uses them to buy goods or withdraw cash, this conduct might at one and the same time amount to a s 15 offence in respect of the goods or cash and an offence of theft in respect of the chose in action represented by P's credit balance at the bank: *cf Chan Man-Sin v R* [1988] 1 All ER 1.

In respect of offences committed by corporations, see also s 18 *infra*.

'dishonestly' Strictly speaking, s 2 of the Act does not apply to offences under this provision; but the concept of dishonesty is in practice essentially the same as that applicable in theft cases. Indeed, *R v Ghosh* [1982] QB 1053 (discussed in the notes to s 2 *supra*) was itself a s 15 case. See also *R v Woolven* [1983] Crim LR 632.

'with the intention of permanently depriving the other' See the notes to s 6 *supra*, which applies to s 15 offences by virtue of s 15(3).

'property' The definition in s 4(1) *supra* applies here by virtue of s 34(1) *infra*. The concept of property is therefore identical to that applicable in cases of theft. s 4(2)–(4) do *not* however apply; there are therefore no rules precluding a charge of obtaining land by deception.

'belonging to another' This concept is again identical to that which applies in cases of theft. S 5 applies by virtue of s 34(1).

'obtains' Note the wide definition of 'obtaining' provided by subs (2). The offence may be committed when (and where) D obtains ownership, even if he does not acquire physical possession or control (and *vice-versa*). It is therefore possible for there to be more than one 'obtaining' of the same property; and it is equally possible for an obtaining to be followed by a latter appropriation which could amount to theft under s 1: *R v Hircock* (1978) 67 Cr App R 278. In cases involving a foreign element, it may well happen that one of these offences is committed within the jurisdiction, even though the essential elements of the other are completed abroad. If, for example, D dishonestly persuades P to let him take P's property abroad, and appropriates it there, a charge of theft would fail (*cf R v Fritschy* [1985] Crim LR 745) but a s 15 offence might still be proved.

'obtaining for another' The other person may, but need not be, a party to the offence or cognisant of the deception: *R v Duru* [1973] 3 All ER 715.

'by any deception' See subs (4). The classic definition of a deception is that of Buckley J in *Re London and Globe Finance Corp Ltd* [1903] 1 Ch 728 at 732: 'to induce a man to believe that a thing is true which is false'. One can deceive without necessarily making false assertions. Half-truths may be calculated to deceive (*cf R v Lord Kylsant* [1932] 1 KB 442) and conduct may induce false beliefs: *DPP v Ray* [1974] AC 370; *R v Williams* [1980] Crim LR 589.

More problematic is the case in which D induces P to believe that something *may* possibly be true. If D knows that it cannot be true, is he accordingly guilty of deception? The authorities suggest that he is, and this may be so even in cases where P is not particularly concerned with the truth of D's representation. A shop assistant may be happy to accept D's cheque and cheque card without concerning himself with the question of D's authority to use them, but he would not be likely to accept them if he knew for a fact that D had no such authority. See *R v Charles* [1977] AC 177; *R v Lambie* [1982] AC 449; *R v King* [1979] Crim LR 122.

Who must be deceived? It is clear that a deception offence may be committed even though the deception is practised against someone other than the person who suffers loss: *Smith v Koumourou* [1979] Crim LR 116; *R v Charles, supra*. On the other hand, some *person* must be deceived. The law does not regard machines or computers as capable of being deceived. If D dishonestly uses a foreign coin to operate a vending machine, the proper charge would be theft, just as it would be if D wrenched open the machine with a crowbar.

'whether deliberate or reckless' In practice, a recklessly misleading statement is only likely to found a deception offence under the Theft Acts if it is reckless in the *Cunningham* sense (i.e. if D realises that his statement may be false). Recklessness in the wider *Caldwell* sense is unlikely to be relevant, because the deception offences all require proof of dishonesty.

Deception by omission See *R v Firth* [1990] Crim LR 326.

Obtaining pecuniary advantage by deception

16. (1) A person who by any deception dishonestly obtains for himself or another any pecuniary advantage shall on conviction on indictment be liable to imprisonment for a term not exceeding five years.

(2) The cases in which a pecuniary advantage within the meaning of this section is to be regarded as obtained for a person are cases where—

(*a*) [*Repealed*]

(*b*) he is allowed to borrow by way of overdraft, or to take out any policy of insurance or annuity contract, or obtains an improvement of the terms on which he is allowed to do so; or

(*c*) he is given the opportunity to earn remuneration or greater remuneration in an office or employment, or to win money by betting.

(3) For purposes of this section "deception" has the same meaning as in section 15 of this Act.

NOTES

Many of the situations which were originally covered by s 16 are now covered by ss 1 and 2 of the Theft Act 1978 (*qv*). That Act repealed subs (2)(a), which had been described as a 'judicial nightmare', and it thereby effected an undoubted improvement in the law. S 16 now applies in only a very limited range of circumstances.

'by any deception' See subs (3) and notes to s 15 *supra*.

'dishonestly' See notes to ss 2 and 15 *supra;* but note that s 2 itself is not strictly speaking applicable to offences under this provision.

'obtains' See notes to s 15 *supra*.

'any pecuniary advantage' The term 'pecuniary advantage' (like the term 'handling' in s 22 *infra*) is a mere term of art, which has no meaning save that given to it in the relevant section. In this case the meaning is set out in subs (2)(b) and (c).

'he is allowed to borrow by way of overdraft' Borrowing cash involves the obtaining of property, and is therefore governed by s 15; but the mere granting of overdraft facilities may be enough as far as s 16 is concerned. It is not necessary that any use should have been made of those facilities. See *R v Watkins* [1976] 1 All ER 578.

The deception will often be practised on someone other than the bank which provides the overdraft, *eg* where D deceives P into accepting a cheque backed by a cheque guarantee card which D is no longer authorised to use, and the bank then becomes obliged to honour the cheque, thereby increasing D's overdraft. See *R v Waites* [1982] Crim LR 369; *R v Bevan* (1987) 84 Cr App R 143.

'opportunity' (subs (2)(c)) The essence of the offence under subs (2)(c) is the gaining of an opportunity to earn remuneration, win money by betting *etc*. It is not necessary that he should actually earn or win anything.

False accounting
17. (1) Where a person dishonestly, with a view to gain for himself or another or with intent to cause loss to another,—
  (*a*) destroys, defaces, conceals or falsifies any account or any record or document made or required for any accounting; or
  (*b*) in furnishing information for any such purpose produces or makes use of any account, or any such record or document as aforesaid, which to his knowledge is or may be misleading, false or deceptive in a material particular;
he shall, on conviction on indictment, be liable to imprisonment for a term not exceeding seven years.

(2) For purposes of this section a person who makes or concurs in making in an account or other document an entry which is or may be misleading, false or deceptive in a material particular, or who omits or concurs in omitting a material particular from an account or other document, is to be treated as falsifying the account or document.

NOTES
The two offences of falsifying accounts (subs (1)(a)) and of using false or deceptive accounts (subs (1)(b)) clearly overlap to some extent with the offences created by ss 1 and 3 of the Forgery and Counterfeiting Act 1981 (*qv*), but there will be many cases in which accounting documents will be 'misleading, false or deceptive' within the meaning of subs (2) without being 'false' in any of the special respects specified by s 9 of the 1981 Act, and the destruction or concealment of records cannot possibly be termed forgery. It is therefore quite wrong to suggest that any case of false accounting necessarily involves forgery: *R v Dodge* [1972] 1 QB 416.
Cases of false accounting are often closely connected with other Theft Act offences, the falsification being a cover for past, contemporaneous or future offences under ss 1, 15 *etc*; but in *R v Monaghan* [1979] Crim LR 673, the Court of Appeal appeared to confuse ss 1 and 17. The appellant's dishonest failure to 'ring up' £3.99 on the supermarket till she was operating, with a view to abstracting an equivalent sum from the till later in the day, was held to constitute theft of the £3.99, but with respect she had done nothing more than falsify the till roll: she had put the money itself in the till where it belonged. If *Monaghan* is correct, there is a very considerable overlap between ss 1 and 17, but the better view must be that the decision is wrong.
A further area of overlap exists in respect of falsified company accounts and records: see the Companies Act 1985 ss 221, 393 and 450. See also s 18 of this Act in respect of the liability of company directors.

'dishonestly' S 2 does not apply; but *R v Ghosh* presumably does (see notes to s 2). It may be dishonest to falsify a record for the purpose of concealing an earlier innocent mistake: *R v Eden* (1971) 55 Cr App R 193.

'with a view to gain' etc. See s 34 (2)(a), under which gain and loss are to be construed in terms only of money or other property; but 'gain' includes keeping what one has, and 'loss' includes not getting what one might otherwise get. An intent to avoid loss on a temporary basis (ie playing for time) may suffice: *R v Eden, supra*; but see *R v Golechha* (1990) 90 Cr App R 241.

Accounts, records and documents A record or account need not necessarily be a document: *Edwards v Coombs* [1983] Crim LR 43, nor need a document be a record or account; but if not accounts in their own right, documents or records must be made or required for an accounting purpose, whether the offender's own or someone elses. This accounting purpose may however be a secondary or incidental one: *Att Gen's Reference (No 1 of 1980)* [1981] 1 WLR 34.

'destroys, defaces, conceals or falsifies' (subs (1)(a)) The concept or falsity is elaborated upon (but not exhaustively defined) in subs (2). The other terms will bear their normal dictionary meanings. As to omissions, see *R v Shama* [1990] Crim LR 411.

Furnishing false information (subs (1)(b)) Whereas subs (1)(a) strikes at the act of falsification, subs (1)(b) strikes at the production or use of misleading, false or deceptive records, accounts *etc*. The falsity *etc* must be material, but it may affect something other than accuracy of accounts: *R v Mallett* [1978] 3 All ER 10.

'misleading, false or deceptive' (subs (1)(b) and (2)) To be false or falsified, the record *etc* in question need not strictly be untrue: a collection of individually correct half-truths may infringe the provision: *cf R v Lord Kylsant* (The *Royal Mail* case) [1932] 1 KB 442.

Liability of company officers for certain offences by company

18. (1) Where an offence committed by a body corporate under section 15, 16 or 17 of this Act is proved to have been committed with the consent or connivance of any director, manager, secretary or other similar officer of the body corporate, or any person who was purporting to act in any such capacity, he as well as the body corporate shall be guilty of that offence, and shall be liable to be proceeded against and punished accordingly.

(2) Where the affairs of a body corporate are managed by its members, this section shall apply in relation to the acts and defaults of a member in connection with his functions of management as if he were a director of the body corporate.

NOTES
This provision now applies in respect of offences under ss 1 & 2 of the Theft Act 1978, in addition to those specifically mentioned. These are all *mens rea* offences: corporations can only be guilty of such offences if the requisite *mens rea* is possessed by the directors, managers or senior officials who actually determine and control its actions, and who are therefore its 'brains'. As Denning LJ said in *H.L. Bolton (Engineering) Co. Ltd v T.J. Graham & Sons Ltd* [1957] 1 QB 159 at 172, 'The state of mind of these directors is the state of mind of the company and is treated as such.' Directors *etc.* who dishonestly cause their companies to commit the specified offences will necessarily be guilty of those same offences as co-principals or a accessories under the general principles of complicity (Accessories & Abettors Act 1861 s 8); but the present provision ensures that other officers who knowingly acquiesce in those offences will be liable as well.

'consent or connivance' One cannot consent or connive at something one is not aware of; but arguably wilful blindness may suffice, and there is clearly no need for any active participation in the offence.

'purporting to act' This ensures that an invalidly appointed director *etc*, or one who has acted as such with no formal appointment at all, cannot use this lack of proper authority as a defence. Note also subs (2).

False statements by company directors, etc.

19. (1) Where an officer of a body corporate or unincorporated association (or person purporting to act as such), with intent to deceive members or creditors of the body corporate or association about its affairs, publishes or concurs in publishing a written statement or account which to his knowledge is or may be misleading, false or deceptive in a material particular, he shall on conviction on indictment be liable to imprisonment for a term not exceeding seven years.

(2) For purposes of this section a person who has entered into a security for the benefit of a body corporate or association is to be treated as a creditor of it.

(3) Where the affairs of a body corporate or association are managed by its members, this section shall apply to any statement which a member publishes or concurs in publishing in connection with his functions of management as if he were an officer of the body corporate or association.

NOTES

This provision overlaps to some extent with the offence of false accounting (s 17 *supra*) and with certain offences under the Companies Act 1985 and the Financial Services Act 1986 (not printed in this book).

'officer of a body corporate or unincorporated association' In relation to a registered company, directors, managers and company secretaries are all 'officers' (Companies Act 1985 s 744). Auditors may aslo be officers; *R v Shacter* [1960] 2 QB 252. Treasurers, secretaries and chairmen may constitute the officers of an unincorporated association, and note subs (3) in relation to management by ordinary members.

'misleading, false or deceptive' See the notes to s 17 *supra*.

'publishes or concurs in publishing a written statement or account' Oral statements are excluded, but it has been argued (Arlidge & Parry, *Fraud* p 195) that an oral statement to the press, with a view to its publication by them, might be within the provision.

'with intent to deceive' On the meaning of deception see the notes to s 15 *supra;* but note that a *successful deception* is not essential for liability under this provision. The intent alone will suffice.

'members or creditors' This would appear to mean existing members or creditors rather than potential ones; but false or misleading statements made with a view to encouraging share purchase or subscription might still be within the scope of the provision on the basis that existing shareholders might be encouraged to invest in further shares.

Suppression, etc of documents

20. (1) A person who dishonestly, with a view to gain for himself or another or with intent to cause loss to another, destroys, defaces or conceals any valuable security, any will or other testamentary document or any original document of or belonging to, or filed or deposited in, any court of justice or any government department shall on conviction on indictment be liable to imprisonment for a term not exceeding seven years.

(2) A person who dishonestly, with a view to gain for himself or another or with intent to cause loss to another, by any deception procures the execution of a valuable security shall on conviction on indictment be liable to imprisonment for a term not exceeding seven years; and this subsection shall apply in relation to the making, acceptance, indorsement, alteration, cancellation or destruction in whole or in part of a valuable security, and in relation to the signing or sealing of any paper or other material in order that it may be made or converted into, or used or dealt with as, a valuable security, as if that were the execution of a valuable security.

(3) For purposes of this section"deception" has the same meaning as in section 15 of this Act, and "valuable security" means any document creating, transferring, surrendering or releasing any right to, in or over property, or authorising the payment of money or delivery of any property, or evidencing the creation, transfer, surrender or release of any such right, or the payment of money or delivery of any property, or the satisfaction of any obligation.

NOTES

This provision creates two distinct offences, which have little in common with each other. The first (the offence of supressing documents) is not a deception offence; the second (that of procuring the execution of a valuable security) is one.

'dishonestly'   s 2 *supra* does not directly apply, but see the notes thereto, and see also *R v Ghosh* [1982] QB 1053.

'with a view to gain' *etc.*   See s 34(2)(a) *infra* and the notes to s 17 *supra*.

'valuable security'   See subs (3). See aslo *R v Benstead* (1982) 75 Cr App R 276 and *R v Beck* [1985] 1 All ER 571.
   A forged instrument may still be a valuable security, and is capable of being executed: *R v Beck supra.*

'execution' (subs (2) only)   Note the extended meaning of execution provided by subs (2) itself. In *Beck* it was held that execution takes place when a valuable security, such as a cheque, is paid, there being 'no good reason' why there should not be several 'executions' of such an instrument during the course of its life. 'Acceptance' in this context means something more than mere receipt of the item in question. See *R v Nanayakkara* [1987] 1 WLR 265.

'procuring'   In *Beck*, Watkins LJ said:

'[Procure] is a word in common usage ... The most common meaning attached to it ... is to cause or to bring about. It has no special meaning for the purpose of s 20(2).'

Blackmail

21. (1) A person is guilty of blackmail if, with a view to gain for himself or another or with intent to cause loss to another, he makes any unwarranted demand with menaces; and for this purpose a demand with menaces is unwarranted unless the person making it does so in the belief—

(*a*) that he has reasonable grounds for making the demand; and

(*b*) that the use of the menaces is a proper means of reinforcing the demand.

(2) The nature of the act or omission is immaterial, and it is also immaterial whether the menaces relate to action to be taken by the person making the demand.

(3) A person guilty of blackmail shall on conviction on indictment be liable to imprisonment for a term not exceeding fourteen years.

NOTES

This provision proscribes the *making* of certain kinds of improper demands. It is deliberately drafted in such a way that the complete offence can be committed even if the blackmailer fails to intimidate the victim or fails to obtain anything from him, and it has been interpreted by the courts as obviating even the need for the successful communication of the demand. Thus, in *Treacy v DPP* [1971] AC 537 it was held that D committed blackmail in England by posting a blackmail letter addressed to a victim in West Germany, the offence being completed by the act of posting the letter.

'with a view to gain ... or intent to cause loss' See s 34(2)(a) of this Act, in which 'gain' and 'loss' are defined as extending only to gain or loss in money or other property. See also *R v Parkes* [1973] Crim LR 358.

The procuring of sexual intercourse by threats or intimidation may amount to an offence under s 2 of the Sexual Offences Act 1956 (*qv*) and may even amount to rape if the threats *etc* cause the women to submit rather than consent (see *R v Olugboja* [1982] QB 320), but will not amount to blackmail. Murder threats may or may not involve an intent to gain *etc*, but may in either event involve an offence under s 16 of the Offences Against the Person Act 1861.

'makes any ... demand' A demand may be expressed or implied. As was pointed out in *R v Studer* (1915) 11 Cr App R 307, 'it may be in language only a request'. See also *R v Collister* (1955) 39 Cr App R 199.

Communication of a demand to the victim is not an essential ingredient of the offence: *Treacy v DPP* (supra).

'with menaces' These need not involve threats of violence, still less immediate violence (*cf* robbery); but at the same time they must ordinarily be 'threats of such a nature and extent that the mind of an ordinary person might be influenced ... so as to accede unwillingly to the demand': *R v Clear* [1968] 1 QB 670.

'unwarranted' D's genuine belief that he is entitled to make the demand and to reinforce it with the particular menaces concerned will be a complete defence, even if the belief is unreasonable; but if D knows the menaces are improper, then he may be guilty even if he is demanding something to which he knows he is perfectly entitled (*eg* repayment of a debt): *R v Lawrence* (1971) 57 Cr App R 64; *R v Harvey* (1981) 72 Cr App R 139.

As far as harassment of debtors is concerned, liability may also be incurred under s 40 of the Administration of Justice Act 1970 (not printed in this work).

Handling stolen goods

22. (1) A person handles stolen goods if (otherwise than in the course of the stealing) knowing or believing them to be stolen goods he dishonestly receives the goods, or dishonestly undertakes or assists in their retention, removal, disposal or realisation by or for the benefit of another person, or if he arranges to do so.

(2) A person guilty of handling stolen goods shall on conviction on indictment be liable to imprisonent for a term not exceeding fourteen years.

NOTES

This provision, which must be read in conjunction with s 24 *infra,* creates an offence of much greater width than the 'old' offence of receiving, and indeed of greater width than its own title suggests: 'goods' can include anything other than land; the property in question need not necessarily be that originally stolen, but may represent the 'proceeds' of that property, and may indeed represent the fruits of blackmail or of an offence under s 15 rather than one of ordinary theft. The maximum penalty under subs (2) is significantly higher than that for theft (though not burglary or robbery); this reflects the fact that some professional handlers are perceived as greater criminals than the theives they deal with.

'goods' 'Goods' are defined in s 34 (2)(b) *infra.* For most purposes the term 'goods' is co-extensive with 'property' as defined in s 4 *supra,* excluding only land. Money and choses in action are within the definition: *Attorney-General's Ref. (No. 4 of 1979)* (1980) 71 Cr App R 341. So too are things which have been stolen by severence from the land.

'stolen goods' are extensively defined in s 24 *infra.*

Forms of handling The term 'handling' is merely a kind of shorthand embracing the various forms of dealing with property specified in subs (1). The basic form of handling is 'receiving' (*infra*). In practice, a charge of receiving or of arranging to receive will be contained in a separate count from any other variants that may be alleged, even though s 22 probably creates only one offence (i.e. handling). See *Griffiths v Freeman* [1970] 1 All ER 1117. Except in cases of receiving or arranging to receive, it must be proved that D assisted or acted for the benefit of some other person.

'receiving' The act provides no definition of 'receiving', but cases on receiving under the Larceny Act defined it as involving the taking of joint or exclusive possession or control of the property (*R v Frost* (1964) 48 Cr App R 284) but not necessarily of direct personal possession or control: receipt of the goods by E on D's behalf and with D's authority could make D guilty of receiving (*R v Miller* (1854) 6 Cox CC 353).

'arranging to receive' A charge of arranging to receive stolen goods may sometimes offer the prosecution advantages over a charge of attempted handling (eg in avoiding problems of 'proximity'). It is not enough, however, that an arrangement is made to receive goods which have yet to be stolen at the time. This might be conspiracy, but cannot be handling: *R v Park, The Times,* 14th December 1987.

'undertaking or assisting etc ... by or for the benefit of another person' In *R v Bloxham* [1983] 1 AC 109 Lord Bridge said, (at pp. 113–4):

"The offence can be committed in relation to any one of these activities in one or other of two ways. First, the offender may himself undertake the activity *for the benefit of* another person. Secondly, the activity may be undertaken *by* another person and the offender may assist him ... The category of other persons contemplated by the subsection is subjected to the same limitations whichever way the offence is committed. Accordingly a purchaser, as such, of stolen goods cannot .. be 'another person' within the subsection, since his act of purchase could not sensibly be described as a disposal or realisation of the stolen goods *by* him.'

It followed that D did not commit the offence of handling merely by selling a stolen car to E at a knockdown price. D had earlier purchased the car without realising it was stolen.

'assisting in retention' This requires some active assistance: merely failing to reveal stolen property during a police search will not suffice (*R v Brown* [1970] 1 QB 105), nor will it suffice that D uses goods he knows E has stolen *etc*: *R v Sanders* [1982] Crim LR 615 (*cf R v Pitchley* (1973) 57 Cr App R 30).

'otherwise than in the course of the stealing' This must mean the *original* stealing: every receiver of stolen goods appropriates another person's property and will therefore be guilty of theft as well as of handling. The two offences cannot be materially exclusive: *R v Sainthouse* [1980] Crim LR 506. There may be problems where there is some doubt as to whether the original appropriation is continuing or finished at the relevant moment—see *R v Pitham* (1976) 65 Cr App R 45 and *R v Cash* [1985] QB 801.

'dishonestly' The test of dishonesty in handling is not directly subject to s 2 of the Act, but will be determined as a question of fact by the jury in accordance with the tests laid down in *R v Ghosh* (see notes to s 2 *supra*).

'knowing or believing them to be stolen' It is not enough that D *believes* goods to be stolen if it cannot be proved they were: *Haughton v Smith* [1975] AC 476 at p 485.

A person may 'believe' goods to be stolen when he does not know for certain that they are (*eg* where this is merely an inference he draws from the circumstances in which he acquires them). Nevertheless, belief means positive belief, not mere suspicion. It is not even enough that D thinks the goods were 'probably' stolen: *R v Griffiths* (1974) 60 Cr App R 14; *R v Pethick* [1980] Crim LR 242; *R v Reader* (1977) 66 Cr App R 33; *R v Lincoln* [1980] Crim LR 575.

Advertising rewards for return of goods stolen or lost

23. Where any public advertisement of a reward for the return of any goods which have been stolen or lost uses any words to the effect that no questions will be asked, or that the person producing the goods will be safe from apprehension or inquiry, or that any money paid for the purchase of the goods or advanced by way of loan on them will be repaid, the person advertising the reward and any person who prints or publishes the advertisement shall on summary conviction be liable to a fine not exceeding level 3 on the standard scale.

NOTES

This provision does not necessarily forbid the offering of rewards for the return of stolen goods, nor does it necessarily prohibit advertisements promising that 'no questions will be asked'. It prohibits only public advertisements containing *both* an offer of a reward *and* a promise of immunity from investigation.

'goods which have been stolen or lost' *Stolen* goods are defined in s 24. The fact that the advertiser may be uncertain whether the goods have been lost or stolen is irrelevant.

'any person who prints or publishes ...'   See *R v Denham* (1983) 77 Cr App
R 210.

mens rea   The offence is one of strict liability—*R v Denham supra.*

Scope of offences relating to stolen goods
   24. (1) The provisions of this Act relating to goods which have been
stolen shall apply whether the stealing occurred in England or Wales or
elsewhere, and whether it occurred before or after the commencement of
this Act, provided that the stealing (if not an offence under this Act)
amounted to an offence where and at the time when the goods were stolen;
and references to stolen goods shall be construed accordingly.
   (2) For purposes of those provisions references to stolen goods shall
include, in addition to the goods originally stolen and parts of them
(whether in their original state or not),—
   (*a*) any other goods which directly or indirectly represent or have at
         any time represented the stolen goods in the hands of the thief as
         being the proceeds of any disposal or realisation of the whole or part
         of the goods stolen or of goods so representing the stolen goods; and
   (*b*) any other goods which directly or indirectly represent or have at
         any time represented the stolen goods in the hands of a handler of
         the stolen goods or any part of them as being the proceeds of any
         disposal or realisation of the whole or part of the stolen goods
         handled by him or of goods so representing them.
   (3) But no goods shall be regarded as having continued to be stolen
goods after they have been restored to the person from whom they were
stolen or to other lawful possession or custody, or after that person and any
other person claiming through him have otherwise ceased as regards those
goods to have any right to restitution in respect of the theft.
   (4) For purposes of the provisions of this Act relating to goods which
have been stolen (including subsections (1) to (3) above) goods obtained
in England or Wales or elsewhere either by blackmail or in the circumstances described in section 15(1) of this Act shall be regarded as stolen;
and "steal", "theft" and "thief" shall be construed accordingly.

NOTES
The principal function of this provision is to supplement s 22 by defining the
concept of stolen goods. The definition provided is very wide and must be read in
conjunction with s 34 (2)(b).

Subs (4)   This extends the concept of stolen goods to cover the fruits of offences of
fraud or blackmail under ss 15 or 21. The fruits of burglary and robbery need no
special mention, because they are obtained by theft.

Subs (1)   This extends the concept to goods stolen (or obtained by fraud *etc*)
outside the jurisdiction, provided that the original stealing *etc* was *either* an
extraterritorial offence under English law (*eg* theft by a seaman from a British ship)
or an offence under the equivalent local law. Thus, if C steals P's goods in France
or Scotland and D in England dishonestly receives them knowing of the circumstances D will be guilty of handling under s 22. Proof may be needed as to the
content of the relevant foreign law.

Subs (2) Although undoubtedly wide-ranging, this is actually more restrictive than the corresponding provisions in the Larceny Act 1916, which it has replaced. In theory the old law tainted any proceeds of the sale of stolen goods, or anything purchased therewith, or anything exchanged for stolen goods, as being itself stolen goods, whether or not it had ever been in the hands of a thief or receiver.

Where stolen cheques or cash are paid into a bank account, the balance in the account may then represent stolen goods under subs (2); but where the proceeds of theft *etc* are mixed with untainted credits, so that perhaps only half of the total balance represents stolen goods, a cheque drawn on that account for less than the 'untainted' half of the balance cannot ordinarily be regarded as being caught by subs (2)—unless there is evidence that the thief or handler drawing the cheque specifically intended it to represent proceeds of theft (*eg* a 'pay out' to another party of his share of the proceeds): *Att. Gen's Reference (No. 4 of 1979)* [1981] 1 All ER 1193.

Subs (3) See *Haughton v Smith* [1975] AC 476 and *Att. Gen's Reference (No. 1 of 1974)* [1974] QB 744 on the issue of what amounts to a restoration to lawful possession.

Loss of right to restitution Where D acquires a negotiable instrument as or from a holder in due course, or where he acquires goods purchased in 'market overt', then he will acquire a good title, notwithstanding any earlier theft of the goods or instruments, and there can be no question of his handling stolen goods. The goods will have ceased to belong to the original owner.

The 'innocent thief' D may be found guilty of handling goods alleged to have been stolen by E notwithstanding E's acquittal on the theft charge. E's acquittal at an earlier trial would not even be admissible evidence for the defence (see Police and Criminal Evidence Act 1984, s 74). Nevertheless, there is a difference between E's acquittal for want of satisfactory evidence (*eg* D has confessed but his confession is inadmissible against E) and a clear finding that he must have been innocent (*eg* because he is under the age of criminal responsibility, as in *Walters v Lunt* [1951] 2 All ER 645.). In the latter case, E's innocence means there has been no theft and D cannot be guilty of handling the proceeds. D might however be guilty of theft.

Possession of housebreaking implements, etc.

Going equipped for stealing, etc.

25. (1) A person shall be guilty of an offence if, when not at his place of abode, he has with him any article for use in the course of or in connection with any burglary, theft or cheat.

(2) A person guilty of an offence under this section shall on conviction on indictment be liable to imprisonment for a term not exceeding three years.

(3) Where a person is charged with an offence under this section, proof that he had with him any article made or adapted for use in committing a burglary, theft or cheat shall be evidence that he had it with him for such use.

(4) Any person may arrest without warrant anyone who is, or whom he, with reasonable cause, suspects to be, committing an offence under this section.

(5) For purposes of this section an offence under section 12(1) of this Act of taking a conveyance shall be treated as theft, and "cheat" means an offence under section 15 of this Act.

NOTES

'when not at his place of abode'　It is not generally an offence under this provision to keep or possess articles intended for use in theft, burglary *etc* as long as these are kept at home. Possession of some such items, including unlicensed firearms and explosives, may however be punishable under other legislation; and see in particular s 3 of the Criminal Damage Act 1971.

As to the meaning of 'place of abode' in respect of gypsies and travellers, see *R v Bundy* [1977] 2 All ER 382 at 384.

'has with him'　See the notes to s 10 *supra*.

'any article for use　... *Ie* intended for such use, whether by D himself or by someone to whom he intends to supply it; *R v Ellames* (1974) 60 Cr App R 7. It would not seem to matter whether the article is intended for use that day. It may suffice if D intends to give it to E so that E can use it the next week.

Apart from the obvious tools of burglary or robbery, proscribed articles may include stolen credit cards and other instruments of deception.

'theft'　Note that the taking of conveyances (other than pedal cycles) is to be treated for the purposes of this section as if it were theft (subs (5)) and that robbery necessarily includes theft.

'cheat'　This means an offence under s 15 of the Act (obtaining by deception). Other deception offences are *not* included. (See subs (5) and *R v Mansfield* [1975] Crim LR 101).

Penalties etc　Apart from the penalties provided for by subs (2), note also the existence of powers of confiscation: Powers of the Criminal Courts Act 1973 s 43.

26–28. [*omitted*]

29. [*repealed*]

General and consequential provisions

Husband and wife

30. (1) This Act shall apply in relation to the parties to a marriage, and to property belonging to the wife or husband whether or not by reason of an interest derived from the marriage, as it would apply if they were not married and any such interest subsisted independently of the marriage.

(2) Subject to subsection (4) below, a person shall have the same right to bring proceedings against that person's wife or husband for any offence (whether under this Act or otherwise), as if they were not married, and a person bringing any such proceedings shall be competent to give evidence for the prosecuion at every stage of the proceedings.

(3) [*repealed*]

(4) Proceedings shall not be instituted against a person for any offence of stealing or doing unlawful damage to property which at the time of the offence belongs to that person's wife or husband, or for any attempt, incitement or conspiracy to commit such an offence, unless the proceedings are instituted by or with the consent of the director of Public Prosecutions:

Provided that—

　(*a*) this subsection shall not apply to preceedings against a person for an offence—

(i) if that person is charged with committing the offence jointly with the wife or husband; or

(ii) if by virtue of any judicial decree or order (wherever made) that person and the wife or husband are at the time of the offence under no obligation to cohabit *and*

(*b*) [*Repealed*]

(5) notwithstanding [section 6 of the Prosecution of Offences Act 1979] subsection (4) of this section shall apply—

(*a*) to an arrest (if without warrant) made by the wife or husband, and

(*b*) to a warrant of arrest issued on an information laid by the wife or husband.

NOTES

The significance of subs (1) is that spouses can commit Theft Act offences in relation to property belonging to their partners; but note subs (4).

'by or with the consent of the Director of Public Prosecutions' These powers can be exercised by Crown prosecutors.

31–33. [*omitted*]

Supplementary

Interpretation

34. (1) Sections 4(1) and 5(1) of this Act shall apply generally for purposes of this Act as they apply for purposes of section 1.

(2) For purposes of this Act—

(*a*) "gain" and "loss" are to be construed as extending only to gain or loss in money or other property, but as extending to any such gain or loss whether temporary or permanent; and —

(i) "gain" includes a gain by keeping what one has, as well as a gain by getting what one has not; and

(ii) "loss" includes a loss by not getting what one might get, as well as a loss by parting with what one has;

(*b*) "goods", except in so far as the context otherwise requires, includes money and every other description of property except land, and includes things severed from the land by stealing.

35. [*omitted*]

Short title, and general provisions as to Scotland and Northern Ireland

36. (1) This Act may be cited as the Theft Act 1968.

(2) [*repealed*]

(3) This Act does not extend to Scotland or ... to Northern Ireland, except as regards any amendment or repeal which in accordance with section 33 above is to extend to Scotland or Northern Ireland.

SCHEDULE 1:
OFFENCES OF TAKING, ETC DEER OR FISH
Taking or killing deer
[1. *repealed*]

Taking or destroying fish
2. (1) Subject to subparagraph (2) below, a person who unlawfully takes or destroys, or attempts to take or destroy, any fish in water which is private property or in which there is any private right or fishery shall on summary conviction be liable to a fine not exceeding fifty pounds or, for an offence committed after a previous conviction of an offence under this subpargraph, to imprisonment for a term not exceeding three months or to a fine not exceeding one hundred pounds or to both.

(2) Subparagraph (1) above shall not apply to taking or destroying fish by angling in the daytime (that is to say, in the period beginning one hour before sunrise and ending one hour after sunset); but a person who by angling in the daytime unlawfully takes or destroys, or attempts to take or destroy, any fish in water which is private property or in which there is any private right of fishery shall on summary conviction be liable to a fine not exceeding twenty pounds.

(3) The court by which a person is convicted of an offence under this paragraph may order the forfeiture of anything which, at the time of the offence, he had with him for use for taking or destroying fish.

(4) Any person may arrest without warrant anyone who is, or whom he, with reasonable cause, suspects to be, committing an offence under subparagraph (1) above, and may seize from any person who is, or whom he, with reasonable cause suspects to be, committing any offence under this paragraph anything which on that person' conviction of the offence would be liable to be forfeited under subparagraph (3) above.

NOTES
S 32 of the Act (not printed here) gives effect to this Schedule, which preserves in a modified form offences formerly contained in the Larceny Act 1861. The protection of deer is now dealt with by the Deer Act 1980; as to other wild birds and animals, see ss 1 and 9 of the Wildlife and Countryside Act 1981.

Criminal Damage Act 1971

(C 48)

Destroying or damaging property
1. (1) A person who without lawful excuse destroys or damages any property belonging to another intending to destroy or damage any such property or being reckless as to whether any such property would be destroyed or damaged shall be guilty of an offence.

(2) A person who without lawful excuse destroys or damages any property, whether belonging to himself or another—

(*a*) intending to destroy or damage any property or being reckless as to whether any property would be destroyed or damaged; and

(*b*) intending by the destruction or damage to endanger the life of another or being reckless as to whether the life of another would be thereby endangered;

shall be guilty of an offence.

(3) An offence committed under this section by destroying or damaging property by fire shall be charged as arson.

NOTES

The offence of criminal damage replaced a variety of offences contained in earlier legislation, including most (but not all) offences under the Malicious Damage Act 1861, and it also replaced the common law offence of arson. Subs (1) creates the basic offence, whilst subs (2) creates an aggravated variant and subs (3) (read in conjunction with s 4) makes special provision for offences involving damage *etc* by fire. Each subsection will be considered separately.

Subs (1): the basic offence   The maximum penalty is 10 years (s 4 *infra*). For mode of trial see notes to that section.

'destroys or damages'   These terms are not defined by the Act, but must bear their ordinary dictionary meanings: to destroy is to 'undo, break up, reduce into a useless form, consume or dissolve'; to damage is to 'hurt, harm, injure—commonly to injure a thing so as to lessen its value' (*Oxford English Dictionary*). No problems need arise as to the subtleties of the distinction between destruction and lesser forms of damage (on which see *Barnet LBC v Eastern Electricity Board* [1973] 2 All ER 319), but problems may arise in cases of marginal or trivial damage. See *Morphitis v Salmon* [1990] Crim LR 48. The *de minimis* rule applies, although the question will ultimately be one of fact.

Damage need not be permanent to constitute an offence. See *R v Kingerlee* [1986] Crim LR 735. In the case of animals, killing involves 'destruction' and injuries are 'damage'.

'property'   See the definition provided by s 10(1) *infra*.

'belonging to another'   As far as subs (1) is concerned, the property in question must belong to another person; but in cases under subs (2) D may incur liability through damage or destruction of his own property. See further s 10(2)–(4) *infra*.

'without lawful excuse'.   See s 5 *infra*.

198

'**intending ... or being reckless**'. On the meaning of intent, see *R v Belfon* [1976] 3 All ER 46; *R v Moloney* [1985] AC 905; *R v Nedrick* [1986] 1 WLR 1025; Criminal Justice Act 1967 s 8.

As to recklessness in this context, see *R v Caldwell* [1982] AC 341, which establishes that a person is reckless if he does an act (or is guilty of an omission) which involves an obvious risk, and he either:

(a) realises that the risk exists, but goes on to take it; or
(b) gives no thought as to the possibility that the risk exists.

It does not matter if, owing to youth, inexperience or ignorance, D would not have realised the risk existed even if he had stopped to think about it—the question is whether it would have been obvious to an ordinary prudent bystander: *Elliot v C (a minor)* [1983] 2 All ER 1005; *R v R (Stephen Malcolm)* (1984) 79 Cr App R 334; *R v Sangha* [1988] 1 WLR 519—but *cf R v Hardie* [1984] 3 All ER 848, which may arguably have been decided wrongly in that it overlooks the objective nature of the *Caldwell* principle. Where D does an act which he knows involves some risk, then unless it is reasonable to take that risk (e.g. because of his act has some greater social utility), he will be accounted reckless, even if he took precautions to minimise the risk and was confident of avoiding any damage: *Chief Constable of Avon & Somerset v Shimmen* [1986] Crim LR 800 (and commentary).

'**any such property**'—This makes it clear that the doctrine of transferred malice applies. If D throws a stone at P's car, but misses and accidentally smashes a window in Q's house, he will be guilty of criminal damage on the basis of the intent to damage P's car. If, however, D throws the stone at P himself, any offence of damage to Q's window would depend on whether D was reckless as to the possibility of such damage. *Cf R v Pembliton* (1874) LR CCR 119.

Subs (2): the aggravated offence This is triable on indictment and the maximum penalty is life imprisonment (s 4 *infra*). The offence may involve:

(a) intentional destruction/damage to property and an intention to endanger life; or
(b) intentional destruction/damage to property and recklessness as to endangering of life; or
(c) reckless destruction/damage to property and recklessness as to endangering of life.

'**without lawful excuse**' S 5 of the Act does *not* apply to offences under s 1(2). Any lawful excuse must therefore be based on general principles (duress, insanity, necessity *etc*). See notes to s 5 *infra*.

'**destroys or damages**' See notes to s 1(1) *supra*.

'**property**' As defined in s 10(1) *infra*.

'**whether belonging to himself or another**' A person's usual right to destroy his own property does not extend to cases where he knows (or ought to know) that other people's lives may be endangered.

'**intending ... or being reckless**' See notes to subs (1).

'**endanger the life of another**' No lives need actually *be* endangered—this is a *mens rea* requirement, not a part of the *actus reus* (*cf R v Sangha supra*).

'**by**' or '**thereby**'—The subs (2) offence is only committed if D intends that (or is reckless whether) life will be endangered as a result of the damage or destruction of property. If D fires a gun at P, but misses and damages property with the shot, his intent to injure P is irrelevant for the purpose of sub (2): *R v Steer* [1988] AC 111.

Subs (3): arson Arson was formerly a common law offence. In this Act, it is defined as an offence under either s 1(1) or s 1(2) in which the damage is caused by fire. The maximum penalty for arson is life imprisonment even where s 1(2) is not infringed, and the simple offence is triable either way even where the value of the property involved does not exceed £2,000 (see notes to s 4 *infra*).

Where s 1(2) *is* infringed, the maximum penalty is unchanged, but sentences are in practice more severe and the offence ceases to be triable summarily. Moreover, whereas D would ordinarily be entitled to destroy his own property (by fire or otherwise), he may not do so if he intends thereby to endanger life or if he is reckless as to that possibility. Note also that s 5 is not directly applicable where D is charged with a s 1(2) offence.

Damage caused by explosives   If D causes damage by explosives, this may well involve contravention of s 1(2) and in some cases arson (petrol bombs, incendiary devices *etc*), but consider also charges under s 2 of the Explosive Substances Act 1883.

Threats to destroy or damage property

2.   A person who without lawful excuse makes to another a threat, intending that that other would fear it would be carried out,—

    (*a*) to destroy or damage any property belonging to that other or a third person; or

    (*b*) to destroy or damage his own property in a way which he knows is likely to endanger life of that other or a third person;

shall be guilty of an offence.

NOTES

See also the notes to s 16 of the Offences Against the Person Act 1861 (threats to murder). The two offences have much in common; in particular the requirement that D must intend P to fear the threat will be carried out.

'without lawful excuse'   See s 5 *infra* and notes thereto.

'property'   See s 10(1) *infra*.

'belonging to another'   See s 10(2) *infra*.

'in a way which he knows is likely ...'   That presumably means 'would be likely', since D need not actually have any intention of carrying out his threats.

Penalty   See s 4 *infra*.

Possessing anything with intent to destroy or damage property

3.   A person who has anything in his custody or under his control intending without lawful excuse to use it or cause or permit another to use it—

    (*a*) to destroy or damage any property belonging to some other person; or

    (*b*) to destroy or damage his own or the user's property in a way which he knows is likely to endanger the life of some other person;

shall be guilty of an offence.

NOTES

This provision is comparable in purpose with s 25 of the Theft Act 1968, but has a wider ambit in that D cannot commit the latter offence as long as he keeps his housebreaking equipment *etc* at his place of abode. If for example the police discover D's jemmy there, they would be better advised to charge him under this provision instead, on the basis that the jemmy would be intended to force open (and therefore damage) locked windows or doors belonging to other persons.

'in his custody or under his control'   D need not have the item in question on his person; it would suffice for it to be kept in D's home or garage *etc*. Problems of inadvertent possession (such as may arise in firearms or drugs cases) should not arise, because the offence requires a specific *mens rea*.

'without lawful excuse'   See s 5 *infra* and the notes thereto.

'destroy or damage'   See notes to s 1 *supra*.

'to use it or cause or permit another to use it'   *Cf* similarly worded offences involving the unlawful use of motor vehicles (such as in s 42 of the Road Traffic Act 1988). These offences establish that 'causing' use by another involves more than simple causation. It requires some directive or order. See *Houston v Buchanan* [1940] 2 All ER 179. Offences of permitting such use differ in that there need be no order: the word bears its ordinary meaning (*ibid*). Permission may be express or implied, but one cannot permit what one cannot in any event prevent or control: *James & Son Ltd v Smee* [1955] 1 QB 78; *Tophams Ltd v Sefton* [1967] 1 AC 50. Many of these road traffic cases involve the question of whether D can cause or permit unlawful use without knowledge of the circumstances making that use unlawful. Such questions will not arise in respect of this offence, because it is expressly stipulated that D must intend the items in question to be used for causing unlawful damage.

Punishment of offences

4. (1) A person guilty of arson under section 1 above or of an offence under section 1(2) above (whether arson or not) shall on conviction on indictment be liable to imprisonment for life.

(2) A person guilty of any other offence under this Act shall on conviction on indictment be liable to imprisonment for a term not exceeding ten years.

NOTES
Offences under s 1(2) are triable only on indictment. Arson, if it does not involve breach of s 1(2), is triable either way, as are offences under ss 2 and 3. Simple damage offences under s 1(1) are also triable either way if the value of the property involved clearly exceeds £2,000 (Magistrates' Courts Act 1980, s 22(3) as amended). If the value of the property clearly does not exceed £2,000 it is generally triable only summarily (Magistrates' Courts Act 1980, s. 22(2)—but see ss. 40 and 41 of the Criminal Justice Act 1988). If it is not clear whether it exceeds £2,000 or not, D can insist on summary trial if he so wishes (Magistrates' Courts Act s 22(5) and (6)).

'Without lawful excuse'

5. (1) This section applies to any offence under section 1(1) above and any offence under section 2 or 3 above other than one involving a threat by the person charged to destroy or damage property in a way which he knows is likely to endanger the life of another or involving an intent by the person charged to use or cause or permit the use of something in his custody or under his control so to destroy or damage property.

(2) A person charged with an offence to which this section applies shall, whether or not he would be treated for the purposes of this Act as having a

lawful excuse apart from this subsection, be treated for those purposes as having a lawful excuse—

(a) if at the time of the act or acts alleged to constitute the offence he believed that the person or persons whom he believed to be entitled to consent to the destruction of or damage to the property in question had so consented, or would have so consented to it if he or they had known of the destruction or damage and its circumstances; or

(b) if he destroyed or damaged or threatened to destroy or damage the property in question or, in the case of a charge of an offence under section 3 above, intended to use or cause or permit the use of something to destroy or damage it, in order to protect property belonging to himself or another or a right or interest in property which was or which he believed to be vested in himself or another, and at the time of the act or acts alleged to constitute the offence he believed—

(i) that the property right or interest was in immediate need of protection; and

(ii) that the means of protection adopted or proposed to be adopted were or would be reasonable having regard to all the circumstances.

(3) For the purposes of this section it is immaterial whether a belief is justified or not if it is honestly held.

(4) For the purposes of subsection (2) above a right or interest in property includes any right or privilege in or over land, whether created by grant, licence or otherwise.

(5) This section shall not be construed as casting doubt on any defence recognised by law as a defence to criminal charges.

NOTES

This provides an enlarged—but not exhaustive—definition of 'lawful excuse' in respect of offences under s 1(1) (including arson) and of some offences under ss 2 and 3; but it has no application in respect of offences under s 1(2) (whether arson or not). As far as s 1(2) is concerned, the concept of lawful excuse is governed ordinarily by general principles: D may therefore plead mistake (see *R v Smith* [1974] 1 All ER 632), self-defence, the prevention of crime (Criminal Law Act 1967, s 3), duress, necessity *etc.*

As far as ss 2 and 3 are concerned, this provision applies only if there is no threat or intent to commit any offence under s 1(2).

'whether or not' See also subs (5). This makes it clear that s 5 supplements, and does not supplant, the general defences that would in any case be available. Thus in *R v Smith* (*supra*) the Court of Appeal held that,

'No offence is committed under [s. 1(1)] if a person destroys or causes a damage to property belonging to another in the honest though mistaken belief that the property is his own and provided the belief is honestly held it is irrelevant to consider whether or not it is a justifiable belief' (*ibid* at p. 36)

D's mistake in that case was not expressly covered by s 5 (the court surprisingly rejected the suggestion that he believed he was the person entitled to consent to its damage), but it nevertheless negatived the *mens rea* required for the offence.

Belief in consent (Subs (2)(a))   See *R v Denton* [1982] 1 All ER 65; *R v Smith, supra*. The only significance of the court's insistence in *Smith* that D must rely on common law mistake rather than on subs (2)(a) might be in a case of mistake induced by voluntary intoxication. Such a defence could not succeed at common law (*DPP v Majewski* [1977] AC 443, *R v O'Grady* [1987] QB 995), but if *Jaggard v Dickinson* [1980] 3 All ER 716 is followed, such intoxication could support a defence where this provision applies.

Defence of property (Subs (2)(b))   If D acts to protect his own safety or the safety of others, and uses such force as is objectively reasonable in the circumstances as he believes them to be, he will have a good defence at common law (cf *Beckford v R* [1987] 3 All ER 425) but the common law defence will not apply where the measures used are unreasonable even having regard to any possible mistake on D's part, Where, however, D acts to protect property rather than personal safety, subs (2)(b) offers him a totally subjective defence to relevant criminal damage charges. As the authors of *Smith & Hogan* put it,

> 'Theoretically, D, given he is acting honestly, would incur no liability in taking the most extravagant measures against the property of another in defence of his own.'

There are limits, however. D must not be reckless as to the possible endangering of lives, and in practice he will doubtless have difficulty in putting forward any credible defence backed on a supposed belief in the necessity for really 'extravagant' measures.

Subs (3)   In *Jaggard v Dickinson* [1980] 3 All ER 716, the Divisional Court held that a belief in a lawful excuse under s 5 is a defence by virtue of subs (3), even when induced by voluntary intoxication. This is very hard to reconcile with the very strict approach to drunken mistake adopted by the courts at common law. In *R v O'Grady* [1987] QB 995, for example, it was held that a drunken mistake could not be relied upon to support a defence such as self-defence, even in respect of a charge involving a crime of specific intent. It is submitted that there is nothing in subs (3) to justify divergence from the normal rules relating to intoxication and drunken mistake, and that *Jaggard v Dickinson* is, accordingly, a doubtful precedent.

6 [*omitted*]

7 [*omitted*]

8 [*repealed*]

9 [*omitted*]

Interpretation
10. (1) In this Act "property" means property of a tangible nature, whether real or personal, including money and—
 (a) including wild creatures which have been tamed or are ordinarily kept in captivity, and any other wild creatures or their carcasses if, but only if, they have been reduced into possession which has not been lost or abandoned or are in the course of being reduced into possession; but
 (b) not including mushrooms growing wild on any land or flowers, fruit or foliage of a plant growing wild on any land.
For the purposes of this subsection "mushroom" includes any fungus and "plant" includes any shrub or tree.

(2) Property shall be treated for the purposes of this Act as belonging to any person—

(*a*) having the custody or control of it;

(*b*) having in it any proprietary right or interest (not being an equitable interest arising only from an agreement to transfer or grant an interest); or

(*c*) having a charge on it.

(3) Where property is subject to a trust, the persons to whom it belongs shall be so treated as including any person having a right to enforce the trust.

(4) Property of a corporation sole shall be so treated as belonging to the corporation notwithstanding a vacancy in the corporation.

NOTES

The definitions provided here have closely followed equivalents in the Theft Act 1968, with some slight differences attributable to the different nature of the offences concerned. (One cannot, for example, damage intangible property.)

'property' Cf s 4 of the Theft Act 1968. Note that the present provision differs from s 4 in that there is no equivalent to s 4(c), restricting the application of the legislation in respect of land or real property; and whereas the picking of wild mushrooms, flowers, fruit *etc* may be theft if committed dishonestly for commercial purposes, the destruction of such things cannot be criminal damage. An offence may however be committed where bushes, stems or branches are damaged in the process, and cultivated flowers or produce are protected in the same way as any other property.

'belonging to ... any person' See also the notes to s 1(1) *supra*. The definition provided here is basically similar to that provided in s 5 of the Theft Act 1968 (*qv*).

Note that the controlling shareholder and director of a 'one man company' is not the owner of the company's property. The company itself is the owner: *R v Appleyard* [1985] Crim LR 723.

11. [*text omitted*]

NOTES

S 11, together with the Schedule to which it gives effect, has repealed *inter alia* the common law offence of arson and the capital offence of arson in Her Majesty's Dockyards and Arsenals (Dockyards *etc*. Protection Act 1772) together with most, but not all, provisions of the Malicious Damage Act 1861 (*qv*.)

12. [*omitted*]

Sexual Offences (Amendment) Act 1976

(C 82)

Meaning of "rape" etc.

1. (1) For the purposes of section 1 of the Sexual Offences Act 1956 (which relates to rape) a man commits rape if—

    (*a*) he has unlawful sexual intercourse with a woman who at the time of the intercourse does not consent to it; and

    (*b*) at that time he knows that she does not consent to the intercourse or he is reckless as to whether she consents to it;

and references to rape in other enactments (including the following provisions of this Act) shall be construed accordingly.

(2) It is hereby declared that if at a trial for a rape offence the jury has to consider whether a man believed that a woman was consenting to sexual intercourse, the presence or absence of reasonable grounds for such a belief is a matter to which the jury is to have regard, in conjunction with any other relevant matters, in considering whether he so believed.

NOTES

This provision provides a basic, but by no means exhaustive, definition of rape, and effectively confirms the controversial decision of the House of Lords in *DPP v Morgan* [1976] AC 182. In particular, it confirms the principle that a man who mistakenly believes that a woman is consenting to intercourse cannot be guilty of raping her, even if his mistake is unreasonable.

It must be read in conjunction with s 7 *infra*, with ss 1, 44 and 46 of the Sexual Offences Act 1956 (*qv*), and with much of the earlier case law.

'man' A boy aged under 14 years is deemed incapable of sexual intercourse, but may be guilty of indecent assault (*R v Williams* [1893] 1 QB 320) or of secondary participation in rape (*R v Eldershaw* (1828) 3 C & P 316), as may a woman (*R v Ram* (1893) 17 Cox CC 609)).

'unlawful sexual intercourse' On sexual intercourse, see s 7(2) *infra*. Intercourse within marriage cannot generally be 'unlawful', but see note on 'marital rape', *infra*.

'woman' Or girl: see s 46 of the 1956 Act.

'consent' Rape need not involve violence or threats of violence. If a woman submits unwillingly (*eg* through blackmail) a jury may decide that there was no real consent: *R v Olugboja* [1982] QB 320. Consent may also be lacking where the woman is unconscious or asleep (*R v Fletcher* (1859) Bell CC 63) or incapacitated by alcohol or drugs (*R v Camplin* (1845) 1 Den 89) or where a child or mental defective submits without understanding what she is submitting to (*cf R v Williams* [1923] 1 KB 340).

If the woman *does* understand what she is consenting to, and with whom, it is not rape, even if that consent has been obtained by deception (*Papadimitropoulos v R* (1958) 98 CLR 249) or as a result of a loosening of inhibitions brought on by alcohol (*R v Lang* (1975) 62 Cr App R 50). On impersonation of a woman's husband, see s 1(2) of the 1956 Act. The same principle probably applies to impersonation of a boyfriend or lover, since true consent will be lacking in such a case.

'at the time' If a man realises at any time during intercourse that the woman is not or might not be consenting, it will be rape if he continues the act without her consent: *Kaitamaki v R* [1985] AC 147. This principle covers (a) the man who belatedly realises that the woman has never consented and (b) the man whose partner withdraws her consent after penetration (*eg* because she is experiencing pain).

Consent and marital rape A husband cannot generally be convicted of raping his wife, because marital intercourse is deemed to be lawful and consensual; but a wife may properly withdraw her consent where a court order, judgment or injunction, or a husband's undertaking in lieu of an injunction, indicates that she is no longer expected to cohabit with him: *R v Steele* (1976) 65 Cr App R 22; *R v Roberts* [1986] Crim LR 188. It is submitted that her consent can also be withheld if there are good medical reasons (*eg* the husband has venereal disease). See *R v Clarence* (1888) 22 QBD 23 *per* Stephen J (*obiter*) at p 41.

Where a rape conviction is impossible, it may sometimes be possible to charge the husband with another offence, such as assault occasioning actual bodily harm: *R v Miller* [1954] 2 QB 282.

There is no rule against the conviction of a husband for secondary participation in a rape perpetrated on his wife by another man: *R v Lord Audley* (1631) Hut 115; *DPP v Morgan* (*supra*); *R v Cogan* [1976] QB 217.

Recklessness In *R v Satnam Singh* (1985) 78 Cr App R 149 the Court of Appeal held that the *Caldwell* definition of recklessness is 'not relevant' to the concept of reckless rape, being wholly incompatible with the principle established in *DPP v Morgan* that a rapist must at least be aware of the possibility that there is no consent. In other words, if it has never occurred to the man that the woman might *not* be consenting, he cannot be guilty of rape. See also *R v Breckenridge* [1984] Crim LR 174; but note that in *R v Seymour* [1983] 2 AC 493 the House of Lords opined that recklessness should be defined uniformly throughout the criminal law.

'It is hereby declared' Subs (2) does no more than reiterate a basic common-sense point which courts and juries would normally be expected to recognise without the need for legislation to remind them of it, but it should be noted that evidence of voluntary intoxication cannot be used on a charge of rape to support a claim of mistaken belief in consent, rape being a crime of basic intent. It may however be 'relevant' on a charge of attempted rape where specific intent is required (*cf DPP v Majewski* [1977] AC 443).

'rape offence' See s 7(2) *infra*.

2–6 [*omitted*]

Citation, interpretation . . . and extent

7. (1) This Act may be cited as the Sexual Offences (Amendment) Act 1976, and this Act and the Sexual Offences Acts 1956 and 1967 may be cited together as the Sexual Offences Acts 1956 to 1976.

(2) In this Act—

"a rape offence" means any of the following, namely rape, attempted rape, aiding, abetting, counselling and procuring rape or attempted rape, incitement to rape, conspiracy to rape and burglary with intent to rape and references to sexual intercourse shall be construed in accordance with section 44 of the Sexual Offences Act 1956 so far as it relates to natural intercourse (under which such intercourse is deemed complete on proof of penetration only):

and section 46 of that Act (which relates to the meaning of "man" and "woman" in that Act) shall have effect as if the reference to that Act included a reference to this Act.

(3) In relation to such a trial as is mentioned in subsection (2) of section 1 of this Act which is a trial by court-martial or a summary trial by a magistrates' court, references to the jury in that subsection shall be construed as references to the court.

[(4)–(6) *omitted*]

NOTES
'natural intercourse'   The combined effect of this provision and s 44 of the 1956 Act is that rape requires some degree of vaginal penetration by the penis, but no ejaculation is required. No other sexual act can be classed as rape.

Criminal Law Act 1977

(C 45)

Part I: Conspiracy

The offence of conspiracy

1. (1) Subject to the following provisions of this Part of this Act, if a person agrees with any other person or persons that a course of conduct shall be pursued which, if the agreement is carried out in accordance with their intentions, either—

(a) will necessarily amount to or involve the commission of any offence or offences by one or more of the parties to the agreement, or

(b) would do so but for the existence of facts which render the commission of the offence or any of the offences impossible,

he is guilty of conspiracy to commit the offence or offences in question.

(2) Where liability for any offence may be incurred without knowledge on the part of the person committing it of any particular fact or circumstance necessary for the commission of the offence, a person shall nevertheless not be guilty of conspiracy to commit that offence by virtue of subsection (1) above unless he and at least one other party to the agreement intend or know that that fact or circumstance shall or will exist at the time when the conduct constituting the offence is to take place.

(3) Where in pursuance of any agreement the acts in question in relation to any offence are to be done in contemplation or furtherance of a trade dispute (within the meaning of the Trade Union and Labour Relations Act 1974) that offence shall be disregarded for the purposes of subsection (1) above provided that it is a summary offence which is not punishable with imprisonment.

(4) In this Part of this Act "offence" means an offence triable in England and Wales, except that it includes murder notwithstanding that the murder in question would not be so triable if committed in accordance with the intentions of the parties to the agreement.

NOTES

The offence created by this provision largely, but not entirely, supplants the common law offence of conspiracy. This is abolished by s 5 of the Act, except where it amounts to conspiracy to defraud, corrupt public morals or outrage public decency. Conspiracy to defraud overlaps to some extent with the statutory offence, but the other common law variants can only be charged where the conduct agreed upon would not involve the commission of any substantive offences. See the notes to s 5 *infra*.

'if a person agrees with any other person' A person may be either an individual or a corporation, and it is possible for a corporation to be convicted of conspiracy (*R v ICR Haulage Ltd* [1944] KB 551), but a company and its director cannot be the only two parties to a conspiracy, there being no possible 'meeting of minds' in such a case. See *R v McDonnell* [1966] 1 QB 233. As to conspiracies involving spouses, children and intended victims, see s 2 *infra*.

'agrees' Agreement is the essence of conspiracy. There is no conspiracy if prolonged negotiations fail to result in firm agreement (*R v Walker* [1962] Crim LR 458), nor is there one between A and B if they each conspire quite separately with C. There may however be a conspiracy in which some parties have never met or directly communicated with some others: *R v Griffiths* [1966] 1 QB 589.

'that a course of conduct shall be pursued which ... will necessarily amount to or involve the commission of any offence' The problem of conditional intent may arise in this context. Almost all conspiracies will involve some element of conditional intent, and an agreement to commit a certain offence 'provided that circumstances are favourable' must still be indictable (*R v Reed* [1982] Crim LR 819); but it is doubtful whether an agreement by robbers to kill anyone who obstructs them amounts to a conspiracy to commit murder. In *R v Kohn* (1864) 4 F & F 68 it was held to be an offence for foreign sailors to agree to scuttle their own ship if they envisaged that the scuttling *might* take place in British waters. It is difficult to see how this could be the case under the present provision.

'or would do so ...' Subs (1)(b) is designed to avoid the kind of problem which can still arise in common law conspiracy where the successful completion of the intended offence is impossible: *cf DPP v Nock* [1978] AC 979. Similar provisions govern impossible attempts: see the notes to s 1 of the Criminal Attempts Act 1981.

'if the agreement is carried out in accordance with their intentions' In *R v Anderson* [1986] AC 27, the House of Lords held that D could be convicted of conspiracy even though he himself did not intend that the offence should be successfully completed:

> 'Beyond the mere fact of agreement, the necessary *mens rea* of the crime is ... established if, and only if ... the accused ... intended to play some part in the agreed course of conduct in furtherance of the criminal purpose which the agreed course of conduct was intended to achieve. Nothing less will suffice; nothing more is required.'

The statement that D must intend to play some part in the agreed conduct is particularly surprising, but is not part of the *ratio* of the case; and see now *R v Siracusa* [1989] Crim LR 712, which backs away from any such conclusion.

Knowledge of facts or circumstances (subs 2(2)) The rule that knowledge or intent is required as to all the relevant circumstances in cases of statutory conspiracy mirrors the common law position, as established in *Churchill v Walton* [1967] 2 AC 224.

Subs (3) The general rule is that an agreement to commit the most minor offence is a conspiracy triable on indictment. This is the only exception to that rule. Note however that prosecutions for conspiracy to commit summary offences require the consent of the DPP under s 4 *infra*.

Jurisdiction (subs (4)) An extraterritorial agreement to commit an offence within the jurisdiction will be an offence if something is done within the jurisdiction in furtherance thereof: *DPP v Doot* [1973] AC 807. An agreement within the jurisdiction to commit an extraterritorial offence (eg hijacking an airliner) would also be an offence under this Act; but an agreement to rob a French or Scottish bank would not be, because the Theft Act 1968 would not apply to such a robbery and it would not be an offence under English Law.
    As to the circumstances in which murder would *not* be triable under English law, see the notes to s 9 of the Offences Against the Person Act 1861.

Penalty See s 3 *infra*.

Exemptions from liability for conspiracy

2. (1) A person shall not by virtue of section 1 above be guilty of conspiracy to commit any offence if he is an intended victim of that offence.

(2) A person shall not by virtue of section 1 above be guilty of conspiracy to commit any offence or offences if the only other person or persons with whom he agrees are (both initially and at all times during the currency of the agreement) persons of any one or more of the following descriptions, that is to say—

(a) his spouse;

(b) a person under the age of criminal responsibility; and

(c) an intended victim of that offence or of each of those offences.

(3) A person is under the age of criminal responsibility for the purposes of subsection (2)(b) above so long as it is conclusively presumed, by virtue of section 50 of the Children and Young Persons Act 1933, that he cannot be guilty of any offence.

NOTES
'an intended victim' The obvious example of such a person is the under-aged girl who agrees to have sexual intercourse with a man. She cannot herself be guilty of complicity in the substantive offence under the Sexual Offences Act, which exists for her protection. The position is less clear where D agrees with E that one will severely whip the other for their mutual sexual gratification. The consent here is invalid, but is there a conspiracy? Probably not.

'a person under the age of criminal responsibility' This is now ten years of age (Children and Young Persons Act 1933 s. 50 as amended). Where D is between ten and fourteen years old, his own liability depends on proof of 'mischievous discretion', but his acquittal would not seem to preclude the conviction of an alleged fellow conspirator under subs (2)(b), even if he is the only other party involved. See further s 5(8) *infra*.

Penalties for conspiracy

3. (1) A person guilty by virtue of section 1 above of conspiracy to commit any offence or offences shall be liable on conviction on indictment—

(a) in a case falling within subsection (2) or (3) below, to imprisonment for a term related in accordance with that subsection to the gravity of the offence or offences in question (referred to below in this section as the relevant offence or offences); and

(b) in any other case, to a fine.

Paragraph (b) above shall not be taken as prejudicing the application of section 30(1) of the Powers of Criminal Courts Act 1973 (general power of court to fine offender convicted on indictment) in a case falling within subsection (2) or (3) below.

(2) Where the relevant offence or any of the relevant offences is an offence of any of the following descriptions, that is to say—

(a) murder, or any other offence the sentence for which is fixed by law;

(b) an offence for which a sentence extending to imprisonment for life is provided; or (*c*) an indictable offence punishable with imprisonment for which no maximum term of imprisonment is provided,

the person convicted shall be liable to imprisonment for life.

(3) Where in a case other than one to which subsection (2) above applies the relevant offence or any of the relevant offences is punishable with imprisonment, the person convicted shall be liable to imprisonment for a term not exceeding the maximum term provided for that offence or (where more than one such offence is in question) for any one of those offences (taking the longer or the longest term as the limit for the purposes of this section where the terms provided differ).

In the case of an offence triable either way the references above in this subsection to the maximum term provided for that offence are references to the maximum term so provided on conviction on indictment.

NOTES

The penalty for conspiracy at common law could notoriously exceed that for any substantive offence involved. This provision seeks to ensure that there is no great disparity between the maximum sentence for the conspiracy and that for the offence conspired at. Conspiracy to commit a summary offence nevertheless remains punishable by a heavier fine than any magistrates' court could impose.

As to the penalty for conspiracy to defraud, this cannot now exceed ten years' imprisonment: Criminal Justice Act 1987 s 12 (*qv*).

Restrictions on the institution of proceedings for conspiracy

4. (1) Subject to subsection (2) below proceedings under section 1 above for conspiracy to commit any offence or offences shall not be instituted against any person except by or with the consent of the Director of Public Prosecutions if the offence or (as the case may be) each of the offences in question is a summary offence.

(2) In relation to the institution of proceedings under section 1 above for conspiracy to commit—

(*a*) an offence which is subject to a prohibition by or under any enactment on the institution of proceedings otherwise than by, or on behalf or with the consent of, the Attorney General, or

(*b*) two or more offences of which at least one is subject to such prohibition,

subsection (1) above shall have effect with the substitution of a reference to the Attorney General for the reference to the Director of Public Prosecutions.

(3) Any prohibition by or under any enactment on the institution of proceedings for any offence which is not a summary offence otherwise than by, or on behalf or with the consent of, the Director of Public Prosecutions or any other person shall apply also in relation to proceedings under section 1 above for conspiracy to commit that offence.

(4) Where—

(*a*) an offence has been committed in pursuance of any agreement; and

(*b*) proceedings may not be instituted for that offence because any time limit applicable to the institution of any such proceedings has expired, proceedings under section 1 above for conspiracy to commit that offence shall not be instituted against any person on the basis of that agreement.

NOTES

Crown Prosecutors may exercise the powers of the DPP in instituting proceedings, but do so under his direction: Prosecution of Offences Act 1985 s 1(6).

Subs (4) A magistrates' court may not try an information unless it is laid within six months of the commission of the alleged offence (Magistrates' Courts Act 1980 s 127). If the substantive offence is not triable on indictment, a conspiracy charge is accordingly barred after this time, but only where the substantive offence has actually been committed.

Abolitions, savings, transitional provisions, consequential amendment and repeals

5. (1) Subject to the following provisions of this section, the offence of conspiracy at common law is hereby abolished.

(2) Subsection (1) above shall not affect the offence of conspiracy at common law so far as relates to conspiracy to defraud.

(3) Subsection (1) above shall not affect the offence of conspiracy at common law if and in so far as it may be committed by entering into an agreement to engage in conduct which—

(a) tends to corrupt public morals or outrages public decency; but

(b) would not amount to or involve the commission of an offence if carried out by a single person otherwise than in pursuance of an agreement.

(4) Subsection (1) above shall not affect—

(a) any proceedings commenced before the time when this Part of this Act comes into force;

(b) any proceedings commenced after that time against a person charged with the same conspiracy as that charged in any proceedings commenced before that time; or

(c) any proceedings commenced after that time in respect of a trespass committed before that time;

but a person convicted of conspiracy to trespass in any proceedings brought by virtue of paragraph (c) above shall not in respect of that conviction be liable to imprisonment for a term exceeding six months.

(5) Sections 1 and 2 above shall apply to things done before as well as to things done after the time when this Part of this Act comes into force, but in the application of section 3 above to a case where the agreement in question was entered into before that time—

(a) subsection (2) shall be read without the reference to murder in paragraph(a); and

(b) any murder intended under the agreement shall be treated as an offence for which a maximum term of imprisonment of ten years is provided.

(6) The rules laid down by sections 1 and 2 above shall apply for determining whether a person is guilty of an offence of conspiracy under any enactment other than section 1 above, but conduct which is an offence

under any such other enactment shall not also be an offence under section 1 above.

(7) Incitement . . . to commit the offence of conspiracy (whether the conspiracy incited . . . would be an offence at common law or under section 1 above or any other enactment) shall cease to be offences.

(8) The fact that the person or persons who, so far as appears from the indictment on which any person has been convicted of conspiracy, were the only other parties to the agreement on which his conviction was based have been acquitted of conspiracy by reference to that agreement (whether after being tried with the person convicted or separately) shall not be a ground for quashing his conviction unless under all the circumstances of the case his conviction is inconsistent with the acquittal of the other person or persons in question.

(9) Any rule of law or practice inconsistent with the provisions of subsection (8) above is hereby abolished.

(10)–(11)–[*omitted*]

NOTES
'conspiracy to defraud' (**subs (2)**) As originally enacted, this provision appeared to prevent a charge of statutory conspiracy succeeding in any case where the agreement in question amounted to a conspiracy to defraud at common law. The House of Lords then ruled that it meant quite the opposite—conspiracy to defraud could only be charged if the object of the conspiracy was to defraud another without necessarily committing any substantive offence (*R v Ayres* [1984] AC 447). Neither interpretation was satisfactory (see *R v Cooke* [1986] AC 909) and s 12 of the Criminal Justice Act 1987 (*qv*) now ensures that the two charges are not mutually exclusive.

As to the scope of the common law offence, see *Scott v Met Police Commissioner* [1975] AC 819 and *R v Cooke supra*.

'conspiracy to corrupt public morals or to outrage public decency' (**subs (3)**) In this case it is clear from para (b) that the common law conspiracy cannot be committed unless the agreement in question does not amount to a statutory conspiracy. This is strange, because there would appear to be substantive common law offences of corrupting public morals and of outraging public decency (see *Shaw v DPP* [1962] AC 220, *Knuller v DPP* [1973] AC 435 and *R v Mayling* [1963] 2 QB 717). If this is correct, such conspiracies must perforce be statutory ones.

Acquittal of all other alleged conspirators (subss (8) & (9)) In some cases, the evidence is such that D 1 and D 2 stand or fall together. In other cases, it may be that D 1 has confessed but D 2 has not, and in those circumstances D 2 may have to be acquitted even though nobody is in any real doubt as to his guilt. Subs (8) ensures that this does not prevent the conviction of D 1.

Part II: Offences relating to entering and remaining on property

Violence for securing entry
6. (1) Subject to the following provisions of this section, any person who, without lawful authority, uses or threatens violence for the purpose of securing entry into any premises for himself or for any other person is guilty of an offence, provided that—

(*a*) there is someone present on those premises at the time who is opposed to the entry which the violence is intended to secure; and

(*b*) the person using or threatening the violence knows that that is the case.

(2) The fact that a person has any interest in or right to possession or occupation of any premises shall not for the purposes of subsection (1) above constitute lawful authority for the use or threat of violence by him or anyone else for the purpose of securing his entry into those premises.

(3) In any proceedings for an offence under this section it shall be a defence for the accused to prove—

(*a*) that at the time of the alleged offence he or any other person on whose behalf he was acting was a displaced residential occupier of the premises in question; or

(*b*) that part of the premises in question constitutes premises of which he or any other person on whose behalf he was acting was a displaced residential occupier and that the part of the premises to which he was seeking to secure entry constitutes an access of which he or, as the case may be, that other person is also a displaced residential occupier.

(4) It is immaterial for the purposes of this section—

(*a*) whether the violence in question is directed against the person or against property; and

(*b*) whether the entry which the violence is intended to secure is for the purpose of acquiring possession of the premises in question or for any other purpose.

(5) A person guilty of an offence under this section shall be liable on summary conviction to imprisonment for a term not exceeding six months or to a fine not exceeding level 5 on the standard scale or to both.

(6) A constable in uniform may arrest without warrant anyone who is, or whom he, with reasonable cause, suspects to be, guilty of an offence under this section.

(7) Section 12 below contains provisions which apply for determining when any person is to be regarded for the purposes of this Part of this Act as a displaced residential occupier of any premises or of any access to any premises.

NOTES

Ss 6–12 supplant the Forcible Entry Acts 1381–1623, together with the common law offences of forcible entry and detainer, which are abolished by s 13 *infra*.

The summary offence created by this provision is one of using or threatening violence in order to secure entry to premises (not necessarily a building) in the knowledge that entry is opposed by someone therein. A person who commits this offence may also commit more serious indictable offences, such as burglary under ss 9–10 of the Theft Act 1968, depending on the circumstances and on his intent etc. A non-violent entry and occupation of residential premises may amount to an offence under s 7 of this Act and/or under s 1 of the Protection from Eviction Act 1977.

'any person' Note that this may in some cases be the lawful owner or occupier of the property (see sub (2) & (3)).

'without lawful authority' A right of ownership or possession does not itself amount to lawful authority for the purpose of this section (subs (2)), but see subs (3) regarding the position of a 'displaced residential occupier'. A police officer or bailiff would be entitled to enter by force in some circumstances. If, however, a police officer enters unlawfully, he might be guilty of an offence under this section, even if he has made a *bona fide* mistake as to the existence of a power of entry in the circumstances. His error would be one of law, and accordingly no excuse.

'uses or threatens violence' This may mean some kind of assault, but the violence etc may be directed against property (subs (4)) and not necessarily against the premises D wishes to enter (eg "let me in or I'll set fire to your car!"). There is nothing to suggest that the threat must be heard or understood by P. (*cf* blackmail demands under s 21 of the Theft Act 1968).

Violence itself is not defined. In some cases the dividing line between this and lesser degrees of force may be a fine one. See Law Com No 76 para 2, 61.

'for the purpose of securing entry' This is a kind of ulterior intent, and the offence may be committed even if that intent is thwarted. D's reasons for wanting to enter are irrelevant unless he has lawful authority: see subs (4)(b).

'premises' see s. 12(1)(a) *infra*.

'someone present ... opposed to the entry' This may be a trespasser or squatter. Such persons must ordinarily be removed by taking legal proceedings against them (see also s 39 of the Public Order Act 1988); but note the special position of the 'displaced residential occupier' under subs (3).

'knows' (subs 1(b)) Even a strong suspicion falls short of being knowledge (cf cases under s 22 of the Theft Act 1968, where the courts have declined to treat suspicion as equivalent to either knowledge or belief). If, however, D knows the premises to be occupied, it should ordinarily be easy to infer knowledge of the occupier's opposition to D's entry.

'displaced residential occupier' See s 12(3)–(7) *infra*.

'access' See s 12(1)(b) *infra*. A trader whose shop has been occupied by squatters may be able to use force, not to regain occupation of his shop, but to secure his right of access to his flat above the shop. If that means ejecting the squatters from the shop, then so much the better for him.

Adverse occupation of residential premises

7. (1) Subject to the following provisions of this section, any person who is on any premises as a trespasser after having entered as such is guilty of an offence if he fails to leave those premises on being required to do so by or on behalf of—

(*a*) a displaced residential occupier of the premises; or

(*b*) an individual who is a protected intending occupier of the premises by virtue of subsection (2) or subsection (4) below.

(2) For the purposes of this section an individual is a protected intending occupier of any premises at any time if at that time—

(*a*) he has in those premises a freehold interest or a leasehold interest with not less than 21 years still to run and he acquired that interest as a purchaser for money or money's worth; and

(*b*) he requires the premises for his own occupation as a residence; and

(*c*) he is excluded from occupation of the premises by a person who entered them, or any access to them, as a trespasser; and

(*d*) he or a person acting on his behalf holds a written statement—

(i) which specifies his interest in the premises; and

(ii) which states that he requires the premises for occupation as a residence for himself; and

(iii) with respect to which the requirements in subsection (3) below are fulfilled.

(3) The requirements referred to in subsection (2)(d)(iii) above are—

(a) that the statement is signed by the person whose interest is specified in it in the presence of a justice of the peace or commissioner for oaths; and

(b) that the justice of the peace or commissioner for oaths has subscribed his name as a witness to the signature;

and a person is guilty of an offence if he makes a statement for the purposes of subsection (2)(d) above which he knows to be false in a material particular or if he recklessley makes such a statement which is false in a material particular.

(4) For the purposes of this section an individual is also a protected intending occupier of any premises at any time if at that time—

(a) he has been authorised to occupy the premises as a residence by an authority to which this subsection applies; and

(b) he is excluded from occupation of the premises by a person who entered the premises, or any access to them as a trespasser; and

(c) there has been issued to him by or on behalf of the authority referred to in paragraph (a) above a certificate stating that the authority is one to which this subsection applies, being of a description specified in the certificate, and that he has been authorised by the authority to occupy the premises concerned as a residence.

(5) Subsection (4) above applies to the following authorities:—

(a) any body mentioned in section 14 of the Rent Act 1977 (landlord's interest belonging to local authority etc.);

(b) the Housing Corporation;

(ba) Housing for Wales; and

(c) a registered housing association within the meaning of the Housing Associations Act 1985.

(6) In any proceedings for an offence under subsection (1) above it shall be a defence for the accused to prove that he believed that the person requiring him to leave the premises was not a displaced residential occupier or protected intending occupier of the premises or a person acting on behalf of a displaced residential occupier or protected intending occupier.

(7) In any proceedings for an offence under subsection (1) above it shall be a defence for the accused to prove—

(a) that the premises in question are or form part of the premises used mainly for non-residential purposes; and

(b) that he was not on any part of the premises used wholly or mainly for residential purposes.

(8) In any proceedings for an offence under subsection (1) above where the accused was requested to leave the premises by a person claiming to be or to act on behalf of a protected intending occupier of the premises—

(*a*) it shall be a defence for the accused to prove that, although asked to do so by the accused at the time the accused was requested to leave, that person failed at that time to produce to the accused such a statement as is referred to in subsection (2)(*d*) above or such a certificate as is referred to in subsection (4)(*c*) above; and

(*b*) any document purporting to be a certificate under subsection (4)(*c*) above shall be received in evidence and, unless the contrary is proved, shall be deemed to have been issued by or on behalf of the authority stated in the certificate.

(9) Any reference in the preceding provisions of this section other than subsections (2) to (4) above, to any premises includes a reference to any access to them, whether or not any such access itself constitutes premises, within the meaning of this Part of this Act; and a person who is a protected intending occupier of any premises shall be regarded for the purposes of this section as a protected intending occupier also of any access to those premises.

(10) A person guilty of an offence under subsection (1) or (3) above shall be liable on summary conviction to imprisonment for a term not exceeding six months or to a fine not exceeding level 5 on the standard scale or to both.

(11) A constable in uniform may arrest without warrant anyone who is, or whom he, with reasonable cause, suspects to be, guilty of an offence under subsection (1) above.

NOTES

It will usually be advisable for a displaced residential occupier to invoke this provision (and the assistance of the police) where squatters etc refuse a demand that they should leave. The occupier may however use reasonable force to eject them if he prefers. See s 6 *supra*.

'premises'   See s 12(1)(*a*) *infra*.

'as a trespasser after having entered as such'   Tenants or licencees staying on after the expiry of their leases or the revocation of their licences cannot commit this offence, not having entered as trespassers in the first place. The ordinary meaning of the term 'trespasser' is supplemented by s 12(4), (6) & (7) *infra*.

'fails'   D need not necessarily refuse to leave; it is enough if he fails to go at once or within any time limit imposed on him. Note that he does not cease to be a trespasser merely because he is given time to arrange for his departure: s 12(7) *infra*.

'displaced residential occupier'   See s 12(3)–(5) *infra*.

'protected intending occupier'   Only an individual can qualify for this protected status, but he may derive that status through a local authority, housing corporation or housing association (subss (4)–(5)). He may also employ another 'person' (possibly a corporation), to issue his requirement under subs (1).

False statements under subs (3)   This offence is analagous in some respects to certain offences under the Perjury Act 1911, (*qv*). 'False in a material particular' means 'false in an important respect; something which matters': *R v Mallett* [1978] 3 All ER 10.

The subs (7) defence   Note that this is subject to subs (9), so that it is no defence for D to prove he is on business premises if part of those premises occupied by him are used wholly or mainly to provide access to residential premises used by a displaced residential occupier.

Trespassing with a weapon of offence
8. (1) A person who is on any premises as a trespasser, after having entered as such, is guilty of an offence if, without lawful authority or reasonable excuse, he has with him on the premises any weapon of offence.

(2) In subsection (1) above "weapon of offence" means any article made or adapted for use for causing injury to or incapacitating a person, or intended by the person having it with him for such use.

(3) A person guilty of an offence under this section shall be liable on summary conviction to imprisonment for a term not exceeding three months or to a fine not exceeding level 5 on the standard scale or to both.

(4) A constable in uniform may arrest without warrant anyone who is, or whom he, with reasonable cause, suspects to be, in the act of committing an offence under this section.

NOTE
A person trespassing in a building and carrying an offensive weapon may well be guilty of aggravated burglary under s 10 of the Theft Act 1968, which is a far more serious offence than the summary one created here. Burglary cannot however be committed on land ancillary to a building, and requires an ulterior intent, or the commission of other offences. This scope of this offence is therefore somewhat wider and it may be easier to prove.

'premises'   See s 12(1)(a) *infra*.

'weapon of offence'   As defined in subs (2), this has the same meaning as in s 10 of the Theft Act 1968 (*qv*) and a wider one than it has in the Prevention of Crime Act 1953.

Trespassing on premises of foreign missions, etc
9. (1) Subject to subsection (3) below, a person who enters or is on any premises to which this section applies as a trespasser is guilty of an offence.

(2) This section applies to any premises which are or form part of—
(*a*) the premises of a diplomatic mission within the meaning of the definition in Article 1(*i*) of the Vienna Convention on Diplomatic Relations signed in 1961 as that Article has effect in the United Kingdom by virtue of section 2 of and Schedule 1 to the Diplomatic Privileges Act 1964;
(*aa*) premises of a closed diplomatic mission;
(*b*) consular premises within the meaning of the definition in paragraph 1(*j*) of Article 1 of the Vienna Convention on Consular Relations signed in 1963 as that Article has effect in the United Kingdom by virtue of section 1 of and Schedule 1 to the Consular Relations Act 1968;
(*bb*) the premises of a closed consular post;
(*c*) any other premises in respect of which any organisation or body is entitled to inviolability by or under any enactment; and

(*d*) any premises which are the private residence of a diplomatic agent (within the meaning of Article 1(*e*) of the Convention mentioned in paragraph (*a*) above) or of any other person who is entitled to inviolability of residence by or under any enactment.

(2A) In subsection (2) above—

"the premises of a closed diplomatic mission" means premises which fall within Article 45 of the Convention mentioned in subsection (2)(*a*) above (as that Article has effect in United Kingdom by virtue of the section and Schedule mentioned in that paragraph); and

"the premises of a closed consular post" means premises which fall within Article 27 of the Convention mentioned in subsection (2)(*b*) above (as that Article has effect in the United Kingdom by virtue of the section and Schedule mentioned in that paragraph).

(3) In any proceedings for an offence under this section it shall be a defence for the accused to prove that he believed that the premises in question were not premises to which this section applies.

(4) In any proceedings for an offence under this section a certificate issued by or under the authority of the Secretary of State stating that any premises were or formed part of premises of any description mentioned in paragraphs (*a*) to (*d*) of subsection (2) above at the time of the alleged offence shall be conclusive evidence that the premises were or formed part of premises of that description at that time.

(5) A person guilty of an offence under this section shall be liable on summary conviction to imprisonment for a term not exceeding six months or to a fine not exceeding [level 5 on the standard scale] or to both.

(6) Proceedings for an offence under this section shall not be instituted against any person except by or with the consent of the Attorney General.

(7) A constable in uniform may arrest without warrant anyone who is, or whom he with reasonable cause, suspects to be, in the act of committing an offence under this section.

NOTES

The protection afforded to premises to which this provision applies is significantly wider than that afforded by ss 6–8 *supra*. D need not have entered as a trespasser if he becomes one thereafter; he need not use or threaten violence to secure entry; he need not displace or obstruct access by any legitimate occupiers, and he need not have failed to comply with any requirement to leave. He need not even attempt to remain on the premises. As *Smith & Hogan* put it, he may do no more than cross an embassy garden as a short cut to a bus stop.

Obstruction of court officers executing process for possession against unauthorised occupiers

10. (1) Without prejudice to section 8(2) of the Sheriffs Act 1887 but subject to the following provisions of this section, a person is guilty of an offence if he resists or intentionally obstructs any person who is in fact an officer of a court engaged in executing any process issued by the High Court or by any county court for the purpose of enforcing any judgment or order for the recovery of any premises or for the delivery of possession of any premises.

(2) Subsection (1) above does not apply unless the judgment or order in question was given or made in proceedings brought under any provisions of rules of court applicable only in circumstances where the person claiming possession of any premises alleges that the premises in question are occupied solely by a person or persons (not being a tenant or tenants holding over after the termination of the tenancy) who entered into or remained in occupation of the premises without the licence or consent of the person claiming possession or any predecessor in title of his.

(3) In any proceedings for an offence under this section it shall be a defence for the accused to prove that he believed that the person he was resisting or obstructing was not an officer of a court.

(4) A person guilty of an offence under this section shall be liable on summary conviction to imprisonment for a term not exceeding six months or to a fine not exceeding [level 5 on the standard scale] or to both.

(5) A constable in uniform or any officer of a court may arrest without warrant anyone who is, or whom he, with reasonable cause, suspects to be, guilty of an offence under this section.

(6) In this section "officer of a court" means—

(a) any sheriff, under sheriff, deputy sheriff, bailiff or officer of a sheriff; and

(b) any bailiff or other person who is an officer of a county court within the meaning of the County Courts Act 1959.

NOTES
The ambit of this offence is confined by subs (2) to squatters (or persons assisting squatters) who resist court orders for the recovery of the premises they have occupied. Tenants who refuse to vacate premises on termination of their tenancies may commit offences in the course of resisting attempts to eject them, but not offences under this part of the Act.

'resists or intentionally obstructs' This wording is analagous to that in s 51(3) of the Police Act 1964 ('resists or wilfully obstructs'). It seems strange that the adverb 'intentionally' only governs obstruction; but this may be explained by the fact that obstruction is potentially a wider concept. Barricades and locks designed to hinder the owner could easily obstruct court officers, whereas 'resistance' postulates something more obviously directed at them. See generally the notes to s 51 of the Police Act.

Subs (3) This defence can only succeed where D can prove a positive belief. It is no defence for him to argue that he did not consider the identity of the persons he was resisting.

11. [*Repealed*]

Supplementary provisions
12. (1) In this Part of this Act—
(a) "premises" means any building, any part of a building under separate occupation, any land ancillary to a building, the site comprising any building or buildings together with any land ancillary thereto, and (for the purposes only of sections 10 and 11 above) any other place; and

(*b*) "access" means, in relation to any premises, any part of any site or building within which those premises are situated which constitutes an ordinary means of access to those premises (whether or not that is its sole or primary use).

(2) References in this section to a building shall apply also to any structure other than a movable one, and to any movable structure, vehicle or vessel designed or adapted for use for residential purposes; and for the purposes of subsection (1) above—

(*a*) part of a building is under separate occupation if anyone is in occupation or entitled to occupation of that part as distinct from the whole; and

(*b*) land is ancillary to a building if it is adjacent to it and used (or intended for use) in connection with the occupation of that building or any part of it.

(3) Subject to subsection (4) below, any person who was occupying any premises as a residence immediately before being excluded from occupation by anyone who entered those premises, or any access to those premises, as a trespasser is a displaced residential occupier of the premises for the purposes of this Part of this Act so long as he continues to be excluded from occupation of the premises by the original trespasser or by any subsequent trespasser.

(4) A person who was himself occupying the premises in question as a trespasser immediately before being excluded from occupation shall not by virtue of subsection (3) above be a displaced residential occupier of the premises for the purposes of this Part of this Act.

(5) A person who by virtue of subsection (3) above is a displaced residential occupier of any premises shall be regarded for the purposes of this Part of this Act as a displaced residential occupier also of any access to those premises.

(6) Anyone who enters or is on or in occupation of any premises by virtue of—

(*a*) any title derived from a trespasser; or

(*b*) any licence or consent given by a trespasser or by a person deriving title from a trespasser,

shall himself be treated as a trespasser for the purposes of this Part of this Act (without prejudice to whether or not he would be a trespasser apart from this provision); and references in this Part of this Act to a person's entering or being on or occupying any premises as a trespasser shall be construed accordingly.

(7) Anyone who is on any premises as a trespasser shall not cease to be a trespasser for the purposes of this Part of this Act by virtue of being allowed time to leave the premises, nor shall anyone cease to be a displaced residential occupier of any premises by virtue of any such allowance of time to a trespasser.

(8) No rule of law ousting the jurisdiction of magistrates' courts to try offences where a dispute of title to property is involved shall preclude magistrates' courts from trying offences under this Part of this Act.

NOTES
'building' and 'structure' As in s 9(3) of the Theft Act 1968, vehicles and vessels may be included in the relevant definition, but note the differences: caravans etc need not actually be inhabited, and even tents may possibly come within subs (2). *Cf Hobday v Nicol* [1944] 1 All ER 303.

Abolition and repeals
13. (1) The offence of forcible entry and any offence of forcible detainer at common law are hereby abolished for all purposes not relating to offences committed before the coming into force of this Part of this Act.
(2) ...

NOTE
This part of the Act came into force on 1 December 1977.

Part IV: Miscellaneous provisions

50. [*repealed*]

Bomb hoaxes
51.—(1) A person who—
(a) places any article in any place whatever; or
(b) dispatches any article by post, rail or any other means whatever of sending things from one place to another,
with the intention (in either case) of inducing in some other person a belief that it is likely to explode or ignite and thereby cause personal injury or damage to property is guilty of an offence.
In this subsection "article" includes substance.
(2) A person who communicates any information which he knows or believes to be false to another person with the intention of inducing in him or any other person a false belief that a bomb or other thing liable to explode or ignite is present in any place or location whatever is guilty of an offence.
(3) For a person to be guilty of an offence under subsection (1) or (2) above it is not necessary for him to have any particular person in mind as the person in whom he intends to induce the belief mentioned in that subsection.
(4) A person guilty of an offence under this section shall be liable—
(a) on summary conviction, to imprisonment for a term not exceeding three months or to a fine not exceeding [the prescribed sum], or both;
(b) on conviction on indictment, to imprisonment for a term not exceeding five years.

NOTES
Bomb hoaxes are often connected with blackmail demands (see Theft Act 1968 s 21) and may also amount to threats to destroy or damage property under the Criminal Damage Act 1971 s 2 and/or causing wasteful employment of the police under the Criminal Law Act 1967 s 5(2).

Subs (1)   creates an offence of specific intent and does not extend to persons who carelessly or recklessly leave cases etc in places where they are likely to be mistaken for terrorist bombs. It could in theory apply to genuine bombers, since there is nothing expressly confining its application to hoaxers, but more serious charges can obviously be brought where it can be proved that it was more than a mere hoax.

Subs (2)   Again creates an offence of specific intent. This is confined to cases in which D knows or believes himself to be lying, but the offence would still be committed if D unwittingly told the truth.

52–53   [*omitted*]

Inciting girl under sixteen to have incestuous sexual intercourse
54. (1) It is an offence for a man to incite to have sexual intercourse with him a girl under the age of sixteen whom he knows to be his granddaughter, daughter or sister.

(2) In the preceding subsection "man" includes boy, "sister" includes half-sister, and for the purposes of that subsection any expression importing a relationship between two people shall be taken to apply notwithstanding that the relationship is not traced through lawful wedlock.

(3) The following provisions of section 1 of the Indecency with Children Act 1960, namely—

[. . .]

subsection (3) (references in Children and Young Persons Act 1933 to the offences mentioned in Schedule 1 to that Act to include offences under that section);

subsection (4) (offences under that section to be deemed offences against the person for the purpose of section 3 of the Visiting Forces Act 1952),

shall apply in relation to offences under this section.

(4) A person guilty of an offence under this section shall be liable—

(*a*) on summary conviction, to imprisonment for a term not exceeding six months or to a fine not exceeding [the prescribed sum], or both;

(*b*) on conviction on indictment, to imprisonment for a term not exceeding two years.

NOTES
Inciting another person to commit an offence of incest would be a common law offence. Inciting a child under the age of fourteen would amount to an offence under the Indecency With Children Act 1960. Inciting a girl of fourteen or fifteen was not however an offence prior to the enactment of this provision, because she cannot herself commit any offence of incest: *R v Whitehouse* (1977) 65 Cr App R 33.

Suppression of Terrorism Act 1978

(C 26)

Jurisdiction in respect of offences committed outside United Kingdom

4. (1) If a person, whether a citizen of the United Kingdom and Colonies or not, does in a convention country any act which, if he had done it in a part of the United Kingdom, would have made him guilty in that part of the United Kingdom of—

(a) an offence mentioned in paragraph 1, 2, 4, 5, 10, 11, [11B,] 12, 13, 14 or 15 of Schedule 1 to this Act; or

(b) an offence of attempting to commit any offence so mentioned,

he shall, in that part of the United Kingdom, be guilty of the offence or offences aforesaid of which the act would have made him guilty if he had done it there.

(2) [*repealed*]

(3) If a person who is a national of a convention country but not a citizen of the United Kingdom and Colonies does outside the United Kingdom and that convention country any act which makes him in that convention country guilty of an offence and which if he had been a citizen of the United Kingdom and Colonies, would have made him in any part of the United Kingdom guilty of an offence mentioned in paragraph 1, 2 or 13 of Schedule 1 to this Act, he shall, in any part of the United Kingdom, be guilty of the offence or offences aforesaid of which the act would have made him guilty if he had been such a citizen.

(4) Proceedings for an offence which (disregarding the provisions of the Internationally Protected Persons Act 1978 and the Nuclear Material (Offences) Act 1983) would not be an offence apart from this section shall not be instituted—

(a) [*omitted*]

(b) in England and Wales, except by or with the consent of the Attorney General:

(5) [*omitted*]

(6) [*repealed*]

(7) For the purposes of this section any act done—

(a) on board a ship registered in a convention country, being an act which, if the ship had been registered in the United Kingdom, would have constituted an offence within the jurisdiction of the Admiralty; or

(b) on board an aircraft registered in a convention country while the aircraft is in flight elsewhere than in or over that country; or

(c) on board a hovercraft registered in a convention country while the hovercraft is in journey elsewhere than in or over that country, shall be treated as done in that convention country; and subsection (4) of section 92 of the Civil Aviation Act 1982 (definition of "in flight" or, as applied to hovercraft, "in journey") shall apply for the purposes of this subsection as it applies for the purposes of that section.

NOTES
This Act was passed to enable the United Kingdom to ratify the 1977 European Convention on the Suppression of Terrorism. Provisions concerning extradition have been omitted here, but subs (1) of this section enables courts throughout the United Kingdom to exercise jurisdiction over certain crimes specified in Sch 1 *infra*, when these are committed in countries which have been designated by the Secretary of State as parties to the Convention. Jurisdiction in such cases does not depend on the nationality of the alleged offender. Subs (3) meanwhile enables nationals of those 'Convention Countries' to be tried in the United Kingdom for homicide or certain explosives offences committed anywhere in the world, provided that their actions also amount to offences under the laws of their own countries and that British citizens would have been punishable in similar circumstances.

This rather unusual jurisdiction can best be explained by reference to the purpose of the 1977 Convention. This is primarily intended to facilitate the extradition of suspected terrorists between those states which are parties to it, by deeming their alleged offences to be of a non-political character, but it recognises that circumstances will still arise in which such extradition will not be possible, and it provides that in designated cases the requested state must refer the matter to its own prosecuting authorities, having previously ensured that these would have jurisdiction to act 'in any case where the requesting state bases its claim to jurisdiction on a basis which exists equally in the requested state'.

Subs (1) ensures that the United Kingdom will be able to fulfil that obligation in respect of cases where the requesting state is basing its claim to jurisdiction on the territorial principle; but since the United Kingdom does not generally claim jurisdiction over the acts of its own citizens abroad, the scope of subs (3) is far narrower. If, for example, a convention country sought the extradition of one of its own citizens for an alleged kidnapping in a non-convention country, and extradition was for some reason refused, there would be no need for the United Kingdom to consider putting him on trial here, since a British citizen could not be tried here for extraterritorial kidnapping either.

Of the designated offences, only homicide, explosives offences and offences under the Aviation Security Act 1982 possess an extraterritorial ambit outside of this Act, and no further provision was needed in respect of the aviation offences, since these are in any case punishable on a universal basis under the 1982 Act.

'citizen of the United Kingdom and Colonies'   This must now be construed as a reference to British citizens, British overseas citizens and citizens of British Dependent Territories (*eg* Hong Kong): British Nationality Act 1981 s 51(3).

'convention country'   See s 8 *infra*.

'offence within the jurisdiction of the Admiralty'   This jurisdiction is exercised by the Crown Court, and has never extended over purely summary offences.

Provisions as to interpretation and orders
  8. (1) In this Act—
  "act" includes omission;
  "convention country" means a country for the time being designated in
    an order made by the Secretary of State as a party to the European

Convention on the Suppression of Terrorism signed at Strasbourg on
the 27th January 1977;
"country" includes any territory;
"enactment" includes an enactment of the Parliament of Northern
Ireland, a Measure of the Northern Ireland Assembly, and an Order
in Council under the Northern Ireland (Temporary Provisions) Act
1972 or the Northern Ireland Act 1974.

(2) Except so far as the context otherwise requires, any reference in this
Act to an enactment is a reference to it as amended by or under any other
enactment, including this Act.

(3) [*omitted*]

(4) Any power to make an order conferred on the Secretary of State by
any provision of this Act—

(a) shall be exercisable by statutory instrument; and

(b) shall include power to revoke or vary a previous order made under
that provision.

(5)–(6) [*omitted*]

NOTE
Convention countries The following countries have been designated by Orders in
Council under this Act:

Country	Order in Council
Austria	1978/1245
Belgium	1986/271
Cyprus	1979/497
Denmark	1978/1245
Federal Republic of Germany (and West Berlin)	1978/1245
France	1987/2137
Iceland	1980/1392
Italy	1986/1137
Liechtenstein	1986/1137
Luxembourg	1981/1507
Netherlands	1986/271
Norway	1980/357
Portugal	1986/271
Spain	1981/1389
Sweden	1978/1245
Switzerland	1986/271
Turkey	1981/1389

[*Other sections omitted or repealed*]

SCHEDULES
SCHEDULE 1

Sections 1, 4

LIST OF OFFENCES

Common law offences

1. Murder.
2. Manslaughter or culpable homicide.
3. Rape.
4. Kidnapping, abduction or plagium.
5. False imprisonment.
6. Assault occasioning actual bodily harm or causing injury.
7. Wilful fire-raising.

Offences against the person

8. An offence under any of the following provisions of the Offences against the Person Act 1861—
 (*az*) Section 4 (soliciting etc to commit murder)
 (*a*) section 18 (wounding with intent to cause grievous bodily harm);
 (*b*) section 20 (causing grievous bodily harm);
 (*c*) section 21 (attempting to choke etc. in order to commit or assist in the committing of any indictable offence);
 (*d*) section 22 (using chloroform etc. to commit or assist in the committing of any indictable offence);
 (*e*) section 23 (maliciously administering poison etc. so as to endanger life or inflict grievous bodily harm);
 (*f*) section 24 (maliciously administering poison etc. with intent to injure etc.);
 (*g*) section 48 (rape).
9. An offence under section 1 of the Sexual Offences Act 1956 (rape).
9A. The offence of Torture under Section 134 of the Criminal Justice Act 1988.

Abduction

10. An offence under any of the following provisions of the Offences against the Person Act 1861—
 (*a*) section 55 (abduction of unmarried girl under 16);
 (*b*) section 56 (child-stealing or receiving stolen child).
11. An offence under section 20 of the Sexual Offences Act 1956 (abduction of unmarried girl under 16).

Taking of hostages

11A. An offence under the Taking of Hostages Act 1982.
11B. An offence under section 2 of the Child Abduction Act 1984 (abduction of child by person other than parent etc.) or any corresponding provision in force in Northern Ireland.

Explosives

12. An offence under any of the following provisions of the Offences against the Person Act 1861—

(a) section 28 (causing bodily injury by gunpowder);

(b) section 29 (causing gunpowder to explode etc. with intent to do grievous bodily harm).

(c) section 30 (placing gunpowder near a building etc. with intent to cause bodily injury).

13. An offence under any of the following provisions of the Explosive Substances Act 1883—

(a) section 2 (causing explosion likely to endanger life or property);

(b) section 3 (doing any act with intent to cause such an explosion, conspiring to cause such an explosion, or making or possessing explosive with intent to endanger life or property).

Nuclear Material

13A. An offence under any provision of the Nuclear Material (Offences) Act 1983

Firearms

14. The following offences under the Firearms Act 1968—

(a) an offence under section 16 (possession of firearm with intent to injure);

(b) an offence under subsection (1) of section 17 (use of firearm or imitation firearm to resist arrest) involving the use or attempted use of a firearm within the meaning of that section.

15. The following offences under the Firearms (Northern Ireland) Order 1981—

(a) an offence under Article 17 consisting of a person's having in his possession any firearm or ammunition (within the meaning of that Article) with intent by means thereof to endanger life, or to enable another person by means thereof to endanger life;

(b) an offence under paragraph (1) of Article 18 (use of firearm or imitation firearm to resist arrest) involving the use or attempted use of a firearm within the meaning of that Article.

Offences against property

16. An offence under section 1(2) of the Criminal Damage Act 1971 (destroying or damaging property intending to endanger life or being reckless as to danger to life).

17. An offence under Article 3(2) of the Criminal Damage (Northern Ireland) Order 1977 (destroying or damaging property intending to endanger life or being reckless as to danger to life).

Offences in relation to aircraft

18. An offence under Part I of the Aviation Security Act 1982 (other than an offence under section 4 or 7 of that Act).

19. (*merged with 18*).

Attempts
20. An offence of attempting to commit any offence mentioned in a preceding paragraph of this Schedule.

Conspiracy
21. An offence of conspiring to commit any offence mentioned in a preceding paragraph of this Schedule.

NOTE
Some of the scheduled offences are not (or are no longer) offences under *English* criminal law, as the Act applies throughout the United Kingdom.

Theft Act 1978

(C 31)

Obtaining services by deception

1. (1) A person who by any deception dishonestly obtains services from another shall be guilty of an offence.

(2) It is an obtaining of services where the other is induced to confer a benefit by doing some act, or causing or permitting some act to be done, on the understanding that the benefit has been or will be paid for.

NOTES

This provision, together with s 2 and (less directly) s 3 of the Act, replaced s 16(2)(a) of the Theft Act 1968, which had been described as a 'judicial nightmare'. The s 16 offence of obtaining property by deception has not entirely disappeared: it survives in the form of s 16(2)(b) and (c) (*qv*).

There would appear to be some degree of overlap between the present provision and ss 15 and 16 of the 1968 Act. Thus the obtaining of property (s 15) or of overdraft facilities (s 16(2)(b)) may also involve the obtaining of services. The prosecution may therefore have some choice in the selection of charges; but see *R v Halai* [1983] Crim LR 624.

'by any deception' S 5(1) of the Act provides that 'deception' has the same meaning as in s 15 of the 1968 Act (*qv*). Note that D must not only practise a deception, but also obtain the services thereby.

'dishonestly' Note that s 2 of the 1968 Act does not directly apply; but the judicial definition provided in *R v Ghosh* [1982] QB 1053 would appear to be applicable. See further the notes to ss 2 and 15 of the 1968 Act.

'obtains' There is a partial definition of this concept in subs (2); it does not, however specify whether the 'obtaining' must be for the benefit of the deceiver. Contrast s 15(2) of the 1968 Act and s 2(4) of this Act.

'services' Subs (2) defines services in terms of benefits, but excludes benefits provided gratuitously. Thus in *R v Halai* [1983] Crim LR 624 the Court of Appeal held that a building society had not provided the appellant with services merely by allowing him to open a savings account: building societies do not charge any fee or expect any payment for the opening or operation of such accounts. The court appeared to doubt whether the society had provided any benefit at all; but, with respect, it surely had. Banks sometimes charge for the operation of such accounts; and the obtaining of banking facilities by deception could therefore come within this provision. If the usual charges are waived as a result of the deception, there could be an offence under s 2(1)(c) of this Act.

'from another / where the other is induced' In respect of the offences created by ss 15 and 16 of the 1968 Act, it has been held that they can be committed where D deceives P and thereby obtains property from Q. See *R v Charles* [1977] AC 177. In the present case, however, it would seem that the person on whom the deception is practised must also be the one from whom the services are obtained, (or his agent, employee, etc.)

'causing, permitting' The victim of the deception may cause (ie order) or permit his agents, employees *etc* to do something for the offender, or he may do something himself. In either case he will be deemed to have provided a benefit.

'on the understanding that the benefit has been or will be paid for' See notes on 'services', *supra*. In many cases, the whole gist of D's offence will be that he deceives P into expecting a payment that D has no intention of making, but the offence is so drafted that it may be committed even where D has no intention of avoiding payment (eg he hires a car by pretending to be the holder of a vaild licence, without which the lender would not be prepared to let him use it).

Penalty See s 4 *infra*. To offences by company directors s 18 of the 1968 Act applies, by virtue of s 5(1) *infra*.

Evasion of liability by deception
2. (1) Subject to subsection (2) below, where a person by any deception—

(*a*) dishonestly secures the remission of the whole or part of any existing liability to make a payment, whether his own liability or another's; or

(*b*) with intent to make permanent default in whole or in part on any existing liability to make a payment, or with intent to let another do so, dishonestly induces the creditor or any person claiming payment on behalf of the creditor to wait for payment (whether or not the due date for payment is deferred) or to forgo payment; or

(*c*) dishonestly obtains any exemption from or abatement of liability to make a payment;

he shall be guilty of an offence.

(2) For purposes of this section "liability" means legally enforceable liability; and subsection (1) shall not apply in relation to liability that has not been accepted or established to pay compensation for a wrongful act or omission.

(3) For purposes of subsection 1(*b*) a person induced to take in payment a cheque or other security for money by way of conditional satisfaction of a pre-existing liability is to be treated not as being paid but as being induced to wait for payment.

(4) For purposes of subsection (1)(*c*) "obtains" includes obtaining for another or enabling another to obtain.

NOTES
Whereas s 1 of the Act penalises the dishonest obtaining of services, this provision generally confines itself to the dishonest evasion of pre-existing liabilities to pay for something. There may however be some degree of overlap between s 1 and s 2(1)(c). Both could apply where D dishonestly deceives P into providing him with some benefit at a reduced price.

Subss (1)(a–c) create three distinct offences, but there are a number of common elements, and the offences again overlap with each other to some extent: *R v Jackson* [1983] Crim LR 617.

'by any deception' S 5(1) of the Act declares that this expression has the same meaning as it bears in s 15 of the 1968 Act. As with s 15, the prosecution must be able to prove causation: liability must be evaded by means of the deception. See *R v Andrews* [1981] Crim LR 106.

'dishonestly'   See the notes to s 1 *supra*.

'liability to make a payment'   All of the offences created by subs (1) involve some kind of evasion of a liability to make a payment. For the purposes of subs (1)(a) and (b) it must be an existing liability, and in all cases it must be a legally enforceable one (subs (2)). Thus, although one may commit an offence under s 1 of this Act or s 16 of the 1968 Act by deceiving another person into providing a benefit or accepting a wager under an unenforceable contract, it will be no offence to practise a further deception afterwards in order to avoid payment for it.

'liability ... for a wrongful act or omission'   Subs (2) distiguishes between cases in which liability has been accepted or established and cases where it has not. Thus, if D negligently damages P's property and dishonestly denies that he was responsible, no offence is committed; but if he admits liability and gives P a false name and address 'to which the bill may be sent', he may be guilty of an offence under subs (1)(b). This distinction seems hard to justify. It could only be avoided if 'informal' admissions of liability (as in the above example) are distinguished from 'formal' or binding admissions, and if only the latter are treated as acceptances of liability.

'secures the remission of ... any existing liability' (subs (1)(a))   Remission means release. If D deceives P into accepting a fake diamond in settlement of his original debt, this would involve remission of that debt. Similarly where D induces P to accept payment by credit card, in circumstances where he has no right to use the card, P accepts the card in settlement of the debt, and may be able to recover from the card company despite D's misconduct. See *R v Jackson* [1983] Crim LR 617.

    It is less clear whether subs (1)(a) applies where D dishonestly persuades P to accept a lesser sum in full payment of the debt. At first sight it would appear to do so; but as a matter of law D remains liable for the remaining amount, there being no valid consideration for the release. A better charge in such circumstances would be under subs (1)(b), assuming that intent to make permanent default can be proved.

Payment by cheque (subs (3))   For the purposes of subs (1)(b) payment by cheque is to be treated as inducing the creditor to wait for payment; but in other cases it could arguably be regarded as payment, even if not backed by a cheque guarantee card. In the event of the cheque being dishonoured, the payee's obvious civil remedy would be to sue on the cheque, and it could be argued that he has at least conditionally exchanged this right for the right to enforce the original debt. (See notes on securing remission of liability, *supra*.)

'induces the creditor ... to wait for ... or forgo payment' (subs (1)(b))   This is the only one of the offences in s 2 which requires an intent to make permanent default on at least part of the liability. In certain other respect it is probably wider than the others, since it does not require that D should be granted either remission or exemption from his liability. It will suffice if the creditor or his agents are deceived into doing without his payment either permanently or (as they imagine) temporarily.

    If D is indeed granted remission or exemption, this does not rule out a conviction under subs (1)(b), as long as his intent to make permanent default can be proved: *R v Holt* [1981] Crim LR 499.

'obtains any exemption from or abatement of liability' (subs (1)(c))   This need not be an existing liability, and in this respect (if in no other) this covers cases not covered by the other subsections. Its scope was considered in *R v Sibartie* [1983] Crim LR 470, where D was convicted of an attempt to commit the offence by showing an invalid season ticket to an inspector on the London Underground. Most commentators have nevertheless taken the view that a better charge in such a case would have been one under subs (1)(b). See also *R v Firth* [1990] Crim LR 326.

Penalty   See s 4 *infra*.

Making off without payment
   3. (1) Subject to subsection (3) below, a person who, knowing that payment on the spot for any goods supplied or service done is required or expected from him, dishonestly makes off without having paid as required or expected and with intent to avoid payment of the amount due shall be guilty of an offence.
   (2) For purposes of this section "payment on the spot" includes payment at the time of collecting goods on which work has been done or in respect of which service has been provided.
   (3) Subsection (1) above shall not apply where the supply of the goods or the doing of the service is contrary to law, or where the service done is such that payment is not legally enforceable.
   (4) Any person may arrest without warrant anyone who is, or whom he, with reasonable cause, suspects to be, committing or attempting to commit an offence under this section.

NOTES
This offence was created in order to fill a gap which had been identified in the 1968 Act. If, for example D fills his car's fuel tank, consumes a meal in a restaurant, or takes a ride in a taxi, and then makes off without paying, he may perhaps be guilty of obtaining the property or service by deception, but only if it can be proved that he practised the deception in order to obtain it. If D's intent to avoid payment is formed only after consuming the meal *etc*, this cannot be the case. D might still be guilty of evading a liability by deception, but not if he simply runs away.
   Such difficulties are avoided by using this provision; and it will sometimes be chosen by the prosecution even when a more serious offence would be proveable on the facts.
   'payment on the spot'   This must in fact be required or expected, and D must be aware that it is. The 'spot' in question is the place where the payment is required—this will usually be the premises (shop, restaurant etc.) where the transaction takes place. See *R v Brooks* (1982) 76 Cr App R 66. Note also subs (2).
   'goods supplied or services done'   Under s 5(2), 'goods' are to be construed in accordance with s 34(2)(b) of the 1968 Act. The goods need no longer belong to another when the offence is committed. 'Service done' is not defined in this context, but must presumably be understood in the same sense as in s 1.
   'dishonestly'   See the notes to s 1 *supra*.
   'makes off without having paid as required or expected'   One may make off with the aid of a deception (which may amount to an offence under s 2) or without one. If D fails to get beyond the door of the 'place' in question, he may be liable for an attempt: *R v Brooks, supra*.
   If D purports to pay by means of a forged or stolen cheque which is worthless to P, it is doubtful whether this can be regarded as 'payment as required' and it may therefore be possible to succeed with a charge under this provision; but it would seem safer and preferable to use s 2(1)(b) in such a case.
   'with intent to avoid payment'   This means an intent permanently to avoid payment; *R v Allen* [1985] AC 1029. This will readily be inferred if D has run away

without leaving any name or address; but if D gives those details to the restauranteur *etc.* and offers to pay when he has found his wallet or chequebook, he will commit no offence by refusing to let the restauranteur detain him.

Illegality and unenforceability (subs (3)) It may be an offence under s 15 of the 1968 Act or s 1 of the present Act to obtain property or services by deception, even if the property or benefit. in question is provided under an illegal or unenforceable agreement; but no offence can be committed under this provision or under s 2 merely by avoiding the unenforceable obligation to pay for what has already been provided.

Punishments

4. (1) Offences under this Act shall be punishable either on conviction on indictment or on summary conviction.

(2) A person convicted on indictment shall be liable—

(*a*) for an offence under section 1 or section 2 of this Act, to imprisonment for a term not exceeding five years; and

(*b*) for an offence under section 3 of this Act, to imprisonment for a term not exceeding two years.

(3) A person convicted summarily of any offence under this Act shall be liable—

(*a*) to imprisonment for a term not exceeding six months; or

(*b*) to a fine not exceeding the prescribed sum for the purposes of [section 32 of the Magistrates' Courts Act 1980],

or to both.

Supplementary

5. (1) For the purposes of sections 1 and 2 above "deception" has the same meaning as in section 15 of the Theft Act 1968, that is to say, it means any deception (whether deliberate or reckless) by words or conduct as to fact or as to law, including a deception as to the present intentions of the persons using the deception or any other person; and section 18 of that Act (liability of company officers for offences by the company) shall apply in relation to sections 1 and 2 above as it applies in relation to section 15 of that Act.

(2) Sections 30(1) (husband and wife), 31(1) (effect on civil proceedings) and 34 (interpretation) of the Theft Act 1968, so far as they are applicable in relation to this Act, shall apply as they apply in relation to that Act.

(3) [*omitted*]

(4) [*omitted*]

Protection of Children Act 1978

(C 37)

Indecent photographs of children
1. (1) It is an offence for a person—

(*a*) to take, or permit to be taken, any indecent photograph of a child (meaning in this Act a person under the age of 16); or

(*b*) to distribute or show such indecent photographs; or

(*c*) to have in his possession such indecent photographs, with a view to their being distributed or shown by himself or others; or

(*d*) to publish or cause to be published any advertisement likely to be understood as conveying that the advertiser distributes or shows such indecent photographs, or intends to do so.

(2) For purposes of this Act, a person is to be regarded as distributing an indecent photograph if he parts with possession of it to, or exposes or offers it for acquisition by, another person.

(3) Proceedings for an offence under this Act shall not be instituted except by or with the consent of the Director of Public Prosecutions.

(4) Where a person is charged with an offence under subsection (1)(*b*) or (*c*), it shall be a defence for him to prove—

(*a*) that he had a legitimate reason for distributing or showing the photographs or (as the case may be) having them in his possession; or

(*b*) that he had not himself seen the photographs and did not know, nor had any cause to suspect, them to be indecent.

(5) References in the Children and Young Persons Act 1933 (except in sections 15 and 99) to the offences mentioned in Schedule 1 to that Act shall include an offence under subsection (1)(*a*) above.

(6) [*omitted*]

NOTES
This Act creates offences carrying similar penalties to those under the Obscene Publications Act 1959, and there is some degree of overlap with the earlier Act in that almost all obscene pictures of children will be indecent within the meaning of this Act. It should nevertheless be noted that a publication may be obscene for other reasons (eg where it promotes the misuse of drugs); and a photograph may easily be indecent without in any sense being obscene under the 1959 Act.

'indecent photograph of a child' In determining whether a photo is indecent, the court should take account of the age of the child. A photo of a bare-breasted woman might be regarded as daring, whilst a similar photo of a fifteen year old girl might be considered indecent. See *R v Owen* [1988] 1 WLR 134. It is submitted that in some cases a court or jury might nevertheless consider the age of the subject to be unimportant on the particular facts before them.

The motives of the photographer or (subject to subs (4)) the possessor *etc* are irrelevant, as long as he has deliberately taken or acquired the photo in question.

Indecency is to be determined by the court or jury by looking at the thing itself and applying recognised standards of propriety: *R v Graham-Kerr* (1989) 88 Cr App R 302. Subs (3) is no doubt intended to prevent over zealous prosecutions in respect of family snapshots *etc*.

Note that s 7(3) covers cases in which a child appears in an indecent photo but is not himself the reason for it being indecent. 'Photograph' includes film and video (s 7(2) & (5)); but one must presume that the Act will not be contravened unless the child is filmed or recorded in an indecent scene.

'possession . . . with a view to their being distributed or shown . . .' Where no such purpose can be proved, D may still be guilty of an offence under s 160 of the Criminal Justice Act 1988 (*qv*).

'permit to be taken' By analogy with cases under other legislation, this must mean 'knowingly permit': see *James & Son Ltd v Smee* [1955] 1 QB 78.

Penalty See s 6 *infra*. There is provision for forfeiture under s 5 (not printed in this work).

2. [*omitted*]

Offences by corporations

3. (1) Where a body corporate is guilty of an offence under this Act and it is proved that the offence occurred with the consent or connivance of, or was attributable to any neglect on the part of, any director, manager, secretary or other officer of the body, or any person who was purporting to act in any such capacity he, as well as the body corporate, shall be deemed to be guilty of that offence and shall be liable to be proceeded against and punished accordingly.

(2) Where the affairs of a body corporate are managed by its members, subsection (1) shall apply in relation to the acts and defaults of a member in connection with his functions of management as if he were a director of the body corporate.

NOTE
See the notes to similar provisions in s 18 of the Theft Act 1968 and s 25 of the Forgery and Counterfeiting Act 1981.

4–5. [*omitted*]

Punishments

6. (1) Offences under this Act shall be punishable either on conviction on indictment or on summary conviction.

(2) A person convicted on indictment of any offence under this Act shall be liable to imprisonment for a term of not more than three years, or to a fine or to both.

(3) A person convicted summarily of any offence under this Act shall be liable—

(*a*) to imprisonment for a term not exceeding six months; or

(*b*) to a fine not exceeding the prescribed sum for the purposes of section 32 of the Magistrates' Courts Act 1980 (punishment on summary conviction of offences triable either way: [£2,000] or other sum substituted by order under that Act), or to both.

Interpretation

7. (1) The following subsections apply for the interpretation of this Act.

(2) References to an indecent photograph include an indecent film, a copy of an indecent photograph or film, and an indecent photograph comprised in a film.

(3) Photographs (including those comprised in a film) shall, if they show children and are indecent, be treated for all purposes of this Act as indecent photographs of children.

(4) References to a photograph include the negative as well as the positive version.

(5) "Film" includes any form of video-recording.

NOTE

See the notes to s 1 *supra*.

8–9 [*omitted*]

Magistrates' Courts Act 1980

(C 43)

Aiders and abettors

44. (1) A person who aids, abets, counsels or procures the commission by another person of a summary offence shall be guilty of the like offence and may be tried (whether or not he is charged as a principal) either by a court having jurisdiction to try that other person or by a court having by virtue of his own offence jurisdiction to try him.

(2) Any offence consisting in aiding, abetting, counselling or procuring the commission of an offence triable either way (other than an offence listed in Schedule 1 to this Act) shall by virtue of this subsection be triable either way.

NOTES

This provision serves a function in relation to summary offences which is largely identical to that served by s 8 of the Accessories and Abettors Act 1861 (*qv*) in relation to indictable offences.

'aids, abets, counsels or procures' The meaning of these terms is explained in the notes to s 8 of the Accessories and Abettors Act 1861.

'guilty of the like offence' Nevertheless, as with indictable offences under the 1861 Act, aiding, abetting, *etc* require *mens rea*, and a secondary party cannot be convicted on the basis of strict liability, even in circumstances where the perpetrator can be: see *Callow v Tillstone* (1900) 83 LT 411.

'whether or not he is charged as a principal' This is the same principle as applies under the 1861 Act. The effect is that a prosecution need not fail merely because it cannot be proved which of D or E was the perpetrator and which the abettor *etc*—nor need D be acquitted merely because he is charged as perpetrator and turns out to have been the abettor: *Du Cross v Lambourne* [1907] 1 KB 40.

'either by a court' Ss 2 and 3 of this Act deal with the jurisdiction of magistrates' courts to try summary offences. Jurisdiction may be claimed (*inter alia*) where the offence is committed within the county, London Commission Area *etc* for which the court sits (s 2(1)) or within 500 yards of the relevant boundary (s 3(1)); and, under s 2(6), once the court has jurisdiction to try D for one offence, they shall have jurisdiction to try him for other summary offences committed outside their ordinary jurisdiction. Under the present provisions, the court will also have jurisdiction to try the secondary offender with him.

'other than an offence listed in Schedule 1 to this Act' This passage is potentially misleading, in that it appears to suggest that, where an offence is triable either way by virtue of Sch 1 (and s 17), the offence of aiding, abetting *etc* that offence is *not* triable either way; but it *is* so triable by virtue of Sch 1, para 3.3, except in the case of offences under ss 4(1) and 5(1) of the Criminal Law Act 1967.

238

Incitement
45. (1) Any offence consisting in the incitement to commit a summary offence shall be triable only summarily.

(2) Subsection (1) above is without prejudice to any other enactment by virtue of which any offence is triable only summarily.

(3) On conviction of an offence consisting in the incitement to commit a summary offence a person shall be liable to the same penalties as he would be liable to on conviction of the last-mentioned offence.

NOTES
'incitement'   Incitement is itself an inchoate offence at common law. Where the offence incited is actually committed, the inciter becomes guilty of it as a secondary party (*ie* liability for 'counselling').

As to what actually amounts to 'incitement', see *R v Higgins* (1801) 2 East 5; *R v Most* (1881) 7 QBD 244, *R v Curr* [1986] Crim LR 470. See also the notes to s 4 of the Offences Against the Person Act 1861.

[*other sections omitted*]

Forgery and Counterfeiting Act 1981

(C 45)

Part I: Forgery and kindred offences

The offence of forgery

1. A person is guilty of forgery if he makes a false instrument, with the intention that he or another shall use it to induce somebody to accept it as genuine, and by reason of so accepting it to do or not to do some act to his own or any other person's prejudice.

NOTES

S 30 of the Act, together with the schedule, repealed a number of older statutory offences of forgery (notably the Forgery under Act 1913), whilst s 13 abolished the offence of forgery at common law. The repealed offences have been supplanted by the single offence created by this provision.

Most of the key terms used, including 'instrument', 'false', 'makes', 'induce' and 'prejudice', are defined in ss 8–10 *infra*.

'with the intention that' Note that this is a 'double intention'. D must intend both that the forged instrument will be accepted as genuine *and* that someone will thereby act to his own or another's prejudice (as defined in s 10). The fact that someone might possibly be prejudiced is not in itself enough: *R v Garcia* [1988] Crim LR 115 (cf *R v Tobierre* [1986] 1 WLR 125 on s 3).

On the other hand, the intention is ulterior, and neither of the intended events need actually happen for the complete offence to be committed. This may have jurisdictional implications: the making of a false instrument in England or Wales will be an offence under this provision, even if intended for use abroad (*cf Treacy v DPP* [1971] AC 537, which concerned the making of a blackmail demand). Conversely, no offence would be committed under this provision if an instrument forged abroad is used within the jurisdiction: the correct charge would be under s 3 (using a false instrument).

'to his own or any other person's prejudice' This is a reference to the person whom the forgery is intended to deceive. In *R v Utting* [1987] 1 WLR 1375, the indictment alleged that D made a false instrument,

> 'with the intention that he should use it to induce somebody to accept it as genuine, and by so accepting it not to do some act to the prejudice of himself' [*ie* the appellant].

The indictment was held to be defective. The case involved the alleged making of a false instrument by the appellant in order to deceive the police into not prosecuting him. Had the indictment alleged an intent that the police should be deceived into prejudicing themselves by not prosecuting him, that would apparently have been satisfactory (*ibid* at p 1340, and see s 10 *infra*).

Penalty See s 6 *infra*,

Dishonesty Note that dishonesty is not an essential ingredient in the *mens rea* of any offence under the Act, albeit that most forgeries will in fact be dishonest: see *R v Campbell* (1984) 80 Cr App R 47.

The offence of copying a false instrument

2. It is an offence for a person to make a copy of an instrument which is, and which he knows or believes to be, a false instrument, with the intention that he or another shall use it to induce somebody to accept it as a copy of a genuine instrument, and by reason of so accepting it to do or not to do some act to his own or any other person's prejudice.

NOTES

A copy of an original instrument may be a false one if it is intended that it should be passed off as the original; a copy of that forgery would equally be a false instrument if made for the same reasons, and the act of making it would therefore be an offence under s 1 of the Act. S 2 covers the situation where the copy of the forgery is not intended to be taken as the original instrument, but as a true copy of the original. It is nevertheless questionable whether this provision is really necessary. A document which purports to be a photocopy of an original certificate etc, but which is really a photocopy of a forgery, would still appear to be a false instrument within s 1: see s 9(1)(g) and *R v Donnelly* [1984] 1 WLR 1017. See also *R v Utting* [1987] 1 WLR 1375, where a s 1 charge was brought but failed for other reasons.

'instrument'　See s 8 *infra*.

'false' and 'makes'　See s 9 *infra*.

'induce' and 'prejudice'　See s 10 *infra*.

'with the intention that'　See notes to s 1 *supra*.

'to his own or any other person's prejudice'　See notes to s 1 *supra*.

'knows or believes'　See notes to s 22 of the Theft Act 1968, where the same words are used.

Penalty　See s 6 *infra*.

The offence of using a false instrument

3. It is an offence for a person to use an instrument which is, and which he knows or believes to be, false, with the intention of inducing somebody to accept it as genuine, and by reason of so accepting it to do or not to do some act to his own or any other person's prejudice.

NOTES

Whereas s 1 penalises the making of a false instrument, even if it is never used for its intended purpose, and even if it is intended for use outside the jurisdiction, this provision penalises the use of such an instrument, even if it was not originally made for any such purpose, and even if it was made abroad. The instrument in question must however be used with the requisite *mens rea* and within the jurisdiction (or by a person subject to a special extraterritorial jurisdiction).

'instrument'　See s 8 *infra*.

'false'　See s 9 *infra*.

'induce' and 'prejudice'　See s 10 *infra*.

'with the intention that'　See the notes to s 1 *supra* and see also *R v Tobierre* [1986] 1 WLR 125.

'knows or believes'   See the notes to s 22 of the Theft Act 1968, where the same words are used.

'uses'   This term is not defined in the Act. Previous legislation used the term 'utters', and 'using' was the principal form of uttering (*cf R v Morris* [1966] 1 QB 184). A dictionary definition of the verb 'use' is 'to put into action or service, avail oneself of . . . to carry out a purpose or transaction by means of' (*Webster*). It seems clear that the use need not be successful: the offence may be committed even if the instrument is at once recognised as a forgery. (See the note on intention in s 1.)

'to his own or any other person's prejudice'   See the notes to s 1 *supra.*

Penalty   See s 6 *infra.*

The offence of using a copy of a false instrument
   4.   It is an offence for a person to use a copy of an instrument which is, and which he knows or believes to be, a false instrument, with the intention of inducing somebody to accept it as a copy of a genuine instrument, and by reason of so accepting it to do or not to do some act to his own or any other person's prejudice.

NOTES
This provision relates to s 2 in the same way that s 3 relates to s 1; and like s 2 it is arguably otiose, since the use of a photocopy etc which purports to be a copy of a genuine instrument, but which is in fact a copy of a forgery, would appear to be an offence under s 3: see s 9(1)(g) as interpreted in *R v Donnelly* [1984] 1 WLR 1017. The actual copying of the original forgery would meanwhile appear to constitute 'use' of that instrument—again an offence under s 3. See *R v Harris* [1966] 1 QB 184.
   On all other matters concerning the meaning of this provision, see the notes to ss 2 and 3 *supra.*

Offences relating to money orders, shares certificates, passports, etc.
   5. (1) It is an offence for a person to have in his custody or under his control an instrument to which this section applies which is, and which he knows or believes to be, false, with the intention that he or another shall use it to induce somebody to accept it as genuine, and by reason of so accepting it to do or not to do some act to his own or any other person's prejudice.
   (2) It is an offence for a person to have in his custody or under his control, without lawful authority or excuse, an instrument to which this section applies which is, and which he knows or believes to be, false.
   (3) It is an offence for a person to make or to have in his custody or under his control a machine or implement, or paper or any other material, which to his knowledge is or has been specially designed or adapted for the making of an instrument to which this section applies, with the intention that he or another shall make an instrument to which this section applies which is false and that he or another shall use the instrument to induce somebody to accept is as genuine, and by reason of so accepting it to do or not to do some act to his own or any other person's prejudice.

(4) It is an offence for a person to make or to have in his custody or under his control any such machine, implement, paper or material, without lawful authority or excuse.

(5) The instruments to which this section applies are—

(*a*) money orders;

(*b*) postal orders;

(*c*) United Kingdom postage stamps;

(*d*) Inland Revenue stamps;

(*e*) share certificates;

(*f*) passports and documents which can be used instead of passports;

(*g*) cheques;

(*h*) travellers' cheques;

(*j*) cheque cards;

(*k*) credit cards;

(*l*) certified copies relating to an entry in a register of births, adoptions, marriages or deaths and issued by the Registrar General, the Registrar General for Northern Ireland, a registration officer or a person lawfully authorised to register marriages; and

(*m*) certificates relating to entries in such registers.

(6) In subsection (5)(*e*) above "share certificate" means an instrument entitling or evidencing the title of a person to a share or interest—

(*a*) in any public stock, annuity, fund or debt of any government or state, including a state which forms part of another state; or

(*b*) in any stock, fund or debt of a body (whether corporate or unincorporated) established in the United Kingdom or elsewhere.

NOTES

This provision creates four different offences; the two involving ulterior intent (subss (1) and (3)) carry the same penalties as ss 1–4; the other two (subss (2) and (4)), which require no such intent, carry lighter penalties.

'in his custody or . . . control'   See the notes to s 3 of the Criminal Damage Act 1971, which similarly uses the concept of 'custody or control'.

'instrument'   See s 8 *infra*.

'false'   see s 9 *infra*.

'knows or believes'   See the notes to s 22 of the Theft Act 1968.

'induce' and 'prejudice'   See s 10 *infra*.

'with the intention that'   See the notes to s 1 *supra*.

'to his own or any other person's prejudice'   See the notes to s 1 *supra*.

'without lawful authority or excuse' (subss (2) and (4))   These concepts are not defined in the Act; but 'lawful excuse' must include general defences such as duress *etc* and would also cover possession of items with intent to hand them over to the police or other authorities at the first reasonable opportunity (*cf R v Wuyts* [1969] 2 QB 476).

Any defence of lawful authority would probably have to be proved on the balance of probabilities.

Penalties for offences under Part I

6. (1) A person guilty of an offence under this Part of this Act shall be liable on summary conviction—

(*a*) to a fine not exceeding the statutory maximum; or

(*b*) to imprisonment for a term not exceeding six months; or

(*c*) to both.

(2) A person guilty of an offence to which this subsection applies shall be liable on conviction on indictment to imprisonment for a term not exceeding ten years.

(3) The offences to which subsection (2) above applies are offences under the following provisions of this Part of this Act—

(*a*) section 1;

(*b*) section 2;

(*c*) section 3;

(*d*) section 4;

(*e*) section 5(1); and

(*f*) section 5(3).

(4) A person guilty of an offence under section 5(2) or (4) above shall be liable on conviction on indictment to imprisonment for a term not exceeding two years.

(5) In this section "statutory maximum," in relation to a fine on summary conviction, means the prescribed sum, within the meaning of section 32 of the Magistrates' Courts Act 1980 (£2,000 or another sum fixed by order under section 143 of that Act to take account of changes in the value of money); and those sections shall extend to Northern Ireland for the purposes of the application of this definition.

7. [*omitted*].

Meaning of instrument

8. (1) Subject to subsection (2) below, in this Part of this Act "instrument" means—

(*a*) any document, whether of a formal or informal character;

(*b*) any stamp issued or sold by the Post Office;

(*c*) any Inland Revenue stamp; and

(*d*) any disc, tape, sound track or other device on or in which information is recorded or stored by mechanical, electronic or other means.

(2) A currency note within the meaning of Part II of this Act is not an instrument for the purposes of this Part of this Act.

(3) A mark denoting payment of postage which the Post Office authorise to be used instead of an adhesive stamp is to be treated for the purposes of this Part of this Act as if it were a stamp issued by the Post Office.

(4) In this Part of this Act "Inland Revenue stamp" means a stamp as defined in section 27 of the Stamp Duties Management Act 1891.

NOTES
This definition is extremely wide; all documents are instruments, not only those such as cheques or wills which perform legal functions or create legal rights or liabilities.

'document' This term is not defined, and there is therefore room for doubt as to whether a forged signature on a work of art is a false instrument: *cf R v Closs* (1857) D and B 460; *R v Douce* [1972] Crim LR 105. See also *R v Smith* (1858) D and B 566 (wrapper on goods not a document at common law).

'disc, tape, sound track or other device ...' A pirated copy of a film or recording would not appear to be a forgery within the meaning of the Act, even though it might appear to fit within the relevant definitions of 'false' and 'instrument'. This is because the information recorded on the pirate copy will not itself be false; any falsity will be in the label or packaging, as to which see *R v Smith supra*.

'currency notes within the meaning of Part II' See the definition in s 27(1) *infra*. Counterfeit notes are covered by the offences contained in Part II.

Meaning of "false" and "making"
9. (1) An instrument is false for the purposes of this Part of this Act—
(a) if it purports to have been made in the form in which it is made by a person who did not in fact make it in that form; or
(b) if it purports to have been made in the form in which it is made on the authority of a person who did not in fact authorise its making in that form; or
(c) if it purports to have been made in the terms in which it is made by a person who did not in fact make it in those terms; or
(d) if it purports to have been made in the terms in which it is made on the authority of a person who did not in fact authorise its making in those terms; or
(e) if it purports to have been altered in any respect by a person who did not in fact alter it in that respect; or
(f) if it purports to have been altered in any respect on the authority of a person who did not in fact authorise the alteration in that respect; or
(g) if it purports to have been made or altered on a date on which, or at a place at which, or otherwise in circumstances in which, it was not in fact made or altered; or
(h) if it purports to have been made or altered by an existing person but he did not in fact exist.
(2) A person is to be treated for the purposes of this Part of this Act as making a false instrument if he alters an instrument so as to make it false in any respect (whether or not it is false in some other respect apart from that alteration).

NOTES
Not all false statements in documents make those documents into forgeries; a false instrument must purport to be something which it is not (*cf R v Windsor* (1865) 10 Cox CC 118 at p 123; *R v More* [1987] 1 WLR 1578). The dividing line between a false instrument and one which merely contains false statements may sometimes be rather subtle: see *R v Donnelly* [1984] 1 WLR 1017, which distinguishes between a deliberately inaccurate valuation certificate (not a forgery) and a valuation certificate purporting to relate to property which does not really exist (a forgery within subs (1)(g)).
   Note that the indictment need not specify the exact ground on which the instrument is alleged to be false, but the variants listed in (a)–(h) are presumably exhaustive.

'purports'   A false instrument must tell a lie about itself, and it is doubtful if this is the case where D signs his name on an instrument in an abnormal way with a view to later denying its authenticity: see *R v Macer* [1979] Crim LR 659, which was decided under earlier but essentially similar provisions. It is clearly not the case where D has adopted an assumed name when opening a bank or building society account and he then uses that assumed name on an instrument withdrawing money from that account: *R v More supra*.

Subs (1)(a)   The obvious example is where D forges P's signature on a cheque etc. See *R v Lack* (1986) 84 Cr App R 342; But *cf R v More supra*.

Subs (1)(c) and (e)   Alteration of an instrument after it has been made so as to change its value etc would come within para (c) if it is intended to be undetected; but if D's illicit alteration purports to be P's lawful one then para (e) applies.

Subs (1)(g)   See *R v Donnelly supra*.

Subs (1)(h)   D's use of an assumed name on an instrument does not in itself make the instrument a forgery, even where D's purpose is fraudulent (see *R v More supra*); but if the instrument purports to come from someone other than him (eg a reference from an imaginary employer) it would then be a clear forgery.

Meaning of "prejudice" and "induce"
   10. (1) Subject to subsections (2) and (4) below, for the purposes of this Part of this Act an act or omission intended to be induced is to a person's prejudice if, and only if, it is one which, if it occurs—
   (*a*) will result—
      (i) in his temporary or permanent loss of property; or
      (ii) in his being deprived of an opportunity to earn remuneration or greater remuneration; or
      (iii) in his being deprived of an opportunity to gain a financial advantage otherwise than by way of remuneration; or
   (*b*) will result in somebody being given an opportunity—
      (i) to earn remuneration or greater remuneration from him; or
      (ii) to gain a financial advantage from him otherwise than by way of remuneration; or
   (*c*) will be the result of his having accepted a false instrument as genuine, or a copy of a false instrument as a copy of a genuine one, in connection with his performance of any duty.
   (2) An act which a person has an enforceable duty to do and an omission to do an act which a person is not entitled to do shall be disregarded for the purposes of this Part of this Act.

(3) In this Part of this Act references to inducing somebody to accept a false instrument as genuine, or a copy of a false instrument as a copy of a genuine one, include references to inducing a machine to respond to the instrument or copy as if it were a genuine instrument or, as the case may be, a copy of a genuine one.

(4) Where subsection (3) above applies, the act or omission intended to be induced by the machine responding to the instrument or copy shall be treated as an act or omission to a person's prejudice.

(5) In this section "loss" includes not getting what one might get as well as parting with what one has.

NOTES

'prejudice' (subs (1))   Note that the definition provided is exhaustive and that what must be intended is that certain prejudice will (not may) result. See *R v Garcia* [1985] Crim LR 115. At the same time, this is only an ulterior intent, and so a successful deception is not an element in the *actus reus* of any offence under this part of the Act.

Where a forged instrument is used to obtain property, services or some other pecuniary advantage, this may involve an offence under the Theft Acts 1968 or 1978.

Subs (1)(a)   This covers situations in which acceptance of a forgery will result in some person losing or failing to profit; subs (1)(b) covers those in which actual profit or loss may be difficult to identify (*cf* s 16(2)(c) of the Theft Act 1968). The scope of subs (1)(c) is illustrated by *R v Campbell* (1984) 80 Cr App R 47: a bank will be prejudiced if it is induced to pay or collect payment on a forged cheque, whether or not it suffers loss by so doing, and whether or not the offender profits thereby.

'property'   This is not defined in the Act, but see the definition in s 5 of the Theft Act 1968, which is probably a good guide to the meaning of the term here.

'loss'   See subs (5).

Subs (2)   The effect of this provision is that it is not an offence under the Act to make or use a false instrument to secure or protect one's lawful rights vis-a-viz anyone it is intended to deceive.

Subss (3)–(4)   These provisions effectively treat machines (such as computers or automatic cash dispensers) as persons who may be deceived by false instruments. It would not however be an offence under this Act to use a stolen cashpoint service card in such a machine, nor would it be a deception offence under the Theft Acts, which have no provisions akin to these. The proper charge would be theft of any money withdrawn. As for the 'deception' of computers, see *R v Gold* [1988] 2 All ER 186. 'Hacking' or gaining unauthorised access by keying in electronic passwords or false user identification numbers cannot be an offence under the Act. The electronic impulses representing the passwords etc are too ephemeral to constitute 'instruments'. A further objection to a charge of forgery was noted in the Court of Appeal ([1987] QB 1116): even if the electronic impulses momentarily lodged in the computer's 'user segment' could be regarded as an instrument, the prosecution would then be alleging that the computer was deceiving itself.

11 and **12** [*omitted*].

Abolition of offence of forgery at common law

13. The offence of forgery at common law is hereby abolished for all purposes not relating to offences committed before the commencement of this Act.

NOTE

The Act came into force on October 28th 1981.

Part II: Counterfeiting and kindred offences

Offences of counterfeiting notes and coins

14. (1) It is an offence for a person to make a counterfeit of a currency note or of a protected coin, intending that he or another shall pass or tender it as genuine.

(2) It is an offence for a person to make a counterfeit of a currency note or of a protected coin without lawful authority or excuse.

NOTES

This provision, like s 5 *supra*, distinguishes between cases in which there is proof of an intent that the fake item shall be passed as genuine and cases in which there is not, but still penalises the latter kind of case unless the maker has lawful authority or excuse. The reason for this is that the manufacture of realistic fakes carries inevitable risks of confusion or of subsequent misuse (*cf Selby v DPP* [1972] AC 515).

'counterfeit'   See s 28 *infra*.

'currency note or protected coin'   These need not be British; see s 27 *infra*.

'intending that' (subs (1))   This is an ulterior intent. The actual passing of the counterfeit need never happen. In contrast to ss 1–4 and s 5(1), there is no need to prove an intent to induce someone to act to his own or another's prejudice.

'pass or tender as genuine' (subs (1))   See the notes to s 15 *infra*.

'without lawful authority or excuse'   See the notes to s 5 *supra*.

Penalties   See s 22(1) *infra* for subs (1); s 22(3), for subs (2).

Offences of passing etc. counterfeit notes and coins

15. (1) It is an offence for a person—

(*a*) to pass or tender as genuine anything which is, and which he knows or believes to be, a counterfeit of a currency note or of a protected coin; or

(*b*) to deliver to another any thing which is, and which he knows or believes to be, such a counterfeit, intending that the person to whom it is delivered or another shall pass or tender it as genuine.

(2) It is an offence for a person to deliver to another, without lawful authority or excuse, any thing which is, and which he knows or believes to be, a counterfeit of a currency note or of a protected coin.

NOTES
This follows the same pattern as s 14 *supra,* in that it distinguishes between cases in which a counterfeit is intended to be passed as genuine and cases in which there is no proof of such intent, the latter kind of case attracting less serious penalties.

'pass or tender as genuine' A counterfeit may be tendered as genuine, even if it is at once rejected, and an offence may be committed even where the item in question is not passed or tendered as legal tender (s 28(3)). Many forms of notes *etc* used as money are not legal tender (*eg* Scottish notes, which are not even legal tender in Scotland itself), and others may have a collectors' value exceeding their value as currency. As to copies of old coins or notes, which are no longer in current use as money, contrast paras (a) and (b) of s 27(1) *infra.*

'counterfeit' See s 28 *infra.*

'currency note or protected coin' See s 27 *infra.*

'knows or believes' See the notes to s 22 of the Theft Act 1968, where the same words are used.

'deliver' This need not involve any intent to deceive as to the nature of the thing delivered, but note that the more serious (subs (1)) offence may still be committed if it is intended that the counterfeits should eventually be tendered as genuine.

'without lawful authority or excuse' See the notes to s 5 *supra.*

Penalties See s 22(1) *infra* for subs (1); s 22(3) for subs (2).

Offences involving the custody or control of counterfeit notes and coins
   16. (1) It is an offence for a person to have in his custody or under his control anything which is, and which he knows or believes to be, a counterfeit of a currency note or of a protected coin, intended either to pass or tender it as genuine or to deliver it to another with the intention that he or another shall pass or tender it as genuine.
   (2) It is an offence for a person to have in his custody or under his control, without lawful authority or excuse, any thing which is, and which he knows or believes to be, a counterfeit of a currency note or of a protected coin.
   (3) It is immaterial for the purposes of subsections (1) and (2) above that a coin or note is not in a fit state to be passed or tendered or that the making or counterfeiting of a coin or note has not been finished or perfected.

NOTES
This provision follows the same format as the preceding two, and serves the same kind of function as that served by s 5(1)–(2) in relation to forgery offences. The only terms requiring further comment are those of 'custody and control', which are themselves considered in the notes to s 3 of the Criminal Damage Act 1971.

Penalties See s 22(1) *infra* for subs (1); s 22(3) for subs (2).

Offences involving the making or custody or control of counterfeiting materials and implements

17. (1) It is an offence to make, or to have in his custody or under his control, any thing which he intends to use, or permit any other person to use, for the purpose of making a counterfeit of a currency note or of a protected coin with the intention that it be passed or tendered as genuine.

(2) It is an offence for a person without lawful authority or excuse—

(*a*) to make; or

(*b*) to have in his custody or under his control,

any thing which, to his knowledge, is or has been specially designed or adapted for the making of a counterfeit of a currency note.

(3) Subject to subsection (4) below, it is an offence for a person to make, or to have in his custody or under his control, any implement which, to his knowledge, is capable of imparting to anything a resemblance—

(*a*) to the whole or part of either side of a protected coin; or

(*b*) to the whole or part of the reverse of the image on either side of a protected coin.

(4) It shall be a defence for a person charged with an offence under subsection (3) above to show—

(*a*) that he made the implement or, as the case may be, had it in his custody or under control, with the written consent of the Treasury; or

(*b*) that he had lawful authority otherwise than by virtue of paragraph (*a*) above, or a lawful excuse, for making it or having it in his custody or under his control.

NOTES

This provision serves the same kind of function as that served by s 5(3)–(4) in relation to forgery offences, and it follows s 5 in distinguishing between cases where there is proof of an intent to pass false items as genuine and cases where there is not. Subs (1) deals with the more serious kind of case; subss (2) & (3) deal with the less serious kind.

Whereas subs (3) is subject to subs (4), which expressly places the burden of proving lawful authority or excuse on the defence, subs (2) is not. This would appear to suggest that proof of lawful authority or excuse is not a defence burden under subs (2), but as pointed out in the notes to s 5, proof of authority, at least might ordinarily be construed as a defence burden (see s 101 of the Magistrates Court Act 1980), so the position is not free from doubt.

'in his custody or ... control'   See the notes to s 3 of the Criminal Damage Act 1971, which uses the same concept.

'counterfeit'   See s 28 *infra*.

'currency note or protected coin'   These need not be British—see s 27 *infra*.

'passed or tendered as genuine'   See the notes to s 15 *supra*.

Penalties   See s 22(1) *infra* for subs(1); s 22(3) for subss (2) & (3).

The offence of reproducing British currency notes

18. (1) It is an offence for any person, unless the relevant authority has previously consented in writing, to reproduce on any substance what-soever, and whether or not on the correct scale, any British currency note or any part of a British currency note.

(2) In this section — "British currency note" means any note which—

(*a*) has been lawfully issued in England and Wales, Scotland or Northern Ireland; and

(*b*) is or has been customarily used as money in the country where it was issued; and

(*c*) is payable on demand; and

"the relevant authority", in relation to a British currency note of any particular description, means the authority empowered by law to issue notes of that description.

NOTES

The difference between this offence and the more serious offence created by s 14(2) *supra* is that the reproduction in this case need not be in the slightest bit capable of passing as a genuine article. It may for example be reproduced at half or double the size of the original, and it may be on board or newspaper. It could arguably be in black and white. This provision was even used on one occasion (with conspic-uous lack of success) against an artist who had painted giant banknotes on canvas. It is difficult to see any sensible use for this provision. The Law Commission argument that counterfeiters could be assisted by newspaper reproductions etc is unconvincing. Counterfeiters would be more greatly assisted by genuine notes, from which they could if they wished obtain their own photo-enlargements.

Penalty See s 22(5) *infra*.

Offences of making etc imitation British coins

19. (1) It is an offence for a person—

(*a*) to make an imitation British coin in connection with a scheme intended to promote the sale of any product or the making of contracts for the supply of any service; or

(*b*) to sell or distribute imitation British coins in connection with any such scheme, or to have imitation British coins in his custody or under his control with a view to such sale or distribution,

unless the Treasury have previously consented in writing to the sale or distribution of such imitation British coins in connection with that scheme.

(2) In this section—

"British coin" means any coin which is legal tender in any part of the United Kingdom; and

"imitation British coin" means any thing which resembles a British coin in shape, size and the substance of which it is made.

NOTES

This offence differs from those created by ss 14(2), 15(2) and 16(2) in two main respects. It can only be committed in connection with the promotion of products or services, and the coins in question need not be reasonably capable of passing as genuine. They must however resemble British coins in shape, size and substance, and it is obvious that any such coin must be capable of causing confusion in a busy store, bar etc, especially where lighting is poor or subdued. See also the notes to s 28 *infra*.

Penalty   See s. 22(5) *infra*.

Prohibition of importation of counterfeit notes and coins
20. The importation, landing or unloading of a counterfeit of a currency note or of a protected coin without the consent of the Treasury is hereby prohibited.

NOTES
'counterfeit'   See s. 28 *infra*.

'curency note or protected coin'   see s. 27 *infra*.

Offence and penalty   See s 50 of the Customs and Excise Management Act 1979. As to acquisition with intent to evade the prohibition, see s 170 of that Act.

Prohibition of exportation of counterfeit notes and coins
21. (1) The exportation of a counterfeit of a currency note or of a protected coin without the consent of the Treasury is hereby prohibited.

(2) A counterfeit of a currency note or of a protected coin which is removed to the Isle of Man from the United Kingdom shall be deemed to be exported from the United Kingdom—
    (*a*) for the purposes of this section; and
    (*b*) for the purposes of the customs and excise Acts, in their application to the prohibition imposed by this section.

(3) In section 9(1) of the Isle of Man Act 1979 (which relates to the removal of goods from the United Kingdom to the Isle of Man) after the word "below" there shall be inserted the words "and section 21(2) of the Forgery and Counterfeiting Act 1981".

NOTE
See the notes to s 20 *supra*. The offence and penalty in this case is however under s 68 of the 1979 Act.

Penalties etc

Penalties for offences under Part II
22. (1) A person guilty of an offence to which this subsection applies shall be liable—
    (*a*) on summary conviction—
        (i) to a fine not exceeding the statutory maximum; or
        (ii) to imprisonment for a term not exceeding six months; or
        (iii) to both; and
    (*b*) on conviction on indictment—
        (i) to a fine; or
        (ii) to imprisonment for a term not exceeding ten years; or
        (iii) to both.

(2) The offences to which subsection (1) above applies are offences under the following provisions of this Part of this Act—

(*a*) section 14(1);
(*b*) section 15(1);
(*c*) section 16(1); and
(*d*) section 17(1);
(3) A person guilty of an offence to which this subsection applies shall be liable—
(*a*) on summary conviction—
    (i) to a fine not exceeding the statutory maximum; or
    (ii) to imprisonment for a term not exceeding six months; or
    (iii) to both; and
(*b*) on conviction on indictment
    (i) to a fine; or
    (ii) to imprisonment for a term not exceeding two years; or
    (iii) to both.
(4) The offences to which subsection (3) above applies are offences under the following provisions of this Part of this Act—
(*a*) section 14(2);
(*b*) section 15(2);
(*c*) section 16(2);
(*d*) section 17(2); and
(*e*) section 17(3);
(5) A person guilty of an offence under section 18 or 19 above shall be liable—
(*a*) on summary conviction, to a fine not exceeding the statutory maximum; and
(*b*) on conviction on indictment, to a fine.
(6) In this section "statutory maximum", in relation to a fine on summary conviction, means—
(*a*) if the offence was committed in England and Wales . . ., the prescribed sum within the meaning of section 32 of the Magistrates' Courts Act 1980 (£2,000 or another sum fixed by order under section 143 of that Act to take account of changes in the value of money);
(b)–(c) [*omitted*].

23–24. [*omitted*].

Directors' etc liability
25. (1) Where an offence under section 18 or 19 of this Act which has been committed by a body corporate is proved to have been committed with the consent or connivance of, or to be attributable to any neglect on the part of, a director, manager, secretary or other similar officer of the body corporate, or any person who was purporting to act in any such capacity, he, as well as the body corporate, shall be guilty of that offence and be liable to be proceeded against and punished accordingly.
(2) Where the affairs of a body corporate are managed by its members, subsection (1) above shall apply in relation to the acts and defaults of a

member in connection with his functions of management as if he were a director of the body corporate.

NOTE
This provision is similar in most respects to s 18 of the Theft Act 1968 (*qv*). It differs slightly in stating that directors *etc*, may incur liability for neglect as well as for connivance, but in other respects the format is identical. See generally the notes to that provision.

26. [*omitted*]

Interpretation of Part II

Meaning of "currency note" and "protected coin"
27. (1) In this Part of this Act—
"currency note" means—
   (*a*) any note which—
      (i) has been lawfully issued in England and Wales, Scotland, Northern Ireland, any of the Channel Islands, the Isle of Man or the Republic of Ireland; and
      (ii) is or has been customarily used as money in the country where it was issued; and
      (iii) is payable on demand; or
   (*b*) any note which—
      (i) has been lawfully issued in some country other than those mentioned in paragraph (*a*)(i) above; and
      (ii) is customarily used as money in that country; and
"protected coin" means any coin which—
   (*a*) is customarily used as money in any country; or
   (*b*) is specified in an order made by the Treasury for the purposes of this Part of this Act.

(2) The power to make an order conferred on the Treasury by subsection (1) above shall be exercisable by statutory instrument.

(3) A statutory instrument containing such an order shall be laid before Parliament after being made.

NOTES
British or Irish notes come within the Act even if no longer customarily used as money (subs (1)(a)); foreign or Commonwealth notes must be in current use (subs (1)(b)). Neither kind need ever have been legal tender; Scottish notes, for example, are not legal tender even in Scotland (and see s 28(3) *infra*).
Coins must either be in current use or be specified by the Treasury for the purpose of this Act (as are Krugerrands, sovereigns *etc*). The making of copies of ancient coins cannot be an offence under this Act, however dishonest the motives.

Meaning of "counterfeit"
28. (1) For the purposes of this Part of this Act a thing is a counterfeit of a currency note or of a protected coin—
   (*a*) if it is not a currency note or a protected coin but resembles a currency note or protected coin (whether on one side only or on

both) to such an extent that it is reasonably capable of passing for a currency note or protected coin of that description; or

(b) if it is a currency note or protected coin which has been so altered that it is reasonably capable of passing for a currency note or protected coin of some other description.

(2) For the purposes of this Part of this Act—

(a) a thing consisting of one side only of a currency note, with or without the addition of other material, is a counterfeit of such a note;

(b) a thing consisting—

(i) of parts of two or more currency notes; or

(ii) of parts of a currency note, or of parts of two or more currency notes, with the addition of other material,

is capable of being a counterfeit of a currency note.

(3) References in this Part of this Act to passing or tendering a counterfeit of a currency note or a protected coin are not to be construed as confined to passing or tendering it as legal tender.

NOTES

'reasonably capable of passing for' It is not possible to argue that a one-sided note or coin is *ipso facto* incapable of passing for a genuine one, but in other respects the question of what kind of imitation can amount to a counterfeit is one of fact. An incompetent counterfeiter whose notes would fool nobody can nevertheless be guilty of an attempt to counterfeit or of an offence under s 17.

S 19 of the Act appears to assume that a coin may imitate a British coin in size, shape and substance, without necessarily being a counterfeit. Since any such coins could, in some circumstances, be confused with the real thing (*eg*, when mixed in a handful of change), it would seem that a counterfeit must be 'reasonably capable' of bearing some direct scrutiny, albeit not close or careful scrutiny.

29–32. [*omitted*]

Commencement

33. This Act shall come into force on the expiration of the period of three months from the date on which it is passed.

NOTE

The Act came into force on 28 October 1981.

Criminal Attempts Act 1981

(C. 47)

Attempting to commit an offence
1. (1) If, with intent to commit an offence to which this section applies, a person does an act which is more than merely preparatory to the commission of the offence, he is guilty of attempting to commit the offence.

(2) A person may be guilty of attempting to commit an offence to which this section applies even though the facts are such that the commission of the offence is impossible.

(3) In any case where—

(*a*) apart from this subsection a person's intention would not be regarded as having amounted to an intent to commit an offence; but

(*b*) if the facts of the case had been as he believed them to be, his intention would be so regarded,

then, for the purposes of subsection (1) above, he shall be regarded as having had an intent to commit that offence.

(4) This section applies to any offence which, if it were completed, would be triable in England and Wales as an indictable offence, other than—

(*a*) conspiracy (at common law or under section 1 of the Criminal Law Act 1977 or any other enactment);

(*b*) aiding, abetting, counselling, procuring or suborning the commission of an offence;

(*c*) offences under section 4(1) (assisting offenders) or 5(1) (accepting or agreeing to accept consideration for not disclosing information about an arrestable offence) of the Criminal Law Act 1967.

NOTES
This provision replaces the former common law offence of attempt, which has been abolished by s 6 *infra* for all purposes not relating to acts done before the commencement of the Act (ie 27 August 1981). The abolition of the common law offence was precipitated by the controversial decision of the House of Lords in *Haughton v Smith* [1975] AC 476, in which it was held that there could be no liability for attempt in circumstances where actual completion of the intended offence was impossible (ie conceptually impossible—not just beyond D's expertise or equipment). The 'impossibility' rule was difficult and unsatisfactory and has been abrogated by subss (2) and (3).

'an offence to which this section applies' The scope of this provision is delimited by sub (4). Note that is excludes purely summary offences. Attempts to commit such offences are only punishable where the statutes creating them make special provision for attempts. See for example s 5 of the Road Traffic Act 1988, which creates excess alcohol offences of driving, *attempting to drive* or being in charge of a motor vehicle whilst 'over' the prescribed limit. As to the interpretation of such provisions see s 3 *infra*.

One cannot generally be guilty of 'attempting to procure' the commission of some other offence (see subs (4)(b)); but this does not preclude liability for attempting to commit a substantive offence which is itself an offence of procuring (as for example where D attempts to procure a woman for sexual purposes contrary to ss 2, 3, 9 or 22 of the Sexual Offences Act 1956). Moreover, although subs (4)(b) precludes charges of attempting to aid, abet *etc*, it does not preclude a charge of aiding and abetting an attempt: see *R v Dunnington* [1984] 1 All ER 676.

'with intent to commit' Attempt is a crime of specific intent, and evidence of intoxication (even self-induced intoxication) may therefore be admissible to show the absence of any such intent.

Recklessness or foresight is not sufficient *mens rea* (*R v Mohan* [1976] 1 QB 1; *R v Pearman* (1985) 80 Cr App R 259), but it is possible that intent as to consequence, coupled with recklessness as to circumstances, may suffice. A man who has intercourse with a woman and is reckless as to her lack of consent is guilty of rape; he can therefore be guilty of attempted rape if he fails to achieve his object. See *R v Pigg* [1982] 2 All ER 591 and *R v Khan*, The Times, 3 February 1990. Where recklessness as to circumstances is not sufficient for the full offence (*eg* handling stolen goods), it cannot of course suffice for the attempt.

'conditional intent' The fact that D's intent may be conditional (*eg* he intends to steal the contents of a safe, provided they are valuable to him) does not mean that he lacks the *mens rea* of attempt. Most intent is conditional in some sense or other. See *Att-General's References (Nos 1 & 2 of 1979)* [1980] QB 180; *R v Bagley* [1980] Crim LR 503.

'an act which is more than merely preparatory' At common law, acts of attempt were distinguished from acts of 'mere preparation' by the concept of 'proximity'. It had to be shown that D actually *tried* to commit the offence before he could be convicted of attempt. Thus, in *R v Robinson* [1915] 2 KB 342 D was not guilty of attempting to defraud his insurers when he had done nothing more than fake a 'robbery' in his own jeweller's shop. Had he made a claim on his insurers it would obviously have been different.

The concept of 'proximity' is not expressly referred to in the statutory offence, but it would appear that the test is similar in principle. See *R v Widdowson* (1985) 82 Cr App R 314. Each case must, however, depend primarily on its own facts, and old cases (such as *Robinson*) must be seen as illustrative rather than as binding precedents. See *R v Boyle* (1986) 84 Cr App R 270.

Where D has performed the last act which he considers necessary on his part, leaving the rest to chance, to the acts of innocent agents (*eg* the Post Office) or to the acts of the victim himself, this will almost inevitably be construed as an attempt; but this does not mean that such an act is essential (*R v Gullefer* [1987] Crim LR 195) and even if such an act is proved the issue remains one of fact for the jury: *DPP v Stonehouse* [1978] AC 55.

Attempting the impossible Even at common law, it has never been any defence to a charge of attempt to show that the means adopted were inadequate or ineffective (see *R v White* [1910] 2 KB 124); but it was held in *Haughton v Smith* [1975] AC 476 that it could not be an offence to attempt to handle goods which D believed to be stolen but which turned out not to be; or to attempt to murder a person who was already dead. Subss (2) and (3) abrogate this rule entirely, so that even where D's actions turn out to be 'objectively innocent' he will be guilty of attempt if, on the facts as he believed them to be, he would have been committing or attempting to commit an offence: *R v Shivpuri* [1987] AC 1, overruling *Anderton v Ryan* [1985] AC 560. If D is not mistaken as to the facts, but mistakenly believes his actions are criminal when they are not, this mistake of law will not render him guilty of any offence. Neither subs (2) nor subs (3) applies in such circumstances.

Jurisdiction over attempts   Subs (4) restates the common law rule that conduct cannot ordinarily amount to an attempt under English law unless it is directed towards the commission of a substantive offence which would itself be indictable under the law. Since, for example, D cannot ordinarily be tried in England for obtaining property by deception in France or Scotland, he cannot be tried in England for attempting to do so, even if he does things in England which would otherwise be regarded as an attempt. If however the proposed crime was one with an extraterritorial ambit (*eg* homicide on land abroad, or hijacking of an aircraft) an attempt instigated from England or Wales would clearly be an offence under the provisions of this Act.

An attempt abroad to commit an indictable offence within the jurisdiction may also be within this provision (*R v Baxter* [1972] 1 QB 1), but probably only if some effect of that attempt is felt within the jurisdiction, thereby furthering the attempt: see *DPP v Stonehouse* [1978] AC 55 *per* Lord Keith at p 93.

Penalty etc   See s 4 *infra*.

Application of procedural and other provisions to offences under s 1

2. (1) Any provision to which this section applies shall have effect with respect to an offence under section 1 above of attempting to commit an offence as it has effect with respect to the offence attempted.

(2) This section applies to provisions of any of the following descriptions made by or under any enactment (whenever passed)—

(*a*) provisions whereby proceedings may not be instituted or carried on otherwise than by, or on behalf or with the consent of, any person (including any provisions which also make other exceptions to the prohibition);

(*b*) provisions conferring power to institute proceedings;

(*c*) provisions as to the venue of proceedings;

(*d*) provisions whereby proceedings may not be instituted after the expiration of a time limit;

(*e*) provisions conferring a power of arrest or search;

(*f*) provisions conferring a power of seizure and detention of property;

(*g*) provisions whereby a person may not be convicted or committed for trial on the uncorroborated evidence of one witness (including any provision requiring the evidence of not less than two credible witnesses);

(*h*) provisions conferring a power of forfeiture, including any power to deal with anything liable to be forfeited;

(*i*) provisions whereby, if an offence committed by a body corporate is proved to have been committed with the consent or connivance of another person, that person also is guilty of the offence.

NOTES
This provision serves the important function of ensuring that most special rules applicable to particular substantive offences (*eg* powers of arrest, or the need for the DPP's consent to the institution of proceedings) apply equally to charges of attempting to commit those offences. There is, however, at least one notable gap: there is nothing in this provision to extend English jurisdiction over acts committed abroad in an attempt to commit an extraterritorial offence: *eg* murder or manslaughter committed on land abroad is punishable under s 9 of the Offences

Against the Person Act 1861, provided that the offender is a British citizen *etc*; but there is nothing in that provision or in this (or indeed in s 1 (4) *supra*) to make an extraterritorial *attempt* so punishable.

Offences of attempt under other enactments
3. (1) Subsections (2) to (5) below shall have effect, subject to subsection (6) below, and to any inconsistent provision in any other enactment, for the purpose of determining whether a person is guilty of an attempt under a special statutory provision.
(2) For the purposes of this Act an attempt under a special statutory provision is an offence which—
  (*a*) is created by an enactment other than section 1 above, including an enactment passed after this Act; and
  (*b*) is expressed as an offence of attempting to commit another offence (in this section referred to as "the relevant full offence").
(3) A person is guilty of an attempt under a special statutory provision if, with intent to commit the relevant full offence, he does an act which is more than merely preparatory to the commission of that offence.
(4) A person may be guilty of an attempt under a special statutory provision even though the facts are such that the commission of the relevant full offence is impossible.
(5) In any case where—
  (*a*) apart from this subsection a person's intention would not be regarded as having amounted to an intent to commit the relevant full offence; but
  (*b*) if the facts of the case had been as he believed them to be, his intention would be so regarded,
then, for the purposes of subsection (3) above, he shall be regarded as having had an intent to commit that offence.
(6) Subsections (2) to (5) above shall not have effect in relation to an act done before the commencement of this Act.

NOTES
This provision ensures that offences of attempt which are *not* covered by s 1 *supra* will nevertheless be construed (in respect of issues such as proximity or impossibility *etc*) in the same way as offences under s 1 itself.
These 'specific' offences of attempt generally take the form of attempts to commit purely summary offences (s 1 applies only in respect of indictable offences). Important examples include ss 4 and 5 of the Road Traffic Act 1988 and s 173 of the Licensing Act 1964. Other forms include specific extraterritorial offences of attempt which, as explained in the notes to s 2 *supra*, do not come within the scope of s 1. See for example the Suppression of Terrorism Act 1978 s 4(1)(b).

'is expressed as an offence of attempting to commit another offence' This excludes from the ambit of this provision offences such as s 21 of the Offences Against the Person Act 1861 (attempting to choke *etc* with intent to commit some other offence). That offence, despite the use of the word 'attempt' is *not* an inchoate version of any other specific offence.

In contrast it does not matter if the full offence and the offence of attempting it are both created by the same provision. Indeed, most specific offences of attempt take precisely that form (*eg* ss 4 and 5 of the Road Traffic Act 1988).

Impossibility etc   See notes to s 1 *supra*.

Trial and penalties

4. (1) A person guilty by virtue of section 1 above of attempting to commit an offence shall—

  (*a*) if the offence attempted is murder or any other offence the sentence for which is fixed by law, be liable on conviction on indictment to imprisonment for life; and

  (*b*) if the offence attempted is indictable but does not fall within paragraph (*a*) above, be liable on conviction on indictment to any penalty to which he would have been liable on conviction on indictment of that offence; and

  (*c*) if the offence attempted is triable either way, be liable on summary conviction to any penalty to which he would have been liable on summary conviction of that offence.

(2) In any case in which a court may proceed to summary trial of an information charging a person with an offence and an information charging him with an offence under section 1 above of attempting to commit it or an attempt under a special statutory provision, the court may without his consent, try the informations together.

(3) Where, in proceedings against a person for an offence under section 1 above, there is evidence sufficient in law to support a finding that he did an act falling within subsection (1) of that section, the question whether or not his act fell within that subsection is a question of fact.

(4) Where, in proceedings against a person for an attempt under a special statutory provision, there is evidence sufficient in law to support a finding that he did an act falling within subsection (3) of section 3 above, the question whether or not his act fell within that subsection is a question of fact.

(5) Subsection (1) above shall have effect—

  (*a*) subject to section 37 of and Schedule 2 to the Sexual Offences Act 1956 (mode of trial of and penalties for attempts to commit certain offences under that Act); and

  (*b*) notwithstanding anything—

    (i) in section 32(1) (no limit to fine on conviction on indictment) of the Criminal Law Act 1977; or

    (ii) in section 31(1) and (2) (maximum of six months' imprisonment on summary conviction unless express provision made to the contrary) of the Magistrates' Courts Act 1980.

NOTES

'or any other offence the sentence for which is fixed by law'   A mandatory penalty of death by hanging is prescribed in cases of high treason (Treason Act 1814 s 1) and sentence of death is also provided in cases of piracy involving certain kinds of violence (Piracy Act 1837 s 2). See also Genocide Act 1969 s 1(2)(a).

'if the offence attempted is indictable . . .' Note that 'either way' offences are indictable, and attempts to commit them may therefore be tried on indictment under subs (1)(b). Subs (1)(c) does not restrict this option: it merely means that, whereas an attempt to commit a purely indictable offence *must* be tried on indictment under (1)(a) or (b), an attempt to commit an offence triable either way *may* be tried summarily if the accused and the court agree.

Subs (2) Following trial on indictment, a jury may convict the accused of an attempt even where he has been charged only with the complete offence (Criminal Law Act 1967 s 6), but this rule does not apply in summary proceedings; nor can the accused ordinarily be obliged to face more than one charge at a time in summary proceedings (*Brangwynne v Evans* [1962] 1 WLR 267).

This subsection avoids the latter difficulty but not the former.

Subss (3) & (4) This confirms the decision of the House of Lords in *DPP v Stonehouse* [1978] AC 55. It means that, even if D concedes that he shot at his victim and missed, the question whether this amounts to an attempt to wound is one of fact for the jury. The judge may perhaps suggest to them that, if this is not an attempt, he cannot imagine what would be, but he cannot decide the point as one of law (*ibid*).

Extension of definition of the offence of conspiracy

5.

[This provision has amended the Criminal Law Act 1977 by substituting a new s 1(1), the amendment having effect as regards all statutory conspiracies entered into or existing on or after 27 August 1981. The text of the substituted provision is reproduced in the 1977 Act (*qv*)].

Effect of Part I on common law

6. (1) The offence of attempt at common law and any offence at common law of procuring materials for crime are hereby abolished for all purposes not relating to acts done before the commencement of this Act.

(2) Except as regards offences committed before the commencement of this Act, references in any enactment passed before this Act which fall to be construed as references to the offence of attempt at common law shall be construed as references to the offence under section 1 above.

NOTES

'before the commencement of this Act' Ie before 27 August 1981.

Amendments consequential on Part I

7. (1) [*repealed*]

(2) In paragraph 3(1) of Part II of Schedule 6 to the Firearms Act 1968 the reference to an offence triable either way listed in Schedule 1 to the Magistrates' Court Act 1980 includes a reference to an offence under section 1 above of attempting to commit the offence so listed.

(3) In section 12(1)(*a*) of the Misuse of Drugs Act 1971 the reference to an offence under that Act includes a reference to an offence under section 1 above of attempting to commit such an offence.

Part II: Suspected persons etc

Abolition of offence of loitering etc with intent
8. The provisions of section 4 of the Vagrancy Act 1824 which apply to suspected persons and reputed thieves frequenting or loitering about the places described in that section with the intent there specified shall cease to have effect.

NOTE
This abolishes the notorious 'sus' law, which in certain circumstances made it an offence merely to loiter suspiciously, and the use of which was widely regarded as a source of racial tension, conflict and discrimination. See however the new offence created by s 9 *infra*.

Interference with vehicles
9. (1) A person is guilty of the offence of vehicle interference if he interferes with a motor vehicle or trailer or with anything carried in or on a motor vehicle or trailer with the intention that an offence specified in subsection (2) below shall be committed by himself or some other person.
(2) The offences mentioned in subsection (1) above are—
(*a*) theft of the motor vehicle or trailer or part of it;
(*b*) theft of anything carried in or on the motor vehicle or trailer; and
(*c*) an offence under section 12(1) of the Theft Act 1968 (taking and driving away without consent);
and, if it is shown that a person accused of an offence under this section intended that one of those offences should be committed, it is immaterial that it cannot be shown which it was.
(3) A person guilty of an offence under this section shall be liable on summary conviction to imprisonment for a term not exceeding three months or to a fine not exceeding [level 4 on the standard scale] or to both.
(4) [*repealed*]
(5) In this section "motor vehicle" and "trailer" have the meanings assigned to them by section 185(1) of the Road Traffic Act 1988.

NOTES
This offence differs from that of attempt in a number of respects. Firstly, it need not be shown that D's actions were 'more than merely preparatory' to the commission of any of the offences specified in subs (2)(a)–(c). Secondly, now that the offence of taking a conveyance without consent *etc* is a purely summary offence, there can be no prosecution for attempting to commit it. Thirdly, any prosecution for attempt would require proof as to which offence D intended to commit. Under this provision, it need only be proved that D intended that one or other such offence should be committed, and it need not be shown which one he had in mind (subs (2)).

'motor vehicle' This is defined in s 185(1) of the Road Traffic Act 1988 as a mechanically propelled vehicle designed or adapted for use on roads (thus excluding Formula One racing cars *etc!*) See further the notes to s 1 of the Road Traffic Act 1988.

'trailer'   This is defined in s 185(1) of the Road Traffic Act 1988 as a 'vehicle drawn by a motor vehicle' (thus excluding horse drawn carts *etc*).

10.   [*omitted*]

11.   [*omitted*]

Civil Aviation Act 1982

(C 16)

Application of criminal law to aircraft

92. (1) Any act or omission taking place on board a British-controlled aircraft while in flight elsewhere than in or over the United Kingdom which, if taking place in, or in a part of, the United Kingdom, would constitute an offence under the law in force in, or in that part of, the United Kingdom shall constitute that offence; but this subsection shall not apply to any act or omission which is expressly or impliedly authorised by or under that law when taking place outside the United Kingdom.

(2) Subject to any provision to the contrary in any Act passed after 14th July 1967, no proceedings for any offence under the law in force in, or in a part of, the United Kingdom committed on board an aircraft while in flight elsewhere than in or over the United Kingdom (other than an offence under, or under any instrument made under, any of the air navigation enactments) shall be instituted—

(a) in England and Wales, except by or with the consent of the Director of Public Prosecutions;

(b) [omitted]

(3) For the purpose of conferring jurisdiction, any offence under the law in force in, or in a part of, the United Kingdom committed on board an aircraft in flight shall be deemed to have been committed in any place in the United Kingdom (or, as the case may be, in that part thereof) where the offender may for the time being be.

(4) For the purposes of this section the period during which an aircraft is in flight shall be deemed to include any period from the moment when power is applied for the purpose of the aircraft taking off on a flight until the moment when the landing run (if any) at the termination of that flight ends; and any reference in this section to an aircraft in flight shall include a reference to an aircraft during any period when it is on the surface of the sea or land but not within the territorial limits of any country.

(5) In this section, except where the context otherwise requires—

"aircraft" means any aircraft, whether or not a British controlled aircraft, other than—

(a) a military aircraft; or

(b) subject to section 101(1)(b) below, an aircraft which, not being a military aircraft, belongs to or is exclusively employed in the service of Her Majesty in right of the United Kingdom;

"the air navigation enactments" mean the enactments contained in sections 60 to 62, 72 to 77, 81 to 83, 87 and 97 of this Act;

"British-controlled aircraft" means an aircraft—

(a) which is for the time being registered in the United Kingdom; or (*b*) which is not for the time being registered in any country but in the case of which either the operator of the aircraft or each person entitled as owner to any legal or beneficial interest in it satisfies the following requirements, namely—

  (i) that he is a person qualified to be the owner of a legal or beneficial interest in an aircraft registered in the United Kingdom; and

  (ii) that he resides or has his principal place of business in the United Kingdom; or

(*c*) which, being for the time being registered in some other country, is for the time being chartered by demise to a person who, or to persons each of whom, satisfies the requirements aforesaid;

"military aircraft" means—

(*a*) an aircraft of the naval, military or air forces of any country; or

(*b*) any other aircraft in respect of which there is in force a certificate issued in accordance with any Order in Council in force under section 60, 87, 89, 91, 101(1)(*a*) or 107(2) of this Act that the aircraft is to be treated for the purposes of that Order in Council as a military aircraft;

and a certificate of the Secretary of State that any aircraft is or is not a military aircraft for the purposes of this section shall be conclusive evidence of the fact certified.

(6) [*omitted*]

NOTES

Under the Civil Aviation Act 1949, there had been considerable doubt as to whether the general corpus of English criminal law was applicable to acts committed aboard British aircraft, unless the aircraft in question was in or above England or Wales at the relevant time. This remained the case until the passing of the Tokyo Convention Act 1967. This provision is largely derived from s 1 of that Act.

'British controlled aircraft'   This includes hovercraft, by virtue of s 100 of this Act and the Hovercraft (Application of Enactments) Order 1972 (SI 1972 No 971), construed in accordance with ss 17(1) and 23(2) of the Interpretation Act 1978.

'in flight'   The definition of this concept in subs (4) differs from that in s 38(3) of the Aviation Security Act 1982 (*qv*). As far as the offence of hijacking is concerned, s 1 of that Act applies from the moment that the aircraft's external doors are closed prior to take-off.

'elsewhere than in or over the United Kingdom'   English courts have no jurisdiction under this Act where crimes are committed in aircraft flying over Scotland or Northern Ireland.

'for the purpose of conferring jurisdiction' (subs (3))   This subsection overcomes difficulties relating to the jurisdiction of magistrates' courts over purely summary offences. It is of no relevance in relation to indictable or 'either way' offences.

'subject to s 101(1)(b)'   The provision referred to enables Orders in Council to be made, applying s 92 (with or without modifications) to such aircraft as are referred to in s 92(2)(b) (*ie* to Crown aircraft *etc*).

[*Other sections omitted*]

Taking of Hostages Act 1982

(C 28)

Hostage-taking

1. (1) A person, whatever his nationality, who, in the United Kingdom or elsewhere—

(a) detains any other person ("the hostage"), and

(b) in order to compel a State, international governmental organisation or person to do or abstain from doing any act, threatens to kill, injure or continue to detain the hostage,

commits an offence.

(2) A person guilty of an offence under this Act shall be liable, on conviction on indictment, to imprisonment for life.

NOTES

This offence overlaps to some extent with the common law offences of kidnapping and false imprisonment, but differs from them in at least two important respects.

Firstly, it is an offence of universal jurisdiction, so that a person may be convicted of it even if he is a foreigner who has committed it entirely abroad.

Secondly, the hostage-taking must be committed for one or more of the reasons specified in sub (1)(b), and must involve threats of the kind there specified.

'international governmental organisation' This term is not defined in the Act, but clearly includes organisations such as the United Nations and the European Economic Community. Many bodies which are not governmental or international may nevertheless constitute corporations, and thus 'persons' within the terms of this provision. Organisations which are not corporations will in practice be run by individuals or corporations, and the hostage takers' threats will no doubt be directed at them.

Prosecution of offences

2. (1) Proceedings for an offence under this Act shall not be instituted—

(a) in England and Wales, execpt by or with the consent of the Attorney General;

(b) [*omitted*]

(2) [*omitted*]

(3) [*omitted*]

3–5. [*omitted*]

Short title and commencement

6. (1) This Act may be cited as the Taking of Hostages Act 1982.

(2) This Act shall come into force on such day as Her Majesty may by Order in Council appoint.

NOTE

The Act was brought into force on 26 November 1982.

Firearms Act 1982

(C 31)

Control of imitation firearms readily convertible into firearms to which section 1 of the 1968 Act applies

1. (1) This Act applies to an imitation firearm if—

(*a*) it has the appearance of being a firearm to which section 1 of the 1968 Act (firearms requiring a firearm certificate) applies; and

(*b*) it is so constructed or adapted as to be readily convertible into a firearm to which that section applies.

(2) Subject to section 2(2) of this Act and the following provisions of this section, the 1968 Act shall apply in relation to an imitation firearm to which this Act applies as it applies in relation to a firearm to which section 1 of that Act applies.

(3) Subject to the modifications in subsection (4) below, any expression given a meaning for the purposes of the 1968 Act has the same meaning in this Act.

(4) For the purposes of this section and the 1968 Act, as it applies by virtue of this section—

(*a*) the definition of air weapon in section 1(3)(*b*) of that Act (air weapons excepted from requirement of firearm certificate) shall have effect without the exclusion of any type declared by rules made by the Secretary of State under section 53 of that Act to be specially dangerous; and

(*b*) the definition of firearms in section 57(1) of that Act shall have effect without paragraphs (*b*) and (*c*) of that subsection (component parts and accessories).

(5) In any proceedings brought by virtue of this section for an offence under the 1968 Act involving an imitation firearm to which this Act applies, it shall be a defence for the accused to show that he did not know and had no reason to suspect that the imitation firearm was so constructed or adapted as to be readily convertible into a firearm to which section 1 of that Act applies.

(6) For the purposes of this section an imitation firearm shall be regarded as readily convertible into a firearm to which section 1 of the 1968 Act applies if—

(*a*) it can be so converted without any special skill on the part of the person converting it in the construction or adaptation of firearms of any description; and

(*b*) the work involved in converting it does not require equipment or tools other than such as are in common use by persons carrying out works of construction and maintenance in their own homes.

NOTES
The possession or use of imitation firearms for a criminal purpose may lead to liability under a number of other enactments, including ss 17 and 18 of the Firearms Act 1968 and s 10 of the Theft Act 1968, whether or not the imitation weapons are readily convertible into working order, and whether or not they resemble firearms to which s 1 of the 1968 Act applies. Plastic toys and dummy shotguns, for example, would both be within the scope of those provisions, but do not come within the scope of this one.

The effect of this provision is to apply the terms of the 1968 Act, with certain exceptions, to those imitation weapons which are 'readily convertible' within the meaning of subs (6). One would therefore need a firearms certificate to possess one; the acquisition of such an article by a person under the age of seventeen is prohibited etc.

SS 16–20 of the 1968 Act are not affected by this Act (although the scope of ss 17 and 18 is in any case wider). See s 2 *infra*.

'imitation firearm' See s 57(4) of the 1968 Act.

'firearm to which s 1 of the 1968 Act applies' Reference must be made to that provision, which excludes most shotguns and most air weapons. High-powered air weapons do come within that provision, but see s 1(4)(a) of this Act, which effectively excludes imitations thereof.

Provisions supplementary to section 1
2. (1) Subject to subsection (2) below, references in the 1968 Act, and in any order made under section 6 of that Act (orders prohibiting movement of firearms or ammunition) before this Act comes into force—

(*a*) to firearms (without qualification); or

(*b*) to firearms to which section 1 of that Act applies;

shall be read as including imitation firearms to which this Act applies.

(2) The following provisions of the 1968 Act do not apply by virtue of this Act to an imitation firearm to which this Act applies, that is to say—

(*a*) section 4(3) and (4) (offence to convert anything having appearance of firearm into a firearm and aggravated offence under section 1 involving a converted firearm); and

(*b*) the provisions of that Act which relate to, or to the enforcement of control over, the manner in which a firearm is used or the circumstances in which it is carried;

but without prejudice, in the case of the provisions mentioned in paragraph (*b*) above, to the application to such an imitation firearm of such of those provisions as apply to imitation firearms apart from this Act.

(3) The provisions referred to in subsection (2)(*b*) are sections 16 to 20 and section 47.

NOTE
Subs (2)(*a*) This means that it is not an offence under s 4(3) of the 1968 Act to carry out a limited or incomplete conversion on a replica firearm, so that it becomes 'readily convertible' (within the meaning of s 1(6) *supra*) into full working order, nor is the unauthorised possession of such a partial conversion an aggravated offence under s 4(4).

3–4. [*omitted*]

Aviation Security Act 1982

(C 36)

Hijacking
1. (1) A person on board an aircraft in flight who unlawfully, by the use of force or by threats of any kind, seizes the aircraft or exercises control of it commits the offence of hijacking, whatever his nationality, whatever the State in which the aircraft is registered and whether the aircraft is in the United Kingdom or elsewhere, but subject to subsection (2) below.

(2) If—

(*a*) the aircraft is used in military, customs or police service, or

(*b*) both the place of take-off and the place of landing are in the territory of the State in which the aircraft is registered,

subsection (1) above shall not apply unless—

(i) the person seizing or exercising control of the aircraft is a United Kingdom national; or

(ii) his act is committed in the United Kingdom; or

(iii) the aircraft is registered in the United Kingdom or is used in the military or customs service of the United Kingdom or in the service of any police force in the United Kingdom.

(3) A person who commits the offence of hijacking shall be liable, on conviction on indictment, to imprisonment for life.

(4) If the Secretary of State by order made by statutory instrument declares—

(*a*) that any two or more States named in the order have established an organisation or agency which operates aircraft; and

(*b*) that one of those States has been designated as exercising, for aircraft so operated, the powers of the State of registration,

the State declared under paragraph (*b*) of this subsection shall be deemed for the purposes of this section to be the State in which any aircraft so operated is registered; but in relation to such an aircraft subsection (2)(*b*) above shall have effect as if it referred to the territory of any one of the States named in the order.

(5) For the purposes of this section the territorial waters of any State shall be treated as part of its territory.

NOTES
Hijacking is a different offence from air piracy (as to which see s 5 *infra*) and was introduced into English law by the Hijacking Act 1971, the provisions of which are re-enacted in this consolidating legislation. The Hijacking Act enabled the United Kingdom to ratify the 1970 Hague Convention on the unlawful seizure of aircraft.

'aircraft' No definition of this term is provided in the Act. For the purpose of s 5 *infra* the definition provided in s 92(5) of the Civil Aviation Act applies, but it does not strictly apply to other sections of the Act. As a result, it would appear that hovercraft are not included. (The Hovercraft (Application of Enactments) Order was never applied to the original Hijacking Act.) Helicopters and airships must, however, be regarded as types of aircraft in the absence of any express indication to the contrary.

'in flight' See s 38(3)(a) *infra*. Note that the definition for these purposes is wider than that adopted in s 92 of the Civil Aviation Act 1982 (*qv*).

'threats of any kind' This might arguably include a threat to commit suicide, even in circumstances which pose no possible danger to any other person.

'seizes or exercises control' It is no defence to show that the pilot or commander of the aircraft was a willing accomplice of the hijacker, if force or threats were used against other members of the crew: *R v Moussa Membar* [1983] Crim LR 618. The pilot may indeed be guilty as an accessory to the offence.

Subs (2) Except where subs (2) applies, hijacking is an offence of universal jurisdiction.

'United Kingdom national' See s 38(1) *infra*.

'military ... service' See s 38(1) *infra*.

'his act is committed in the United Kingdom' Hijacking includes, not only the seizure of an aircraft, but also the subsequent exercise of control over it, so if a foreign military aircraft is hijacked abroad and flown to England, jurisdiction may be claimed under subs (2)(ii).

Destroying, damaging or endangering safety of aircraft
2. (1) It shall, subject to subsection (4) below, be an offence for any person unlawfully and intentionally—

(*a*) to destroy an aircraft in service or so to damage such an aircraft as to render it incapable of flight or as to be likely to endanger its safety in flight; or

(*b*) to commit on board an aircraft in flight any act of violence which is likely to endanger the safety of the aircraft.

(2) It shall also, subject to subsection (4) below, be an offence for any person unlawfully and intentionally to place, or cause to be placed, on an aircraft in service any device or substance which is likely to destroy the aircraft, or is likely so to damage it as to render it incapable of flight or as to be likely to endanger its safety in flight; but nothing in this subsection shall be construed as limiting the circumstances in which the commission of any act—

(*a*) may constitute an offence under subsection (1) above, or

(*b*) may constitute attempting or conspiring to commit, or aiding, abetting, counselling or procuring, or being art and part in, the commission of such an offence.

(3) Except as provided by subsection (4) below, subsections (1) and (2) above shall apply whether any such act as is therein mentioned is committed in the United Kingdom or elsewhere, whatever the nationality of the person committing the act and whatever the State in which the aircraft is registered.

(4) Subsections (1) and (2) above shall not apply to any act committed in relation to an aircraft used in military, customs or police service unless—

(a) the act is committed in the United Kingdom, or

(b) where the act is committed outside the United Kingdom, the person committing it is a United Kingdom national.

(5) A person who commits an offence under this section shall be liable, on conviction on indictment, to imprisonment for life.

(6) In this section "unlawfully"—

(a) in relation to the commission of an act in the United Kingdom, means so as (apart from this Act) to constitute an offence under the law of the part of the United Kingdom in which the act is committed, and

(b) in relation to the commission of an act outside the United Kingdom, means so that the commission of the act would (apart from this Act) have been an offence under the law of England and Wales if it had been committed in England and Wales or of Scotland if it had been committed in Scotland.

(7) In this section "act of violence" means—

(a) any act done in the United Kingdom which constitutes the offence of murder, attempted murder, manslaughter, culpable homicide or assault or an offence under section 18, 20, 21, 22, 23, 24, 28 or 29 of the Offences against the Person Act 1861 or under section 2 of the Explosive Substances Act 1883, and

(b) any act done outside the United Kingdom which, if done in the United Kingdom, would constitute such an offence as is mentioned in paragraph (a) above.

NOTES

This provision replaces those originally contained in the Protection of Aircraft Act 1973, which themselves had enabled the United Kingdom to ratify the Montreal Convention of 1971.

Where acts of damage or destruction are committed in England and Wales, there is an overlap between this provision and those of the Criminal Damage Act 1971 or the Explosive Substances Act 1883 (*qqv*), but subs (3) gives this provision a universal ambit not shared by the others.

'aircraft' See the notes to s 1 *supra*.

'in flight'; 'in service' See s 38(3) *infra*.

'intentionally'; 'likely' Reckless acts resulting in the destruction etc of an aircraft do not create liability under this provision (but may do under the Criminal Damage Act). If, however, an intentional act of damage or violence is likely to endanger the safety of an aircraft in flight, there would appear to be no need to prove that the person responsible appreciated that danger, or even that he should have done. It may be enough that it proves objectively dangerous.

Subs (4) This subsection serves the same purpose as s 1(2) serves in relation to hijacking; but note that, whereas the hijacking of a foreign aircraft is no offence under s 1 if it both takes off and lands in its own country, there is no corresponding limitation on the scope of s 2. Many hijackings will involve acts of violence which may endanger the safety of the aircraft, and thus amount to offences under s 2 even if s 1(2) prevents a charge of hijacking.

'United Kingdom national' See s 38(1) *infra*.

Other acts endangering or likely to endanger safety of aircraft

3. (1) It shall, subject to subsections (5) and (6) below, be an offence for any person unlawfully and intentionally to destroy or damage any property to which this subsection applies, or to interfere with the operation of any such property, where the destruction, damage or interference is likely to endanger the safety of aircraft in flight.

(2) Subsection (1) above applies to any property used for the provision of air navigation facilities, including any land, building or ship so used, and including any apparatus or equipment so used, whether it is on board an aircraft or elsewhere.

(3) It shall also, subject to subsections (4) and (5) below, be an offence for any person intentionally to communicate any information which is false, misleading or deceptive in a material particular, where the communication of the information endangers the safety of an aircraft in flight or is likely to endanger the safety of aircraft in flight.

(4) It shall be a defence for a person charged with an offence under subsection (3) above to prove—

(a) that he believed, and had reasonable grounds for believing, that the information was true; or

(b) that, when he communicated the information, he was lawfully employed to perform duties which consisted of or included the communication of information and that he communicated the information in good faith in the performance of those duties.

(5) Subsections (1) and (3) above shall not apply to the commission of any act unless either the act is committed in the United Kingdom, or, where it is committed outside the United Kingdom—

(a) the person committing it is a United Kingdom national; or

(b) the commission of the act endangers or is likely to endanger the safety in flight of a civil aircraft registered in the United Kingdom or chartered by demise to a lessee whose principal place of business, or (if he has no place of business) whose permanent residence, is in the United Kingdom; or

(c) the act is committed on board a civil aircraft which is so registered or so chartered; or

(d) the act is committed on board a civil aircraft which lands in the United Kingdom with the person who committed the act still on board.

(6) Subsection (1) above shall also not apply to any act committed outside the United Kingdom and so committed in relation to property which is situated outside the United Kingdom and is not used for the provision of air navigation facilities in connection with international air navigation, unless the person committing the act is a United Kingdom national.

(7) A person who commits an offence under this section shall be liable, on conviction on indictment, to imprisonment for life.

(8) In this section "civil aircraft" means any aircraft other than an aircraft used in military, customs or police service and "unlawfully" has the same meaning as in section 2 of this Act.

NOTES
This provision is also derived from the 1973 Act (see the notes to s 2 *supra*). As with s 2, the offence created by subs (1) overlaps with offences under the Criminal Damage Act, but enjoys a wider jurisdictional ambit by virtue of subss (5)–(6). That ambit is not, however as wide as those of ss 1 & 2.

'intentionally'; 'likely' See the notes to s 2 *supra*.

'aircraft' See the notes to s 1 *supra*.

'in flight' See s 38(3) *infra*.

Subs (3) Bomb hoaxes are the obvious examples of offences under this subsection (and see also s 51 of the Criminal Law Act 1977). The prosecution must prove that the information communicated was false, deceptive or misleading, and that D intentionally communicated it; but if D wishes to rely on one of the defences created by subs (4), the burden of proving it (on the balance of probabilities) will lie on the defence. This means that a jury may be required to find D guilty of an offence punishable with life imprisonment, even though they consider it quite possible that he communicated a false warning in the honest belief that it was true. Even if they are satisfied as to his honest belief, subs (4)(a) offers D no defence unless that belief was based on reasonable grounds.

'United Kingdom national' See s 38(1) *infra*.

Offences in relation to certain dangerous articles
4. (1) It shall be an offence for any person without lawful authority or reasonable excuse (the proof of which shall lie on him) to have with him—

   (*a*) in any aircraft registered in the United Kingdom, whether at a time when the aircraft is in the United Kingdom or not, or

   (*b*) in any other aircraft at a time when it is in, or in flight over, the United Kingdom, or

   (*c*) in any part of an aerodrome in the United Kingdom, or

   (*d*) in any air navigation installation in the United Kingdom which does not form part of an aerodrome,

any article to which this section applies.

(2) This section applies to the following articles, that is to say—

   (*a*) any firearm, or any article having the appearance of being a firearm, whether capable of being discharged or not;

   (*b*) any explosive, any article manufactured or adapted (whether in the form of a bomb, grenade or otherwise) so as to have the appearance of being an explosive, whether it is capable of producing a practical effect by explosion or not, or any article marked or labelled so as to indicate that it is or contains an explosive; and

   (*c*) any article (not falling within either of the preceding paragraphs) made or adapted for use for causing injury to or incapacitating a person or for destroying or damaging property, or intended by the person having it with him for such use, whether by him or by any other person.

(3) For the purposes of this section a person who is for the time being in an aircraft, or in part of an aerodrome, shall be treated as having with him in the aircraft, or in that part of the aerodrome, as the case may be, an article to which this section applies if—

(*a*) where he is in an aircraft, the article, or an article in which it is contained, is in the aircraft and has been caused (whether by him or by any other person) to be brought there as being, or as forming part of, his baggage on a flight in the aircraft or has been caused by him to be brought there as being, or as forming part of, any other property to be carried on such a flight, or

(*b*) where he is in part of an aerodrome (otherwise than in an aircraft), the article, or an article in which it is contained, is in that or any other part of the aerodrome and has been caused (whether by him or by any other person) to be brought into the aerodrome as being, or as forming part of, his baggage on a flight from that aerodrome or has been caused by him to be brought there as being, or as forming part of, any other property to be carried on such a flight on which he is also to be carried,

notwithstanding that the circumstances may be such that (apart from this subsection) he would not be regarded as having the article with him in the aircraft or in a part of the aerodrome, as the case may be.

(4) A person guilty of an offence under this section shall be liable—

(*a*) on summary conviction, to a fine not exceeding the statutory maximum or to imprisonment for a term not exceeding three months or to both;

(*b*) on conviction on indictment, to a fine or to imprisonment for a term not exceeding five years or to both.

(5) Nothing in subsection (3) above shall be construed as limiting the circumstances in which a person would, apart from that subsection, be regarded as having an article with him as mentioned in subsection (1) above.

NOTES

Unlike ss 1–3, this section is primarily territorial in application: but subs (1)(a) is capable of applying to UK registered aircraft anywhere in the world, even when they are not in flight.

'aerodrome'; **'air navigation installation';** **'firearm';** **'article';** **'explosive'** See s 38(1) *infra*.

'in flight over the United Kingdom' This includes flight over adjacent territorial waters: see s 38(4) *infra*.

'article having the appearance of being a firearm' This could include a plastic toy if it was brandished in such a way or in such circumstances that it might be mistaken for a real weapon.

Jurisdiction of courts in respect of air piracy

5. (1) Any court in the United Kingdom having jurisdiction in respect of piracy committed on the high seas shall have jurisdiction in respect of piracy committed by or against an aircraft, wherever that piracy is committed.

(2) In subsection (1) above, "aircraft" has the same meaning as in section 92 of the Civil Aviation Act 1982 (application of criminal law to aircraft); and, for the purposes of this definition, section 101 of that Act

(Crown aircraft) shall apply to this section as it applies to the said section 92.

NOTES
Piracy *jure gentium* was defined for the purposes of international law by the 1958 Geneva Convention on the High Seas, and this definition was incorporated into English law by s 4 of the Tokyo Convention Act 1967, the relevant articles of the Convention being reproduced in the schedule to that Act. Air piracy, as opposed to hijacking, would appear to be a difficult offence to commit, since the seizure of an aircraft by its own passengers or crew is not capable of being an act of piracy. One could perhaps envisage a helicopter being used to plunder a ship; this would be piracy under art 15(1) of the Convention.

'any court ... having jurisdiction in respect of piracy' In England and Wales this means the Crown Court: see s 46(2) of the Supreme Court Act 1981.

'wherever that piracy is committed' Piracy *jure gentium* can only be committed on or over the High Seas or in a place outside the jurisdiction of any state (*eg* in Antarctica): art 15 *supra*.

Ancillary offences
  6. (1) Without prejudice to section 92 of the Civil Aviation Act 1982 (application of criminal law to aircraft) or to section 2(1)(*b*) of this Act, where a person (of whatever nationality) does on board any aircraft (wherever registered) and while outside the United Kingdom any act which, if done in the United Kingdom would constitute the offence of murder, attempted murder, manslaughter, culpable homicide or assault or an offence under section 18, 20, 21, 22, 23, 28 or 29 of the Offences against the Person Act 1861 or section 2 of the Explosive Substances Act 1883, his act shall constitute that offence if it is done in connection with the offence of hijacking committed or attempted by him on board that aircraft.
  (2) It shall be an offence for any person in the United Kingdom to induce or assist the commission outside the United Kingdom of any act which—
  (*a*) would, but for subsection (2) of section 1 of this Act, be an offence under that section; or
  (*b*) would, but for subsection (4) of section 2 of this Act, be an offence under that section; or
  (*c*) would, but for subsection (5) or (6) of section 3 of this Act, be an offence under that section.
  (3) A person who commits an offence under subsection (2) above shall be liable, on conviction on indictment, to imprisonment for life.
  (4) Subsection (2) above shall have effect without prejudice to the operation, in relation to any offence under section 1, 2 or 3 of this Act—
  (*a*) in England and Wales, or in Northern Ireland, of section 8 of the Accessories and Abettors Act 1861; or
  (*b*) [*omitted*]

NOTES
Subs (1) This provides British courts with jurisdiction over any of the specified offences which might be committed in the course of a hijacking attempt that itself

comes within British jurisdiction under s 1 *supra*. In view of the possible life sentence that may be imposed for hijacking, the importance of a power to deal with other offences is not enormous; but it is clearly desirable that any really serious additional offence, such as murder, may be charged as a separate count to the indictment.

Subss (2)–(3) The Hague and Montreal Conventions do not authorise states to claim jurisdiction over foreigners who hijack or sabotage foreign military, customs or police aircraft in foreign countries; but the United Kingdom has every right to exercise jurisdiction over persons who induce or assist in such offences whilst they themselves are within its territorial limits.

'induce or assist' The nearest equivalent terms in the Accessories and Abettors Act 1861 (*qv*) are 'counsel or procure'.

7. [*omitted*]

Prosecution of offences and proceedings
8. (1) Proceedings for an offence under any of the preceding provisions of this Part of this Act (other than sections 4 and 7) shall not be instituted—
    (*a*) in England and Wales, except by, or with the consent of, the Attorney General; and
    (*b*) in Northern Ireland, except by, or with the consent of, the Attorney General for Northern Ireland.
    (2) [*omitted*]

9–37. [*omitted*]

Interpretation etc
38. (1) In this Act, except in so far as the context otherwise requires—
"act of violence" shall be construed in accordance with section 2(7) or, as the case may require, section 10(2) of this Act;
"aerodrome" means the aggregate of the land, buildings and works comprised in an aerodrome within the meaning of the Civil Aviation Act 1982 and (if and so far as not comprised in an aerodrome as defined in that Act) any land, building or works situated within the boundaries of an area designated, by an order made by the Secretary of State which is for the time being in force, as constituting the area of an aerodrome for the purposes of this Act;
"air navigation installation" means any building, works, apparatus or equipment used wholly or mainly for the purpose of assisting air traffic control or as an aid to air navigation, together with any land contiguous or adjacent to any such building, works, apparatus or equipment and used wholly or mainly for purposes connected therewith;
"aircraft registered or operating in the United Kingdom" means any aircraft which is either—

(a) an aircraft registered in the United Kingdom, or

(b) an aircraft not so registered which is for the time being allocated for use on flights which (otherwise than in exceptional circumstances) include landing at or taking off from one or more aerodromes in the United Kingdom;

"article" includes any substance, whether in solid or liquid form or in the form of a gas or vapour;

"constable" includes any person having the powers and privileges of a constable;

"explosive" means any article manufactured for the purpose of producing a practical effect by explosion, or intended for that purpose by a person having the article with him;

"firearm" includes an airgun or air pistol;

"manager", in relation to an aerodrome, means the person (whether ... the Civil Aviation Authority, a local authority or any other person) by whom the aerodrome is managed;

"military service" includes naval and air force service;

"measures" (without prejudice to the generality of that expression) includes the construction, execution, alteration, demolition or removal of buildings or other works and also includes the institution or modification, and the supervision and enforcement, of any practice or procedure;

"operator" has the same meaning as in the Civil Aviation Act 1982;

"property" includes any land, buildings or works, any aircraft or vehicle and any baggage, cargo or other article of any description;

"the statutory maximum" means—

(a) in England and Wales, the prescribed sum within the meaning of section 32 of the Magistrates' Courts Act 1980 (that is to say, [£2,000] or another sum fixed by order under section 143 of that Act to take account of changes in the value of money);

(b) [omitted]

(c) [omitted]

"United Kingdom national" means an individual who is—

(a) a British citizen, a British Dependent Territories citizen [, a British National (Overseas)] or a British Overseas citizen;

(b) a person who under the British Nationality Act 1981 is a British subject; or

(c) a British protected person (within the meaning of that Act).

(2) For the purposes of this Act—

(a) in the case of an air navigation installation provided by, or used wholly or mainly by, the Civil Aviation Authority, that Authority, and

(b) in the case of any other air navigation installation, the manager of an aerodrome by whom it is provided, or by whom it is wholly or mainly used,

shall be taken to be the authority responsible for that air navigation installation.

(3) For the purposes of this Act—

(a) the period during which an aircraft is in flight shall be deemed to include any period from the moment when all its external doors are closed following embarkation until the moment when any such door is opened for disembarkation, and, in the case of a forced landing, any period until the competent authorities take over responsibility for the aircraft and for persons and property on board; and

(b) an aircraft shall be taken to be in service during the whole of the period which begins with the pre-flight preparation of the aircraft for a flight and ends 24 hours after the aircraft lands having completed that flight, and also at any time (not falling within that period) while, in accordance with the preceding paragraph, the aircraft is in flight,

and anything done on board an aircraft while in flight over any part of the United Kingdom shall be treated as done in that part of the United Kingdom.

(4) For the purposes of this Act the territorial waters adjacent to any part of the United Kingdom shall be treated as included in that part of the United Kingdom.

(5) Any power to make an order under subsection (1) above shall be exercisable by statutory instrument; and any statutory instrument containing any such order shall be subject to annulment in pursuance of a resolution of either House of Parliament.

(6) Any power to give a direction under any provision of this Act shall be construed as including power to revoke or vary any such direction by a further direction given under that provision.

(7) Subject to section 18 of the Interpretation Act 1978 (which relates to offences under two or more laws), Part I of this Act shall not be construed as—

(a) conferring a right of action in any civil proceedings in respect of any contravention of this Act, or

(b) derogating from any right of action or other remedy (whether civil or criminal) in proceedings instituted otherwise than under this Act.

(8) [omitted]

39–40. [omitted]

Short title and commencement
41. (1) This Act may be cited as the Aviation Security Act 1982.

(2) This Act shall come into force on the expiration of the period of three months beginning with its passing.

NOTE
The Act came into force on 23 October 1982, but offences under the Act were previously subject to identical penalties under the Hijacking Act 1971 or the Protection of Aircraft Act 1973.

Child Abduction Act 1984

(C 37)

Offences under law of England and Wales

Offence of abduction of child by parent, etc.

1. (1) Subject to subsections (5) and (8) below, a person connected with a child under the age of sixteen commits an offence if he takes or sends the child out of the United Kingdom without the appropriate consent.

(2) A person is connected with a child for the purposes of this section if—

(a) he is a parent or guardian of the child; or

(b) there is in force an order of [a court in the United Kingdom] awarding custody of the child to him, whether solely or jointly with any other person; or

(c) in the case of an illegitimate child, there are reasonable grounds for believing that he is the father of the child.

(3) In this section "the appropriate consent," in relation to a child, means—

(a) the consent of each person—

(i) who is a parent or guardian of the child; or

(ii) to whom custody of the child has been awarded (whether solely or jointly with any other person) by an order of [a court in the United Kingdom], or

(b) if the child is the subject of such a custody order, the leave of the court which made the order; or

(c) the leave of the court granted on an application for a direction under section 7 of the Guardianship of Minors Act 1971 or section 1(3) of the Guardianship Act 1973.

(4) In the case of a custody order made by a magistrates' court, subsection (3)(b) above shall be construed as if the reference to the court which made the order included a reference to any magistrates' court acting for the same petty sessions area as that court.

(5) A person does not commit an offence under this section by doing anything without the consent of another person whose consent is required under the foregoing provisions if—

(a) he does it in the belief that the other person—

(i) has consented; or

(ii) would consent if he was aware of all the relevant circumstances; or

(b) he has taken all reasonable steps to communicate with the other person but has been unable to communicate with him; or

(c) the other person has unreasonably refused to consent,

279

but paragraph (*c*) of this subsection does not apply where what is done relates to a child who is the subject of a custody order made by [a court in the United Kingdom], or where the person who does it acts in breach of any direction under section 7 of the Guardianship of Minors Act 1971 or section 1(3) of the Guardianship Act 1973.

(6) Where, in proceedings for an offence under this section, there is sufficient evidence to raise an issue as to the application of subsection (5) above, it shall be for the prosecution to prove that that subsection does not apply.

(7) In this section—

(*a*) "guardian" means a person appointed by deed or will or by order of a court of competent jurisdiction to be the guardian of a child; and

(*b*) a reference to a custody order or an order awarding custody includes a reference to an order awarding legal custody and a reference to an order awarding care and control.

(8) This section shall have effect subject to the provisions of the Schedule to this Act in relation to a child who is in the care of a local authority or voluntary organisation or who is committed to a place of safety or who is the subject of custodianship proceedings or proceedings or an order relating to adoption.

NOTES

This offence must be distinguished both from the common law offence of kidnapping, and from the offence created by s 2 *infra*. A parent cannot commit the s 2 offence, even if he has no legal right of access to his child. He can under certain circumstances be guilty of kidnapping his own child (*R v D* [1984] AC 778), but kidnapping involves taking by force or fraud, without the consent of the victim. A parent without legal custody who entices his child away from the custodial parent or foster home *etc* therefore commits none of these offences unless he takes or sends the child out of the United Kingdom, or unless the child is regarded as too young or immature to give effective consent.

As to restrictions on prosecutions for kidnapping by parents *etc*, see s 5 *infra*.

'takes or sends' See s 3 *infra*.

'United Kingdom' This does not include the Channel Islands or the Isle of Man.

Subs (8) Where the schedule (*infra*) applies, the main effects are that a different consent is needed from that specified in subs (3), and no defence may be raised under subs (5).

Penalty etc See s 4 *infra*.

Offence of abduction of child by other persons

2. (1) Subject to subsection (2) below, a person not falling within section 1(2)(*a*) or (*b*) above commits an offence if, without lawful authority or reasonable excuse, he takes or detains a child under the age of sixteen—

(*a*) so as to remove him from the lawful control of any person having lawful control of the child; or

(*b*) so as to keep him out of the lawful control of any person entitled to lawful control of the child.

(2) In proceedings against any person for an offence under this section, it shall be a defence for that person to show that at the time of the alleged offence—

(*a*) he believed that the child had attained the age of sixteen; or

(*b*) in the case of an illegitimate child, he had reasonable grounds for believing himself to be the child's father.

NOTES

As to the relationship between this offence and kidnapping, see the notes to s 1 *supra*. There is also a potential overlap with abduction offences under the Sexual Offences Act 1956, particularly s 20 (*qv*), which does not specifically require there to be any sexual motive for the abduction of a girl under sixteen years of age. The present offence nevertheless has a somewhat wider scope, in that it covers acts which interfere with the responsibilities of persons (such as school teachers) who have lawful control of the child at the time. It may also cover very brief interferences, which would not be sufficient for liability under the 1956 Act (see *R v Jones* [1973] Crim LR 621), and of course the sex of the child is unimportant.

'takes or detains' See s 3 *infra*.

'without lawful authority' This would most obviously include the consent of the person having lawful control of the child.

Subs (2) These defences would have to be proved on the balance of probability. It is not intended that putative fathers should incur liability under s 2, since they are regarded as connected with the child under s 1(2) *supra*.

Penalty etc See s 4 *infra*.

Construction of references to taking, sending and detaining

3. For the purposes of this Part of this Act—

(*a*) a person shall be regarded as taking a child if he causes or induces the child to accompany him or any other person or causes the child to be taken;

(*b*) a person shall be regarded as sending a child if he causes the child to be sent; and

(*c*) a person shall be regarded as detaining a child if he causes the child to be detained or induces the child to remain with him or any other person.

NOTES

It would not seem necessary that the taking *etc* should last for more than a short time, although the *de minimis* rule would apply so as to exclude insignificant incidents.

'causes or induces' 'Causing' the act of another usually means ordering or directing it (*Houston v Buchanan* [1940] 2 All ER 179). A person who agrees to a child's request to drive him away from a hated school or home would not therefore appear either to cause or to induce the child to accompany him. If s 3 is construed as providing an exhaustive definition of the terms 'taking', 'sending', *etc*, that person would not incur liability under this Act.

Penalties and prosecutions
4. (1) A person guilty of an offence under this Part of this Act shall be liable—

(a) on summary conviction, to imprisonment for a term not exceeding six months or to a fine not exceeding the statutory maximum, as defined in section 74 of the Criminal Justice Act 1982, or to both such imprisonment and fine;

(b) on conviction on indictment, to imprisonment for a term not exceeding seven years.

(2) No prosecution for an offence under section 1 above shall be instituted except by or with the consent of the Director of Public Prosecutions.

Restriction on prosecutions for offence of kidnapping
5. Except by or with the consent of the Director of Public Prosecutions no prosecutions shall be instituted for an offence of kidnapping if it was committed—

(a) against a child under the age of sixteen; and

(b) by a person connected with the child, within the meaning of section 1 above.

NOTES
As to the common law offence of kidnapping, see *R v D* [1984] AC 778 and the notes to s 1 *supra*. The restriction imposed by this provision matches that imposed by s 4(2) in respect of s 1 offences.

6–13. [*omitted*]

SCHEDULE
(Section 1(8))

Modifications of section 1 for children in certain cases

Children in care of local authorities and voluntary organisations
1. (1) This paragraph applies in the case of a child who is in the care of a local authority or voluntary organisation in England or Wales.

(2) Where this paragraph applies, section 1 of this Act shall have effect as if—

(a) the reference in subsection (1) to the appropriate consent were a reference to the consent of the local authority or voluntary organisation in whose care the child is; and

(b) subsections (3) to (6) were omitted.

Children in places of safety
2. (1) This paragraph applies in the case of a child who is committed to a place of safety in England or Wales in pursuance of—

(a) section 40 of the Children and Young Persons Act 1933; or

(b) section 43 of the Adoption Act 1958; or

(c) section 2(5) or (10), 16(3) or 28(1) or (4) of the Children and Young Persons Act 1969; or

(d) section 12 of the Foster Children Act 1980.

(2) Where this paragraph applies, section 1 of this Act shall have effect as if—

(a) the reference in subsection (1) to the appropriate consent were a reference to the leave of any magistrates' court acting for the area in which the place of safety is; and

(b) subsections (3) to (6) were omitted.

Adoption and custodianship

3. (1) This paragraph applies in the case of a child—

(a) who is the subject of an order under section 14 of the Children Act 1975 freeing him for adoption; or

(b) who is the subject of a pending application for such an order; or

(c) who is the subject of a pending application for an adoption order; or

(d) who is the subject of an order under section 25 of the Children Act 1975 or section 53 of the Adoption Act 1958 relating to adoption abroad or of a pending application for such an order; or

(e) who is the subject of a pending application for a custodianship order.

(2) Where this paragraph applies, section 1 of this Act shall have effect as if—

(a) the reference in subsection (1) to the appropriate consent were a reference—

(i) in a case within sub-paragraph (1)(a) above, to the consent of the adoption agency which made the application for the order or, if the parental rights and duties in respect of the child have been transferred from that agency to another agency by an order under section 23 of the Children Act 1975, to the consent of that other agency;

(ii) in a case within sub-paragraph (1)(b), (c) or (e) above, to the leave of the court to which the application was made; and

(iii) in a case within sub-paragraph (1)(d) above, to the leave of the court which made the order or, as the case may be, to which the application was made; and

(b) subsections (3) to (6) were omitted.

Cases within paragraphs 1 and 3

4. In the case of a child falling within both paragraph 1 and paragraphm 3 above, the provisions of paragraph 3 shall apply to the exclusion of those in paragraph 1.

Interpretation

5. (1) In this Schedule—

(a) subject to sub-paragraph (2) below, "adoption agency" has the same meaning as in section 1 of the Children Act 1975;

(b) "adoption order" means an order under section 8(1) of that Act;

(c) "custodianship order" has the same meaning as in Part II of that Act; and

(d) "local authority" and "voluntary organisation" have the same meanings as in section 87 of the Child Care Act 1980.

(2) Until the coming into force of section 1 of the Children Act 1975, for the words "adoption agency" in this Schedule there shall be substituted "approved adoption society or local authority"; and in this Schedule "approved adoption society" means an adoption society approved under Part I of that Act.

(3) In paragraph 3(1) above references to an order or to an application for an order are references to an order made by, or to an application to, a court in England and Wales.

(4) Paragraph 3(2) above shall be construed as if the references to the court included, in any case where the court is a magistrates' court, a reference to any magistrates' court acting for the same petty sessions area as that court.

NOTES
'Children Act 1975'; 'Adoption Act 1958' The relevant provisions are now contained in the Adoption Act 1976.

Companies Act 1985

(C 6)

Punishment for fraudulent trading

458. If any business of a company is carried on with intent to defraud creditors of the company or creditors of any other person, or for any fraudulent purpose, every person who was knowingly a party to the carrying on of the business in that manner is liable to imprisonment or a fine, or both.

This applies whether or not the company has been, or is in the course of being wound up.

NOTES

This provision, in contrast to most other company law offences, is closely related to 'mainstream' fraud offences under the Theft Acts, a point recently demonstrated in *R v Philippou* [1989] Crim LR 559. The concept of fraudulent trading has a significance beyond the criminal liability which may arise under this provision. Under s 213 of the Insolvency Act 1986, the persons responsible for fraudulent trading may also be declared liable to make contributions to the assets of a company in liquidation. Fraudulent trading was previously dealt with under s 332 of the Companies Act 1948, from which the present provisions are largely derived.

'company' This means a company registered under this Act or a previous Companies Act, but does not include one registered under the Joint Stock Companies Acts, the Companies Act 1862, or the Companies (Consolidation) Act 1908 in Ireland (s 735(1)).

'any business ... is carried on' A single fraudulent transaction in the course of what is otherwise an honest business may suffice to create liability under this section; see the civil case of *Re Gerald Cooper Chemicals Ltd* [1978] Ch 262 and *R v Lockwood* [1986] Crim LR 244. See also *R v Philippou* [1989] Crim LR 559 where the fraudulent obtaining of an air travel operator's licence was held to be within the scope of this offence.

'with intent to defraud' Note that the scope of the offence extends beyond the defrauding of the company's own creditors. Any fraudulent purpose suffices. As to what amounts to an intent to defraud, see *R v Grantham* [1984] QB 675 and *R v Cox* (1982) 75 Cr App R 291. It is clear that there can be such an intent even though D does not mean to profit for himself or to cause loss to another; it suffices if D dishonestly puts P's economic interests in jeopardy. If the directors of a company realise that it is incapable of meeting its financial obligations, but nevertheless cause it to incur further liabilities in the hope of delaying its final collapse, this may be considered fraudulent. The position is less clear where the directors hope that the company may eventually ride out the crisis; fraud may still be present if, for example, the new creditors are deceived as to the prospects of prompt repayment. See *R v Grantham, supra*.

285

'person' This may mean another company, which could be deemed to possess the requisite *mens rea* through its own directors and managers.

Penalty etc The maximum penalty following conviction on indictment is seven years' imprisonment and/or a fine. Following summary conviction it is six months and/or the statutory maximum fine (Sch 24). Conviction may also result in disqualification as a company director under s 2 of the Company Directors Disqualification Act 1986; and see s 4 of that Act.

Sexual Offences Act 1985

(C 44)

Soliciting of women by men

Kerb-crawling

1. (1) A man commits an offence if he solicits a woman (or different women) for the purpose of prostitution—

(*a*) from a motor vehicle while it is in a street or public place; or

(*b*) in a street or public place while in the immediate vicinity of a motor vehicle that he has just got out of or off,

persistently or, subject to section 5(6) below, in such manner or in such circumstances as to be likely to cause annoyance to the woman (or any of the women) solicited, or nuisance to other persons in the neighbourhood.

(2) A person guilty of an offence under this section shall be liable on summary conviction to a fine not exceeding level 3 on the standard scale (as defined in section 75 of the Criminal Justice Act 1982).

(3) In this section "motor vehicle" has the same meaning as in the Road Traffic Act 1988.

NOTES

There is a large area of overlap between this provision and s 2 *infra*. If there is persistent soliciting, then s 2 applies, whether D is kerb crawling or not; it is therefore only in cases of non-persistent kerb crawling that this provision has any separate utility.

'man', 'woman'. See s 4(2) & (3) *infra*.

'solicits ... for the purpose of prostitution' See s 4(1) *infra*. Soliciting may take place without words and/or without success (*Horton v Mead* [1913] 1 KB 154).

'street' See s 4(4) *infra*.

'public place' It has been held in the context of other legislation that this includes privately owned property to which the public have unimpeded access (*e.g. Williams v Boyle* [1963] Crim LR 204).

'motor vehicle' It might suffice if D has just alighted from a bus which has not yet moved off, although this is hardly the mischief against which the section is aimed.

'likely to cause annoyance to the woman ...' It is presumably only where D correctly identifies actual prostitutes first time that he would *not* be likely to cause annoyance.

'or nuisance to other persons in the neighbourhood' Even if D correctly identifies actual prostitutes, he may not be safe from prosecution, since it is likely that the very presence of kerb crawlers and prostitutes will cause obstruction, irritation *etc* in some localities.

Persistent soliciting of women for the purpose of prostitution

2. (1) A man commits an offence if in a street or public place he persistently solicits a woman (or different women) for the purpose of prostitution.

(2) A person guilty of an offence under this section shall be liable on summary conviction to a fine not exceeding level 3 on the standard scale (as defined in section 75 of the Criminal Justice Act 1982).

NOTES

Most of the terms used in this provision have been considered in the notes to s 1 *supra*. Apart from the overlap with that section, there is an apparent overlap with s 32 of the Sexual Offences Act 1956 (*qv*) but it was held in *Crook v Edmondson* [1966] 1 All ER 833 that the s 32 offence is not committed by soliciting for prostitutes, and despite doubts as to the correctness of that decision, it was considered necessary to plug the gap it appeared to leave.

'persistently' It would suffice if D persists in soliciting women, even if he never persists in soliciting any particular woman. It was said in *Dale v Smith* [1967] 2 All ER 1133 that persistence implies repetition, but a prolonged attempt to procure a single woman would doubtless involve repeated requests etc. It is submitted that persistence may also be measured over a period of days or weeks. See further *Darroch v DPP*, The Times, 11 May 1990.

3. [*omitted*]

Supplementary

Interpretation

4. (1) References in this Act to a man soliciting a woman for the purpose of prostitution are references to his soliciting her for the purpose of obtaining her services as a prostitute.

(2) The use in any provision of this Act of the word "man" without the addition of the word "boy" shall not prevent the provision applying to any person to whom it would have applied if both words had been used, and similarly with the words "woman" and "girl".

(3) Paragraphs (*a*) and (*b*) of section 6 of the Interpretation Act 1978 (words importing the masculine gender to include the feminine, and vice versa) do not apply this Act.

(4) For the purpose of this Act "street" includes any bridge, road, lane, footway, subway, square, court, alley or passage, whether a thoroughfare or not, which is for the time being open to the public; and the doorways and entrances of premises abutting on a street (as hereinbefore defined), and any ground adjoining and open to a street, shall be treated as forming part of the street.

Public Order Act 1986

(C 64)

Part I: new offences

Riot

1. (1) Where 12 or more persons who are present together use or threaten unlawful violence for a common purpose and the conduct of them (taken together) is such as would cause a person of reasonable firmness present at the scene to fear for his personal safety, each of the persons using unlawful violence for the common purpose is guilty of riot.

(2) It is immaterial whether or not the 12 or more use or threaten unlawful violence simultaneously.

(3) The common purpose may be inferred from conduct.

(4) No person of reasonable firmness need actually be, or be likely to be, present at the scene.

(5) Riot may be committed in private as well as in public places.

(6) A person guilty of riot is liable on conviction on indictment to imprisonment for a term not exceeding ten years or a fine or both.

NOTES

S 9 of the Act abolishes the common law offence of riot, together with rout, affray and unlawful assembly. Riot and affray have been recast as statutory offences (ss 1 and 3); unlawful assembly has been replaced with the new offence of violent disorder (s 2), and rout has disappeared entirely.

The Law Commission, in proposing the new statutory offences, sought primarily to restate the main features of the old ones; but there are certain, mostly minor, changes, so the new offences are not merely declaratory of the old law.

'twelve or more persons who are present together' At common law, as few as three persons could form a riot, but it was felt that the concept of the three-man riot was inappropriate. The question whether a given number of persons are 'present together' must be one of fact in every case.

'use or threaten unlawful violence' Violence is defined in s 8 *infra*. One must discount the contribution of any innocent persons who have been unwittingly caught up in the incident and have been forced to use or threaten violence in self-defence.

'person of reasonable firmness' This is a hypothetical character. No such person need actually be at the scene, or even be likely to be there (subs (4)). Indeed, it would seem that no person at all, other than the rioters themselves, needs to be present or likely to be so.

The concept of the hypothetical bystander is borrowed from the common law offence of affray. Riot at common law probably required at least one actual person to be present and alarmed (see *Field v Met Police Receiver* [1907] 2 KB 853).

Mens rea. See s 6(1) *infra*, which requires intent to use violence or awareness that conduct may be violent. As for the position where awareness is impaired by intoxication, see s 6(5). Note that proof of *mens rea* is needed only in respect of the

289

defendant himself; the other persons making up the minimum twelve involved need not themselves be guilty or even criminally responsible. (See s 6(7)).

Consent of the DPP. See s 7(1) *infra*.

Violent disorder

2. (1) Where 3 or more persons who are present together use or threaten unlawful violence and the conduct of them (taken together) is such as would cause a person of reasonable firmness present at the scene to fear for his personal safety, each of the persons using or threatening unlawful violence is guilty of violent disorder.

(2) It is immaterial whether or not the 3 or more use or threaten unlawful violence simultaneously.

(3) No person of reasonable firmness need actually be, or be likely to be, present at the scene.

(4) Violent disorder may be committed in private as well as in public places.

(5) A person guilty of violent disorder is liable on conviction on indictment to imprisonment for a term not exceeding 5 years or a fine or both, or on summary conviction to imprisonment for a term not exceeding 6 months or a fine not exceeding the statutory maximum or both.

NOTES

This new offence replaces that of unlawful assembly, and has many features in common with riot, as defined in s 1 *supra*. Riot is in fact an aggravated form of violent disorder, and in introducing the Public Order Bill in the Commons, the Home Secretary stated that the latter offence 'will be used in future as the normal charge for serious outbreaks of disorder' (*H.C. Deb. 13.1.86*).

'three or more persons present together' This contrasts with the twelve who are required in cases of riot. If there is no evidence that anyone other than the defendants were involved in the alleged offence, it will normally be necessary for at least three of them to be convicted, or none (*R v Mahroof* [1989] Crim LR 72; *R v Fleming* [1989] Crim LR 658); but it is nevertheless submitted that, as in conspiracy cases, a single conviction may sometimes be correct (e.g. when based on a confession which is inadmissible against other defendants).

'use or threaten unlawful violence' Violence is defined in s 8 *infra*. As in riot, one must discount the contributions of any innocent persons who have been caught up in the violence and have been forced to use or threaten violence in lawful self defence.

Whereas riot can only be perpetrated by persons who actually use violence, violent disorder does not require anyone to do more than threaten it. Nor need there be any common purpose on the part of any of those involved.

'persons of reasonable firmness' See the notes to s 1 *supra*. It may in fact be relevant to know if any actual bystanders were frightened, but evidence of their reactions would not in theory be decisive.

Mens rea See s 6(2) *infra*. The offence requires intent to use or threaten violence, or awareness that one's conduct may be violent or threaten violence. As to the position where intoxication affects awareness, see s 6(5). Note that only the defendant must be proved to have acted with *mens rea*; other persons involved need not even be criminally responsible (see s 6(7)).

Affray
3. (1) A person is guilty of affray if he uses or threatens unlawful violence towards another and his conduct is such as would cause a person of reasonable firmness present at the scene to fear for his personal safety.

(2) Where 2 or more persons use or threaten the unlawful violence, it is the conduct of them taken together that must be considered for the purposes of subsection (1).

(3) For the purposes of this section a threat cannot be made by the use of words alone.

(4) No person of reasonable firmness need actually be, or be likely to be, present at the scene.

(5) Affray may be committed in private as well as in public places.

(6) A constable may arrest without warrant anyone he reasonably suspects is committing affray.

(7) A person guilty of affray is liable on conviction on indictment to imprisonment for a term not exceeding 3 years or a fine or both, or on summary conviction to imprisonment for a term not exceeding 6 months or a fine not exceeding the statutory maximum or both.

NOTES
Whereas ss 1 and 2 of the Act have introduced significant changes in the offences with which they deal, this provision does little more than restate the essential elements of the common law offence it replaces, and in *R v Plastow* [1988] Crim LR 604 the Court of Appeal referred to this provision for the purpose of deciding an appeal against a conviction for the old common law offence. The enactment of the statutory offence does of course help to resolve uncertainties, and it has also reduced the maximum penalty which can be imposed, whilst making the offence triable either way.

'if he uses or threatens'   Affray differs from the offences defined in ss 1 and 2 in that there need be no collective action; it is thus possible for a single person to cause an affray by attacking or threatening another (*cf Taylor v DPP* [1973] AC 964), but in practice two or more persons so doing are more likely to instill fear in bystanders of reasonable firmness.

'unlawful violence towards another'   Note that violence directed against property is excluded from the scope of this offence. This is apparent from the wording of this provision and from s 8 *infra*.

'person of reasonable firmness'   See the notes to ss 1 and 2 *supra*. Although the presence of such persons is not necessary, it may nevertheless be helpful if the prosecution can produce witnesses who were indeed frightened by the incident in question.

Arrest without warrant   The power of arrest created by subs (6) is necessary because the three year maximum penalty is not sufficient to make it a full 'arrestable offence'. Private citizens have no power of arrest for affray itself, but they do have the power to arrest for a breach or threatened breach of the peace, and an affray will inevitably involve one of these (*cf R v Howell* [1982] QB 416).

Threats by words alone (subs (3))   The rule that words alone cannot suffice to create an affray is derived from the common law (see *Taylor v DPP supra*), but note that the position is different in other offences under this Act.

Fear or provocation of violence

4. (1) A person is guilty of an offence if he—

(*a*) uses towards another person threatening, abusive or insulting words or behaviour, or

(*b*) distributes or displays to another person any writing, sign or other visible representation which is threatening, abusive or insulting,

with intent to cause that person to believe that immediate unlawful violence will be used against him or another by any person, or to provoke the immediate use of unlawful violence by that person or another, or whereby that person is likely to believe that such violence will be used or it is likely that such violence will be provoked.

(2) An offence under this section may be committed in a public or a private place, except that no offence is committed where the words or behaviour are used, or the writing, sign or other visible representation is distributed or displayed, by a person inside a dwelling and the other person is also inside that or another dwelling.

(3) A constable may arrest without warrant anyone he reasonably suspects is committing an offence under this section.

(4) A person guilty of an offence under this section is liable on summary conviction to imprisonment for a term not exceeding 6 months or a fine not exceeding level 5 on the standard scale or both.

NOTES

This provision replaces s 5 of the Public Order Act 1936, which is repealed twice, by s 40(3) and Sch 3 of this Act, as well as by s 9(2).

The old offence was broadly similar to the new one, but required an intent to provoke a breach of the peace, or a likelihood that such a breach would be occasioned, and it could only be committed in a public place or at a public meeting. Its replacement was not a Law Commission initiative, but a Government one.

'if he uses etc.' This is not a group offence and can be committed by a single person.

'threatening, abusive or insulting' Under the old law, these words were held to be capable of applying to overt homosexual or exhibitionist behaviour (see *Masterson v Holden* [1986] 1 WLR 1017 and *Parkin v Norman* [1983] QB 92), but whether particular conduct or writing fits this description is ultimately a question of fact in every case; the words have no special legal meaning. See *Brutus v Cozens* [1973] AC 854.

'uses towards another ... distributes or displays to another' In contrast to the offence created by s 5 *infra*, the most provocative behaviour cannot constitute this offence unless used or displayed 'towards' another. This means that it must be directed or aimed at others, in their presence (*Atkin v DPP* [1989] Crim LR 581), thus excluding threats to distant third parties or conduct which is merely insensitive. Note also the *mens rea* required by s 6(3).

Intended or likely consequences D may intend to cause fear of violence or he may intend to provoke it. In either case he may be guilty of this offence notwithstanding that the intended consequence is unlikely or even impossible. Alternatively, D may become guilty where such consequences are likely. In such cases there need be no such specific intent on his part, but under s 6(3) *infra*, D must at least be aware that his conduct may be threatening, abusive or insulting. As to cases where D's awareness is impaired by intoxication, see s 6(5) and (6).

'**inside a dwelling**' See s 8 *infra*. A malicious letter pushed through a letterbox cannot be within the scope of this provision or s 5 *infra*, since only the recipient is inside the dwelling (*Chappell v DPP* (1989) 89 Cr App R 82); but see s 1 of the Malicious Communications Act 1988.

Arrest without warrant See the notes to s 3 *supra*. In this case a private citizen may similarly be able to arrest for actual or threatened breach of the peace, but there may be occasions when no such ground would exist.

Harassment, alarm or distress
  5. (1) A person is guilty of an offence if he—
  (a) uses threatening, abusive or insulting words or behaviour, or disorderly behaviour, or
  (b) displays any writing, sign or other visible representation which is threatening, abusive or insulting,
within the hearing or sight of a person likely to be caused harassment, alarm or distress thereby.
  (2) An offence under this section may be committed in a public or a private place, except that no offence is committed where the words or behaviour are used, or the writing, sign or other visible representation is displayed, by a person inside a dwelling and the other person is also inside that or another dwelling.
  (3) It is a defence for the accused to prove—
  (a) that he had no reason to believe that there was any person within hearing or sight who was likely to be caused harassment, alarm or distress, or
  (b) that he was inside a dwelling and had no reason to believe that the words or behaviour used, or the writing, sign or other visible representation displayed, would be heard or seen by a person outside that or any other dwelling, or
  (c) that his conduct was reasonable.
  (4) A constable may arrest a person without warrant if—
  (a) he engages in offensive conduct which the constable warns him to stop, and
  (b) he engages in further offensive conduct immediately or shortly after the warning.
  (5) In subsection (4) "offensive conduct" means conduct the constable reasonably suspects to constitute an offence under this section, and the conduct mentioned in paragraph (a) and the further conduct need not be of the same nature.
  (6) A person guilty of an offence under this section is liable on a summary conviction to a fine not exceeding level 3 on the standard scale.

NOTES
This is the least serious of the offences created under this Part of the Act. It is closely related to the s 4 offence, but the conduct in question need not be directed against anyone else and, subject to subs (3), D need have no *mens rea* beyond an awareness that his behaviour may be threatening, abusive, insulting, or just

disorderly (s 6(4)). As to the position where D's awareness is impaired by intoxication, see s 6(5) and (6) *infra*.

'threatening, abusive or insulting'   See the notes to s 4 *supra*.

'disorderly'   This term has no special legal meaning; whether conduct is disorderly is a question of fact in every case.

'within the hearing or sight . . .'   Although the conduct in question need not be directed against any person (as in s 4), it is necessary that the prosecution prove the presence of a potential 'victim'. They need not, however, prove that this person suffered any actual alarm *etc*.

'a person likely to be caused'   Police officers can themselves be the 'victims' of behaviour which contravenes subs (1), but it may sometimes be hard to prove that they were 'likely' to be affected. See *R v Orum* [1988] Crim LR 848.

'inside a dwelling'   See the notes to s 4 *supra*.

Mental element: miscellaneous

6. (1) A person is guilty of riot only if he intends to use violence or is aware that his conduct may be violent.

(2) A person is guilty of violent disorder or affray only if he intends to use or threaten violence or is aware that his conduct may be violent or threaten violence.

(3) A person is guilty of an offence under section 4 only if he intends his words or behaviour, or the writing, sign or other visible representation, to be threatening, abusive or insulting, or is aware that it may be threatening, abusive or insulting.

(4) A person is guilty of an offence under section 5 only if he intends his words or behaviour, or the writing, sign or other visible representation, to be threatening, abusive or insulting, or is aware that it may be threatening, abusive or insulting or (as the case may be) he intends his behaviour to be or is aware that it may be disorderly.

(5) For the purposes of this section a person whose awareness is impaired by intoxication shall be taken to be aware of that of which he would be aware if not intoxicated, unless he shows either that his intoxication was not self-induced or that it was caused solely by the taking or administration of a substance in the course of medical treatment.

(6) In subsection (5) "intoxication" means any intoxication, whether caused by drink, drugs or other means, or by a combination of means.

(7) Subsections (1) or (2) do not affect the determination for the purposes of riot or violent disorder of the number of persons who use or threaten violence.

NOTES

Subs (5) is an interesting statutory version of the *Majewski* principle (*DPP v Majewski* [1977] AC 433). The burden of proof it places on the defence appears to go beyond the common law position.

Procedure: miscellaneous

7. (1) No prosecution for an offence of riot or incitement to riot may be instituted except by or with the consent of the Director of Public Prosecutions.

(2) For the purposes of the rules against charging more than one offence in the same count or information, each of sections 1 to 5 creates one offence.

(3) If on the trial on indictment of a person charged with violent disorder or affray the jury find him not guilty of the offence charged, they may (without prejudice to section 6(3) of the Criminal Law Act 1967) find him guilty of an offence under section 4.

(4) The Crown Court has the same powers and duties in relation to a person who is by virtue of subsection (3) convicted before it of an offence under section 4 as a magistrates' court would have on convicting him of the offence.

Interpretation

8. In this Part—

"dwelling" means any structure or part of a structure occupied as a person's home or as other living accommodation (whether the occupation is separate or shared with others) but does not include any part not so occupied, and for this purpose "structure" includes a tent, caravan, vehicle, vessel or other temporary or movable structure;

"violence" means any violent conduct, so that—

(*a*) except in the context of affray, it includes violent conduct towards property as well as violent conduct towards persons, and

(*b*) it is not restricted to conduct causing or intended to cause injury or damage but includes any other violent conduct (for example, throwing at or towards a person a missile of a kind capable of causing injury which does not hit or falls short).

Offences abolished

9. (1) The common law offences of riot, rout, unlawful assembly and affray are abolished.

(2) The offences under the following enactments are abolished—

(*a*) section 1 of the Tumultuous Petitioning Act 1661 (presentation of petition to monarch or Parliament accompanied by excessive number of persons),

(*b*) section 1 of the Shipping Offences Act 1793 (interference with operation of vessel by persons riotously assembled),

(*c*) section 23 of the Seditious Meetings Act 1817 (prohibition of certain meetings within one mile of Westminster Hall when Parliament sitting), and

(*d*) section 5 of the Public Order Act 1936 (conduct conducive to breach of the peace).

10. [*omitted*]

Part II [*omitted*]

Part III: Racial hatred

Meaning of "racial hatred"
17. In this Part "racial hatred" means hatred against a group of persons in Great Britain defined by reference to colour, race, nationality (including citizenship) or ethnic or national origins.

NOTES
'Great Britain' This does not include Northern Ireland. Offences under the Act can generally be committed only in England or Wales, although they may relate to racial groups in Scotland.

'colour, race, etc.' Religious hatred is not as such within the scope of this Part of the Act, except to the extent that religion may be associated with racial or ethnic groups. Sikhs have been held to be a distinct ethnic group under the Race Relations Act 1976 (*Mandla v Dowell Lee* [1983] 2 AC 548) and one could hardly stir up hatred against Judaism, or even Islam, without it being 'likely' that racial hatred would also be stirred. As to the significance of such likelihood, see the notes to s 18 *infra*.

Acts intended or likely to stir up racial hatred

Use of words or behaviour or display of written material
18. (1) A person who uses threatening, abusive or insulting words or behaviour, or displays any written material which is threatening, abusive or insulting, is guilty of an offence if—
   (*a*) he intends thereby to stir up racial hatred, or
   (*b*) having regard to all the circumstances racial hatred is likely to be stirred up thereby.
   (2) An offence under this section may be committed in a public or a private place, except that no offence is committed where the words or behaviour are used, or the written material is displayed, by a person inside a dwelling and are not heard or seen except by other persons in that or another dwelling.
   (3) A constable may arrest without warrant anyone he reasonably suspects is committing an offence under this section.
   (4) In proceedings for an offence under this section it is a defence for the accused to prove that he was inside a dwelling and had no reason to believe that the words or behaviour used, or the written material displayed, would be heard or seen by a person outside that or any other dwelling.
   (5) A person who is not shown to have intended to stir up racial hatred is not guilty of an offence under this section if he did not intend his words or behaviour, or the written material, to be, and was not aware that it might be, threatening, abusive or insulting.

(6) This section does not apply to words or behaviour used, or written material displayed, solely for the purpose of being included in a programme broadcast or included in a cable programme service.

NOTES
This provision, together with s 19 *infra*, has replaced s 5A of the Public Order Act 1936.

'threatening, abusive or insulting' See the notes to s 4 *supra*.

'racial hatred' See s 17 *supra*.

'written material'; **'programme'**; **'broadcast'**; **'cable programme service'** See s 29 *infra*. Broadcasting and cable services are dealt with under s 22 (not included in this work).

Intended or likely consequences D may intend to stir up racial hatred, in which case he may be guilty of this offence even where he has no real chance of success. Alternatively, he may become guilty where he is likely to stir up such hatred, notwithstanding a lack of any specific intent on his part; but in such a case he must at least be aware that his behaviour *etc* might be threatening, abusive or insulting (subs (5)).

'in a dwelling' See the notes to s 4 *supra*.

Penalties etc. See s 27 *infra*.

Publishing or distributing written material
19. (1) A person who publishes or distributes written material which is threatening, abusive or insulting is guilty of an offence if—
(a) he intends thereby to stir up racial hatred, or
(b) having regard to all the circumstances racial hatred is likely to be stirred up thereby.
(2) In proceedings for an offence under this section it is a defence for an accused who is not shown to have intended to stir up racial hatred to prove that he was not aware of the content of the material and did not suspect, and had no reason to suspect, that it was threatening, abusive or insulting.
(3) References in this Part to the publication or distribution of written material are to its publication or distribution to the public or a section of the public.

NOTES
Most of the terms used in this provision are also found in s 18 *supra*; and little further annotation is needed; but note that, whereas s 18(5) leaves the prosecution with the burden of proving intent or awareness, subs (2) of the present provision requires the publisher of offending material to prove that he was unaware of its content, did not suspect it and had no reason to suspect it.

'person' A corporation which publishes or distributes offending material may commit this offence. As far as subs (1)(a) and subs (2) are concerned, the requisite intent, awareness or suspicion is that of its directors or managers. See further s 28 *infra*.

Penalties See s 27 *infra*.

Public performance of a play
   20. [*omitted*]

Distributing, showing or playing a recording
   21. [*omitted*]

Broadcasting and cable services
   22. [*omitted*]

Racially inflammatory material

Possession of racially inflammatory material
   23. (1) A person who has in his possession written material which is threatening, abusive or insulting, or a recording of visual images or sounds which are threatening, abusive or insulting, with a view to—
   (*a*) in the case of written material, its being displayed, published, distributed, broadcast or included in a cable programme service, whether by himself or another, or
   (*b*) in the case of a recording, its being distributed, shown, played, broadcast or included in a cable programme service, whether by himself or another,
is guilty of an offence if he intends racial hatred to be stirred up thereby or, having regard to all the circumstances, racial hatred is likely to be stirred up thereby.
   (2) For this purpose regard shall be had to such display, publication, distribution, showing, playing, broadcasting or inclusion in a cable programme service as he has, or it may reasonably be inferred that he has, in view.
   (3) In proceedings for an offence under this section it is a defence for an accused who is not shown to have intended to stir up racial hatred to prove that he was not aware of the content of the written material or recording and did not suspect, and had no reason to suspect, that it was threatening, abusive or insulting.
   (4) This section does not apply to the possession of written material or a recording by or on behalf of the British Broadcasting Corporation or the Independent Broadcasting Authority or with a view to its being broadcast by either of those authorities.

NOTES

'person' As to corporations, see the notes to s 19 *supra*.

'possession' This presumably has the same wide meaning as in other legislation (see for example s 1 of the Firearms Act 1968), and to some extent the offence is one of strict liability; but note subs (3).

'threatening, abusive or insulting' See the notes to s 4 *supra*.

'racial hatred' See s 17 *supra*.

'publication and distribution' See s 19(3) *supra*.

'broadcast'; 'cable programme service'; 'written material' See s 29 *infra*.

Penalties etc See s 27 *infra*.

24–25. [*omitted*]

Supplementary provisions

Savings for reports of Parliamentary or judicial proceedings
   26. (1) Nothing in this Part applies to a fair and accurate report of proceedings in Parliament.

   (2) Nothing in this Part applies to a fair and accurate report of proceedings publicly heard before a court or tribunal exercising judicial authority where the report is published contemporaneously with the proceedings or, if it is not reasonably practicable or would be unlawful to publish a report of them contemporaneously, as soon as publication is reasonably practicable and lawful.

NOTES
This provision serves a similar function to that served by s 3 of the Law of Libel Amendment Act 1888 in respect of defamatory material in such reports.

'fair and accurate report' To be protected, a report need not reproduce every word of the proceedings in question, but it must give a balanced and impartial account which reflects the substance of what has taken place. See *Turner v Sullivan* (1862) 6 LT 130.

Procedure and punishment
   27. (1) No proceedings for an offence under this Part may be instituted in England and Wales except by or with the consent of the Attorney General.

   (2) For the purposes of the rules in England and Wales against charging more than one offence in the same count or information, each of sections 18 to 23 creates one offence.

   (3) A person guilty of an offence under this Part is liable—
   (*a*) on conviction on indictment to imprisonment for a term not exceeding two years or a fine or both;
   (*b*) on summary conviction to imprisonment for a term not exceeding six months or a fine not exceeding the statutory maximum, or both.

Offences by corporations
   28. (1) Where a body corporate is guilty of an offence under this Part and it is shown that the offence was committed with the consent or connivance of a director, manager, secretary or other similar officer of the body, or a person purporting to act in any such capacity, he as well as the body corporate is guilty of the offence and liable to be proceeded against and punished accordingly.

(2) Where the affairs of a body corporate are managed by its members, subsection (1) applies in relation to the acts and defaults of a member in connection with his functions of management as it applies to a director.

NOTE
See generally the notes to s 18 of the Theft Act 1968, which is in similar terms.

Interpretation
29. In this Part—
'broadcast' means broadcast by wireless telegraphy (within the meaning of the Wireless Telegraphy Act 1949) for general reception, whether by way of sound broadcasting or television;
'cable programme service' has the same meaning as in the Cable and Broadcasting Act 1984;
'distribute', and related expressions, shall be construed in accordance with section 19(3) (written material) and section 21(2) (recordings);
'dwelling' means any structure or part of a structure occupied as a person's home or other living accommodation (whether the occupation is separate or shared with others) but does not include any part not so occupied, and for this purpose 'structure' includes a tent, caravan, vehicle, vessel or other temporary or movable structure;
'programme' means any item which is broadcast or included in a cable programme service;
'publish', and related expressions, in relation to written material, shall be construed in accordance with section 19(3);
'racial hatred' has the meaning given by section 17;
'recording' has the meaning given by section 21(2), and 'play' and 'show', and related expressions, in relation to a recording, shall be construed in accordance with that provision;
'written material' includes any sign or other visible representation.

Part IV [*omitted*]

Part V: Miscellaneous and general

Contamination of or interference with goods with intention of causing public alarm or anxiety, etc
38. (1) It is an offence for a person, with the intention—
(a) of causing public alarm or anxiety, or
(b) of causing injury to members of the public consuming or using the goods, or
(c) of causing economic loss to any person by reason of the goods being shunned by members of the public, or
(d) of causing economic loss to any person by reason of steps taken to avoid any such alarm or anxiety, injury or loss,

to contaminate or interfere with goods, or make it appear that goods have been contaminated or interfered with, or to place goods which have been contaminated or interfered with, or which appear to have been contaminated or interfered with, in a place where goods of that description are consumed, used, sold or otherwise supplied.

(2) It is also an offence for a person, with any such intention as is mentioned in paragraph (*a*), (*c*) or (*d*) of subsection (1), to threaten that he or another will do, or claim that he or another has done, any of the acts mentioned in that subsection.

(3) It is an offence for a person to be in possession of any of the following articles with a view to the commission of an offence under subsection (1)—

(*a*) materials to be used for contaminating or interfering with goods or making it appear that goods have been contaminated or interfered with, or

(*b*) goods which have been contaminated or interfered with, or which appear to have been contaminated or interfered with.

(4) A person guilty of an offence under this section is liable—

(*a*) on conviction on indictment to imprisonment for a term not exceeding 10 years or a fine or both, or

(*b*) on summary conviction to imprisonment for a term not exceeding six months or a fine not exceeding the statutory maximum or both.

(5) In this section 'goods' includes substances whether natural or manufactured and whether or not incorporated in or mixed with other goods.

(6) The reference in subsection (2) to a person claiming that certain acts have been committed does not include a person who in good faith reports or warns that such acts have been, or appear to have been, committed.

NOTES

This provision deals with something that has become a fairly major problem, particularly in relation to foodstuffs and other items intended for human consumption. The contamination of such goods may in some cases represent an attempt to commit an offence under ss 23 or 24 of the Offences Against the Person Act 1861, and the demands which usually accompany such acts or purported acts will often constitute blackmail under s 21 of the Theft Act 1968. Charges under the Criminal Damage Act 1971 may also be appropriate; but if D tampers with foodstuffs he has previously purchased, and then replaces them in the store, a basic criminal damage offence could not be made out. Damaging one's own property is only an offence where s 1(2) of the 1971 Act applies.

This provision may therefore have closed some loopholes; but it does not appear to apply where, as often happens, D hears that a certain product has been affected by such contamination, and pretends to have suffered harm in the hope of an offer of compensation. Recklessness as to the risk of causing further public alarm *etc* does not suffice under subs (1).

'possession ... with a view to' Possession must bear the same wide meaning as in other legislation (see the notes to s 1 of the Firearms Act 1968), but problems of strict liability will not arise, since the prosecution must prove an ulterior intent.

39–43. [*omitted*]

Crossbows Act 1987

(C 32)

Sale and letting on hire
1. A person who sells or lets on hire a crossbow or a part of a crossbow to a person under the age of seventeen is guilty of an offence, unless he believes him to be seventeen years of age or older and has reasonable ground for the belief.

NOTES
'crossbow' The Act does not apply to crossbows with a draw weight of less than 1.4 kilograms (s 5). The prosecution would have the burden of proving that the crossbow in question was more powerful than this (*cf R v Hunt* [1987] 1 All ER 1).

'unless he believes' The section says nothing about a mistaken belief that the weapon is a toy or a low-powered one exempted under s 5. This would presumably be no defence (*cf R v Pierre* [1963] Crim LR 513).

Penalty See s 6 *infra.*

Purchasing and hiring
2. A person under the age of seventeen who buys or hires a crossbow or a part of a crossbow is guilty of an offence.

NOTE
See the notes to s 1 *supra.*

Possession
3. A person under the age of seventeen who has with him—
(a) a crossbow which is capable of discharging a missile, or
(b) parts of a crossbow which together (and without any other parts) can be assembled to form a crossbow capable of discharging a missile,
is guilty of an offence, unless he is under the supervision of a person who is twenty-one years of age or older.

NOTES
'has with him' This is a narrower concept than that of possession. D must either be carrying the weapon or have it ready to hand (*eg* in the vehicle he is travelling in). This offence would appear to be one of strict liability to the extent that D might commit it despite believing the weapon to be a toy or a low powered one exempted under s 5. D does not commit the offence if he is unaware that the weapon is there at all; *Cf R v Cugullere* [1961] 1 WLR 858.

'**crossbow**' See the notes to s 1 *supra*.

Penalty See s 6 *infra*.

4. [*omitted*]

Exception

5. This Act does not apply to crossbows with a draw weight of less than 1.4 kilograms.

NOTE
See the notes to s 1 *supra*.

Punishments

6. (1) A person guilty of an offence under section 1 shall be liable, on summary conviction, to imprisonment for a term not exceeding six months, to a fine not exceeding level 5 on the standard scale, or to both.

(2) A person guilty of an offence under section 2 or 3 shall be liable, on summary conviction, to a fine not exceeding level 3 on the standard scale.

(3) The court by which a person is convicted of an offence under this Act may make such order as it thinks fit as to the forfeiture or disposal of any crossbow or part of a crossbow in respect of which the offence was committed.

Criminal Justice Act 1987

(C 38)

Charges of and penalty for conspiracy to defraud

12. (1) If—

(a) a person agrees with any other person or persons that a course of conduct shall be pursued; and

(b) that course of conduct will necessarily amount to or involve the commission of any offence or offences by one or more of the parties to the agreement if the agreement is carried out in accordance with their intentions,

the fact that it will do so shall not preclude a charge of conspiracy to defraud being brought against any of them in respect of the agreement.

(2) In section 5(2) of the Criminal Law Act 1977, the words from "and" to the end are hereby repealed.

(3) A person guilty of conspiracy to defraud is liable on conviction on indictment to imprisonment for a term not exceeding 10 years or a fine or both.

NOTES

This provision was enacted in order to remedy the unsatisfactory situation spawned by s 5(2) of the Criminal Law Act 1977, as originally enacted. This attempted to draw a rigid distinction between the offence of statutory conspiracy and the common law offence of conspiracy to defraud, and it was interpreted by the House of Lords as precluding a conviction for the latter unless it could be shown that the conspiracy in question was not capable of being classed as one of the former kind. (See *R v Ayres* [1984] 1 All ER 691 and the notes to s 5 of the 1977 Act).

'if a person agrees etc' See the notes to s 1 of the 1977 Act.

'shall not preclude a charge of conspiracy to defraud' As to what may amount to a conspiracy to defraud, see *Scott v Met. Police Commissioner* [1975] AC 819; *Attorney General's Reference (No. 1 of 1982)* [1983] 2 All ER 721; *R v Cooke* [1986] AC 909. The importance of the reform introduced by this provision is that, in a case such as *Scott*, a major fraud operation may involve the planned commission of relatively minor substantive offences. In such a case, a charge of statutory conspiracy would be possible but would not adequately reflect the seriousness of the criminal enterprise.

Malicious Communications Act 1988

(C 27)

Offence of sending letters etc. with intent to cause distress or anxiety

1. (1) Any person who sends to another person—

(a) a letter or other article which conveys—

  (i) a message which is indecent or grossly offensive;

  (ii) a threat; or

  (iii) information which is false and known or believed to be false by the sender; or

(b) any other article which is, in whole or part, of an indecent or grossly offensive nature,

is guilty of an offence if his purpose, or one of his purposes, in sending it is that is should, so far as falling within paragraph (a) or (b) above, cause distress or anxiety to the recipient or to any other person to whom he intends that it or its contents or nature should be communicated.

(2) A person is not guilty of an offence by virtue of subsection (1)(a)(ii) above if he shows—

(a) that the threat was used to reinforce a demand which he believed he had reasonable grounds for making; and

(b) that he believed that the use of the threat was a proper means of reinforcing the demand.

(3) In this section references to sending include references to delivering and to causing to be sent or delivered and "sender" shall be construed accordingly.

(4) A person guilty of an offence under this section shall be liable on summary conviction to a fine not exceeding level 4 on the standard scale.

NOTES

This provision, which came into force on 29 September 1988, deals with the sending of poison-pen letters and any other articles which are sent with the purpose of causing distress or anxiety. It is not by any means confined to written communications or to articles delivered by post: a dead rat, for example, could be a 'grossly offensive' article within subs (1)(b) if pushed through a letterbox.

'person' A corporation is a person and may commit this offence through its employees if its directors or managers possess the requisite *mens rea* under subs (1).

'sends' See subs (3) and the general note, supra. A message fixed to a brick thrown through a window is presumably 'sent' or 'delivered' within the meaning of this section.

'letter or other article' see the general note, *supra*. A telephone message is not within the scope of this Act; but might be covered by s 43 of the Telecommunications Act 1984 (not printed in this work).

'purpose' This is a narrower concept than intention, in that it excludes what is sometimes called 'oblique intent'. If D deliberately acts, knowing that his actions

306

will inevitably have a certain side effect, he arguably intends that side effect, but it could not be described as his purpose to cause it. Note that the purpose need not be achieved for the offence to be committed.

'distress or anxiety' An intent to cause offence or annoyance is not enough. An intent to extort money or other property might make the offence one of blackmail contrary to s 21 of the Theft Act 1968 (*qv*).

Subs (2) Note the subjective nature of this test (and *cf* s 21 of the Theft Act 1968, which adopts a similar one). Note also that the burden of proof in establishing it lies on the defence.

Criminal Justice Act 1988

(C 33)

Common assault and battery to be summary offences

39. Common assault and battery shall be summary offences and a person guilty of either of them shall be liable to a fine not exceeding level 5 on the standard scale, to imprisonment for a term not exceeding six months, or to both.

NOTES

Assault and battery are common law offences, the penalties and procedure for which were previously governed by ss 42 and 47 of the Offences Against the Person Act 1861. S 42 governed summary trial and s 47, besides creating an aggravated statutory offence of assault occasioning actual bodily harm, provided for common assault to be tried on indictment.

S 42 (together with ss 43 and 46) is repealed under s 151 and Sch 14 of this Act; and s 47 has been amended so that it now only deals with the statutory offence.

Under s 40 of the present Act (not printed here) a count for common assault may still be included in an indictment where based on the same facts as an indictable offence, or where it is part of a series of similar offences to an indictable one which is also charged; and note also s 41 (power of Crown Court to deal with summary offence where person committed for offence triable either way). See also *R v Mearns*, The Times, 4 May 1990.

'assault and battery' See the notes to s 47 of the 1861 Act.

Commencement This provision came into force on 12 October 1988.

Torture

134. (1) A public official or person acting in an official capacity, whatever his nationality, commits the offence of torture if in the United Kingdom or elsewhere he intentionally inflicts severe pain or suffering on another in the performance or purported performance of his offical duties.

(2) A person not falling within subsection (1) above commits the offence of torture, whatever his nationality, if—

(a) in the United Kingdom or elsewhere he intentionally inflicts severe pain or suffering on another at the instigation or with the consent or asquiescence—
   (i) of a public official; or
   (ii) of a person acting in an official capacity; and
(b) the official or other person is performing or purporting to perform his official duties when he instigates the commission of the offence or consents to or acquiesces in it.

(3) It is immaterial whether the pain or suffering is physical or mental and whether it is caused by an act or an omission.

(4) It shall be a defence for a person charged with an offence under this section in respect of any conduct of his to prove that he had lawful authority, justification or excuse for that conduct.

(5) For the purposes of this section "lawful authority or excuse" means—

(a) in relation to pain or suffering inflicted in the United Kingdom, lawful authority, justification or excuse under the law of the part of the United Kingdom where it was inflicted

(b) in relation to pain or suffering inflicted outside the United Kingdom—

   (i) if it was inflicted by a United Kingdom official acting under the law of the United Kingdom or by a person acting in an official capacity under that law, lawful authority, justification or excuse under the law;

   (ii) if it was inflicted by a United Kingdom official acting under the law of any part of the United Kingdom or by a person in an official capacity under such law, lawful authority, justification or excuse under the law of the part of the United Kingdom under whose law he was acting; and

   (iii) in any other case, lawful authority, justification or excuse under the law of the place where it was inflicted.

(6) A person who commits the offence of torture shall be liable on conviction on indictment to imprisonment for life.

NOTES

This provision, which came into force on 29 September 1988, was enacted so that the United Kingdom could ratify the 1984 United Nations Convention against Torture *etc.* Although the offence of torture is new to English law, it overlaps with a number of existing offences, and the most significant feature of the new law is that it is of universal extent, applicable to the acts or omissions of persons in other countries, where English law might not otherwise be applicable.

'performance or purported performance' This wording ensures that the offence may still be committed even where D's actions pull him outside the proper performance of his offical duties.

'it shall be a defence ... to prove' (subs (4)) This means proof on balance of probabilities. It is submitted that D would not be precluded from raising a defence, such as duress, independently of subss (4) and (5); and, if raised, the burden of disproving such a defence would be on the prosecution in the usual way.

'lawful authority ... under the law of the place where it was inflicted' The new offence does not apply where the pain is inflicted in accordance with local law, as where a flogging is administered under the law of an Islamic country.

Requirement of Attorney General's consent for prosecutions

135. Proceedings for an offence under section 134 above shall not be begun—

(a) in England and Wales, except by, or with the consent of, the Attorney General;

(*b*) [*omitted*]

136–138. [*omitted*]

Articles with blades or points and offensive weapons

Offence of having article with blade or point in public place
139. (1) Subject to subsections (4) and (5) below, any person who has an article to which this section applies with him in a public place shall be guilty of an offence.

(2) Subject to subsection (3) below, this section applies to any article which has a blade or is sharply pointed except a folding pocketknife.

(3) This section applies to a folding pocketknife if the cutting edge of its blade exceeds 3 inches.

(4) It shall be a defence for a person charged with an offence under this section to prove that he had good reason or lawful authority for having the article with him in a public place.

(5) Without prejudice to the generality of subsection (4) above, it shall be a defence for a person charged with an offence under this section to prove that he had the article with him—

(*a*) for use at work;

(*b*) for religious reasons; or

(*c*) as part of any national constume.

(6) A person guilty of an offence under subsection (1) above shall be liable on summary conviction to a fine not exceeding level 3 on the standard scale.

(7) In this section "public place" includes any place to which at the material time the public have or are permitted access, whether on payment or otherwise.

(8) This section shall not have effect in relation to anything done before it comes into force.

NOTES
This provision, which came into force on 29 September 1988, supplements s 1 of the Prevention of Crime Act 1953 (*qv*), and many of the terms used must bear the same meanings as in that Act. The significance of the new provision is that many dangerous knives are not inherently offensive weapons, and in prosecutions under the older legislation it will then be necessary for the prosecution to prove the knife was carried for the purpose of causing injury. In the new provision, it is for the defence to prove, on balance of probabilities, that the knife was carried for a legitimate purpose.

'has with him'; 'public place' See the notes to s 1 of the 1953 Act.

140. [*omitted*]

Offensive weapons

141. (1) Any person who manufactures, sells or hires or offers for sale or hire, exposes or has in his possession for the purpose of sale or hire, or lends or gives to any other person, a weapon to which this section applies shall be guilty of an offence and liable on summary conviction to imprisonment for a term not exceeding six months or to a fine not exceeding level 5 on the standard scale or both.

(2) The Secretary of State may by order made by statutory instrument direct that this section shall apply to any description of weapon specified in the order except—

(*a*) any weapon subject to the Firearms Act 1968; and

(*b*) crossbows.

(3) A statutory instrument containing an order under this section shall not be made unless a draft of the instrument has been laid before Parliament and has been approved by a resolution of each House of Parliament.

(4) The importation of a weapon to which this section applies is hereby prohibited.

(5) It shall be a defence for any person charged in respect of any conduct of his relating to a weapon to which this section applies—

(*a*) with an offence under subsection (1) above; or

(*b*) with an offence under section 50(2) or (3) of the Customs and Excise Management Act 1979 (improper importation),

to prove that his conduct was only for the purposes of functions carried out on behalf of the crown or a visiting force.

(6) In this section the reference to the Crown includes the Crown in right of Her Majesty's Government in Northern Ireland; and "visiting force" means any body, contingent or detachment of the forces of a country—

(*a*) mentioned in subsection (1)(*a*) of section 1 of the Visiting Forces Act 1952; or

(*b*) designated for the purposes of any provision of that Act by Order in Council under subsection (2) of that section,

which is present in the United Kingdom (including United Kingdom territorial waters) or in any place to which subsection (7) below applies on the invitation of Her Majesty's Government in the United Kingdom.

(7) This subsection applies to any place on, under or above an installation in a designated area within the meaning of section 1(7) of the Continental Shelf Act 1964 or any waters within 500 metres of such an installation.

(8) It shall be a defence for any person charged in respect of any conduct of his relating to a weapon to which this section applies—

(*a*) with an offence under subsection (1) above; or

(*b*) with an offence under section 50(2) or (3) of the Customs and Excise Management Act 1979,

to prove that the conduct in question was only for the purpose of making the weapon available to a museum or gallery to which this subsection applies.

(9) If a person acting on behalf of a museum or gallery to which subsection (8) above applies is charged with hiring or lending a weapon to which this section applies, it shall be a defence for him to prove that he has reasonable grounds for believing that the person to whom he lent or hired it would use it only for cultural, artistic or educational purposes.

(10) Subsection (8) above applies to a museum or gallery only if it does not distribute profits.

(11) In this section "museum or gallery" includes any institution which has as its purpose, or one of its purposes, the preservation, display and interpretation of material of historical, artistic or scientific interest and gives the public access to it.

(12) This section shall not have effect in relation to anything done before it comes into force.

(13) [*omitted*]

NOTES
This provision came into force on 29 July 1988, and is designed to restrict the availability of offensive weapons. The carrying of such weapons is still controlled primarily by the Prevention of Crime Act 1953 (*qv*); but see also s 139 *supra* in respect of knives etc.
It will clearly apply as much to companies as to natural persons.

'weapons to which this section applies' See subss (2)–(3), together with the Criminal Justice Act 1988 (Offensive Weapons) Order (SI 1988 No 2019).

Subs (4) This does not itself create any offence, but it brings relevant items within the scope of ss 49–50 of the Customs and Excise Management Act 1979.

Crossbows These are subject to separate control under the Crossbows Act 1989 (*qv*).

142–159. [*omitted*]

Summary offences of possession of indecent photograph of child
160. (1) It is an offence for a person to have any indecent photograph of a child (meaning in this section a person under the age of 16) in his possession.

(2) Where a person is charged with an offence under subsection (1) above, it shall be a defence for him to prove—

(a) that he had a legitimate reason for having the photograph in his possession; or

(b) that he had not himself seen the photograph and did not know, nor had any cause to suspect, it to be indecent; or

(c) that the photograph was sent to him without any prior request made by him or on his behalf and that he did not keep it for an unreasonable time.

(3) A person shall be liable on summary conviction of an offence under this section to a fine not exceeding level 5 on the standard scale.

(4) Sections 1(3), 2(3), 3 and 7 of the Protection of Children Act 1978 shall have effect as if any reference in them to that Act included a reference to this section.

(5) Possession before this section comes into force is not an offence.

NOTE

See generally the Protection of Children Act 1978 and the notes thereto. This provision supplements the more serious offence created by s 1(c) of that Act, and differs in that it is not necessary in this case to prove that D intended to show or distribute the photos to others.

Subs (5) Possession prior to commencement of this section (which came into force on 29 September 1988) may still be an offence under s 1(c) of the 1978 Act if the requirements of that Act are satisfied.

Road Traffic Act 1988

(C 52)

Causing death by reckless driving

1. A person who causes the death of another person by driving a motor vehicle on a road recklessly is guilty of an offence.

NOTES
Road traffic law generally lies outside the scope of this work; but this particular offence can equally well be categorised as a part of mainstream criminal law as a form of manslaughter.

'person who causes' A corporation cannot 'drive' a vehicle, but it can incur liability through the actions of its directors or senior managers. See, for example, *R v Robert Millar (Contractors) Ltd* [1970] 1 All ER 577, where the company, through its managing director, counselled and procured its employee to commit the offence by driving a dangerously defective lorry, which caused a fatal accident.

'causes the death of another' The same principles of causation are applicable here as apply in other cases of unlawful homicide. Where P is injured by D's reckless driving, and dies following faulty medical treatment, the question is whether the original injuries were an operating and substantial cause of death: see *R v Smith* [1959] 2 QB 35: *R v Jordan* (1956) 40 Cr App R 152. See also *R v Malcherek* [1981] 2 All ER 422.
    Where other persons are in part to blame for a fatal accident it need not be shown that D was primarily to blame, as long as his recklessness was a substantial causative factor, rather than an insignificant or minimal one: *R v Henningan* [1971] 3 All ER 133.

'driving' This is a rather narrower concept than that of 'using' a vehicle. See generally *R v Macdonagh* [1974] RTR 372; *McKeon v Ellis* [1987] RTR 26.

'motor vehicle' This is defined in s 185 of the Act as 'a mechanically propelled vehicle intended or adapted for use on roads'. The engine need not be in proper working order (*eg* where D is coasting in it or where he is receiving a tow): *McEachran v Hurst* [1978] RTR 462. Problems may however arise where the vehicle is not one ordinarily used on roads at all. A go-cart, for example does not come within this definition merely because D intentionally uses it on a public road. It must be a vehicle which a reasonable man might contemplate would be used on a road as one of its functions: *Burns v Currell* [1963] 2 All ER 297; *O'Brien v Anderton* [1979] RTR 388.

'road' This is defined in s 192 of the Act as 'any highway and any other road to which the public has access, and includes bridges over which a road passes'.
    Paths and footways which are highways (i.e. over which the public have a right of way) are thus roads within this section. See *Lang v Hindhaugh* [1986] RTR 271. In other cases, the question is whether the public have access to a road. If they do (and this is largely a question of fact) a privately owned road may be within the scope of the Road Traffic Act. See *Harrison v Hill* 1932 SC(J) 13; *Cox v White* [1976] RTR 248: *Adams v Met. Police Commissioner* [1980] RTR 289.
    Foreign roads are generally outside the scope of the Act but offences under this section may be committed abroad be servicemen *etc* who are subject to English criminal law. See *Cox v Army Council* [1962] 1 All ER 880.

Finally, it should be noted that some private roads to which the public do not have access are nevertheless deemed to be within the scope of the Road Traffic Acts. These include various airport, Ministry of Defence and dockyard roads. See *R v Murray* [1984] RTR 203.

'recklessly' According to the House of Lords in *R v Lawrence* [1982] AC 510, D's driving must be of a kind that involves an obvious and serious risk of causing injury to other road users or serious damage to property, and D must either appreciate this risk or have failed to consider it. The reckless or deliberate use of a dangerously defective vehicle or a dangerously loaded one may in itself amount to reckless driving: *R v Crossman* [1986] Crim LR 406.

There is little difference between the essential elements of this offence and those of reckless 'motor' manslaughter. The latter offence requires recklessness as to the risk of killing or at least injuring someone, not just recklessness as to the risk of damaging property; but in practice a motorist is unlikely to be reckless as to the one without being reckless as to the other. Manslaughter charges tend to be brought only in the most serious cases of reckless killing on the roads. See generally *R v Seymour* [1983] 2 AC 493: *Kong Cheuk Kwan v R* (1985) 82 Cr App R 18.

Prevention of Terrorism (Temporary Provisions) Act 1989

(C 4)

Part I: Proscribed Organisations

1. [*omitted*]

Membership, support and meetings

2. (1) Subject to subsection (3) below, a person is guilty of an offence if he—

(a) belongs or professes to belong to a proscribed organisation;

(b) solicits or invites support for a proscribed organisation other than support with money or other property; or

(c) arranges or assists in the arrangement or management of, or addresses, any meeting of three or more persons (whether or not it is a meeting to which the public are admitted) knowing that the meeting is—

(i) to support a proscribed organisation;

(ii) to further the activities of such an organisation; or

(iii) to be addressed by a person belonging or professing to belong to such an organisation.

(2) A person guilty of an offence under subsection (1) above is liable—

(a) on conviction on indictment, to imprisonment for a term not exceeding ten years or a fine or both;

(b) on summary conviction, to imprisonment for a term not exceeding six months or a fine not exceeding the statutory maximum or both.

(3) A person belonging to a proscribed organisation is not guilty of an offence under this section by reason of belonging to the organisation if he shows—

(a) that he became a member when it was not a proscribed organisation under the current legislation; and

(b) that he has not since he became a member taken part in any of its activities at any time while it was a proscribed organisation under that legislation.

(4) In subsection (3) above "the current legislation", in relation to any time, means whichever of the following was in force at that time—

(a) the Prevention of Terrorism (Temporary Provisions) Act 1974;

(b) the Prevention of Terrorism (Temporary Provisions) Act 1976;

(c) the Prevention of Terrorism (Temporary Provisions) Act 1984; or

(d) this Act.

(5) The reference in subsection (3) above to a person becoming a member of an organisation is a reference to the only or last occasion on which he became a member.

NOTES
Under s 1 and Sch 1 of this Act, the Irish Republican Army and the Irish National Liberation Army are both proscribed organisations. Other organisations may in future be proscribed if they appear to be connected with terrorism in Northern Ireland, but note subs (3) of this section.

'other than support with money or other property'   This kind of support is dealt with in ss 9 and 10 *infra.*

'property'   See s 20(1) *infra.*

Display of support in public
3. (1) Any person who in a public place—
(*a*) wears any item of dress; or
(*b*) wears, carries or displays any article,
in such a way or in such circumstances as to arouse reasonable apprehension that he is a member or supporter of a proscribed organisation, is guilty of an offence and liable on summary conviction to imprisonment for a term not exceeding six months or a fine not exceeding level 5 on the standard scale or both.
(2) [*Applies to Scotland only.*]
(3) In this section "public place" includes any highway or, in Scotland, any road within the meaning of the Roads (Scotland) Act 1984 and any premises to which at the material time the public have, or are permitted to have, access, whether on payment or otherwise.

NOTES
In *R v O'Moran* [1975] QB 864 it was stated (*obiter*) that the wearing of a badge could not amount to an offence of wearing a uniform, contrary to s 1 of the Public Order Act 1936. The present offence would appear to fill any gap revealed by that decision, since the display of any article could suffice for liablility under subs (1).

'proscribed organisation'   See the notes to s 2 *supra*

'premises'   See s. 20(1) *infra.*

Part II: Exclusion Orders

4–7. [*omitted—see the notes to s 8*]

Offences in respcect of exclusion orders
8. (1) A person who is subject to an exclusion order is guilty of an offence if he fails to comply with the order at a time after he has been, or has become liable to be, removed under Schedule 2 to this Act.
(2) A person is guilty of an offence—
(*a*) if he is knowingly concerned in arrangements for securing or facilitating the entry into Great Britain, Northern Ireland or the

United Kingdom of a person whom he knows, or has reasonable grounds for believing, to be an excluded person; or

(b) if he knowingly harbours such a person in Great Britain, Northern Ireland or the United Kingdom.

(3) In subsection (2) above "excluded person" means—

(a) in relation to Great Britain, a person subject to an exclusion order made under section 5 above who has been, or has become liable to be, removed from Great Britain under Schedule 2 to this Act;

(b) in relation to Northern Ireland, a person subject to an exclusion order made under section 6 above who has been, or has become liable to be, removed from Northern Ireland under that Schedule; and

(c) in relation to the United Kingdom, a person subject to an exclusion order made under section 7 above who has been, or has become liable to be, removed from the United Kingdom under that Schedule.

(4) A person guilty of an offence under this section is liable—

(a) on conviction on indictment, to imprisonment for a term not exceeding five years or a fine or both;

(b) on summary conviction, to imprisonment for a term not exceeding six months or a fine not exceeding the statutory maximum or both.

NOTES

Ss 4–7 of this Act empower the Secretary of State to make orders excluding persons from Great Britain (s 5), Northern Ireland (s 6) or the United Kingdom (s 7). He may make such orders when he is satisfied that the persons excluded are or have been concerned in acts of terrorism connected with Northern Ireland and that their exclusion would be expedient in order to prevent further such acts (s 4). The Act does not empower the Secretary of State to make orders excluding persons he suspects to be concerned with terrorism that has no Northern Ireland connection.

An exclusion order may be served on someone already within the relevant territory, and that person may then become liable to removal under Sch 2.

Part III: Financial Assistance for Terrorism

Contributions towards acts of terrorism

9. (1) A person is guilty of an offence if he—

(a) solicits or invites any other person to give, lend or otherwise make available, whether for consideration or not, any money or other property; or

(b) receives or accepts from any other person, whether for consideration or not, any money or other property,

intending that it shall be applied or used for the commission of, or in furtherance of, or in connection with, acts of terrorism to which this section applies or having reasonable cause to suspect that it may be so used or applied.

(2) A person is guilty of an offence if he— .

(a) gives, lends or otherwise makes available to any other person, whether for consideration or not, any money or other property; or (*b*) enters into or is otherwise concerned in an arrangement whereby money or other property is or is to be made available to another person,

knowing or having reasonable cause to suspect that it will or may be applied or used as mentioned in subsection (1) above.

(3) The acts of terrorism to which this section applies are—

(*a*) acts of terrorism connected with the affairs of Northern Ireland; and

(*b*) subject to subsection (4) below, acts of terrorism of any other description except acts connected solely with the affairs of the United Kingdom or any part of the United Kingdom other than Northern Ireland.

(4) Subsection (3)(*b*) above does not apply to an act done or to be done outside the United Kingdom unless it constitutes or would constitute an offence triable in the United Kingdom.

(5) In proceedings against a person for an offence under this section in relation to an act within subsection (3)(*b*) above done or to be done outside the United Kingdom—

(*a*) the prosecution need not prove that that person knew or had reasonable cause to suspect that the act constituted or would constitute such an offence as is mentioned in subsection (4) above; but

(*b*) it shall be a defence to prove that he did not know and had no reasonable cause to suspect that the facts were such that the act constituted or would constitute such an offence.

NOTES

Whereas s 10 *infra* deals with financial and material support for proscribed organisations, this provision deals with the provision of such support for terrorist activities. It does not confine itself to support for terrorist acts by proscribed organisations, nor does it confine itself to support for terrorism in connection with Northern Ireland. Various kinds of international terrorism come within the scope of subs (3)(b), including many that have no direct link with the United Kingdom at all. Subs (4) excludes some acts of terrorism; but there are many pieces of legislation that extend English jurisdiction over terrorist crimes committed abroad. See for example the Aviation Security Act 1982 and s 4 of the Suppression of Terrorism Act 1978.

Support for terrorism exclusively concerned with other parts of the United Kingdom (e.g. the burning of holiday homes in Wales) is *not* within the scope of this provision.

'property'; **'terrorism'**   See s. 20(1) *infra*.

Further defences   See s 12(2)–(3) *infra*,

Penalties etc   See s 13 *infra*

Contributions to resources of proscribed organisations

10. (1) A person is guilty of an offence if he—

(*a*) solicits or invites any other person to give, lend or otherwise make available, whether for consideration or not, any money or other property for the benefit of a proscribed organisation;

(b) gives, lends or otherwise makes available or receives or accepts, whether for consideration or not, any money or other property for the benefit of such an organisation; or

(c) enters into or is otherwise concerned in an arrangement whereby money or other property is or is to be made available for the benefit of such an organisation.

(2) In proceedings against a person for an offence under subsection (1)(b) above it is a defence to prove that he did not know and had no reasonable cause to suspect that the money or property was for the benefit of a proscribed organisation; and in proceedings against a person for an offence under subsection (1)(c) above it is a defence to prove that he did not know and had no reasonable cause to suspect that the arrangement related to a proscribed organisation.

(3) In this section and sections 11 and 13 below "proscribed organisation" includes a proscribed organisation for the purposes of section 21 of the Northern Ireland (Emergency Provisions) Act 1978.

NOTES
See the notes to s 9 *supra*. Note that the list of organisations proscribed under the 1978 Act is somewhat longer and includes certain 'loyalist' groups such as the Ulster Freedom Fighters and the Ulster Volunteer Force.

Further defences   See s 12(2)–(3) *infra*.

Penalties etc   See s 13 *infra*.

Assisting in retention or control of terrorist funds
11. (1) A person is guilty of an offence if he enters into or is otherwise concerned in an arrangement whereby the retention of control by or on behalf of another person of terrorist funds is facilitated, whether by concealment, removal from the jurisdiction, transfer to nominees or otherwise.

(2) In proceedings against a person for an offence under the section it is a defence to prove that he did not know and had no reasonable cause to suspect that the arrangement related to terrorist funds.

(3) In this section and section 12 below "terrorist funds" means—

(a) funds which may be applied or used for the commission of, or in furtherance of or in connection with, acts of terrorism to which section 9 above applies;

(b) the proceeds of the commission of such acts of terrorism or of activities engaged in in furtherance of or in connection with such acts; and

(c) the resources of a proscribed organisation.

(4) Paragraph (b) of subsection (3) includes any property which in whole or in part directly or indirectly represents such proceeds as are mentioned in that paragraph; and paragraph (c) of that subsection includes any money or other property which is or is to be applied or made available for the benefit of a proscribed organisation.

NOTES
'property'; **'terrorism'**   See s 20(1) *infra.*

'proscribed organisation'   Note that this has the wider meaning imposed by s 10(3) *supra.*

Further defences   See s 12(2)–(3) *infra.*

Penalties etc.   See s 13 *infra.*

Disclosure of information about terrorist funds
   12. (1) A person may notwithstanding any restriction on the disclosure of information imposed by contract disclose to a constable a suspicion or belief that any money or other property is or is derived from terrorist funds or any matter on which such a suspicion or belief is based.

   (2) A person who enters into or is otherwise concerned in any such transaction or arrangement as is mentioned in section 9, 10 and 11 above does not commit an offence under that section if he is acting with the express consent of a constable or if—

   (a) he discloses to a constable his suspicion or belief that the money or other property concerned is or is derived from terrorist funds or any matter on which such a suspicion or belief is based; and

   (b) the disclosure is made after he enters into or otherwise becomes concerned in the transaction or arrangement in question but is made on his own initiative and as soon as it is reasonable for him to make it,

but paragraphs (a) and (b) above do not apply in a case where, having disclosed any such suspicion, belief or matter to a constable and having been forbidden by a constable to enter into or otherwise be concerned in the transaction or arrangement in question, he nevertheless does so.

   (3) In proceedings against a person for an offence under section 9(1)(b) or (2), 10(1)(b) or (c) or 11 above it is a defence to prove—

   (a) that he intended to disclose to a constable such a suspicion, belief or matter as is mentioned in paragraph (a) of subsection (2) above; and

   (b) that there is a reasonable excuse for his failure to make the disclosure as mentioned in paragraph (b) of that subsection.

NOTES
S 18 *infra* makes it an offence in certain circumstances to fail to disclose material information to the police; but subs (1) of the present provision is facilitative rather than coercive. Subss (2) and (3) differ from each other in that the former narrows the scope of the offences under ss 9–11, whereas the latter merely provides a defence which the accused must establish on balance of probabilities. The two provisions help to make life easier for banks *etc.*, which may find themselves in a position where they have cause to believe that they are involved in transactions proscribed under ss 9–11, but without being able to take action in the absence of direct proof.

'terrorist funds'   See s 11(3) *infra,*

'property'   see s 20(1) *infra.*

Penalties and forfeiture

13. (1) A person guilty of an offence under section 9, 10 or 11 above is liable—

(a) on conviction on indictment, to imprisonment for a term not exceeding fourteen years or a fine or both;

(b) on summary conviction, to imprisonment for a term not exceeding six months or a fine not exceeding the statutory maximum or both.

(2) Subject to the provisions of this section, the court by or before which a person is convicted of an offence under section 9(1) or (2)(a) above may order the forfeiture of any money or other property—

(a) which, at the time of the offence, he had in his possession or under his control; and

(b) which, at the time—

(i) in the case of an offence under subsection (1) of section 9, he intended should be applied or used, or had reasonable cause to suspect might be applied or used, as mentioned in that subsection;

(ii) in the case of an offence under subsection (2)(a) of that section, he knew or had reasonable cause to suspect would or might be applied or used as mentioned in subsection (1) of that section.

(3) Subject to the provisions of this section, the court by or before which a person is convicted of an offence under section 9(2)(b), 10(1)(c) or 11 above may order a forfeiture of the money or other property to which the arrangement in question related and which, in the case of an offence under section 9(2)(b), he knew or had reasonable cause to suspect would or might be applied or used as mentioned in section 9(1) above.

(4) Subject to the provisions of this section, the court by or before which a person is convicted of an offence under section 10(1)(a) of (b) above may order the forfeiture of any money or other property which, at the time of the offence he had in his possession or under his control for the use or benefit of a proscribed organisation.

(5) The court shall not under this section make an order forfeiting any money or other property unless the court considers that the money or property may, unless forfeited, be applied or used as mentioned in section 9(1) above but the court may, in the absence of evidence to the contrary, assume that any money or property may be applied or used as there mentioned.

(6) Where a person other than the convicted person claims to be the owner of or otherwise interested in anything which can be forfeited by an order under this section, the court shall, before making such an order in respect of it, gave him an opportunity to be heard.

(7) [*omitted*]

(8) Schedule 4 to this Act shall have effect in relation to orders under this section.

NOTES
Sch 4 (not printed in this work) contains detailed provisions governing the implementation and enforcement of forfeiture orders, together with rules relating

to restraint orders and to the payment of compensation following acquittals or the quashing of convictions.

'proscribed organisation'   Note that this has the wider meaning imposed by s 10(3) *supra*.

'terrorist funds'   See s 11(3) *supra*.

'property'   See s 20(1) *infra*.

14–16 [*omitted*]

Part V: Information, proceedings and interpretation

Investigation of terrorist activities

17. (1) [*omitted*]

(2) Where in relation to a terrorist investigation a warrant or order under Schedule 7 to this Act has been issued or made or has been applied for and not refused, a person is guilty of an offence if, knowing or having reasonable cause to suspect that the investigation is taking place, he—

(a) makes any disclosure which is likely to prejudice the investigation; or

(b) falsifies, conceals or destroys or otherwise disposes of, or causes or permits the falsification, concealment, destruction or disposal of, material which is or is likely to be relevant to the investigation.

(3) In proceedings against a person for an offence under subsection (2)(a) above it is a defence to prove—

(a) that he did not know and had no reasonable cause to suspect that the disclosure was likely to prejudice the investigation; or

(b) that he had lawful authority or reasonable excuse for making the disclosure.

(4) In proceedings against a person for an offence under subsection (2)(b) above it is a defence to prove that he had no intention of concealing any information contained in the material in question from the persons carrying out the investigation.

(5) A person guilty of an offence under subsection (2) above is liable—

(a) on conviction on indictment, to imprisonment for a term not exceeding five years or a fine or both;

(b) on summary conviction, to imprisonment for a term not exceeding six months or a fine not exceeding the statutory maximum or both.

NOTES

Subs (1) and Sch 7 provide in detail for investigations into terrorist activities, for searches and for the seizure of material.

'falsifies, conceals or destroys'   *Cf* s 17(1) of the Theft Act 1968, and the notes thereto.

'causes or permits'   'Causes' must here bear its imperative meaning. A person causes another person's act when he orders it. 'Permitting' the act involves some awareness of it and a failure to prevent it where prevention would be within one's power. See *Houston v Buchanan* [1940] 2 All ER 179.

Information about acts of terrorism
18. (1) A person is guilty of an offence if he has information which he knows or believes might be of material assistance—
  (a) in preventing the commission by any person of an act of terrorism connected with the affairs of Northern Ireland; or
  (b) in securing the apprehension, prosecution or conviction of any other person for an offence involving the commission, preparation or instigation of such an act,
and fails without reasonable excuse to disclose that information as soon as reasonably practicable—
    (i) in England and Wales, to a constable;
    (ii) [omitted]
    (iii) [omitted]
(2) A person guilty of an offence under this section is liable—
  (a) on conviction on indictment, to imprisonment for a term not exceeding five years or a fine or both;
  (b) on summary conviction, to imprisonment for a term not exceeding six months or a fine not exceeding the statutory maximum or both.
(3) Proceedings for an offence under this section may be taken, and the offence may for purposes of those proceedings be treated as having been committed, in any place where the person to be charged is or has at anytime been since he first knew or believed that the information might be of material assistance as mentioned in subsection (1) above.

NOTES
The imposition of criminal liability for omissions of this kind is most unusual under English law; but there is a similar offence at common law known as misprision of treason, and there was formerly an offence of misprision of felony. Cases on the latter offence established that partial disclosure of relevant information might not absolve D from liability, and that friendship or family relationship might not constitute a reasonable excuse for non-disclosure at least in the case of serious offences. The position of a lawyer in relation to his clients was more doubtful. See generally *Sykes v DPP* [1962] AC 528.
  Further difficulties arise where D would incriminate himself if he informed upon others who were his accomplices. This might be regarded as a reasonable excuse for inaction. See *R v King* [1965] 1 All ER 1053.

Prosecutions and evidence
19. (1) Proceedings shall not be instituted—
  (a) in England and Wales for an offence under section 2, 3, 8, 9, 10, 11, 17 or 18 above or Schedule 7 to this Act except by or with the consent of the Attorney General:
  (b)–(c) [omitted]
(2) [omitted]
(3) [omitted]

Interpretation
20. (1) In this Act—
"exclusion order" has the meaning given by section 4(3) above but subject to section 25(3) below;

"premises" includes any place and in particular includes—
  (*a*) any vehicle, vessel or aircraft;
  (*b*) any offshore installation as defined in section 1 of the Mineral
      Workings (Offshore Installations) Act 1971; and
  (*c*) any tent or movable structure;
"property" includes property wherever situated and whether real or
  personal, heritable or moveable and things in action and other
  intangible or incorporeal property;
"terrorism" means the use of violence for political ends, and includes
  any use of violence for the purpose of putting the public or any
  section of the public in fear; [. . .]
  (2) A constable or examining officer may, if necessary, use reasonable
force for the purpose of exercising any powers conferred on him under or
by virtue of any provision of this Act other than paragraph 2 of Schedule
5; but this subsection is without prejudice to any provision of this Act, or of
any instrument made under it, which implies that a person may use
reasonable force in connection with that provision.
  (3) [*omitted*]
  (4) Any reference in a provision of this Act to a person having been
concerned in the commission, preparation or instigation of acts of
terrorism shall be taken to be a reference to his having been so concerned
at any time, whether before or after the passing of this Act.

21–26. [*omitted*]

Commencement and duration
  27. (1) Subject to subsection (2), (3) and (4) below, this Act shall come
into force on 22nd March 1989.
  (2)–(4) [*omitted*]
  (5) The provisions of Parts I to V of this Act and of subsection (6)(*c*)
below shall remain in force until 22nd March 1990 and shall then expire
unless continued in force by an order under subsection (6) below.
  (6) The Secretary of State may by order made by statutory instrument
provide—
  (*a*) that all or any of those provisions which are for the time being in
      force (including any in force by virtue of an order under this
      paragraph or paragraph (*c*) below) shall continue in force for a
      period not exceeding twelve months from the coming into operation
      of the order;
  (*b*) that all or any of those provisions which are for the time being in
      force shall cease to be in force; or
  (*c*) that all or any of those provisions which are not for the time being
      in force shall come into force again and remain in force for a period
      not exceeding twelve months from the coming into operation of the
      order.
  (7) No order shall be made under subsection (6) above unless—
  (*a*) a draft of the order has been laid before and approved by a
      resolution of each House of Parliament; or

(*b*) it is declared in the order that it appears to the Secretary of State that by reason of urgency it is necessary to make the order without a draft having been so approved.

(8) An order under that subsection of which a draft has not been approved under subsection (7) above—

(*a*) shall be laid before Parliament; and

(*b*) shall cease to have effect at the end of the period of forty days beginning with the day on which it was made unless, before the end of that period, the order has been approved by a resolution of each House of Parliament, but without prejudice to anything previously done or to the making of a new order.

(9) In reckoning for the purposes of subsection (8) above the period of forty days no account shall be taken of any period during which Parliament is dissolved or prorogued or during which both Houses are adjourned for more than four days.

(10) In subsection (5) above the reference to Parts I to V of this Act does not include a reference to the provisions of Parts III and V so far as they have effect in Northern Ireland and relate to proscribed organisations for the purposes of section 21 of the Northern Ireland (Emergency Provisions) Act 1978 or offences or orders under that section.

(11) The provisions excluded by subsection (10) above from subsection (5) and the provisions of sections 21 to 24 above shall remain in force until 22nd March 1990 and then expire but shall be—

(*a*) included in the provisions to which subsection (3) of section 33 of the said Act of 1978 applies (provisions that can be continued in force, repealed or revived by order); and

(*b*) treated as part of that Act for the purposes of subsection (9) of that Act (repeal on 14th May 1992).

(12) [*omitted*]

NOTE
All the sections printed here came into force on 22 March 1989. There is no fixed expiry date, as long as orders under subs (6) are made and approved each year.

28. [*omitted*]

Official Secrets Act 1989

(C 6)

Security and intelligence

1. (1) A person who is or has been—

(*a*) a member of the security and intelligence services; or

(*b*) a person notified that he is subject to the provisions of this subsection,

is guilty of an offence if without lawful authority he discloses any information, document or other article relating to security or intelligence which is or has been in his possession by virtue of his position as a member of any of those services or in the course of his work while the notification is or was in force.

(2) The reference in subsection (1) above to disclosing information relating to security or intelligence includes a reference to making any statement which purports to be a disclosure of such information or is intended to be taken by those to whom it is adressed as being such a disclosure.

(3) A person who is or has been a Crown servant or government contractor is guilty of an offence if without lawful authority he makes a damaging disclosure of any information, document or other article relating to security or intelligence which is or has been in his possession by virtue of his position as such but otherwise than as mentioned in subsection (1) above.

(4) For the purposes of subsection (3) above a disclosure is damaging if—

(*a*) it causes damage to the work of, or any part of, the security and intelligence services; or

(*b*) it is of information or a document or other article which is such that its unauthorised disclosure would be likely to cause such damage or which falls within a class or description of information, documents or articles the unauthorised disclosure of which would be likely to have that effect.

(5) It is a defence for a person charged with an offence under this section to prove that at the time of the alleged offence he did not know, and had no reasonable cause to believe, that the information, document or article in question related to security or intelligence or, in the case of an offence under subsection (3), that the disclosure would be damaging within the meaning of that subsection.

(6) Notification that a person is subject to subsection (1) above shall be effected by a notice in writing served on him by a Minister of the Crown; and such a notice may be served if, in the Minister's opinion, the work undertaken by a person in question is or includes work connected with the

security and intelligence services and its nature is such that the interests of national security require that he should be subject to the provisions of that subsection.

(7) Subject to subsection (8) below, a notification for the purposes of subsection (1) above shall be in force for the period of five years beginning with the day on which it is served but may be renewed by further notices under subsection (6) above for periods of five years at a time.

(8) A notification for the purposes of subsection (1) above may at any time be revoked by a further notice in writing served by the Minister on the person concerned; and the Minister shall serve such a further notice as soon as, in his opinion, the work undertaken by that person ceases to be such as is mentioned in subsection (6) above.

(9) In this section "security or intelligence" means the work of, or in support of, the security and intelligence services or any part of them, and references to information relating to security or intelligence include references to information held or transmitted by those services or by persons in support of, or of any part of, them.

NOTES

The Act replaces the absurdly wide s 2 of the Official Secrets Act 1911 with more detailed provisions protecting more limited classes of official information. This provision deals specifically with matters relating to security and intelligence, other provisions dealing with defence, international relations, criminal investigation, *etc*. Note that important distinctions are made between persons coming within subs (1) and those coming only within subs (3). Unauthorised disclosures by the former may be criminal without necessarily being damaging within the meaning of subs (4), and under subs (2) such persons may incur liability by making statements which merely *purport* to disclose information covered by subs (1) itself. This may save the prosecution from having to make awkward disclosures on sensitive issues in order to prove its case.

'without lawful authority' See s 7 *infra,*

'Crown servant'; 'government contractor' See s 12 *infra,*

'Disclose/disclosure' See s 13 *infra*

'damaging' For the purpose of subs (4)(*b*) a disclosure may be regarded as 'damaging' if an unauthorised disclosure of that material or that kind of material would be likely to cause damage to the work of the security or intelligence services. Actual damage clearly need not be proved, nor will it always be necessary to identify the precise content of the material disclosed. Furthermore, it would not appear to be possible for D to escape liability by arguing that his disclosure, although unauthorised, was to a person of undoubted loyalty and discretion (perhaps D's own spouse). The subsection refers to the danger of unauthorised disclosure generally, not to the danger of the particular disclosure in question.

Penalty See s 10 *infra,*

Acts done abroad See s 15 *infra*

Defence
2. (1) A person who is or has been a Crown servant or government contractor is guilty of an offence if without lawful authority he makes a damaging disclosure of any information, document or other article

relating to defence which is or has been in his possession by virtue of his position as such.

(2) For the purposes of subsection (1) above a disclosure is damaging if—

(a) it damages the capability of, or of any part of, the armed forces of the Crown to carry out their tasks or leads to loss of life or injury to members of those forces or serious damage to the equipment or installations of those forces; or

(b) otherwise than as mentioned in paragraph (a) above, it endangers the interests of the United Kingdom abroad, seriously obstructs the promotion or protection by the United Kingdom of those interests or endangers the safety of British citizens abroad; or

(c) it is of information or of a document or article which is such that its unauthorised disclosure would be likely to have any of those effects.

(3) It is a defence for a person charged with an offence under this section to prove that at the time of the alleged offence he did not know, and had no reasonable cause to believe, that the information, document or article in question related to defence or that its disclosure would be damaging within the meaning of subsection (1) above.

(4) In this section "defence" means—

(a) the size, shape, organisation, logistics, order of battle, employment, operations, state of readiness and training of the armed forces of the Crown;

(b) the weapons, stores or other equipment of those forces and the invention, development, production and operation of such equipment and research relating to it;

(c) defence policy and strategy and military planning and intelligence;

(d) plans and measures for the maintenance of essential supplies and services that are or would be needed in time of war.

NOTES
This provision follows the same general pattern as s 1, except that it is always necessary for the prosecution to prove that an unauthorised disclosure was 'damaging' (within the extended meaning provided by subs (2)). See generally the notes to s 1 *supra*.

International relations
3. (1) A person who is or has been a Crown servant or government contractor is guilty of an offence if without lawful authority he makes a damaging disclosure of—

(a) any information, document or other article relating to international relations; or

(b) any confidential information, document or other article which was obtained for a State other than the United Kingdom or an international organisation,

being information or a document or article which is or has been in his possession by virtue of his position as a Crown servant or government contractor.

(2) For the purposes of subsection (1) above a disclosure is damaging if—

(a) it endangers the interests of the United Kingdom abroad, seriously obstructs the promotion or protection by the United Kingdom of those interests or endangers the safety of British citizens abroad; or

(b) it is of information or of a document or article which is such that its unauthorised disclosure would be likely to have any of those effects.

(3) In the case of information or a document or article within subsection (1)(b) above—

(a) the fact that it is confidential, or

(b) its nature or contents,

may be sufficient to establish for the purposes of subsection (2)(b) above that the information, document or article is such that its unauthorised disclosure would be likely to have any of the effects there mentioned.

(4) It is a defence for a person charged with an offence under this section to prove that at the time of the alleged offence he did not know, and had no reasonable cause to believe, that the information, document or article in question was such as is mentioned in subsection (1) above or that its disclosure would be damaging within the meaning of that subsection.

(5) In this section "international relations" means the relations between States, between international organisations or between one or more States and one or more such organisations and includes any matter relating to a State other than the United Kingdom or to an international organisation which is capable of affecting the relations of the United Kingdom with another State or with an international organisation.

(6) For the purposes of this section any information, document or article obtained from a State or organisation is confidential at any time while the terms on which it was obtained require it to be held in confidence or while the circumstances in which it was obtained make it reasonable for the State or organisation to expect that it would be so held.

NOTES

This offence involves *either* unauthorised disclosure of material relating to international relations, *or* unauthorised disclosure of confidential material obtained from another state or from an international organisation. Material in the latter category need not itself have anything to do with international relations, but the failure of the United Kingdom to prevent leaks of such material may have damaging effects in that area.

'damaging' As in ss 1 and 2, actual damage need not be proved; and subs (3) is designed to save the prosecution from the need to make embarrasing disclosures of its own. See further the notes to s 1 *supra*.

'without lawful authority' See s 7 *infra*.

'Crown servant'; government contractor' See s 12 *infra*.

'disclose/disclosure'; 'international organisation'; 'state' See s 13 *infra*.

Penalty See s 10 *infra*,

Acts done abroad See s 15 *infra*.

Crime and special investigation powers

4. (1) A person who is or has been a Crown servant or government contractor is guilty of an offence if without lawful authority he discloses any information, document or other article to which this section applies and which is or has been in his possession by virtue of his position as such.

(2) This section applies to any information, document or other article—

(*a*) the disclosure of which—

    (i) results in the commission of an offence; or

    (ii) facilitates an escape from legal custody or the doing of any other act prejudicial to the safekeeping of persons in legal custody; or

    (iii) impedes the prevention or detection of offences or the apprehension or prosecution of suspected offenders; or

(*b*) which is such that its unauthorised disclosure would be likely to have any of those effects.

(3) This section also applies to—

(*a*) any information obtained by reason of the interception of any communication in obedience to a warrant issued under section 2 of the Interception of Communications Act 1985, any information relating to the obtaining of information by reason of any such interception and any document or other article which is or has been used or held for use in, or has been obtained by reason of, any such interception; and

(*b*) any information obtained by reason of action authorised by a warrant issued under section 3 of the Security Service Act 1989, any information relating to the obtaining of information by reason of any such action and any document or other article which is or has been used or held for use in, or has been obtained by reason of, any such action.

(4) It is a defence for a person charged with an offence under this section in respect of a disclosure falling within subsection (2)(*a*) above to prove that at the time of the alleged offence he did not know, and had no reasonable cause to believe, that the disclosure would have any of the effects there mentioned.

(5) It is a defence for a person charged with an offence under this section in respect of any other disclosure to prove that at the time of the alleged offence he did not know, and had no reasonable cause to believe, that the information, document or article in question was information or a document or article to which this section applies.

(6) In this section "legal custody" includes detention in pursuance of any enactment or any instrument made under an enactment.

NOTES
This provision is aimed primarily, but not exclusively, at police officers and civilian police employees, and covers a range of possible disclosures, from 'tip-offs' which frustrate police raids (conduct which may also amount to an offence under s 51 of the Police Act 1964) to the disclosure of information needed by criminals in order

to commit a future offence (conduct which may in certain cases give rise to liability as an accessory to that offence). Liability under this provision may however be incurred where such wider liability would not be, as where D is merely indiscreet and has no intention of assisting criminals or of frustrating law enforcement. Note that under subs (2)(*b*) no actual consequences of the disclosure need be proved, and where a disclosure falls within subs(2)(*b*), the defence provided by subs (4) is unavailable.

'information ... to which this section applies' Note that information *etc* covered by subs (3) need not also fall within subs (2). In either cases it would appear that the identity and character of the person to whom unauthorised disclosure is made is irrelevant. In other words disclosure to one's spouse may be as much an offence as disclosure to a known criminal (*cf* the notes to s 1 *supra*).

'without lawful authority' See s 7 *infra*.

'Crown servant'; 'government contractor' See s 12 *infra*.

'disclose/disclosure' See s 13 *infra*.

Penalty See s 10 *infra*.

Acts done abroad See s 15 *infra*.

Information resulting from unauthorised disclosures or entrusted in confidence
5. (1) Subsection (2) below applies where—
  (*a*) any information, document of other article protected against disclosure by the foregoing provisions of this Act has come into a person's possession as a result of having been—
    (i) disclosed (whether to him or another) by a Crown servant or government contractor without lawful authority; or
    (ii) entrusted to him by a Crown servant or government contractor on terms requiring it to be held in confidence or in circumstances in which the Crown servant or government contractor could reasonably expect that it would be so held; or
    (iii) disclosed (whether to him or another) without lawful authority by a person to whom it was entrusted as mentioned in subparagraph (ii) above; and
  (*b*) the disclosure without lawful authority of the information, document or article by the person into whose possession it has come is not an offence under any of those provisions.
(2) Subject to subsections (3) and (4) below, the person into whose possession the information, document or article has come is guilty of an offence if he discloses it without lawful authority knowing, or having reasonable cause to believe, that it is protected against disclosure by the foregoing provisions of this Act and that it has come into his possession as mentioned in subsection (1) above.
(3) In the case of information or a document or article protected against disclosure by sections 1 to 3 above, a person does not commit an offence under subsection (2) above unless—
  (*a*) the disclosure by him is damaging; and
  (*b*) he makes it knowing, or having reasonable cause to believe, that it would be damaging;

and the question whether a disclosure is damaging shall be determined for the purposes of this subsection as it would be in relation to a disclosure of that information, document or article by a Crown servant in contravention of section 1(3), 2(1) of 3(1) above.

(4) A person does not commit an offence under subsection (2) above in respect of information or a document or other article which has come into his possession as a result of having been disclosed—

(*a*) as mentioned in subsection (1)(*a*)(i) above by a government contractor; or

(*b*) as mentioned in subsection (1)(*a*)(iii) above,

unless that disclosure was by a British citizen or took place in the United Kingdom, in any of the Channel Islands or in the Isle of Man or a colony.

(5) For the purposes of this section information or a document or article is protected against disclosure by the foregoing provisions of this Act if—

(*a*) it relates to security or intelligence, defence or international relations within the meaning of section 1, 2 or 3 above or is such as is mentioned in section 3(1)(*b*) above; or

(*b*) it is information or a document or article to which section 4 above applies;

and information or a document or article is protected against disclosure by sections 1 to 3 above if it falls within paragraph (*a*) above.

(6) A person is guilty of an offence if without lawful authority he discloses any information, document or other article which he knows, or has reasonable cause to believe, to have come into his possession as a result of a contravention of section 1 of the Official Secrets Act 1911.

NOTES

This provision is designed to prohibit the wider disclosure of secret and confidential material by persons (particularly the media) into whose hands it may have fallen (directly or indirectly) following an initial disclosure by a Crown servant of government contractor (subss (1)–(5)), or (sub (6)) following a contravention of s 1 of the Official Secrets Act 1911 (*qv*). Somewhat suprisingly, an offence under the first part of this section does not appear to be possible unless the initial disclosure was by a serving Crown servant or government contractor within the meaning of s 12 *infra*. This contrasts with the wider scope of the four previous sections, which apply to former Crown servants *etc* as well. The contrast may perhaps be the result of an oversight; but there is a further, deliberate, contrast, in that the prosecution must prove *mens rea* under sub (2); and in the case of material protected under ss 1–3, the additional *mens rea* specified in sub (3)(*b*). (In ss 1–4 the defence has the burden of proving the absence of any such *mens rea*.)

Subs (4) This limitation on the scope of the sub (2) offence is apparently designed to prevent the British media from remaining gagged by it once the original disclosure has resulted in the protected information *etc* being common knowledge elsewhere in the world (*cf* the *Spycatcher* case, where attempts were made to supress reproduction of Peter Wright's memoirs in the UK, long after they had become a bestseller elsewhere).

'Crown servant'; 'government contractor' See s 12 *infra*.

'without lawful authority'—See s 7 *infra*.

'disclose/disclosure' See s 13 *infra.*

Penalty See s 10 *infra.*

Acts done abroad See s 15 *infra.*

Information entrusted in confidence to other States or international organisations
6. (1) This section applies where—
(*a*) any information, document or other article which—
  (i) relates to security or intelligence, defence or international relations; and
  (ii) has been communicated in confidence by or on behalf of the United Kingdom to another State or to an international organisation,
  has come into a person's possession as a result of having been disclosed (whether to him or another) without the authority of that State or organisation or, in the case of an organisation, of a member of it; and
(*b*) the disclosure without lawful authority of the information, document or article by the person into whose possession it has come is not an offence under any of the foregoing provisions of this Act.

(2) Subject to subsection (3) below, the person into whose possession the information, document or article has come is guilty of an offence if he makes a damaging disclosure of it knowing, or having reasonable cause to believe, that it is such as is mentioned in subsection (1) above, that it has come into his possession as there mentioned and that its disclosure would be damaging.

(3) A person does not commit an offence under subsection (2) above if the information, document or article is disclosed by him with lawful authority or has previously been made available to the public with the authority of the State or organisation concerned or, in the case of an organisation, of a member of it.

(4) For the purposes of this section "security or intelligence", "defence" and "international relations" have the same meaning as in sections 1, 2 and 3 above and the question whether a disclosure is damaging shall be determined as it would be in relation to a disclosure of the information, document or article in question by a Crown servant in contravention of sections 1(3), 2(1) and 3(1) above.

(5) For the purposes of this section information or a document or article is communicated in confidence if it is communicated on terms requiring it to be held in confidence or in circumstances in which the person communicating it could reasonably expect that it would be so held.

NOTES
This provision complements s 5 *supra* by making it an offence to give wider circulation to protected material which has been improperly leaked after being entrusted to another state or to an international organisation. As in s 5, and in contrast to ss 1–4, the prosecution must prove *mens rea* (see subs (2)), rather than it being left for the defence to prove its absence.

'state'; **'international organisation'**; **'disclose/disclosure'** See s 13 *infra*.

'without lawful authority'; **'official authorisation'** See s 7 *infra*.

Acts done abroad See s 15 *infra*.

Penalty See s 10 *infra*.

Authorised disclosures
7. (1) For the purposes of this Act a disclosure by—
(*a*) a Crown servant; or
(*b*) a person, not being a Crown servant or government contractor, in whose case a notification for the purposes of section 1(1) above is in force,
is made with lawful authority if, and only if, it is made in accordance with his official duty.

(2) For the purposes of this Act a disclosure by a government contractor is made with lawful authority if, and only if, it is made—
(*a*) in accordance with an official authorisation; or
(*b*) for the purposes of the functions by virtue of which he is a government contractor and without contravening an official restriction.

(3) For the purposes of this Act a disclosure made by any other person is made with lawful authority if, and only if, it is made—
(*a*) to a Crown servant for the purposes of his functions as such; or
(*b*) in accordance with an official authorisation.

(4) It is a defence for a person charged with an offence under any of the foregoing provisions of this Act to prove that at the time of the alleged offence he believed that he had lawful authority to make the disclosure in question and had no reasonable cause to believe otherwise.

(5) In this section "official authorisation" and "official restriction" mean, subject to subsection (6) below, an authorisation or restriction duly given or imposed by a Crown servant or government contractor or by or on behalf of a prescribed body or a body of a prescribed class.

(6) In relation to section 6 above "official authorisation" includes an authorisation duly given by or on behalf of the State or organisation concerned or, in the case of an organisation, a member of it.

NOTES
Apart from defining authorised disclosure, this provision creates a defence of reasonable belief in such authorisation (subs (5)). As with the defences created under ss 1–4, this defence must be proved on balance of probabilities.

'Crown servant'; **'government contractor'** See s 12 *infra*.

'Prescribed' See s 13 *infra*.

Safeguarding of information

8. (1) Where a Crown servant or government contractor, by virtue of his position as such, has in his possession or under his control any document or other article which it would be an offence under any of the foregoing provisions of this Act for him to disclose without lawful authority he is guilty of an offence if—

(a) being a Crown servant, he retains the document or article contrary to his official duty; or

(b) being a government contractor, he fails to comply with an official direction for the return or disposal of the document or article,

or if he fails to take such care to prevent the unauthorised disclosure of the document or article as a person in his position may reasonably be expected to take.

(2) It is a defence for a Crown servant charged with an offence under subsection (1)(a) above to prove that at the time of the alleged offence he believed that he was acting in accordance with his official duty and had no reasonable cause to believe otherwise.

(3) In subsections (1) and (2) above references to a Crown servant include any person, not being a Crown servant or government contractor, in whose case a notification for the purposes of section 1(1) above is in force.

(4) Where a person has in his possession or under his control any document or other article which it would be an offence under section 5 above for him to disclose without lawful authority, he is guilty of an offence if—

(a) he fails to comply with an official direction for its return or disposal or

(b) where he obtained it from a Crown servant or government contractor on terms requiring it to be held in confidence or in circumstances in which that servant or contractor could reasonably expect that it would be so held, he fails to take such care to prevent its unauthorised disclosure as a person in his position may reasonably be expected to take.

(5) Where a person has in his possession or under his control any document or other article which it would be an offence under section 6 above for him to disclose without lawful authority, he is guilty of an offence if he fails to comply with an official direction for its return or disposal.

(6) A person is guilty of an offence if he discloses any official information, document or other article which can be used for the purpose of obtaining access to any information, document or other article protected against disclosure by the foregoing provisions of this Act and the circumstances in which it is disclosed are such that it would be reasonable to expect that it might be used for that purpose without authority.

(7) For the purposes of subsection (6) above a person discloses information or a document or article which is official if—

(a) he has or had it in his possession by virtue of his position as a Crown servant or government contractor; or (*b*) he knows or has reasonable cause to believe that a Crown servant or government contractor has or has had it in his possession by virtue of his position as such.

(8) Subsection (5) of section 5 above applies for the purposes of subsection (6) above as it applies for the purposes of that section.

(9) In this section "official direction" means a direction duly given by a Crown servant or government contractor or by or on behalf of a prescribed body or a body of a prescribed class.

NOTES

This section creates a number of summary offences dealing with improper retention of protected materials and with failure to take reasonable care of such materials (subss 1–5). It also creates a further indictable offence of disclosing official information *etc* which may give access to such protected materials (subs 6)).

'Crown servant'; 'government contractor'   See s 12 *infra;* and note also subs (3) of this section.

'unauthorised disclosure'   See s 7 *supra.*

Acts done abroad   See s 15 *infra.*

Penalties   See s. 10 *infra.*

Prosecutions

9. (1) Subject to subsection (2) below, no prosecution for an offence under this Act shall be instituted in England and Wales or in Northern Ireland except by or with the consent of the Attorney General or, as the case may be, the Attorney General for Northern Ireland.

(2) Subsection (1) above does not apply to an offence in respect of any such information, document or article as is mentioned in section 4(2) above but no prosecution for such an offence shall be instituted in England and Wales or in Northern Ireland except by or with the consent of the Director of Public Prosecutions or, as the case may be, the Director of Public Prosecutions for Northern Ireland.

NOTE

The Act also applies to Scotland, where the Lord Advocate is responsible for all prosecutions.

Penalties

10. (1) A person guilty of an offence under any provision of this Act other than section 8(1), (4) or (5) shall be liable—

    (*a*) on conviction on indictment, to imprisonment for a term not exceeding two years or a fine or both;

    (*b*) on summary conviction, to imprisonment for a term not exceeding six months or a fine not exceeding the statutory maximum or both.

(2) A person guilty of an offence under section 8(1), (4) or (5) above shall be liable on summary conviction to imprisonment for a term not

exceeding three months or a fine not exceeding level 5 on the standard scale or both.

11. [*omitted*]

"Crown servant" and "government contractor"
12. (1) In this Act "Crown servant" means—
(*a*) a Minister of the Crown;
(*b*) a person appointed under section 8 of the Northern Ireland Constitution Act 1973 (the Northern Ireland Excutive etc.);
(*c*) any person employed in the civil service of the Crown, including Her Majesty's Diplomatic Service, Her Majesty's Overseas Civil Service, the Civil Service of Northern Ireland and the Northern Ireland Court Service;
(*d*) any member of the naval, military or air forces of the Crown, including any person employed by an association established for the purposes of the Reserve Forces Act 1980;
(*e*) any constable and any other person employed or appointed in or for the purposes of any police force (including a police force within the meaning of the Police Act (Northern Ireland) 1970);
(*f*) any person who is a member or employee of a prescribed body or a body of a prescribed class and either is prescribed for the purposes of this paragraph or belongs to a prescribed class of members or employees of any such body;
(*g*) any person who is the holder of a prescribed office or who is an employee of such a holder and either is prescribed for the purpose of this paragraph or belongs to a prescribed class of such employees.
(2) In this Act "government contractor" means, subject to subsection (3) below, any person who is not a Crown servant but who provides, or is employed in the provision of, goods or services—
(*a*) for the purposes of any Minister or person mentioned in paragraph (a) or (b) of subsection (1) above, of any of the services, forces or bodies mentioned in that subsection or of the holder of any office prescribed under that subsection; or
(*b*) under an agreement or arrangement certified by the Secretary of State as being one to which the government of a State other than the United Kingdom or an international organisation is a party or which is subordinate to, or made for the purposes of implementing, any such agreement or arrangement.
(3) Where an employee or class of employees of any body, or of any holder of an office, is prescribed by an order made for the purposes of subsection (1) above—
(*a*) any employee of that body, or of the holder of that office, who is not prescribed or is not within the prescribed class; and
(*b*) any person who does not provide, or is not employed in the provision of, goods or services for the purposes of the performance of those functions of the body or the holder of the office in connection

with which the employee or prescribed class of employees is
  engaged,
shall not be a government contractor for the purposes of this Act.

NOTE
'prescribed' See s 13 *infra.*

Other interpretation provisions
  13. (1) In this Act—
"disclose" and "disclosure", in relation to a document or other article,
  include parting with possession of it;
"international organisation" means, subject to subsections (2) and (3)
  below, an organisation of which only States are members and
  includes a reference to any organ of such an organisation;
"prescribed" means prescribed by an order made by the Secretary of
  State;
"State" includes the government of a State and any organ or its
  government and references to a State other than the United Kingdom
  include references to any territory outside the United Kingdom.
  (2) In section 12(2)(*b*) above the references to an international organisation includes a reference to any such organisation whether or not one of
which only States are members and includes a commercial organisation.
  (3) In determining for the purposes of subsection (1) above whether
only States are members of an organisation, any member which is itself an
organisation of which only States are members, or which is an organ of
such an organisation, shall be treated as a State.

Orders
  14. (1) Any power of the Secretary of State under this Act to make
orders shall be exercisable by statutory instrument.
  (2) No order shall be made by him for the purposes of section 7(5), 8(9)
or 12 above unless a draft of it has been laid before, and approved by a
resolution of, each House of Parliament.
  (3) If, apart from the provisions of this subsection, the draft of an order
under any of the provisions mentioned in subsection (2) above would be
treated for the purposes of the Standing Orders of either House of
Parliament as a hybrid instrument it shall proceed in that house as if it
were not such an instrument.

Acts done abroad and extent
  15. (1) Any act—
  (*a*) done by a British citizen or Crown servant; or
  (*b*) done by a person in any of the Channel Islands or the Isle of Man
    or any colony,
shall, if it would be an offence by that person under any provision of this
Act other than section 8(1), (4) or (5) when done by him in the United
Kingdom, be an offence under that provision.
  (2) This Act extends to Northern Ireland.

(3) Her Majesty may by Order in Council provide that any provision of this Act shall extend, with such exceptions, adaptations and modifications as may be specified in the Order, to any of the Channel Islands or the Isle of Man or any colony.

NOTE
Under s 11(5) (not printed here), proceedings for an offence under the Act may be instituted in any place in the UK.

Short title, citation, consequential amendments, repeals, revocation and commencement
16. (1) This Act may be cited as the Official Secrets Act 1989.

(2) This Act and the Official Secrets Acts 1911 to 1939 may be cited together as the Official Secrets Acts 1911 to 1989.

(3) Schedule 1 to this Act shall have effect for making amendments consequential on the provisions of this Act.

(4) The enactments and Order mentioned in Schedule 2 to this Act are hereby repealed or revoked to the extent specified in the third column of that Schedule.

(5) Subject to any Order under subsection (3) of section 15 above the repeals in the Official Secrets Act 1911 and the Official Secrets Act 1920 do not extend to any of the territories mentioned in that subsection.

(6) This Act shall come into force on such day as the Secretary of State may by order appoint.

NOTE
The Act was brought into force on 1 March 1990 (SI 1990 no 199).

Index

abduction, women and girls, of 91–2
accounts, falsification of 186
abortion 32–3, 142–7
admiralty jurisdiction 35–8, 47–8
affray 291
aircraft,
    crimes aboard 224–5, 264, 275
    hijacking of 269, 275
    sabotage and endangerment of
        270–2
    dangerous articles aboard 273
aiding and abetting 8–9, 238–9
appropriation, definition of in theft
    170–1
arrest,
    use of force in making 130
    causing GBH resisting 18
    use of firearms to resist 154
assault and battery 308
    occasioning actual bodily harm
        29–30
    on police 126
    with intent to resist arrest etc 28
    with intent to rob 175–6
    with intent to commit buggery 91
assisting offenders 10, 131–4
attempts,
    to commit indictable offences
        256–61
    to commit summary offences 259
    to procure abortion 32–3

bigamy 30
blackmail (see also threats) 189–90
bomb hoaxes 222
British nationality 77
brothels 100–2
    children in 74
    detention of women in 95
    homosexual 138
buggery 88
    assault with intent to commit 91
burglary 176–8
    aggravated 178–9

child destruction 70–1
children,
    abduction of 279–84
    concealing birth of 33–4

brothels, in 74
    criminal responsibility of 74
    cruelty and neglect of 22–23
    indecency with 123
    indecent photos of 235, 312
coercion, of wives by husbands 69
companies,
    fraudulent trading by 285–6
    liability of directors 187, 236, 253
    false statements by directors 187
conspiracy 208–13, 305
contaminating goods 300–2
conveyances, taking of without consent
    180–2
corrosive fluid, throwing 23–4
corruption 44–6, 49–50, 63
counselling and procuring offences
    8–10, 238–9
counterfeiting etc 248–55
criminal damage 12, 198–204
crossbows 303–4

damaging property (see malicious
    damage and criminal damage)
deception,
    definition of 183, 234
    evading liability by 231
    obtaining pecuniary advantage by
        185
    obtaining property by 183–4
    obtaining services by 230–1
    procuring execution of valuable
        security by 188–9
defectives, intercourse with etc 86, 96
dishonesty, definition of 168–9, 230
directors of companies, offences
    by 187, 236, 253
documents, suppression of 188–9
driving,
    furious 27–8
    causing death by reckless 314–5
drugs,
    administering for criminal purposes
        20
    administering for sexual purposes
        83

electricity, abstraction of 182
espionage 58–62, 64

explosives,
  manufacture or possession of 34–5,
    40–1
  misuse of 23–4, 49–51
extraterritorial jurisdiction 1–3, 9,
    47–8, 57, 60–1, 77, 182–3, 224–8,
    264, 266, 269–78

false accounting 186–7
felonies, abolition of 130
firearms (*see also* offensive weapons)
    148–167
  air weapons 148–9
  certificates 148–9, 162
  imitation 154–5, 160, 267
  minors and 157–159
  prohibited 151–2
  shotguns 148–9, 161
forgery offences 13–14, 54–5, 240–7
fortune telling 4–5
fraud and deception 183–5, 230–2

garrotting 20
going equipped for theft etc 194
grievous bodily harm and wounding
    18–19

handling stolen goods 190–4
harrassment 293
housebreaking equipment, possession
    of 194
homosexual acts 88–9, 135–7
hostage taking 266
husband and wife,
  coercion and 69
  conspiracy between 210
  rape offences 205–6
  theft offences between 195

incitement (soliciting) to murder 15
  to incest 223
  to summary offences 239
incest 87
indecency, homosexual 88
indecent exposure 4–5
indecent photographs of
    children 235, 312
infanticide 75–6
insanity, special verdict of 43
intent, proof of 140–1

kerb crawling 287–90
knives and blades (*see also* offensive
    weapons) 310, 311

loitering with intent, abolition of
    offence 262

making off without payment 233
malicious communications 306–7
malicious damage 13–4
manslaughter,
  abroad 16
  diminished responsibility 111–3
  infanticide and 75
  penalty for 16
  provocation 113–4
  reckless driving and 314–5
  suicide pact 115
murder,
  abroad 16
  child destruction and 70–1
  conspiracy to 208, 210
  constructive malice, abolition 111
  infanticide and 75

obscene publications *etc* 80–1,
    119–22, 128–9, 235–7
obtaining by deception (*see* deception)
offensive weapons (*see also* aggravated
    burglary) 78–9, 116, 311
official secrets 58–62, 64–68,
    327–340

perjury 51–2
  offences related to 52–7
piracy 37, 274–5
police,
  assault on 126
  causing wasteful employment of
    133–4
  obstruction of or resistance to 126–7
poisoning, malicious 20–22
procuring (accessories) 8–9, 238–9
procuring women,
  for sexual purposes 82, 95
  for prostitution 93–5
prostitution (*see also* brothels, kerb
    crawling) 93–8, 117–8
  living off earnings of 98–9
  soliciting by prostitutes 117–8

racial hatred, inciting *etc* 296–99
railways, vandalism, obstruction *etc* 11,
    26–7
rape 82, 205–7
  marital 206
reckless driving, causing death by
    314–5
removing exhibition items 179
riot 289–90
robbery 175–6

sexual intercourse, unlawful 84–6,
    96–7, 102
ships, offences on 47–8

soliciting,
   (inciting) murder   15
   for immoral purposes   99
   of women by men   287
spring guns and traps   24–5
spying   58–62, 64
suicide and suicide pacts   115, 124–5
suppressing documents   188–9

taking conveyance without consent
   180–2
territorial waters   36–8
terrorism,
   extraterritorial jurisdiction over
      224–8
   exclusion orders   317–8
   financial assistance for   318–22
   information concerning   323–4
   proscribed organisations   316–326
theft   168–175

threats to kill   17
threatening or abusive behaviour
   292–3
threatening communications   306
torture   308–9
traps   24–5
trespassing and squatting   4, 213–222
   with firearm or offensive weapon
      155, 218
   on foreign missions   218–9
treason   1–3, 6–7
   misprision of   133, 324

vagrancy offences   4–5
vehicles, interference with   262
violent disorder   290

wounding and grievous bodily harm
   18–19